Grosset's **UNIVERSAL** Library

Four Plays

AN ENEMY OF THE PEOPLE

THE WILD DUCK

HEDDA GABLER

THE LADY FROM THE SEA

Henrik Ibsen

Grosset's UNIVERSAL Library

GROSSET & DUNLAP

NEW YORK

CONTENTS

FOUR PLAYS

INTRODUCTION

IBSEN told stories to be acted on the stage. He had, it is true, a less theatrical mind than the dramatists of his day ordinarily had, and he insisted on telling his stories as if they came from actual life and not as if they were merely intended for the theater. From this arose the confusions and arguments, the resistances and partisanships which marked the rise of his reputation and which still are not forgotten. Audiences, used to certain kinds of stories and characters in plays, resented other kinds, most often on the ground that they were not fit to be shown. Ibsen himself was influenced by the controversies. He seems to have chosen some of his stories partly out of a determination to prove that this or that subject was suitable for drama. Too often his choice affected his treatment, or dictated the things his men and women were made to say. For this reason some of his stories now seem uninteresting or unconvincing. The arguments in them have soured or turned to dust. But the best of his dramatic stories still have the vitality which lasts, in spite of time, in all truthful stories of realistic human beings. They should be read, or seen, for what they are, not solemnly mumbled over as obscure debates or ominous prophecies.

An Enemy of the People (1882), for instance, is the story of a man who learns that the water of the municipal baths in a town in Norway is infected, supposes that the authorities will at once move to do away with the public menace, finds that, because of the necessary expense, they refuse to pay any attention to him or even to accept his scientific evidence, tries single-handed to correct the abuse, is defeated and mobbed, and has to take refuge in the assurance that only those who stand alone are strong. No doubt there were local and temporary allusions in the play. Ibsen had scores to pay off. He may well have seen that Stockmann was typical, even symbolical, of the individual at outs with society. And yet the play is first of all a story, and only after that a document. Misfortunes more or less like Stockmann's would come to any man of his disposition and attitude in any conceivable community in the world. But the misfortunes of the play are too highly individualized to be looked upon as allegorical, symbolical, or even purely typical. Such moral conclusions as may be drawn from them are simply such as may be drawn, by moralists, from any individual's story when it is presented with dramatic force in full detail.

Whoever finds himself looking too hard for a moral in *An Enemy of the People* should read *The Wild Duck* (1884). In a sense, it is the other side of a similar argument. As Stockmann has insisted that the truth must be spoken at any cost, so Gregers Werle in the later play talks about the "demands of the ideal." Having learned that the marriage of Gina and Hjalmar Ekdal, though now happy and successful, has a scandal in its past, he cannot rest till he has dug up the old truth. What follows is the consequence of his high-minded obstinacy, which is matched by Hjalmar's. The cloudy significance of the wild duck in the attic, mystifying as it is, cannot hide the plain implications of the story. In this case the truth is superfluous and mischievous. But Ibsen no more means to say that in general the truth is dangerous than he meant in *An Enemy of the People* to say that the truth in general is sacred. Telling two different stories, about human beings differently situated, he is pointing different, not to say contradictory, morals. It is enough to say that he was telling different stories.

To read the innumerable commentaries on *Hedda Gabler* (1890) and then to read the play is to emerge from a jungle to a straight road. Perhaps there was some excuse for the difficulty which contemporaries had with the character of the heroine. They were, in spite of themselves, comparing her with the simple creatures whom they had been accustomed to on the stage. But there is no excuse for such difficulties in any reader who will compare Hedda with actual, though not very usual, women. She is a complex, neurotic woman who has married a commonplace man, chiefly from boredom. He expects her to settle at once into a smug domestic pattern which is unendurable to her. Bored and more bored, she lets her frustrate energies carry her into meddling with other lives, gets involved too deeply, is not strong enough, or concerned enough, to see her way out, and commits suicide. The story does not prove that dull men should not marry neurotic women, or that women unwilling to bear children should not marry, or that complicated persons should not try to lead conventional lives, or that only virtue triumphs. It is the story of a particular woman in particular circumstances. Ibsen was not to blame if his story was so life-like that it set tongues wagging.

The Lady from the Sea (1888) is, again in a sense, to *Hedda Gabler* what *The Wild Duck* is to *An Enemy of the People*. That is, it is the other side of an argument. Ellida is almost as much obsessed as Hedda. But whereas Hedda is kept bound by the stupidity of her husband, who cannot comprehend her restless longings, Ellida has in Wangel a husband who is wise enough to give her her freedom. Once free to choose, she realizes that what she has desired is not the lover of her youth but the sense that nothing outside herself is compelling her in either direction. Believing herself compelled both ways, she inclines to the older compulsion. Believing herself free, whether that is an illusion or not, she prefers the life which she has tested to the life she has only brooded about. Her story is not, strictly speaking, more symbolical than Hedda's. It is only more poetical.

The paradox of Ibsen is the paradox which goes with the most realistic art. His plots and characters are so individual that they seem actual, and so rouse in their readers or their audiences the moralizing impulse which real events arouse. Whether the stories are symbolical or not, they become so in the discussions which they start. Those discussions are now a part of the phenomenon of Ibsen. But in the end it should always be remembered that what he did was to tell stories.

CARL VAN DOREN.

AN ENEMY OF THE PEOPLE

CAST OF CHARACTERS

DR. THOMAS STOCKMANN, *Medical Officer of the Municipal Baths.*

MRS. STOCKMANN, *his wife.*

PETRA, *their daughter, a teacher.*

EJLIF
MORTEN } *their sons (aged 13 and 10 respectively).*

PETER STOCKMANN, *the Doctor's elder brother; Mayor of the Town and Chief Constable, Chairman of the Baths' Committee, etc., etc.*

MORTEN KIIL, *a tanner (Mrs. Stockmann's adoptive father).*

HOVSTAD, *editor of the "People's Messenger."*

BILLING, *sub-editor.*

CAPTAIN HORSTER.

ASLAKSEN, *a printer.*

Men of various conditions and occupations, some few women, and a troop of schoolboys—the audience at a public meeting.

The action takes place in a coast town in southern Norway.

ACT I

(SCENE.—DR. STOCKMANN's *sitting-room. It is evening. The room is plainly but neatly appointed and furnished. In the right-hand wall are two doors; the farther leads out to the hall, the nearer to the doctor's study. In the left-hand wall, opposite the door leading to the hall, is a door leading to the other rooms occupied by the family. In the middle of the same wall stands the stove, and, further forward, a couch with a looking-glass hanging over it and an oval table in front of it. On the table, a lighted lamp, with a lampshade. At the back of the room, an open door leads to the dining-room.* BILLING *is seen sitting at the dining table, on which a lamp is burning. He has a napkin tucked under his chin, and* MRS. STOCKMANN *is standing by the table handing him a large plateful of roast beef. The other places at the table are empty, and the table somewhat in disorder, a meal having evidently recently been finished.*)

MRS. STOCKMANN. You see, if you come an hour late, Mr. Billing, you have to put up with cold meat.

BILLING (*as he eats*). It is uncommonly good, thank you —remarkably good.

MRS. STOCKMANN. My husband makes such a point of having his meals punctually, you know——

BILLING. That doesn't affect me a bit. Indeed, I almost think I enjoy a meal all the better when I can sit down and eat all by myself and undisturbed.

MRS. STOCKMANN. Oh well, as long as you are enjoying it——. (*Turns to the hall door, listening.*) I expect that is Mr. Hovstad coming too.

BILLING. Very likely.

3

(PETER STOCKMANN *comes in. He wears an overcoat and his official hat, and carries a stick.*)

PETER STOCKMANN. Good evening, Katherine.

MRS. STOCKMANN (*coming forward into the sitting-room*). Ah, good evening—is it you? How good of you to come up and see us!

PETER STOCKMANN. I happened to be passing, and so— (*looks into the dining-room*). But you have company with you, I see.

MRS. STOCKMANN (*a little embarrassed*). Oh, no—it was quite by chance he came in. (*Hurriedly.*) Won't you come in and have something, too?

PETER STOCKMANN. I! No, thank you. Good gracious—hot meat at night! Not with my digestion.

MRS. STOCKMANN. Oh, but just once in a way——

PETER STOCKMANN. No, no, my dear lady; I stick to my tea and bread and butter. It is much more wholesome in the long run—and a little more economical, too.

MRS. STOCKMANN (*smiling*). Now you mustn't think that Thomas and I are spendthrifts.

PETER STOCKMANN. Not you, my dear; I would never think that of you. (*Points to the Doctor's study.*) Is he not at home?

MRS. STOCKMANN. No, he went out for a little turn after supper—he and the boys.

PETER STOCKMANN. I doubt if that is a wise thing to do. (*Listens.*) I fancy I hear him coming now.

MRS. STOCKMANN. No, I don't think it is he. (*A knock is heard at the door.*) Come in! (HOVSTAD *comes in from the hall.*) Oh, it is you, Mr. Hovstad!

HOVSTAD. Yes, I hope you will forgive me, but I was delayed at the printer's. Good evening, Mr. Mayor.

PETER STOCKMANN (*bowing a little distantly*). Good evening. You have come on business, no doubt.

HOVSTAD. Partly. It's about an article for the paper.

PETER STOCKMANN. So I imagined. I hear my brother has become a prolific contributor to the "People's Messenger."

HOVSTAD. Yes, he is good enough to write in the "People's Messenger" when he has any home truths to tell.

MRS. STOCKMANN (*to* HOVSTAD). But won't you——? (*Points to the dining-room.*)

PETER STOCKMANN. Quite so, quite so. I don't blame him in the least, as a writer, for addressing himself to the quarters where he will find the readiest sympathy. And, besides that, I personally have no reason to bear any ill will to your paper, Mr. Hovstad.

HOVSTAD. I quite agree with you.

PETER STOCKMANN. Taking one thing with another, there is an excellent spirit of toleration in the town—an admirable municipal spirit. And it all springs from the fact of our having a great common interest to unite us—an interest that is in an equally high degree the concern of every right-minded citizen——

HOVSTAD. The Baths, yes.

PETER STOCKMANN. Exactly—our fine, new, handsome Baths. Mark my words, Mr. Hovstad—the Baths will become the focus of our municipal life! Not a doubt of it!

MRS. STOCKMANN. That is just what Thomas says.

PETER STOCKMANN. Think how extraordinarily the place has developed within the last year or two! Money has been flowing in, and there is some life and some business doing in the town. Houses and landed property are rising in value every day.

HOVSTAD. And unemployment is diminishing.

PETER STOCKMANN. Yes, that is another thing. The burden of the poor rates has been lightened, to the great relief of the propertied classes; and that relief will be even greater if only we get a really good summer this year, and lots of visitors—plenty of invalids, who will make the Baths talked about.

HOVSTAD. And there is a good prospect of that, I hear.

PETER STOCKMANN. It looks very promising. Enquiries about apartments and that sort of thing are reaching us every day.

HOVSTAD. Well, the doctor's article will come in very suitably.

PETER STOCKMANN. Has he been writing something just lately?

HOVSTAD. This is something he wrote in the winter; a recommendation of the Baths—an account of the excellent sanitary conditions here. But I held the article over, temporarily.

PETER STOCKMANN. Ah,—some little difficulty about it, I suppose?

HOVSTAD. No, not at all; I thought it would be better to wait till the spring, because it is just at this time that people begin to think seriously about their summer quarters.

PETER STOCKMANN. Quite right; you were perfectly right, Mr. Hovstad.

HOVSTAD. Yes, Thomas is really indefatigable when it is a question of the Baths.

PETER STOCKMANN. Well—remember, he is the Medical Officer to the Baths.

HOVSTAD. Yes, and what is more, they owe their existence to him.

PETER STOCKMANN. To him? Indeed! It is true I have heard from time to time that some people are of that opinion. At the same time I must say I imagined that I took a modest part in the enterprise.

MRS. STOCKMANN. Yes, that is what Thomas is always saying.

HOVSTAD. But who denies it, Mr. Stockmann? You set the thing going and made a practical concern of it; we all know that. I only meant that the idea of it came first from the doctor.

PETER STOCKMANN. Oh, ideas—yes! My brother has had

plenty of them in his time—unfortunately. But when it is a question of putting an idea into practical shape, you have to apply to a man of different mettle, Mr. Hovstad. And I certainly should have thought that in this house at least——

MRS. STOCKMANN. My dear Peter——

HOVSTAD. How can you think that——?

MRS. STOCKMANN. Won't you go in and have something, Mr. Hovstad? My husband is sure to be back directly.

HOVSTAD. Thank you, perhaps just a morsel. (*Goes into the dining-room.*)

PETER STOCKMANN (*lowering his voice a little*). It is a curious thing that these farmers' sons never seem to lose their want of tact.

MRS. STOCKMANN. Surely it is not worth bothering about! Cannot you and Thomas share the credit as brothers?

PETER STOCKMANN. I should have thought so; but apparently some people are not satisfied with a share.

MRS. STOCKMANN. What nonsense! You and Thomas get on so capitally together. (*Listens.*) There he is at last, I think. (*Goes out and opens the door leading to the hall.*)

DR. STOCKMANN (*laughing and talking outside*). Look here—here is another guest for you, Katherine. Isn't that jolly! Come in, Captain Horster; hang your coat up on this peg. Ah, you don't wear an overcoat. Just think, Katherine; I met him in the street and could hardly persuade him to come up! (CAPTAIN HORSTER *comes into the room and greets* MRS. STOCKMANN. *He is followed by* DR. STOCK-MANN.) Come along in, boys. They are ravenously hungry again, you know. Come along, Captain Horster; you must have a slice of beef. (*Pushes* HORSTER *into the dining-room.* EJLIF *and* MORTEN *go in after them.*)

MRS. STOCKMANN. But, Thomas, don't you see——?

DR. STOCKMANN (*turning in the doorway*). Oh, is it you, Peter? (*Shakes hands with him.*) Now that is very delightful.

PETER STOCKMANN. Unfortunately I must go in a moment——

DR. STOCKMANN. Rubbish! There is some toddy just coming in. You haven't forgotten the toddy, Katherine?

MRS. STOCKMANN. Of course not; the water is boiling now. (*Goes into the dining-room.*)

PETER STOCKMANN. Toddy too!

DR. STOCKMANN. Yes, sit down and we will have it comfortably.

PETER STOCKMANN. Thanks, I never care about an evening's drinking.

DR. STOCKMANN. But this isn't an evening's drinking.

PETER STOCKMANN. It seems to me——. (*Looks towards the dining-room.*) It is extraordinary how they can put away all that food.

DR. STOCKMANN (*rubbing his hands*). Yes, isn't it splendid to see young people eat? They have always got an appetite, you know! That's as it should be. Lots of food—to build up their strength! They are the people who are going to stir up the fermenting forces of the future, Peter.

PETER STOCKMANN. May I ask what they will find here to "stir up," as you put it?

DR. STOCKMANN. Ah, you must ask the young people that —when the time comes. We shan't be able to see it, of course. That stands to reason—two old fogies, like us——

PETER STOCKMANN. Really, really! I must say that is an extremely odd expression to——

DR. STOCKMANN. Oh, you mustn't take me too literally, Peter. I am so heartily happy and contented, you know. I think it is such an extraordinary piece of good fortune to be in the middle of all this growing, germinating life. It is a splendid time to live in! It is as if a whole new world were being created around one.

PETER STOCKMANN. Do you really think so?

DR. STOCKMANN. Ah, naturally you can't appreciate it as

keenly as I. You have lived all your life in these surroundings, and your impressions have got blunted. But I, who have been buried all these years in my little corner up north, almost without ever seeing a stranger who might bring new ideas with him—well, in my case it has just the same effect as if I had been transported into the middle of a crowded city.

PETER STOCKMANN. Oh, a city——!

DR. STOCKMANN. I know, I know; it is all cramped enough here, compared with many other places. But there is life here —there is promise—there are innumerable things to work for and fight for; and that is the main thing. (*Calls.*) Katherine, hasn't the postman been here?

MRS. STOCKMANN (*from the dining-room*). No.

DR. STOCKMANN. And then to be comfortably off, Peter! That is something one learns to value, when one has been on the brink of starvation, as we have.

PETER STOCKMANN. Oh, surely——

DR. STOCKMANN. Indeed I can assure you we have often been very hard put to it, up there. And now to be able to live like a lord! To-day, for instance, we had roast beef for dinner—and, what is more, for supper too. Won't you come and have a little bit? Or let me show it you, at any rate? Come here——

PETER STOCKMANN. No, no—not for worlds!

DR. STOCKMANN. Well, but just come here then. Do you see, we have got a table-cover?

PETER STOCKMANN. Yes, I noticed it.

DR. STOCKMANN. And we have got a lamp-shade too. Do you see? All out of Katherine's savings! It makes the room so cosy. Don't you think so? Just stand here for a moment —no, no, not there—just here, that's it! Look now, when you get the light on it altogether—I really think it looks very nice, doesn't it?

PETER STOCKMANN. Oh, if you can afford luxuries of this kind——

DR. STOCKMANN. Yes, I can afford it now. Katherine tells me I earn almost as much as we spend.

PETER STOCKMANN. Almost—yes!

DR. STOCKMANN. But a scientific man must live in a little bit of style. I am quite sure an ordinary civil servant spends more in a year than I do.

PETER STOCKMANN. I daresay. A civil servant—a man in a well-paid position——

DR. STOCKMANN. Well, any ordinary merchant, then! A man in that position spends two or three times as much as——

PETER STOCKMANN. It just depends on circumstances.

DR. STOCKMANN. At all events I assure you I don't waste money unprofitably. But I can't find it in my heart to deny myself the pleasure of entertaining my friends. I need that sort of thing, you know. I have lived for so long shut out of it all, that it is a necessity of life to me to mix with young, eager, ambitious men, men of liberal and active minds; and that describes every one of those fellows who are enjoying their supper in there. I wish you knew more of Hovstad——

PETER STOCKMANN. By the way, Hovstad was telling me he was going to print another article of yours.

DR. STOCKMANN. An article of mine?

PETER STOCKMANN. Yes, about the Baths. An article you wrote in the winter.

DR. STOCKMANN. Oh, that one! No, I don't intend that to appear just for the present.

PETER STOCKMANN. Why not? It seems to me that this would be the most opportune moment.

DR. STOCKMANN. Yes, very likely—under normal conditions. (*Crosses the room.*)

PETER STOCKMANN (*following him with his eyes*). Is there anything abnormal about the present conditions?

DR. STOCKMANN (*standing still*). To tell you the truth, Peter, I can't say just at this moment—at all events not to-night. There may be much that is very abnormal about the present conditions—and it is possible there may be nothing abnormal about them at all. It is quite possible it may be merely my imagination.

PETER STOCKMANN. I must say it all sounds most mysterious. Is there something going on that I am to be kept in ignorance of? I should have imagined that I, as Chairman of the governing body of the Baths——

DR. STOCKMANN. And I should have imagined that I——. Oh, come, don't let us fly out at one another, Peter.

PETER STOCKMANN. Heaven forbid! I am not in the habit of flying out at people, as you call it. But I am entitled to request most emphatically that all arrangements shall be made in a business-like manner, through the proper channels, and shall be dealt with by the legally constituted authorities. I can allow no going behind our backs by any roundabout means.

DR. STOCKMANN. Have I ever at any time tried to go behind your backs!

PETER STOCKMANN. You have an ingrained tendency to take your own way, at all events; and that is almost equally inadmissible in a well-ordered community. The individual ought undoubtedly to acquiesce in subordinating himself to the community—or, to speak more accurately, to the authorities who have the care of the community's welfare.

DR. STOCKMANN. Very likely. But what the deuce has all this got to do with me?

PETER STOCKMANN. That is exactly what you never appear to be willing to learn, my dear Thomas. But, mark my words, some day you will have to suffer for it—sooner or later. Now I have told you. Good-bye.

DR. STOCKMANN. Have you taken leave of your senses? You are on the wrong scent altogether.

PETER STOCKMANN. I am not usually that. You must excuse me now if I—(*calls into the dining-room*). Good night, Katherine. Good night, gentlemen. (*Goes out.*)

MRS. STOCKMANN (*coming from the dining-room*). Has he gone?

DR. STOCKMANN. Yes, and in such a bad temper.

MRS. STOCKMANN. But, dear Thomas, what have you been doing to him again?

DR. STOCKMANN. Nothing at all. And, anyhow, he can't oblige me to make my report before the proper time.

MRS. STOCKMANN. What have you got to make a report to him about?

DR. STOCKMANN. Hm! Leave that to me, Katherine.—It is an extraordinary thing that the postman doesn't come.

(HOVSTAD, BILLING *and* HORSTER *have got up from the table and come into the sitting-room.* EJLIF *and* MORTEN *come in after them.*)

BILLING (*stretching himself*). Ah!—one feels a new man after a meal like that.

HOVSTAD. The mayor wasn't in a very sweet temper to-night, then.

DR. STOCKMANN. It is his stomach; he has a wretched digestion.

HOVSTAD. I rather think it was us two of the "People's Messenger" that he couldn't digest.

MRS. STOCKMANN. I thought you came out of it pretty well with him.

HOVSTAD. Oh yes; but it isn't anything more than a sort of truce.

BILLING. That is just what it is! That word sums up the situation.

DR. STOCKMANN. We must remember that Peter is a lonely man, poor chap. He has no home comforts of any kind; nothing but everlasting business. And all that infernal weak tea wash that he pours into himself! Now then, my boys, bring chairs up to the table. Aren't we going to have that toddy, Katherine?

MRS. STOCKMANN (*going into the dining-room*). I am just getting it.

DR. STOCKMANN. Sit down here on the couch beside me, Captain Horster. We so seldom see you—. Please sit down, my friends. (*They sit down at the table.* MRS. STOCKMANN *brings a tray, with a spirit-lamp, glasses, bottles, etc., upon it.*)

MRS. STOCKMANN. There you are! This is arrack, and this is rum, and this one is the brandy. Now every one must help himself.

DR. STOCKMANN (*taking a glass*). We will. (*They all mix themselves some toddy.*) And let us have the cigars. Ejlif, you know where the box is. And you, Morten, can fetch my pipe. (*The two boys go into the room on the right.*) I have a suspicion that Ejlif pockets a cigar now and then!—but I take no notice of it. (*Calls out.*) And my smoking-cap too, Morten. Katherine, you can tell him where I left it. Ah, he has got it. (*The boys bring the various things.*) Now, my friends. I stick to my pipe, you know. This one has seen plenty of bad weather with me up north. (*Touches glasses with them.*) Your good health! Ah, it is good to be sitting snug and warm here.

MRS. STOCKMANN (*who sits knitting*). Do you sail soon, Captain Horster?

HORSTER. I expect to be ready to sail next week.

MRS. STOCKMANN. I suppose you are going to America?

HORSTER. Yes, that is the plan.

MRS. STOCKMANN. Then you won't be able to take part in the coming election.

HORSTER. Is there going to be an election?

BILLING. Didn't you know?

HORSTER. No, I don't mix myself up with those things.

BILLING. But do you not take an interest in public affairs?

HORSTER. No, I don't know anything about politics.

BILLING. All the same, one ought to vote, at any rate.

HORSTER. Even if one doesn't know anything about what is going on?

BILLING. Doesn't know! What do you mean by that? A

community is like a ship; every one ought to be prepared to take the helm.

HORSTER. Maybe that is all very well on shore; but on board ship it wouldn't work.

HOVSTAD. It is astonishing how little most sailors care about what goes on on shore.

BILLING. Very extraordinary.

DR. STOCKMANN. Sailors are like birds of passage; they feel equally at home in any latitude. And that is only an additional reason for our being all the more keen, Hovstad. Is there to be anything of public interest in to-morrow's "Messenger"?

HOVSTAD. Nothing about municipal affairs. But the day after to-morrow I was thinking of printing your article——

DR. STOCKMANN. Ah, devil take it—my article! Look here, that must wait a bit.

HOVSTAD. Really? We had just got convenient space for it, and I thought it was just the opportune moment——

DR. STOCKMANN. Yes, yes, very likely you are right; but it must wait all the same. I will explain to you later. (PETRA *comes in from the hall, in hat and cloak and with a bundle of exercise books under her arm.*)

PETRA. Good evening.

DR. STOCKMANN. Good evening, Petra; come along.

(*Mutual greetings;* PETRA *takes off her things and puts them down on a chair by the door.*)

PETRA. And you have all been sitting here enjoying yourselves, while I have been out slaving!

DR. STOCKMANN. Well, come and enjoy yourself too!

BILLING. May I mix a glass for you?

PETRA (*coming to the table*). Thanks, I would rather do it; you always mix it too strong. But I forgot, father—I have a letter for you. (*Goes to the chair where she has laid her things.*)

DR. STOCKMANN. A letter? From whom?

PETRA (*looking in her coat pocket*). The postman gave it to me just as I was going out——

DR. STOCKMANN (*getting up and going to her*). And you only give it to me now!

PETRA. I really had not time to run up again. There it is!

DR. STOCKMANN (*seizing the letter*). Let's see, let's see, child! (*Looks at the address.*) Yes, that's all right!

MRS. STOCKMANN. Is it the one you have been expecting so anxiously, Thomas?

DR. STOCKMANN. Yes, it is. I must go to my room now and——. Where shall I get a light, Katherine? Is there no lamp in my room again?

MRS. STOCKMANN. Yes, your lamp is all ready lit on your desk.

DR. STOCKMANN. Good, good. Excuse me for a moment——. (*Goes into his study.*)

PETRA. What do you suppose it is, mother?

MRS. STOCKMANN. I don't know; for the last day or two he has always been asking if the postman has not been.

BILLING. Probably some country patient.

PETRA. Poor old dad!—he will overwork himself soon. (*Mixes a glass for herself.*) There, that will taste good!

HOVSTAD. Have you been teaching in the evening school again to-day?

PETRA (*sipping from her glass*). Two hours.

BILLING. And four hours of school in the morning——

PETRA. Five hours.

MRS. STOCKMANN. And you have still got exercises to correct, I see.

PETRA. A whole heap, yes.

HORSTER. You are pretty full up with work too, it seems to me.

PETRA. Yes—but that is good. One is so delightfully tired after it.

BILLING. Do you like that?

PETRA. Yes, because one sleeps so well, then.

MORTEN. You must be dreadfully wicked, Petra.

PETRA. Wicked?

MORTEN. Yes, because you work so much. Mr. Rörlund says work is a punishment for our sins.

EJLIF. Pooh, what a duffer you are, to believe a thing like that!

MRS. STOCKMANN. Come, come, Ejlif!

BILLING (*laughing*). That's capital!

HOVSTAD. Don't you want to work as hard as that Morten?

MORTEN. No, indeed I don't.

HOVSTAD. What do you want to be, then?

MORTEN. I should like best to be a Viking.

EJLIF. You would have to be a pagan then.

MORTEN. Well, I could become a pagan, couldn't I?

BILLING. I agree with you, Morten! My sentiments, exactly.

MRS. STOCKMANN (*signalling to him*). I am sure that is not true, Mr. Billing.

BILLING. Yes, I swear it is! I am a pagan, and I am proud of it. Believe me, before long we shall all be pagans.

MORTEN. And then shall be allowed to do anything we like?

BILLING. Well, you see, Morten——.

MRS. STOCKMANN. You must go to your room now, boys; I am sure you have some lessons to learn for to-morrow.

EJLIF. I should like so much to stay a little longer——

MRS. STOCKMANN. No, no; away you go, both of you.
    (*The boys say good night and go into the room on the left.*)

HOVSTAD. Do you really think it can do the boys any harm to hear such things?

MRS. STOCKMANN. I don't know, but I don't like it.

PETRA. But you know, mother, I think you really are wrong about it.

Mrs. Stockmann. Maybe, but I don't like it—not in our own home.

Petra. There is so much falsehood both at home and at school. At home one must not speak, and at school we have to stand and tell lies to the children.

Horster. Tell lies?

Petra. Yes, don't you suppose we have to teach them all sorts of things that we don't believe?

Billing. That is perfectly true.

Petra. If only I had the means I would start a school of my own, and it would be conducted on very different lines.

Billing. Oh, bother the means——!

Horster. Well, if you are thinking of that, Miss Stockmann, I shall be delighted to provide you with a schoolroom. The great big old house my father left me is standing almost empty; there is an immense dining-room downstairs——

Petra (*laughing*). Thank you very much; but I am afraid nothing will come of it.

Hovstad. No, Miss Petra is much more likely to take to journalism, I expect. By the way, have you had time to do anything with that English story you promised to translate for us?

Petra. No, not yet; but you shall have it in good time.

(Dr. Stockmann *comes in from his room with an open letter in his hand.*)

Dr. Stockmann (*waving the letter*). Well, now the town will have something new to talk about, I can tell you!

Billing. Something new?

Mrs. Stockmann. What is this?

Dr. Stockmann. A great discovery, Katherine.

Hovstad. Really?

Mrs. Stockmann. A discovery of yours?

Dr. Stockmann. A discovery of mine. (*Walks up and down.*) Just let them come saying, as usual, that it is all fancy and a crazy man's imagination! But they will be careful what they say this time, I can tell you!

PETRA. But, father, tell us what it is.

DR. STOCKMANN. Yes, yes—only give me time, and you shall know all about it. If only I had Peter here now! It just shows how we men can go about forming our judgments, when in reality we are as blind as any moles——

HOVSTAD. What are you driving at, Doctor?

DR. STOCKMANN (*standing still by the table*). Isn't it the universal opinion that our town is a healthy spot?

HOVSTAD. Certainly.

DR. STOCKMANN. Quite an unusually healthy spot, in fact —a place that deserves to be recommended in the warmest possible manner either for invalids or for people who are well——

MRS. STOCKMANN. Yes, but my dear Thomas——

DR. STOCKMANN. And we have been recommending it and praising it—I have written and written, both in the "Messenger" and in pamphlets——

HOVSTAD. Well, what then?

DR. STOCKMANN. And the Baths—we have called them the "main artery of the town's life-blood," the "nerve-center of our town," and the devil knows what else——

BILLING. "The town's pulsating heart" was the expression I once used on an important occasion——

DR. STOCKMANN. Quite so. Well, do you know what they really are, these great, splendid, much-praised Baths, that have cost so much money—do you know what they are?

HOVSTAD. No, what are they?

MRS. STOCKMANN. Yes, what are they?

DR. STOCKMANN. The whole place is a pesthouse!

PETRA. The Baths, father?

MRS. STOCKMANN (*at the same time*). Our Baths!

HOVSTAD. But, Doctor——

BILLING. Absolutely incredible!

DR. STOCKMANN. The whole Bath establishment is a whited, poisoned sepulcher, I tell you—the gravest possible danger to the public health! All the nastiness up at Mölle-dal, all that stinking filth, is infecting the water in the conduit-pipes leading to the reservoir; and the same cursed, filthy poison oozes out on the shore too——

HORSTER. Where the bathing-place is?

DR. STOCKMANN. Just there.

HOVSTAD. How do you come to be so certain of all this, Doctor?

DR. STOCKMANN. I have investigated the matter most conscientiously. For a long time past I have suspected some-thing of the kind. Last year we had some very strange cases of illness among the visitors—typhoid cases, and cases of gastric fever——

MRS. STOCKMANN. Yes, that is quite true.

DR. STOCKMANN. At the time, we supposed the visitors had been infected before they came; but later on, in the winter, I began to have a different opinion; and so I set myself to examine the water, as well as I could.

MRS. STOCKMANN. Then that is what you have been so busy with?

DR. STOCKMANN. Indeed I have been busy, Katherine. But here I had none of the necessary scientific apparatus; so I sent samples, both of the drinking-water and of the sea-water, up to the University, to have an accurate analysis made by a chemist.

HOVSTAD. And have you got that?

DR. STOCKMANN (showing him the letter). Here it is! It proves the presence of decomposing organic matter in the water—it is full of infusoria. The water is absolutely dan-gerous to use, either internally or externally.

MRS. STOCKMANN. What a mercy you discovered it in time.

DR. STOCKMANN. You may well say so.

HOVSTAD. And what do you propose to do now, Doctor?

DR. STOCKMANN. To see the matter put right—naturally.

HOVSTAD. Can that be done?

DR. STOCKMANN. It must be done. Otherwise the Baths will be absolutely useless and wasted. But we need not anticipate that; I have a very clear idea what we shall have to do.

MRS. STOCKMANN. But why have you kept this all so secret, dear?

DR. STOCKMANN. Do you suppose I was going to run about the town gossiping about it, before I had absolute proof? No, thank you. I am not such a fool.

PETRA. Still, you might have told us——

DR. STOCKMANN. Not a living soul. But to-morrow you may run round to the old Badger——

MRS. STOCKMANN. Oh, Thomas! Thomas!

DR. STOCKMANN. Well, to your grandfather, then. The old boy will have something to be astonished at! I know he thinks I am cracked—and there are lots of other people think so too, I have noticed. But now these good folks shall see— they shall just see——! (*Walks about, rubbing his hands.*) There will be a nice upset in the town, Katherine; you can't imagine what it will be. All the conduit-pipes will have to be relaid.

HOVSTAD (*getting up*). All the conduit-pipes——?

DR. STOCKMANN. Yes, of course. The intake is too low down; it will have to be lifted to a position much higher up.

PETRA. Then you were right after all.

DR. STOCKMANN. Ah, you remember, Petra—I wrote opposing the plans before the work was begun. But at that time no one would listen to me. Well, I am going to let them have it, now! Of course I have prepared a report for the Baths Committee; I have had it ready for a week, and was only waiting for this to come. (*Shows the letter.*) Now it shall go off at once. (*Goes into his room and comes back with some papers.*) Look at that! Four closely written sheets!—and the letter shall go with them. Give me a bit of paper, Katherine—something to wrap them up in. That will do! Now give it to—to—(*stamps his foot*)—what the deuce is her name?—give it to the maid, and tell her to take it at once to the Mayor.

(MRS. STOCKMANN *takes the packet and goes out through the dining-room.*)

PETRA. What do you think uncle Peter will say, father?

DR. STOCKMANN. What is there for him to say? I should think he would be very glad that such an important truth has been brought to light.

HOVSTAD. Will you let me print a short note about your discovery in the "Messenger"?

DR. STOCKMANN. I shall be very much obliged if you will.

HOVSTAD. It is very desirable that the public should be informed of it without delay.

DR. STOCKMANN. Certainly.

MRS. STOCKMANN (*coming back*). She has just gone with it.

BILLING. Upon my soul, Doctor, you are going to be the foremost man in the town!

DR. STOCKMANN (*walking about happily*). Nonsense! As a matter of fact I have done nothing more than my duty. I have only made a lucky find—that's all. Still, all the same——

BILLING. Hovstad, don't you think the town ought to give Dr. Stockmann some sort of testimonial?

HOVSTAD. I will suggest it, anyway.

BILLING. And I will speak to Aslaksen about it.

DR. STOCKMANN. No, my good friends, don't let us have any of that nonsense. I won't hear of anything of the kind. And if the Baths Committee should think of voting me an increase of salary, I will not accept it. Do you hear, Katherine?—I won't accept it.

MRS. STOCKMANN. You are quite right, Thomas.

PETRA (*lifting her glass*). Your health, father!

HOVSTAD *and* BILLING. Your health, Doctor! Good health!

HORSTER (*touches glasses with* DR. STOCKMANN). I hope it will bring you nothing but good luck.

DR. STOCKMANN. Thank you, thank you, my dear fellows! I feel tremendously happy! It is a splendid thing for a man to be able to feel that he has done a service to his native town and to his fellow-citizens. Hurrah, Katherine! (*He puts his arms round her and whirls her round and round, while she protests with laughing cries. They all laugh, clap their hands, and cheer the* DOCTOR. *The boys put their heads in at the door to see what is going on.*)

ACT II

(SCENE—*The same. The door into the dining-room is shut. It is morning.* MRS. STOCKMANN, *with a sealed letter in her hand, comes in from the dining-room, goes to the door of the* DOCTOR'S *study, and peeps in.*)

MRS. STOCKMANN. Are you in, Thomas?

DR. STOCKMANN (*from within his room*). Yes, I have just come in. (*Comes into the room.*) What is it?

MRS. STOCKMANN. A letter from your brother.

DR. STOCKMANN. Aha, let us see! (*Opens the letter and reads:*) "I return herewith the manuscript you sent me"— (*Reads on in a low murmur.*) Hm!——

MRS. STOCKMANN. What does he say?

DR. STOCKMANN (*putting the papers in his pocket*). Oh, he only writes that he will come up here himself about midday.

MRS. STOCKMANN. Well, try and remember to be at home this time.

DR. STOCKMANN. That will be all right; I have got through all my morning visits.

MRS. STOCKMANN. I am extremely curious to know how he takes it.

DR. STOCKMANN. You will see he won't like it's having been I, and not he, that made the discovery.

MRS. STOCKMANN. Aren't you a little nervous about that?

DR. STOCKMANN. Oh, he really will be pleased enough, you know. But, at the same time, Peter is so confoundedly afraid of anyone's doing any service to the town except himself.

MRS. STOCKMANN. I will tell you what, Thomas—you

23

should be good natured, and share the credit of this with him. Couldn't you make out that it was he who set you on the scent of this discovery?

DR. STOCKMANN. I am quite willing. If only I can get the thing set right. I——

(MORTEN KIIL *puts his head in through the door leading from the hall, looks round in an enquiring manner, and chuckles.*)

MORTEN KIIL (*slyly*). Is it—is it true?

MRS. STOCKMANN (*going to the door*). Father!—is it you?

DR. STOCKMANN. Ah, Mr. Kiil—good morning, good morning!

MRS. STOCKMANN. But come along in.

MORTEN KIIL. If it is true, I will; if not, I am off.

DR. STOCKMANN. If what is true?

MORTEN KIIL. This tale about the water supply. Is it true?

DR. STOCKMANN. Certainly it is true. But how did you come to hear it?

MORTEN KIIL (*coming in*). Petra ran in on her way to the school——

DR. STOCKMANN. Did she?

MORTEN KIIL. Yes; and she declares that——. I thought she was only making a fool of me, but it isn't like Petra to do that.

DR. STOCKMANN. Of course not. How could you imagine such a thing!

MORTEN KIIL. Oh well, it is better never to trust anybody; you may find you have been made a fool of before you know where you are. But it is really true, all the same?

DR. STOCKMANN. You can depend upon it that it is true. Won't you sit down? (*Settles him on the couch.*) Isn't it a real bit of luck for the town——

MORTEN KIIL (*suppressing his laughter*). A bit of luck for the town?

DR. STOCKMANN. Yes, that I made the discovery in good time.

MORTEN KIIL (*as before*). Yes, yes, yes!—But I should never have thought you the sort of man to pull your own brother's leg like this!

DR. STOCKMANN. Pull his leg!

MRS. STOCKMANN. Really, father dear——

MORTON KIIL (*resting his hands and his chin on the handle of his stick and winking slyly at the* DOCTOR). Let me see, what was the story? Some kind of beast that had got into the water-pipes, wasn't it?

DR. STOCKMANN. Infusoria—yes.

MORTEN KIIL. And a lot of these beasts had got in, according to Petra—a tremendous lot.

DR. STOCKMANN. Certainly; hundreds of thousands of them, probably.

MORTEN KIIL. But no one can see them—isn't that so?

DR. STOCKMANN. Yes; you can't see them.

MORTEN KIIL (*with a quiet chuckle*). Damme—it's the finest story I have ever heard!

DR. STOCKMANN. What do you mean?

MORTEN KIIL. But you will never get the Mayor to believe a thing like that.

DR. STOCKMANN. We shall see.

MORTEN KIIL. Do you think he will be fool enough to—?

DR. STOCKMANN. I hope the whole town will be fools enough.

MORTEN KIIL. The whole town! Well, it wouldn't be a bad thing. It would just serve them right, and teach them a lesson. They think themselves so much cleverer than we old fellows. They hounded me out of the council; they did, I tell you—they hounded me out. Now they shall pay for it. You pull their legs too, Thomas!

DR. STOCKMANN. Really, I——

MORTEN KIIL. You pull their legs! (*Gets up.*) If you can work it so that the Mayor and his friends all swallow the same bait, I will give ten pounds to a charity—like a shot!

DR. STOCKMANN. That is very kind of you.

MORTEN KIIL. Yes, I haven't got much money to throw away, I can tell you; but if you can work this, I will give five pounds to a charity at Christmas.

(HOVSTAD *comes in by the hall door.*)

HOVSTAD. Good morning! (*Stops.*) Oh, I beg your pardon——

DR. STOCKMANN. Not at all; come in.

MORTEN KIIL (*with another chuckle*). Oho!—is he in this too?

HOVSTAD. What do you mean?

DR. STOCKMANN. Certainly he is.

MORTEN KIIL. I might have known it! It must get into the papers. You know how to do it, Thomas! Set your wits to work. Now I must go.

DR. STOCKMANN. Won't you stay a little while?

MORTEN KIIL. No, I must be off now. You keep up this game for all it is worth; you won't repent it, I'm damned if you will!

(*He goes out;* MRS. STOCKMANN *follows him into the hall.*)

DR. STOCKMANN (*laughing*). Just imagine—the old chap doesn't believe a word of all this about the water supply.

HOVSTAD. Oh, that was it, then?

DR. STOCKMANN. Yes, that was what we were talking about. Perhaps it is the same thing that brings you here?

HOVSTAD. Yes, it is. Can you spare me a few minutes, Doctor?

DR. STOCKMANN. As long as you like, my dear fellow.

HOVSTAD. Have you heard from the Mayor yet?

DR. STOCKMANN. Not yet. He is coming here later.

HOVSTAD. I have given the matter a great deal of thought since last night.

DR. STOCKMANN. Well?

HOVSTAD. From your point of view, as a doctor and a

man of science, this affair of the water-supply is an isolated matter. I mean, you do not realize that it involves a great many other things.

DR. STOCKMANN. How, do you mean?—Let us sit down, my dear fellow. No, sit here on the couch. (HOVSTAD *sits down on the couch,* DR. STOCKMANN *on a chair on the other side of the table.*) Now then. You mean that——?

HOVSTAD. You said yesterday that the pollution of the water was due to impurities in the soil.

DR. STOCKMANN. Yes, unquestionably it is due to that poisonous morass up at Mölledal.

HOVSTAD. Begging your pardon, doctor, I fancy it is due to quite another morass altogether.

DR. STOCKMANN. What morass?

HOVSTAD. The morass that the whole life of our town is built on and is rotting in.

DR. STOCKMANN. What the deuce are you driving at, Hovstad?

HOVSTAD. The whole of the town's interests have, little by little, got into the hands of a pack of officials.

DR. STOCKMANN. Oh, come!—they are not all officials.

HOVSTAD. No, but those that are not officials are at any rate the officials' friends and adherents; it is the wealthy folk, the old families in the town, that have got us entirely in their hands.

DR. STOCKMANN. Yes, but after all they are men of ability and knowledge.

HOVSTAD. Did they show any ability or knowledge when they laid the conduit-pipes where they are now?

DR. STOCKMANN. No, of course that was a great piece of stupidity on their part. But that is going to be set right now.

HOVSTAD. Do you think that will be all such plain sailing?

DR. STOCKMANN. Plain sailing or no, it has got to be done, anyway.

HOVSTAD. Yes, provided the press takes up the question.

DR. STOCKMANN. I don't think that will be necessary, my dear fellow, I am certain my brother——

HOVSTAD. Excuse me, doctor; I feel bound to tell you I am inclined to take the matter up.

DR. STOCKMANN. In the paper?

HOVSTAD. Yes. When I took over the "People's Messenger" my idea was to break up this ring of self-opinionated old fossils who had got hold of all the influence.

DR. STOCKMANN. But you know you told me yourself what the result had been; you nearly ruined your paper.

HOVSTAD. Yes, at the time we were obliged to climb down a peg or two, it is quite true; because there was a danger of the whole project of the Baths coming to nothing if they failed us. But now the scheme has been carried through, and we can dispense with these grand gentlemen.

DR. STOCKMANN. Dispense with them, yes; but we owe them a great debt of gratitude.

HOVSTAD. That shall be recognized ungrudgingly. But a journalist of my democratic tendencies cannot let such an opportunity as this slip. The bubble of official infallibility must be pricked. This superstition must be destroyed, like any other.

DR. STOCKMANN. I am whole-heartedly with you in that, Mr. Hovstad; if it is a superstition, away with it!

HOVSTAD. I should be very reluctant to bring the Mayor into it, because he is your brother. But I am sure you will agree with me that truth should be the first consideration.

DR. STOCKMANN. That goes without saying. (*With sudden emphasis.*) Yes, but—but——

HOVSTAD. You must not misjudge me. I am neither more self-interested nor more ambitious than most men.

DR. STOCKMANN. My dear fellow—who suggests anything of the kind?

HOVSTAD. I am of humble origin, as you know; and that

has given me opportunities of knowing what is the most crying need in the humbler ranks of life. It is that they should
be allowed some part in the direction of public affairs, Doctor. That is what will develop their faculties and intelligence
and self-respect——

DR. STOCKMANN. I quite appreciate that.

HOVSTAD. Yes—and in my opinion a journalist incurs a
heavy responsibility if he neglects a favorable opportunity of
emancipating the masses—the humble and oppressed. I know
well enough that in exalted circles I shall be called an agitator,
and all that sort of thing; but they may call what they like.
If only my conscience doesn't reproach me, then——

DR. STOCKMANN. Quite right! Quite right, Mr. Hovstad.
But all the same—devil take it! (*A knock is heard at the
door.*) Come in!

    (ASLAKSEN *appears at the door. He is poorly but de-
    cently dressed, in black, with a slightly crumpled white
    neckcloth; he wears gloves and has a felt hat in his
    hand.*)

ASLAKSEN (*bowing*). Excuse my taking the liberty, Doctor——

DR. STOCKMANN (*getting up*). Ah, it is you, Aslaksen!

ASLAKSEN. Yes, Doctor.

HOVSTAD (*standing up*). Is it me you want, Aslaksen?

ASLAKSEN. No; I didn't know I should find you here. No,
it was the Doctor I——

DR. STOCKMANN. I am quite at your service. What is it?

ASLAKSEN. Is what I heard from Mr. Billing true, sir—
that you mean to improve our water-supply?

DR. STOCKMANN. Yes, for the Baths.

ASLAKSEN. Quite so, I understand. Well, I have come to
say that I will back that up by every means in my power.

HOVSTAD (*to the* DOCTOR). You see!

DR. STOCKMANN. I shall be very grateful to you, but——

ASLAKSEN. Because it may be no bad thing to have us

small tradesmen at your back. We form, as it were, a compact majority in the town—if we choose. And it is always a good thing to have the majority with you, Doctor.

DR. STOCKMANN. That is undeniably true; but I confess I don't see why such unusual precautions should be necessary in this case. It seems to me that such a plain, straightforward thing——

ASLAKSEN. Oh, it may be very desirable, all the same. I know our local authorities so well; officials are not generally very ready to act on proposals that come from other people. That is why I think it would not be at all amiss if we made a little demonstration.

HOVSTAD. That's right.

DR. STOCKMANN. Demonstration, did you say? What on earth are you going to make a demonstration about?

ASLAKSEN. We shall proceed with the greatest moderation, Doctor. Moderation is always my aim; it is the greatest virtue in a citizen—at least, I think so.

DR. STOCKMANN. It is well known to be a characteristic of yours, Mr. Aslaksen.

ASLAKSEN. Yes, I think I may pride myself on that. And this matter of the water-supply is of the greatest importance to us small tradesmen. The Baths promise to be a regular gold-mine for the town. We shall all make our living out of them, especially those of us who are householders. That is why we will back up the project as strongly as possible. And as I am at present Chairman of the Householders' Association——

DR. STOCKMANN. Yes——?

ASLAKSEN. And, what is more, local secretary of the Temperance Society—you know, sir, I suppose, that I am a worker in the temperance cause?

DR. STOCKMANN. Of course, of course.

ASLAKSEN. Well, you can understand that I come into contact with a great many people. And as I have the reputation

of a temperate and law-abiding citizen—like yourself Doctor
—I have a certain influence in the town, a little bit of power,
If I may be allowed to say so.

DR. STOCKMANN. I know that quite well, Mr. Aslaksen.

ASLAKSEN. So you see it would be an easy matter for me
to set on foot some testimonial, if necessary.

DR. STOCKMANN. A testimonial?

ASLAKSEN. Yes, some kind of an address of thanks from
the townsmen for your share in a matter of such importance
to the community. I need scarcely say that it would have to
be drawn up with the greatest regard to moderation, so as
not to offend the authorities—who, after all, have the reins in
their hands. If we pay strict attention to that, no one can
take it amiss, I should think!

HOVSTAD. Well, and even supposing they didn't like it——

ASLAKSEN. No, no, no; there must be no discourtesy to
the authorities, Mr. Hovstad. It is no use falling foul of
those upon whom our welfare so closely depends. I have done
that in my time, and no good ever comes of it. But no one
can take exception to a reasonable and frank expression of a
citizen's views.

DR. STOCKMANN (shaking him by the hand). I can't tell
you, dear Mr. Aslaksen, how extremely pleased I am to find
such hearty support among my fellow-citizens. I am delighted—delighted! Now, you will take a small glass of
sherry, eh?

ASLAKSEN. No, thank you; I never drink alcohol of that
kind.

DR. STOCKMANN. Well, what do you say to a glass of
beer, then?

ASLAKSEN. Nor that either, thank you, Doctor. I never
drink anything as early as this. I am going into town now
to talk this over with one or two householders, and prepare
the ground.

DR. STOCKMANN. It is tremendously kind of you, Mr.

Aslaksen; but I really cannot understand the necessity for all these precautions. It seems to me that the thing should go of itself.

ASLAKSEN. The authorities are somewhat slow to move, Doctor. Far be it from me to seem to blame them——

HOVSTAD. We are going to stir them up in the paper to-morrow, Aslaksen.

ASLAKSEN. But not violently, I trust, Mr. Hovstad. Proceed with moderation, or you will do nothing with them. You may take my advice; I have gathered my experience in the school of life. Well, I must say good-bye, Doctor. You know now that we small tradesmen are at your back at all events, like a solid wall. You have the compact majority on your side, Doctor.

DR. STOCKMANN. I am very much obliged, dear Mr. Aslaksen. (*Shakes hands with him.*) Good-bye, good-bye.

ASLAKSEN. Are you going my way, towards the printing-office, Mr. Hovstad?

HOVSTAD. I will come later; I have something to settle up first.

ASLAKSEN. Very well. (*Bows and goes out;* STOCKMANN *follows him into the hall.*)

HOVSTAD (*as* STOCKMANN *comes in again*). Well, what do you think of that, Doctor? Don't you think it is high time we stirred a little life into all this slackness and vacillation and cowardice?

DR. STOCKMANN. Are you referring to Aslaksen?

HOVSTAD. Yes, I am. He is one of those who are floundering in a bog—decent enough fellow though he may be, otherwise. And most of the people here are in just the same case——see-sawing and edging first to one side and then to the other, so overcome with caution and scruple that they never dare to take any decided step.

DR. STOCKMANN. Yes, but Aslaksen seemed to me so thoroughly well-intentioned.

HOVSTAD. There is one thing I esteem higher than that; and that is for a man to be self-reliant and sure of himself.

DR. STOCKMANN. I think you are perfectly right there.

HOVSTAD. That is why I want to seize this opportunity, and try if I cannot manage to put a little virility into these well-intentioned people for once. The idol of Authority must be shattered in this town. This gross and inexcusable blunder about the water-supply must be brought home to the mind of every municipal voter.

DR. STOCKMANN. Very well; if you are of opinion that it is for the good of the community, so be it. But not until I have had a talk with my brother.

HOVSTAD. Anyway, I will get a leading article ready; and if the Mayor refuses to take the matter up——

DR. STOCKMANN. How can you suppose such a thing possible?

HOVSTAD. It is conceivable. And in that case——

DR. STOCKMANN. In that case I promise you——. Look here, in that case you may print my report—every word of it.

HOVSTAD. May I? Have I your word for it?

DR. STOCKMANN (*giving him the* MS.). Here it is; take it with you. It can do no harm for you to read it through, and you can give it me back later on.

HOVSTAD. Good, good! That is what I will do. And now good-bye, Doctor.

DR. STOCKMANN. Good-bye, good-bye. You will see everything will run quite smoothly, Mr. Hovstad—quite smoothly.

HOVSTAD. Hm!—we shall see. (*Bows and goes out.*)

DR. STOCKMANN (*opens the dining-room door and looks in*). Katherine! Oh, you are back, Petra?

PETRA (*coming in*). Yes, I have just come from the school.

MRS. STOCKMANN (*coming in*). Has he not been here yet?

DR. STOCKMANN. Peter? No. But I have had a long talk with Hovstad. He is quite excited about my discovery. I find it has a much wider bearing than I at first imagined. And he has put his paper at my disposal if necessity should arise.

MRS. STOCKMANN. Do you think it will?

DR. STOCKMANN. Not for a moment. But at all events it makes me feel proud to know that I have the liberal-minded independent press on my side. Yes, and—just imagine—I have had a visit from the Chairman of the Householders' Association!

MRS. STOCKMANN. Oh! What did he want?

DR. STOCKMANN. To offer me his support too. They will support me in a body if it should be necessary. Katherine—do you know what I have got behind me?

MRS. STOCKMANN. Behind you? No, what have you got behind you?

DR. STOCKMANN. The compact majority.

MRS. STOCKMANN. Really? Is that a good thing for you, Thomas?

DR. STOCKMANN. I should think it was a good thing. (*Walks up and down rubbing his hands.*) By Jove, it's a fine thing to feel this bond of brotherhood between oneself and one's fellow citizens!

PETRA. And to be able to do so much that is good and useful, father!

DR. STOCKMANN. And for one's own native town into the bargain, my child!

MRS. STOCKMANN. That was a ring at the bell.

DR. STOCKMANN. It must be he, then. (*A knock is heard at the door.*) Come in!

PETER STOCKMANN (*comes in from the hall*). Good morning.

DR. STOCKMANN. Glad to see you, Peter!

MRS. STOCKMANN. Good morning, Peter. How are you?

PETER STOCKMANN. So so, thank you. (*To* DR. STOCK-
MANN.) I received from you yesterday, after office hours,
a report dealing with the condition of the water at the Baths.

DR. STOCKMANN. Yes. Have you read it?

PETER STOCKMANN. Yes, I have.

DR. STOCKMANN. And what have you to say to it?

PETER STOCKMANN (*with a sidelong glance*). Hm!——

MRS. STOCKMANN. Come along, Petra. (*She and* PETRA
go into the room on the left.)

PETER STOCKMANN (*after a pause*). Was it necessary to
make all these investigations behind my back?

DR. STOCKMANN. Yes, because until I was absolutely certain about it——

PETER STOCKMANN. Then you mean that you are absolutely certain now?

DR. STOCKMANN. Surely you are convinced of that.

PETER STOCKMANN. Is it your intention to bring this
document before the Baths Committee as a sort of official
communication?

DR. STOCKMANN. Certainly. Something must be done in
the matter—and that quickly.

PETER STOCKMANN. As usual, you employ violent expressions in your report. You say, amongst other things, that
what we offer visitors in our Baths is a permanent supply of
poison.

DR. STOCKMANN. Well, can you describe it any other
way, Peter! Just think—water that is poisonous, whether
you drink it or bathe in it! And this we offer to the poor
sick folk who come to us trustfully and pay us at an ex-
orbitant rate to be made well again!

PETER STOCKMANN. And your reasoning leads you to this
conclusion, that we must build a sewer to draw off the alleged
impurities from Mölledal and must relay the water-conduits.

DR. STOCKMANN. Yes. Do you see any other way out of
it? I don't.

PETER STOCKMANN. I made a pretext this morning to go and see the town engineer, and, as if only half seriously, broached the subject of these proposals as a thing we might perhaps have to take under consideration some time later on.

DR. STOCKMANN. Some time later on!

PETER STOCKMANN. He smiled at what he considered to be my extravagance, naturally. Have you taken the trouble to consider what your proposed alterations would cost? According to the information I obtained, the expenses would probably mount up to fifteen or twenty thousand pounds.

DR. STOCKMANN. Would it cost so much?

PETER STOCKMANN. Yes; and the worst part of it would be that the work would take at least two years.

DR. STOCKMANN. Two years? Two whole years?

PETER STOCKMANN. At least. And what are we to do with the Baths in the meantime? Close them? Indeed we should be obliged to. And do you suppose any one would come near the place after it had got about that the water was dangerous?

DR. STOCKMANN. Yes, but, Peter, that is what it is.

PETER STOCKMANN. And all this at this juncture—just as the Baths are beginning to be known. There are other towns in the neighborhood with qualifications to attract visitors for bathing purposes. Don't you suppose they would immediately strain every nerve to divert the entire stream of strangers to themselves? Unquestionably they would; and then where should we be? We should probably have to abandon the whole thing, which has cost us so much money—and then you would have ruined your native town.

DR. STOCKMANN. I—should have ruined—!

PETER STOCKMANN. It is simply and solely through the Baths that the town has before it any future worth mentioning. You know that just as well as I.

DR. STOCKMANN. But what do you think ought to be done, then?

PETER STOCKMANN. Your report has not convinced me

that the condition of the water at the Baths is as bad as you represent it to be.

DR. STOCKMANN. I tell you it is even worse!—or at all events it will be in summer, when the warm weather comes.

PETER STOCKMANN. As I said, I believe you exaggerate the matter considerably. A capable physician ought to know what measures to take—he ought to be capable of preventing injurious influences or of remedying them if they become obviously persistent.

DR. STOCKMANN. Well? What more?

PETER STOCKMANN. The water supply for the Baths is now an established fact, and in consequence must be treated as such. But probably the Committee, at its discretion, will not be disinclined to consider the question of how far it might be possible to introduce certain improvements consistently with a reasonable expenditure.

DR. STOCKMANN. And do you suppose that I will have anything to do with such a piece of trickery as that?

PETER STOCKMANN. Trickery!!

DR. STOCKMANN. Yes, it would be a trick—a fraud, a lie, a downright crime towards the public, towards the whole community!

PETER STOCKMANN. I have not, as I remarked before, been able to convince myself that there is actually any imminent danger.

DR. STOCKMANN. You have! It is impossible that you should not be convinced. I know I have represented the facts absolutely truthfully and fairly. And you know it very well, Peter, only you won't acknowledge it. It was owing to your action that both the Baths and the water-conduits were built where they are; and that is what you won't acknowledge—that damnable blunder of yours. Pooh! —do you suppose I don't see through you?

PETER STOCKMANN. And even if that were true? If I perhaps guard my reputation somewhat anxiously, it is in the interests of the town. Without moral authority I am powerless to direct public affairs as seems, to my judgment, to be best for the common good. And on that account— and for various other reasons too—it appears to me to be a matter of importance that your report should not be delivered to the Committee. In the interests of the public, you must withhold it. Then, later on, I will raise the question and we will do our best, privately; but nothing of this unfortunate affair—not a single word of it—must come to the ears of the public.

DR. STOCKMANN. I am afraid you will not be able to prevent that now, my dear Peter.

PETER STOCKMANN. It must and shall be prevented.

DR. STOCKMANN. It is no use, I tell you. There are too many people that know about it.

PETER STOCKMANN. That know about it? Who? Surely you don't mean those fellows on the "People's Messenger"?

DR. STOCKMANN. Yes, they know. The liberal-minded independent press is going to see that you do your duty.

PETER STOCKMANN (*after a short pause*). You are an extraordinarily independent man, Thomas. Have you given no thought to the consequences this may have for yourself?

DR. STOCKMANN. Consequences?—for me?

PETER STOCKMANN. For you and yours, yes.

DR. STOCKMANN. What the deuce do you mean?

PETER STOCKMANN. I believe I have always behaved in a brotherly way to you—have always been ready to oblige or to help you?

DR. STOCKMANN. Yes, you have, and I am grateful to you for it.

PETER STOCKMANN. There is no need. Indeed, to some extent I was forced to do so—for my own sake. I always hoped that, if I helped to improve your financial position, I should be able to keep some check on you.

DR. STOCKMANN. What!! Then it was only for your own sake—!

PETER STOCKMANN. Up to a certain point, yes. It is painful for a man in an official position to have his nearest relative compromising himself time after time.

DR. STOCKMANN. And do you consider that I do that?

PETER STOCKMANN. Yes, unfortunately, you do, without even being aware of it. You have a restless, pugnacious, rebellious disposition. And then there is that disastrous propensity of yours to want to write about every sort of possible and impossible thing. The moment an idea comes into your head, you must needs go and write a newspaper article or a whole pamphlet about it.

DR. STOCKMANN. Well, but is it not the duty of a citizen to let the public share in any new ideas he may have?

PETER STOCKMANN. Oh, the public doesn't require any new ideas. The public is best served by the good, old-established ideas it already has.

DR. STOCKMANN. And that is your honest opinion?

PETER STOCKMANN. Yes, and for once I must talk frankly to you. Hitherto I have tried to avoid doing so, because I know how irritable you are; but now I must tell you the truth, Thomas. You have no conception what an amount of harm you do yourself by your impetuosity. You complain of the authorities, you even complain of the government—you are always pulling them to pieces; you insist that you have been neglected and persecuted. But what else can such a cantankerous man as you expect?

DR. STOCKMANN. What next! Cantankerous, am I?

PETER STOCKMANN. Yes, Thomas, you are an extremely cantankerous man to work with—I know that to my cost. You disregard everything that you ought to have consideration for. You seem completely to forget that it is me you have to thank for your appointment here as medical officer to the Baths——

DR. STOCKMANN. I was entitled to it as a matter of course! —I and nobody else! I was the first person to see that the town could be made into a flourishing watering-place, and I was the only one who saw it at that time. I had to fight single-handed in support of the idea for many years; and I wrote and wrote——

PETER STOCKMANN. Undoubtedly. But things were not ripe for the scheme then—though, of course, you could not judge of that in your out-of-the-way corner up north. But as soon as the opportune moment came I—and the others— took the matter into our hands——

DR. STOCKMANN. Yes, and made this mess of all my beautiful plan. It is pretty obvious now what clever fellows you were!

PETER STOCKMANN. To my mind the whole thing only seems to mean that you are seeking another outlet for your combativeness. You want to pick a quarrel with your superiors—an old habit of yours. You cannot put up with any authority over you. You look askance at anyone who occupies a superior official position; you regard him as a personal enemy, and then any stick is good enough to beat him with. But now I have called your attention to the fact that the town's interests are at stake—and, incidentally, my own too. And therefore I must tell you, Thomas, that you will find me inexorable with regard to what I am about to require you to do.

DR. STOCKMANN. And what is that?

PETER STOCKMANN. As you have been so indiscreet as to speak of this delicate matter to outsiders, despite the fact that you ought to have treated it as entirely official and confidential, it is obviously impossible to hush it up now. All sorts of rumors will get about directly, and everybody who has a grudge against us will take care to embellish these rumors. So it will be necessary for you to refute them publicly.

DR. STOCKMANN. I! How? I don't understand.

PETER STOCKMANN. What we shall expect is that, after making further investigations, you will come to the conclusion that the matter is not by any means as dangerous or as critical as you imagined in the first instance.

DR. STOCKMANN. Oho!—so that is what you expect!

PETER STOCKMANN. And, what is more, we shall expect you to make public profession of your confidence in the Committee and in their readiness to consider fully and conscientiously what steps may be necessary to remedy any possible defects.

DR. STOCKMANN. But you will never be able to do that by patching and tinkering at it—never! Take my word for it, Peter; I mean what I say, as deliberately and emphatically as possible.

PETER STOCKMANN. As an officer under the Committee, you have no right to any individual opinion.

DR. STOCKMANN (*amazed*). No right?

PETER STOCKMANN. In your official capacity, no. As a private person, it is quite another matter. But as a subordinate member of the staff of the Baths, you have no right to express any opinion which runs contrary to that of your superiors.

DR. STOCKMANN. This is too much! I, a doctor, a man of science, have no right to——!

PETER STOCKMANN. The matter in hand is not simply a scientific one. It is a complicated matter, and has its economic as well as its technical side.

DR. STOCKMANN. I don't care what it is! I intend to be free to express my opinion on any subject under the sun.

PETER STOCKMANN. As you please—but not on any subject concerning the Baths. That we forbid.

DR. STOCKMANN (*shouting*). You forbid—! You! A pack of——

PETER STOCKMANN. *I* forbid it—I, your chief; and if I forbid it, you have to obey.

DR. STOCKMANN (*controlling himself*). Peter—if you were not my brother——

PETRA (*throwing open the door*). Father, you shan't stand this!

MRS. STOCKMANN (coming in after her). Petra, Petra!

PETER STOCKMANN. Oh, so you have been eavesdropping.

MRS. STOCKMANN. You were talking so loud, we couldn't help——

PETRA. Yes, I was listening.

PETER STOCKMANN. Well, after all, I am very glad——

DR. STOCKMANN (*going up to him*). You were saying something about forbidding and obeying?

PETER STOCKMANN. You obliged me to take that tone with you.

DR. STOCKMANN. And so I am to give myself the lie, publicly?

PETER STOCKMANN. We consider it absolutely necessary that you should make some such public statement as I have asked for.

DR. STOCKMANN. And if I do not—obey?

PETER STOCKMANN. Then we shall publish a statement ourselves to reassure the public.

DR. STOCKMANN. Very well; but in that case I shall use my pen against you. I stick to what I have said; I will show that I am right and that you are wrong. And what will you do then?

PETER STOCKMANN. Then I shall not be able to prevent your being dismissed.

DR. STOCKMANN. What——?

PETRA. Father—dismissed!

MRS. STOCKMANN. Dismissed!

PETER STOCKMANN. Dismissed from the staff of the Baths. I shall be obliged to propose that you shall immediately be given notice, and shall not be allowed any further participation in the Baths' affairs.

DR. STOCKMANN. You would dare to do that!

PETER STOCKMANN. It is you that are playing the daring game.

PETRA. Uncle, that is a shameful way to treat a man like father!

MRS. STOCKMANN. Do hold your tongue, Petra!

PETER STOCKMANN (*looking at* PETRA). Oh, so we volunteer our opinions already, do we? Of course. (*To* MRS. STOCKMANN.) Katherine, I imagine you are the most sensible person in this house. Use any influence you may have over your husband, and make him see what this will entail for his family as well as——

DR. STOCKMANN. My family is my own concern and nobody else's!

PETER STOCKMANN. ——for his own family, as I was saying, as well as for the town he lives in.

DR. STOCKMANN. It is I who have the real good of the town at heart! I want to lay bare the defects that sooner or later must come to the light of day. I will show whether I love my native town.

PETER STOCKMANN. You, who in your blind obstinacy want to cut off the most important source of the town's welfare?

DR. STOCKMANN. The source is poisoned, man! Are you mad? We are making our living by retailing filth and corruption! The whole of our flourishing municipal life derives its sustenance from a lie!

PETER STOCKMANN. All imagination—or something even worse. The man who can throw out such offensive insinuations about his native town must be an enemy to our community.

DR. STOCKMANN (*going up to him*). Do you dare to——!

MRS. STOCKMANN (*throwing herself between them*). Thomas!

PETRA (*catching her father by the arm*). Don't lose your temper, father!

PETER STOCKMANN. I will not expose myself to violence. Now you have had a warning; so reflect on what you owe to yourself and your family. Good-bye. (*Goes out.*)

DR. STOCKMANN (*walking up and down*). Am I to put

up with such treatment as this? In my own house, Katherine! What do you think of that!

MRS. STOCKMANN. Indeed it is both shameful and absurd. Thomas——

PETRA. If only I could give uncle a piece of my mind——

DR. STOCKMANN. It is my own fault. I ought to have flown out at him long ago!—shown my teeth!—bitten! To hear him call me an enemy to our community! Me! *I* shall not take that lying down, upon my soul!

MRS. STOCKMANN. But, dear Thomas, your brother has power on his side——

DR. STOCKMANN. Yes, but I have right on mine, I tell you.

MRS. STOCKMANN. Oh yes, right—right. What is the use of having right on your side if you have not got might?

PETRA. Oh, mother!—how can you say such a thing!

DR. STOCKMANN. Do you imagine that in a free country it is no use having right on your side? You are absurd, Katherine. Besides, haven't I got the liberal-minded, independent press to lead the way, and the compact majority behind me? That is might enough, I should think!

MRS. STOCKMANN. But, good heavens, Thomas, you don't mean to——?

DR. STOCKMANN. Don't mean to what?

MRS. STOCKMANN. To set yourself up in opposition to your brother.

DR. STOCKMANN. In God's name, what else do you suppose I should do but take my stand on right and truth?

PETRA. Yes, I was just going to say that.

MRS. STOCKMANN. But it won't do you any earthly good. If they won't do it, they won't.

DR. STOCKMANN. Oho, Katherine! Just give me time, and you will see how I will carry the war into their camp.

MRS. STOCKMANN. Yes, you carry the war into their camp, and you get your dismissal—that is what you will do.

DR. STOCKMANN. In any case I shall have done my duty towards the public—towards the community. I, who am called its enemy!

MRS. STOCKMANN. But towards your family, Thomas? Towards your own home! Do you think that is doing your duty towards those you have to provide for?

PETRA. Ah, don't think always first of us, mother.

MRS. STOCKMANN. Oh, it is easy for you to talk; you are able to shift for yourself, if need be. But remember the boys, Thomas; and think a little too of yourself, and of me——

DR. STOCKMANN. I think you are out of your senses, Katherine! If I were to be such a miserable coward as to go on my knees to Peter and his damned crew, do you suppose I should ever know an hour's peace of mind all my life afterwards?

MRS. STOCKMANN. I don't know anything about that; but God preserve us from the peace of mind we shall have, all the same, if you go on defying him! You will find yourself again without the means of subsistence, with no income to count upon. I should think we had had enough of that in the old days. Remember that, Thomas; think what that means.

DR. STOCKMANN (*collecting himself with a struggle and clenching his fists*). And this is what this slavery can bring upon a free, honorable man! Isn't it horrible, Katherine?

MRS. STOCKMANN. Yes, it is sinful to treat you so, it is perfectly true. But, good heavens, one has to put up with so much injustice in this world.—There are the boys, Thomas! Look at them! What is to become of them? Oh, no, no, you can never have the heart——.

(EJLIF *and* MORTEN *have come in while she was speaking, with their school books in their hands.*)

DR. STOCKMANN. The boys——! (*Recovers himself suddenly.*) No, even if the whole world goes to pieces, I will never bow my neck to this yoke! (*Goes towards his room.*)

MRS. STOCKMANN (*following him*). Thomas—what are you going to do!

DR. STOCKMANN (*at his door*). I mean to have the right to look my sons in the face when they are grown men. (*Goes into his room.*)

MRS. STOCKMANN (*bursting into tears*). God help us all!

PETRA. Father is splendid! He will not give in.

(*The boys look on in amazement;* PETRA *signs to them not to speak.*)

ACT III

(SCENE.—*The editorial office of the "People's Messenger."
The entrance door is on the left-hand side of the back
wall; on the right-hand side is another door with glass
panels through which the printing-room can be seen.
Another door in the right-hand wall. In the middle of
the room is a large table covered with papers, newspapers
and books. In the foreground on the left a window,
before which stand a desk and a high stool. There are a
couple of easy chairs by the table, and other chairs standing along the wall. The room is dingy and uncomfort-
able; the furniture is old, the chairs stained and torn. In
the printing-room the compositors are seen at work, and
a printer is working a hand-press.* HOVSTAD *is sitting at
the desk, writing.* BILLING *comes in from the right with*
DR. STOCKMANN'S *manuscript in his hand.*)

BILLING. Well, I must say!

HOVSTAD (*still writing.*) Have you read it through?

BILLING (*laying the MS. on the desk.*) Yes, indeed I have.

HOVSTAD. Don't you think the Doctor hits them pretty
hard?

BILLING. Hard? Bless my soul, he's crushing! Every word
falls like—how shall I put it?—like the blow of a sledge-
hammer.

HOVSTAD. Yes, but they are not the people to throw up the
sponge at the first blow.

BILLING. That is true; and for that reason we must strike
blow upon blow until the whole of this aristocracy tumbles
to pieces. As I sat in there reading this, I almost seemed to
see a revolution in being.

HOVSTAD (*turning round*). Hush!—Speak so that Aslaksen cannot hear you.

BILLING (*lowering his voice*). Aslaksen is a chicken-hearted chap, a coward; there is nothing of the man in him. But this time you will insist on your own way, won't you? You will put the Doctor's article in?

HOVSTAD. Yes, and if the Mayor doesn't like it——

BILLING. That will be the devil of a nuisance.

HOVSTAD. Well, fortunately we can turn the situation to good account, whatever happens. If the Mayor will not fall in with the Doctor's project, he will have all the small tradesmen down on him—the whole of the Householders' Association and the rest of them. And if he does fall in with it, he will fall out with the whole crowd of large shareholders in the Baths, who up to now have been his most valuable supporters——

BILLING. Yes, because they will certainly have to fork out a pretty penny——

HOVSTAD. Yes, you may be sure they will. And in this way the ring will be broken up, you see, and then in every issue of the paper we will enlighten the public on the Mayor's incapability on one point and another, and make it clear that all the positions of trust in the town, the whole control of municipal affairs, ought to be put in the hands of the Liberals.

BILLING. That is perfectly true! I see it coming—I see it coming; we are on the threshold of a revolution!

(*A knock is heard at the door.*)

HOVSTAD. Hush! (*Calls out.*) Come in! (DR. STOCKMANN *comes in by the street door.* HOVSTAD *goes to meet him.*) Ah, it is you, Doctor! Well?

DR. STOCKMANN. You may set to work and print it, Mr. Hovstad!

HOVSTAD. Has it come to that, then?

BILLING. Hurrah!

DR. STOCKMANN. Yes, print away. Undoubtedly it has

come to that. Now they must take what they get. There is going to be a fight in the town, Mr. Billing!

BILLING. War to the knife, I hope! We will get our knives to their throats, Doctor!

DR. STOCKMANN. This article is only a beginning. I have already got four or five more sketched out in my head. Where is Aslaksen?

BILLING (*calls into the printing-room*). Aslaksen, just come here for a minute!

HOVSTAD. Four or five more articles, did you say? On the same subject?

DR. STOCKMANN. No—far from it, my dear fellow. No, they are about quite another matter. But they all spring from the question of the water-supply and the drainage. One thing leads to another, you know. It is like beginning to pull down an old house, exactly.

BILLING. Upon my soul, it's true; you find you are not done till you have pulled all the old rubbish down.

ASLAKSEN (*coming in*). Pulled down? You are not thinking of pulling down the Baths surely, Doctor?

HOVSTAD. Far from it, don't be afraid.

DR. STOCKMANN. No, we meant something quite different. Well, what do you think of my article, Mr. Hovstad?

HOVSTAD. I think it is simply a masterpiece——

DR. STOCKMANN. Do you really think so? Well, I am very pleased, very pleased.

HOVSTAD. It is so clear and intelligible. One need have no special knowledge to understand the bearing of it. You will have every enlightened man on your side.

ASLAKSEN. And every prudent man too, I hope?

BILLING. The prudent and the imprudent—almost the whole town.

ASLAKSEN. In that case we may venture to print it.

DR. STOCKMANN. I should think so!

HOVSTAD. We will put it in to-morrow morning.

DR. STOCKMANN. Of course—you must not lose a single day. What I wanted to ask you, Mr. Aslaksen, was if you would supervise the printing of it yourself.

ASLAKSEN. With pleasure.

DR. STOCKMANN. Take care of it as if it were a treasure! No misprints—every word is important. I will look in again a little later; perhaps you will be able to let me see a proof. I can't tell you how eager I am to see it in print, and see it burst upon the public——

BILLING. Burst upon them—yes, like a flash of lightning!

DR. STOCKMANN. ——and to have it submitted to the judgment of my intelligent fellow-townsmen. You cannot imagine what I have gone through to-day. I have been threatened first with one thing and then with another; they have tried to rob me of my most elementary rights as a man——

BILLING. What! Your rights as a man!

DR. STOCKMANN. ——they have tried to degrade me, to make a coward of me, to force me to put personal interests before my most sacred convictions——

BILLING. That is too much—I'm damned if it isn't.

HOVSTAD. Oh, you mustn't be surprised at anything from that quarter.

DR. STOCKMANN. Well, they will get the worst of it with me; they may assure themselves of that. I shall consider the "People's Messenger" my sheet-anchor now, and every single day I will bombard them with one article after another, like bomb-shells——

ASLAKSEN. Yes, but——

BILLING. Hurrah!—it is war, it is war!

DR. STOCKMANN. I shall smite them to the ground—I shall crush them—I shall break down all their defenses, before the eyes of the honest public! That is what I shall do!

ASLAKSEN. Yes, but in moderation, Doctor—proceed with moderation——

BILLING. Not a bit of it, not a bit of it! Don't spare the dynamite!

DR. STOCKMANN. Because it is not merely a question of water-supply and drains now, you know. No—it is the whole of our social life that we have got to purify and disinfect——

BILLING. Spoken like a deliverer!

DR. STOCKMANN. All the incapables must be turned out, you understand—and that in every walk of life! Endless vistas have opened themselves to my mind's eye to-day. I cannot see it all quite clearly yet, but I shall in time. Young and vigorous standard-bearers—those are what we need and must seek, my friends; we must have new men in command at all our outposts.

BILLING. Hear, hear!

DR. STOCKMANN. We only need to stand by one another, and it will all be perfectly easy. The revolution will be launched like a ship that runs smoothly off the stocks. Don't you think so?

HOVSTAD. For my part I think we have now a prospect of getting the municipal authority into the hands where it should lie.

ASLAKSEN. And if only we proceed with moderation, I cannot imagine that there will be any risk.

DR. STOCKMANN. Who the devil cares whether there *is* any risk or not! What I am doing, I am doing in the name of truth and for the sake of my conscience.

HOVSTAD. You are a man who deserves to be supported, Doctor.

ASLAKSEN. Yes, there is no denying that the Doctor is a true friend to the town—a real friend to the community, that he is.

BILLING. Take my word for it, Aslaksen, Dr. Stockmann is a friend of the people.

ASLAKSEN. I fancy the Householders' Association will make use of that expression before long.

DR. STOCKMANN (*affected, grasps their hands*). Thank you, thank you, my dear staunch friends. It is very refreshing to me to hear you say that; my brother called me something quite different. By Jove, he shall have it back, with interest! But now I must be off to see a poor devil——. I will come back, as I said. Keep a very careful eye on the manuscript, Aslaksen, and don't for worlds leave out any of my notes of exclamation! Rather put one or two more in! Capital, capital! Well, good-bye for the present—good-bye, good-bye!

(*They show him to the door, and bow him out.*)

HOVSTAD. He may prove an invaluably useful man to us.

ASLAKSEN. Yes, so long as he confines himself to this matter of the Baths. But if he goes farther afield, I don't think it would be advisable to follow him.

HOVSTAD. Hm!—that all depends——

BILLING. You are so infernally timid, Aslaksen!

ASLAKSEN. Timid? Yes, when it is a question of the local authorities, I am timid, Mr. Billing; it is a lesson I have learnt in the school of experience, let me tell you. But try me in higher politics, in matters that concern the government itself, and then see if I am timid.

BILLING. No, you aren't, I admit. But this is simply contradicting yourself.

ASLAKSEN. I am a man with a conscience, and that is the whole matter. If you attack the government, you don't do the community any harm, anyway; those fellows pay no attention to attacks, you see—they go on just as they are, in spite of them. But *local* authorities are different; they *can* be turned out, and then perhaps you may get an ignorant lot into office who may do irreparable harm to the householders and everybody else.

HOVSTAD. But what of the education of citizens by self-government—don't you attach any importance to that?

ASLAKSEN. When a man has interests of his own to protect, he cannot think of everything, Mr. Hovstad.

HOVSTAD. Then I hope I shall never have interests of my own to protect!

BILLING. Hear, hear!

ASLAKSEN (*with a smile*). Hm! (*Points to the desk.*) Mr.
Sheriff Stensgaard was your predecessor at that editorial desk.

BILLING (*spitting*). Bah! That turncoat.

HOVSTAD. I am not a weathercock—and never will be.

ASLAKSEN. A politician should never be too certain of
anything, Mr. Hovstad. And as for you, Mr. Billing, I should
think it is time for you to be taking in a reef or two in your
sails, seeing that you are applying for the post of secretary
to the Bench.

BILLING. I——!

HOVSTAD. Are you, Billing?

BILLING. Well, yes—but you must clearly understand I am
doing it only to annoy the bigwigs.

ASLAKSEN. Anyhow, it is no business of mine. But if I am
to be accused of timidity and of inconsistency in my principles, this is what I want to point out: my political past is an
open book. I have never changed, except perhaps to become
a little more moderate, you see. My heart is still with the
people; but I don't deny that my reason has a certain bias
towards the authorities—the local ones, I mean. (*Goes into
the printing-room.*)

BILLING. Oughtn't we to try and get rid of him, Hovstad?

HOVSTAD. Do you know anyone else who will advance the
money for our paper and printing bill?

BILLING. It is an infernal nuisance that we don't possess
some capital to trade on.

HOVSTAD (*sitting down at his desk*). Yes, if we only had
that, then——

BILLING. Suppose you were to apply to Dr. Stockmann?

HOVSTAD (*turning over some papers*). What is the use?
He has got nothing.

BILLING. No, but he has got a warm man in the background, old Morten Kiil—"the Badger," as they call him.

HOVSTAD (*writing*). Are you so sure *he* has got anything?

BILLING. Good Lord, of course he has! And some of it

must come to the Stockmanns. Most probably he will do something for the children, at all events.

HOVSTAD (*turning half round*). Are you counting on that?

BILLING. Counting on it? Of course I am not counting on anything.

HOVSTAD. That is right. And I should not count on the secretaryship to the Bench either, if I were you; for I can assure you—you won't get it.

BILLING. Do you think I am not quite aware of that? My object is precisely *not* to get it. A slight of that kind stimulates a man's fighting power—it is like getting a supply of fresh bile—and I am sure one needs that badly enough in a hole-and-corner place like this, where it is so seldom anything happens to stir one up.

HOVSTAD (*writing*). Quite so, quite so.

BILLING. Ah, I shall be heard of yet!——Now I shall go and write the appeal to the Householders' Association. (*Goes into the room on the right.*)

HOVSTAD (*sitting at his desk, biting his penholder, says slowly*). Hm!—that's it, is it? (*A knock is heard.*) Come in! (PETRA *comes in by the outer door.* HOVSTAD *gets up.*) What, you!—here?

PETRA. Yes, you must forgive me——

HOVSTAD (*pulling a chair forward*). Won't you sit down?

PETRA. No, thank you; I must go again in a moment.

HOVSTAD. Have you come with a message from your father, by any chance?

PETRA. No, I have come on my own account. (*Takes a book out of her coat pocket.*) Here is the English story.

HOVSTAD. Why have you brought it back?

PETRA. Because I am not going to translate it.

HOVSTAD. But you promised me faithfully——

PETRA. Yes, but then I had not read it. I don't suppose you have read it either?

HOVSTAD. No, you know quite well I don't understand English; but——

PETRA. Quite so. That is why I wanted to tell you that you must find something else. (*Lays the book on the table.*) You can't use this for the "People's Messenger."

HOVSTAD. Why not?

PETRA. Because it conflicts with all your opinions.

HOVSTAD. Oh, for that matter——

PETRA. You don't understand me. The burden of this story is that there is a supernatural power that looks after the so-called good people in this world and makes everything happen for the best in their case—while all the so-called bad people are punished.

HOVSTAD. Well, but that is all right. That is just what our readers want.

PETRA. And are you going to be the one to give it to them? For myself, I do not believe a word of it. You know quite well that things do not happen so in reality.

HOVSTAD. You are perfectly right; but an editor cannot always act as he would prefer. He is often obliged to bow to the wishes of the public in unimportant matters. Politics are the most important thing in life—for a newspaper, anyway; and if I want to carry my public with me on the path that leads to liberty and progress, I must not frighten them away. If they find a moral tale of this sort in the serial at the bottom of the page, they will be all the more ready to read what is printed above it; they feel more secure, as it were.

PETRA. For shame! You would never go and set a snare like that for your readers; you are not a spider!

HOVSTAD (*smiling*). Thank you for having such a good opinion of me. No; as a matter of fact that is Billing's idea and not mine.

PETRA. Billing's!

HOVSTAD. Yes; anyway he propounded that theory here one day. And it is Billing who is so anxious to have that story in the paper; I don't know anything about the book.

PETRA. But how can Billing, with his emancipated views——

HOVSTAD. Oh, Billing is a many-sided man. He is applying for the post of secretary to the Bench, too, I hear.

PETRA. I don't believe it, Mr. Hovstad. How could he possibly bring himself to do such a thing?

HOVSTAD. Ah, you must ask him that.

PETRA. I should never have thought it of him.

HOVSTAD (*looking more closely at her*). No? Does it really surprise you so much?

PETRA. Yes. Or perhaps not altogether. Really, I don't quite know——

HOVSTAD. We journalists are not much worth, Miss Stockmann.

PETRA. Do you really mean that?

HOVSTAD. I think so sometimes.

PETRA. Yes, in the ordinary affairs of everyday life, perhaps; I can understand that. But now, when you have taken a weighty matter in hand——

HOVSTAD. This matter of your father's, you mean?

PETRA. Exactly. It seems to me that now you must feel you are a man worth more than most.

HOVSTAD. Yes, to-day I do feel something of that sort.

PETRA. Of course you do, don't you? It is a splendid vocation you have chosen—to smooth the way for the march of unappreciated truths, and new and courageous lines of thought. If it were nothing more than because you stand fearlessly in the open and take up the cause of an injured man——

HOVSTAD. Especially when that injured man is—ahem!—I don't rightly know how to——

PETRA. When that man is so upright and so honest, you mean?

HOVSTAD (*more gently*). Especially when he is your father, I meant.

PETRA (*suddenly checked*). *That?*

HOVSTAD. Yes, Petra—Miss Petra.

PETRA. Is it *that*, that is first and foremost with you? Not the matter itself? Not the truth?—not my father's big generous heart?

HOVSTAD. Certainly—of course—that too.

PETRA. No, thank you; you have betrayed yourself, Mr. Hovstad, and now I shall never trust you again in anything.

HOVSTAD. Can you really take it so amiss in me that it is mostly for your sake——?

PETRA. What I am angry with you for, is for not having been honest with my father. You talked to him as if the truth and the good of the community were what lay nearest to your heart. You have made fools of both my father and me. You are not the man you made yourself out to be. And that I shall never forgive you—never!

HOVSTAD. You ought not to speak so bitterly, Miss Petra— least of all now.

PETRA. Why not now, especially?

HOVSTAD. Because your father cannot do without my help.

PETRA (*looking him up and down*). Are you that sort of man too? For shame!

HOVSTAD. No, no, I am not. This came upon me so unexpectedly—you must believe that.

PETRA. I know what to believe. Good-bye.

ASLAKSEN (*coming from the printing-room, hurriedly and with an air of mystery*). Damnation, Hovstad!——(*Sees* PETRA.) Oh, this is awkward——

PETRA. There is the book; you must give it to some one else. (*Goes towards the door.*)

HOVSTAD (*following her*). But, Miss Stockmann——

PETRA. Good-bye. (*Goes out.*)

ASLAKSEN. I say—Mr. Hovstad——

HOVSTAD. Well, well!—what is it?

ASLAKSEN. The Mayor is outside in the printing-room.

HOVSTAD. The Mayor, did you say?

ASLAKSEN. Yes, he wants to speak to you. He came in by the back door—didn't want to be seen, you understand.

HOVSTAD. What can he want? Wait a bit—I will go myself. (*Goes to the door of the printing-room, opens it, bows and invites* PETER STOCKMANN *in.*) Just see, Aslaksen, that no one——

ASLAKSEN. Quite so. (*Goes into the printing-room.*)

PETER STOCKMANN. You did not expect to see me here, Mr. Hovstad?

HOVSTAD. No, I confess I did not.

PETER STOCKMANN (*looking round*). You are very snug in here—very nice indeed.

HOVSTAD. Oh——

PETER STOCKMANN. And here I come, without any notice, to take up your time!

HOVSTAD. By all means, Mr. Mayor. I am at your service. But let me relieve you of your—— (*takes* STOCKMANN'S *hat and stick and puts them on a chair*). Won't you sit down?

PETER STOCKMANN (*sitting down by the table*). Thank you. (HOVSTAD *sits down.*) I have had an extremely annoying experience to-day, Mr. Hovstad.

HOVSTAD. Really? Ah well, I expect with all the various business you have to attend to——

PETER STOCKMANN. The Medical Officer of the Baths is responsible for what happened to-day.

HOVSTAD. Indeed? The Doctor?

PETER STOCKMANN. He has addressed a kind of report to the Baths Committee on the subject of certain supposed defects in the Baths.

HOVSTAD. Has he indeed?

PETER STOCKMANN. Yes—has he not told you? I thought he said——

HOVSTAD. Ah, yes—it is true he did mention something about——

ASLAKSEN (*coming from the printing-room*). I ought to have that copy——

HOVSTAD (*angrily*). Ahem!—there it is on the desk.

ASLAKSEN (*taking it*). Right.

PETER STOCKMANN. But look there—that is the thing I was speaking of!

ASLAKSEN. Yes, that is the Doctor's article, Mr. Mayor.

HOVSTAD. Oh, is *that* what you were speaking about?

PETER STOCKMANN. Yes, that is it. What do you think of it?

HOVSTAD. Oh, I am only a layman—and I have only taken a very cursory glance at it.

PETER STOCKMANN. But you are going to print it?

HOVSTAD. I cannot very well refuse a distinguished man——

ASLAKSEN. I have nothing to do with editing the paper, Mr. Mayor——

PETER STOCKMANN. I understand.

ASLAKSEN. I merely print what is put into my hands.

PETER STOCKMANN. Quite so.

ASLAKSEN. And so I must——(*moves off towards the printing-room*).

PETER STOCKMANN. No, but wait a moment, Mr. Aslaksen. You will allow me, Mr. Hovstad?

HOVSTAD. If you please, Mr. Mayor.

PETER STOCKMANN. You are a discreet and thoughtful man, Mr. Aslaksen.

ASLAKSEN. I am delighted to hear you think so, sir.

PETER STOCKMANN. And a man of very considerable influence.

ASLAKSEN. Chiefly among the small tradesmen, sir.

PETER STOCKMANN. The small tax-payers are the majority—here as everywhere else.

ASLAKSEN. That is true.

PETER STOCKMANN. And I have no doubt you know the general trend of opinion among them, don't you?

ASLAKSEN. Yes, I think I may say I do, Mr. Mayor.

PETER STOCKMANN. Yes. Well, since there is such a

praiseworthy spirit of self-sacrifice among the less wealthy citizens of our town——

ASLAKSEN. What?

HOVSTAD. Self-sacrifice?

PETER STOCKMANN. It is pleasing evidence of a public-spirited feeling, extremely pleasing evidence. I might almost say I hardly expected it. But you have a closer knowledge of public opinion than I.

ASLAKSEN. But, Mr. Mayor——

PETER STOCKMANN. And indeed it is no small sacrifice that the town is going to make.

HOVSTAD. The town?

ASLAKSEN. But I don't understand. Is it the Baths——?

PETER STOCKMANN. At a provisional estimate, the alterations that the Medical Officer asserts to be desirable will cost somewhere about twenty thousand pounds.

ASLAKSEN. That is a lot of money, but——

PETER STOCKMANN. Of course it will be necessary to raise a municipal loan.

HOVSTAD (getting up). Surely you never mean that the town must pay——?

ASLAKSEN. Do you mean that it must come out of the municipal funds?—out of the ill-filled pockets of the small tradesmen?

PETER STOCKMANN. Well, my dear Mr. Aslaksen, where else is the money to come from?

ASLAKSEN. The gentlemen who own the Baths ought to provide that.

PETER STOCKMANN. The proprietors of the Baths are not in a position to incur any further expense.

ASLAKSEN. Is that absolutely certain, Mr. Mayor?

PETER STOCKMANN. I have satisfied myself that it is so. If the town wants these very extensive alterations, it will have to pay for them.

ASLAKSEN. But, damn it all—I beg your pardon—this is quite another matter, Mr. Hovstad!

HOVSTAD. It is, indeed.

PETER STOCKMANN. The most fatal part of it is that we shall be obliged to shut the Baths for a couple of years.

HOVSTAD. Shut them? Shut them altogether?

ASLAKSEN. For two years?

PETER STOCKMANN. Yes, the work will take as long as that—at least.

ASLAKSEN. I'm damned if we will stand that, Mr. Mayor! What are we householders to live upon in the meantime?

PETER STOCKMANN. Unfortunately that is an extremely difficult question to answer, Mr. Aslaksen. But what would you have us do? Do you suppose we shall have a single visitor in the town, if we go about proclaiming that our water is polluted, that we are living over a plague spot, that the entire town——

ASLAKSEN. And the whole thing is merely imagination?

PETER STOCKMANN. With the best will in the world, I have not been able to come to any other conclusion.

ASLAKSEN. Well then I must say it is absolutely unjustifiable of Dr. Stockmann—I beg your pardon, Mr. Mayor——

PETER STOCKMANN. What you say is lamentably true, Mr. Aslaksen. My brother has unfortunately always been a head-strong man.

ASLAKSEN. After this, do you mean to give him your support, Mr. Hovstad?

HOVSTAD. Can you suppose for a moment that I——?

PETER STOCKMANN. I have drawn up a short *résumé* of the situation as it appears from a reasonable man's point of view. In it I have indicated how certain possible defects might suitably be remedied without outrunning the resources of the Baths Committee.

HOVSTAD. Have you got it with you, Mr. Mayor.

PETER STOCKMANN (*fumbling in his pocket*). Yes, I brought it with me in case you should——

ASLAKSEN. Good Lord, there he is!

PETER STOCKMANN. Who? My brother?

HOVSTAD. Where? Where?

ASLAKSEN. He has just gone through the printing-room.

PETER STOCKMANN. How unlucky! I don't want to meet him here, and I had still several things to speak to you about.

HOVSTAD (*pointing to the door on the right*). Go in there for the present.

PETER STOCKMANN. But——?

HOVSTAD. You will only find Billing in there.

ASLAKSEN. Quick, quick, Mr. Mayor—he is just coming.

PETER STOCKMANN. Yes, very well; but see that you get rid of him quickly. (*Goes out through the door on the right, which* ASLAKSEN *opens for him and shuts after him.*)

HOVSTAD. Pretend to be doing something, Aslaksen. (*Sits down and writes.* ASLAKSEN *begins foraging among a heap of newspapers that are lying on a chair.*)

DR. STOCKMANN (*coming in from the printing-room*). Here I am again. (*Puts down his hat and stick.*)

HOVSTAD (*writing*). Already, Doctor? Hurry up with what we were speaking about, Aslaksen. We are very pressed for time to-day.

DR. STOCKMANN (*to* ASLAKSEN). No proof for me to see yet, I hear.

ASLAKSEN (*without turning round*). You couldn't expect it yet, Doctor.

DR. STOCKMANN. No, no; but I am impatient, as you can understand. I shall not know a moment's peace of mind till I see it in print.

HOVSTAD. H'm!—It will take a good while yet, won't it, Aslaksen?

ASLAKSEN. Yes, I am almost afraid it will.

DR. STOCKMANN. All right, my dear friends; I will come back. I do not mind coming back twice if necessary. A matter of such great importance—the welfare of the town at stake—it is no time to shirk trouble. (*Is just going, but stops and comes back*). Look here—there is one thing more I want to speak to you about.

HOVSTAD. Excuse me, but could it not wait till some other time?

DR. STOCKMANN. I can tell you in half a dozen words. It is only this. When my article is read to-morrow and it is realized that I have been quietly working the whole winter for the welfare of the town——

HOVSTAD. Yes, but, Doctor——

DR. STOCKMANN. I know what you are going to say. You don't see how on earth it was any more than my duty—my obvious duty as a citizen. Of course it wasn't; I know that as well as you. But my fellow citizens, you know——! Good Lord, think of all the good souls who think so highly of me——!

ASLAKSEN. Yes, our townsfolk have had a very high opinion of you so far, Doctor.

DR. STOCKMANN. Yes, and that is just why I am afraid they——. Well, this is the point; when this reaches them, especially the poorer classes, and sounds in their ears like a summons to take the town's affairs into their own hands for the future——

HOVSTAD (*getting up*). Ahem! Doctor, I won't conceal from you the fact——

DR. STOCKMANN. Ah!—I knew there was something in the wind! But I won't hear a word of it. If anything of that sort is being set on foot——

HOVSTAD. Of what sort?

DR. STOCKMANN. Well, whatever it is—whether it is a demonstration in my honor, or a banquet, or a subscription list for some presentation to me—whatever it is, you must promise me solemnly and faithfully to put a stop to it. You too, Mr. Aslaksen; do you understand?

HOVSTAD. You must forgive me, Doctor, but sooner or later we must tell you the plain truth——

(*He is interrupted by the entrance of* MRS. STOCKMANN, *who comes in from the street door.*)

MRS. STOCKMANN (*seeing her husband*). Just as I thought!

HOVSTAD (*going towards her*). You too, Mrs. Stockmann?

DR. STOCKMANN. What on earth do *you* want here, Katherine?

MRS. STOCKMANN. I should think you know very well what I want.

HOVSTAD. Won't you sit down? Or perhaps——

MRS. STOCKMANN. No, thank you; don't trouble. And you must not be offended at my coming to fetch my husband; I am the mother of three children, you know.

DR. STOCKMANN. Nonsense!—we know all about that.

MRS. STOCKMANN. Well, one would not give you credit for much thought for your wife and children to-day; if you had had that, you would not have gone and dragged us all into misfortune.

DR. STOCKMANN. Are you out of your senses, Katherine! Because a man has a wife and children, is he not to be allowed to proclaim the truth—is he not to be allowed to be an actively useful citizen—is he not to be allowed to do a service to his native town!

MRS. STOCKMANN. Yes, Thomas—in reason.

ASLAKSEN. Just what I say. Moderation is everything.

MRS. STOCKMANN. And that is why you wrong us, Mr. Hovstad, in enticing my husband away from his home and making a dupe of him in all this.

HOVSTAD. I certainly am making a dupe of no one——

DR. STOCKMANN. Making a dupe of me! Do you suppose *I* should allow myself to be duped!

MRS. STOCKMANN. It is just what you do. I know quite well you have more brains than anyone in the town, but you are extremely easily duped, Thomas. (*To* HOVSTAD.) Please to realize that he loses his post at the Baths if you print what he has written——

ASLAKSEN. What!

HOVSTAD. Look here, Doctor——

DR. STOCKMANN (*laughing*). Ha—ha!—just let them try! No, no—they will take good care not to. I have got the compact majority behind me, let me tell you!

MRS. STOCKMANN. Yes, that is just the worst of it—your having any such horrid thing behind you.

DR. STOCKMANN. Rubbish, Katherine!—Go home and look after your house and leave me to look after the community. How can you be so afraid, when I am so confident and happy? (*Walks up and down, rubbing his hands.*) Truth and the People will win the fight, you may be certain! I see the whole of the broadminded middle class marching like a victorious army——! (*Stops beside a chair.*) What the deuce is that lying there?

ASLAKSEN. Good Lord!

HOVSTAD. Ahem!

DR. STOCKMANN. Here we have the topmost pinnacle of authority! (*Takes the Mayor's official hat carefully between his finger-tips and holds it up in the air.*)

MRS. STOCKMANN. The Mayor's hat!

DR. STOCKMANN. And here is the staff of office too. How in the name of all that's wonderful——?

HOVSTAD. Well, you see——

DR. STOCKMANN. Oh, I understand. He has been here trying to talk you over. Ha—ha!—he made rather a mistake there! And as soon as he caught sight of me in the printing-room——. (*Bursts out laughing.*) Did he run away, Mr. Aslaksen?

ASLAKSEN (*hurriedly*). Yes, he ran away, Doctor.

DR. STOCKMANN. Ran away without his stick or his——

Fiddlesticks! Peter doesn't run away and leave his belongings behind him. But what the deuce have you done with him? Ah!—in there, of course. Now you shall see, Katherine!

MRS. STOCKMANN. Thomas—please don't——!

ASLAKSEN. Don't be rash, Doctor.

(DR. STOCKMANN *has put on the Mayor's hat and taken his stick in his hand. He goes up to the door, opens it, and stands with his hand to his hat at the salute.* PETER STOCKMANN *comes in, red with anger.* BILLING *follows him.*)

PETER STOCKMANN. What does this tomfoolery mean?

DR. STOCKMANN. Be respectful, my good Peter. I am the chief authority in the town now. (*Walks up and down.*)

MRS. STOCKMANN (*almost in tears*). Really, Thomas!

PETER STOCKMANN (*following him about*). Give me my hat and stick.

DR. STOCKMANN (*in the same tone as before*). If you are chief constable, let me tell you that I am the Mayor—I am the master of the whole town, please understand!

PETER STOCKMANN. Take off my hat, I tell you. Remember it is part of an official uniform.

DR. STOCKMANN. Pooh! Do you think the newly awakened lion-hearted people are going to be frightened by an official hat? There is going to be a revolution in the town to-morrow, let me tell you. You thought you could turn me out; but now I shall turn you out—turn you out of all your various offices. Do you think I cannot? Listen to me. I have triumphant social forces behind me. Hovstad and Billing will thunder in the "People's Messenger," and Aslaksen will take the field at the head of the whole Householders' Association——

ASLAKSEN. That I won't, Doctor.

DR. STOCKMANN. Of course you will——

PETER STOCKMANN. Ah!—may I ask then if Mr. Hovstad intends to join this agitation?

HOVSTAD. No, Mr. Mayor.

ASLAKSEN. No, Mr. Hovstad is not such a fool as to go and ruin his paper and himself for the sake of an imaginary grievance.

DR. STOCKMANN (*looking round him*). What does this mean?

HOVSTAD. You have represented your case in a false light, Doctor, and therefore I am unable to give you my support.

BILLING. And after what the Mayor was so kind as to tell me just now, I——

DR. STOCKMANN. A false light! Leave that part of it to me. Only print my article; I am quite capable of defending it.

HOVSTAD. I am not going to print it. I cannot and will not and dare not print it.

DR. STOCKMANN. You dare not? What nonsense!—you are the editor; and an editor controls his paper, I suppose!

ASLAKSEN. No, it is the subscribers, Doctor.

PETER STOCKMANN. Fortunately, yes.

ASLAKSEN. It is public opinion—the enlightened public—householders and people of that kind; they control the newspapers.

DR. STOCKMANN (*composedly*). And I have all these influences against me?

ASLAKSEN. Yes, you have. It would mean the absolute ruin of the community if your article were to appear.

DR. STOCKMANN. Indeed.

PETER STOCKMANN. My hat and stick, if you please. (DR. STOCKMANN *takes off the hat and lays it on the table with the stick*. PETER STOCKMANN *takes them up*.) Your authority as mayor has come to an untimely end.

DR. STOCKMANN. We have not got to the end yet. (*To* HOVSTAD.) Then it is quite impossible for you to print my article in the "People's Messenger"?

HOVSTAD. Quite impossible—out of regard for your family as well.

MRS. STOCKMANN. You need not concern yourself about his family, thank you, Mr. Hovstad.

PETER STOCKMANN (*taking a paper from his pocket*). It will be sufficient, for the guidance of the public, if this appears. It is an official statement. May I trouble you?

HOVSTAD (*taking the paper*). Certainly; I will see that it is printed.

DR. STOCKMANN. But not mine. Do you imagine that you can silence me and stifle the truth! You will not find it so easy as you suppose. Mr. Aslaksen, kindly take my manuscript at once and print it as a pamphlet—at my expense. I will have four hundred copies—no, five—six hundred.

ASLAKSEN. If you offered me its weight in gold, I could not lend my press for any such purpose, Doctor. It would be flying in the face of public opinion. You will not get it printed anywhere in the town.

DR. STOCKMANN. Then give it me back.

HOVSTAD (*giving him the* MS.) Here it is.

DR. STOCKMANN (*taking his hat and stick*). It shall be made public all the same. I will read it out at a mass meeting of the townspeople. All my fellow-citizens shall hear the voice of truth!

PETER STOCKMANN. You will not find any public body in the town that will give you the use of their hall for such a purpose.

ASLAKSEN. Not a single one, I am certain.

BILLING. No, I'm damned if you will find one.

MRS. STOCKMANN. But this is too shameful! Why should every one turn against you like that?

DR. STOCKMANN (*angrily*). I will tell you why. It is because all the men in this town are old women—like you; they all think of nothing but their families, and never of the community.

MRS. STOCKMANN (*putting her arm into his*). Then I will show them that an—an old woman can be a man for once. I am going to stand by you, Thomas!

DR. STOCKMANN. Bravely said, Katherine! It shall be made public—as I am a living soul! If I can't hire a hall, I shall hire a drum, and parade the town with it and read it at every street-corner.

PETER STOCKMANN. You are surely not such an arrant fool as that!

DR. STOCKMANN. Yes, I am.

ASLAKSEN. You won't find a single man in the whole town to go with you.

BILLING. No, I'm damned if you will.

MRS. STOCKMANN. Don't give in, Thomas. I will tell the boys to go with you.

DR. STOCKMANN. That is a splendid idea!

MRS. STOCKMANN. Morten will be delighted; and Ejlif will do whatever he does.

DR. STOCKMANN. Yes, and Petra!—and you too, Katherine!

MRS. STOCKMANN. No, I won't do that; but I will stand at the window and watch you, that's what I will do.

DR. STOCKMANN (*puts his arms round her and kisses her*). Thank you, my dear! Now you and I are going to try a fall, my fine gentlemen! I am going to see whether a pack of cowards can succeed in gagging a patriot who wants to purify society! (*He and his wife go out by the street door.*)

PETER STOCKMANN (*shaking his head seriously*). Now he has sent *her* out of her senses, too.

ACT IV

(SCENE.—*A big old-fashioned room in* CAPTAIN HORSTER'S
*house. At the back folding-doors, which are standing
open, lead to an ante-room. Three windows in the left-
hand wall. In the middle of the opposite wall a platform
has been erected. On this is a small table with two
candles, a water-bottle and glass, and a bell. The room
is lit by lamps placed between the windows. In the foreground on the left there is a table with candles and a
chair. To the right is a door and some chairs standing
near it. The room is nearly filled with a crowd of townspeople of all sorts, a few women and schoolboys being
amongst them. People are still streaming in from the
back, and the room is soon filled.*)

1ST CITIZEN (*meeting another*). Hullo, Lamstad! You
here too?

2ND CITIZEN. I go to every public meeting, I do.

3RD CITIZEN. Brought your whistle too, I expect!

2ND CITIZEN. I should think so. Haven't you?

3RD CITIZEN. Rather! And old Evensen said he was going
to bring a cow-horn, he did.

2ND CITIZEN. Good old Evensen! (*Laughter among the
crowd*).

4TH CITIZEN (*coming up to them*). I say, tell me what is
going on here to-night.

2ND CITIZEN. Dr. Stockmann is going to deliver an address attacking the Mayor.

4TH CITIZEN. But the Mayor is his brother.

1ST CITIZEN. That doesn't matter; Dr. Stockmann's not
the chap to be afraid.

70

3RD CITIZEN. But he is in the wrong; it said so in the "People's Messenger."

2ND CITIZEN. Yes, I expect he must be in the wrong this time, because neither the Householders' Association nor the Citizens' Club would lend him their hall for his meeting.

1ST CITIZEN. He couldn't even get the loan of the hall at the Baths.

2ND CITIZEN. No, I should think not.

A MAN IN ANOTHER PART OF THE CROWD. I say—who are we to back up in this?

ANOTHER MAN, BESIDE HIM. Watch Aslaksen, and do as he does.

BILLING (*pushing his way through the crowd, with a writing-case under his arm*). Excuse me, gentlemen—do you mind letting me through? I am reporting for the "People's Messenger." Thank you very much! (*He sits down at the table on the left.*)

A WORKMAN. Who was that?

SECOND WORKMAN. Don't you know him? It's Billing, who writes for Aslaksen's paper.

(CAPTAIN HORSTER *brings in* MRS. STOCKMANN *and* PETRA *through the door on the right.* EJLIF *and* MORTON *follow them in.*)

HORSTER. I thought you might all sit here; you can slip out easily from here, if things get too lively.

MRS. STOCKMANN. Do you think there will be a disturbance?

HORSTER. One can never tell—with such a crowd. But sit down, and don't be uneasy.

MRS. STOCKMANN (*sitting down*). It was extremely kind of you to offer my husband the room.

HORSTER. Well, if nobody else would——

PETRA (*who has sat down beside her mother*). And it was a plucky thing to do, Captain Horster.

HORSTER. Oh, it is not such a great matter as all that.

(HOVSTAD *and* ASLAKSEN *make their way through the crowd.*)

ASLAKSEN (*going up to* HORSTER). Has the Doctor not come yet?

HORSTER. He is waiting in the next room. (*Movement in the crowd by the door at the back.*)

HOVSTAD. Look—here comes the Mayor!

BILLING. Yes, I'm damned if he hasn't come after all!

(PETER STOCKMANN *makes his way gradually through the crowd, bows courteously, and takes up a position by the wall on the left. Shortly afterwards* DR. STOCK- MANN *comes in by the right-hand door. He is dressed in a black frock-coat, with a white tie. There is a little feeble applause, which is hushed down. Silence is obtained.*)

DR. STOCKMANN (*in an undertone*). How do you feel, Katherine?

MRS. STOCKMANN. All right, thank you. (*Lowering her voice.*) Be sure not to lose your temper, Thomas.

DR. STOCKMANN. Oh, I know how to control myself. (*Looks at his watch, steps on to the platform, and bows.*) It is a quarter past—so I will begin. (*Takes his MS. out of his pocket.*)

ASLAKSEN. I think we ought to elect a chairman first.

DR. STOCKMANN. No, it is quite unnecessary.

SOME OF THE CROWD. Yes—yes!

PETER STOCKMANN. I certainly think too that we ought to have a chairman.

DR. STOCKMANN. But I have called this meeting to de- liver a lecture, Peter.

PETER STOCKMANN. Dr. Stockmann's lecture may possibly lead to a considerable conflict of opinion.

VOICES IN THE CROWD. A chairman! A chairman!

HOVSTAD. The general wish of the meeting seems to be that a chairman should be elected.

DR. STOCKMANN (*restraining himself*). Very well—let the meeting have its way.

ASLAKSEN. Will the Mayor be good enough to undertake the task?

THREE MEN (*clapping their hands*). Bravo! Bravo!

PETER STOCKMANN. For various reasons, which you will easily understand, I must beg to be excused. But fortunately we have amongst us a man who I think will be acceptable to you all. I refer to the President of the Householders' Association, Mr. Aslaksen.

SEVERAL VOICES. Yes—Aslaksen! Bravo Aslaksen!

(DR. STOCKMANN *takes up his MS. and walks up and down the platform.*)

ASLAKSEN. Since my fellow-citizens choose to entrust me with this duty, I cannot refuse.

(*Loud applause.* ASLAKSEN *mounts the platform.*)

BILLING (*writing*). "Mr. Aslaksen was elected with enthusiasm."

ASLAKSEN. And now, as I am in this position, I should like to say a few brief words. I am a quiet and peaceable man, who believes in discreet moderation, and—and—in moderate discretion. All my friends can bear witness to that.

SEVERAL VOICES. That's right! That's right, Aslaksen!

ASLAKSEN. I have learnt in the school of life and experience that moderation is the most valuable virtue a citizen can possess——

PETER STOCKMANN. Hear, hear!

ASLAKSEN. —And moreover that discretion and moderation are what enable a man to be of most service to the community. I would therefore suggest to our esteemed fellow-citizen, who has called this meeting, that he should strive to keep strictly within the bounds of moderation.

A MAN BY THE DOOR. Three cheers for the Moderation Society!

A VOICE. Shame!

SEVERAL VOICES. Sh!—Sh!

ASLAKSEN. No interruptions, gentlemen, please! Does anyone wish to make any remarks?

PETER STOCKMANN. Mr. Chairman.

ASLAKSEN. The Mayor will address the meeting.

PETER STOCKMANN. In consideration of the close relationship in which, as you all know, I stand to the present Medical Officer of the Baths, I should have preferred not to speak this evening. But my official position with regard to the Baths and my solicitude for the vital interests of the town compel me to bring forward a motion. I venture to presume that there is not a single one of our citizens present who considers it desirable that unreliable and exaggerated accounts of the sanitary condition of the Baths and the town should be spread abroad.

SEVERAL VOICES. No, no! Certainly not! We protest against it!

PETER STOCKMANN. Therefore I should like to propose that the meeting should not permit the Medical Officer either to read or to comment on his proposed lecture.

DR. STOCKMANN (*impatiently*). Not permit——! What the devil——!

MRS. STOCKMANN (*coughing*). Ahem!—ahem!

DR. STOCKMANN (*collecting himself*). Very well. Go ahead!

PETER STOCKMANN. In my communication to the "People's Messenger," I have put the essential facts before the public in such a way that every fair-minded citizen can easily form his own opinion. From it you will see that the main result of the Medical Officer's proposals—apart from their constituting a vote of censure on the leading men of the town —would be to saddle the ratepayers with an unnecessary expenditure of at least some thousands of pounds.

(*Sounds of disapproval among the audience, and some cat-calls.*)

ASLAKSEN (*ringing his bell*). Silence, please, gentlemen!
I beg to support the Mayor's motion. I quite agree with him
that there is something behind this agitation started by the
Doctor. He talks about the Baths; but it is a revolution he is
aiming at—he wants to get the administration of the town
put into new hands. No one doubts the honesty of the Doctor's intentions—no one will suggest that there can be any
two opinions as to that. I myself am a believer in self-government for the people, provided it does not fall too heavily on
the ratepayers. But that would be the case here; and that is
why I will see Dr. Stockmann damned—I beg your pardon—
before I go with him in the matter. You can pay too dearly
for a thing sometimes; that is my opinion.

(*Loud applause on all sides.*)

HOVSTAD. I, too, feel called upon to explain my position.
Dr. Stockmann's agitation appeared to be gaining a certain
amount of sympathy at first, so I supported it as impartially
as I could. But presently we had reason to suspect that we
had allowed ourselves to be misled by misrepresentation of
the state of affairs——

DR. STOCKMANN. Misrepresentation——!

HOVSTAD. Well, let us say a not entirely trustworthy
representation. The Mayor's statement has proved that. I
hope no one here has any doubt as to my liberal principles;
the attitude of the "People's Messenger" towards important
political questions is well known to every one. But the advice
of experienced and thoughtful men has convinced me that in
purely local matters a newspaper ought to proceed with a
certain caution.

ASLAKSEN. I entirely agree with the speaker.

HOVSTAD. And, in the matter before us, it is now an un-
doubted fact that Dr. Stockmann has public opinion against
him. Now, what is an editor's first and most obvious duty,
gentlemen? Is it not to work in harmony with his readers?
Has he not received a sort of tacit mandate to work persist-

ently and assiduously for the welfare of those whose opinions he represents? Or is it possible I am mistaken in that?

VOICES FROM THE CROWD. No, no! You are quite right!

HOVSTAD. It has cost me a severe struggle to break with a man in whose house I have been lately a frequent guest— a man who till to-day has been able to pride himself on the undivided goodwill of his fellow-citizens—a man whose only, or at all events whose essential, failing is that he is swayed by his heart rather than his head.

A FEW SCATTERED VOICES. That is true! Bravo, Stockmann!

HOVSTAD. But my duty to the community obliged me to break with him. And there is another consideration that impels me to oppose him, and, as far as possible, to arrest him on the perilous course he has adopted; that is, consideration for his family——

DR. STOCKMANN. Please stick to the water-supply and drainage!

HOVSTAD. —consideration, I repeat, for his wife and his children for whom he has made no provision.

MORTEN. Is that us, mother?

MRS. STOCKMANN. Hush!

ASLAKSEN. I will now put the Mayor's proposition to the vote.

DR. STOCKMANN. There is no necessity! To-night I have no intention of dealing with all that filth down at the Baths. No; I have something quite different to say to you.

PETER STOCKMANN (aside). What is coming now?

A DRUNKEN MAN (by the entrance door). I am a rate-payer! And therefore I have a right to speak too! And my entire—firm—inconceivable opinion is——

A NUMBER OF VOICES. Be quiet, at the back there!

OTHERS. He is drunk! Turn him out! (They turn him out.)

DR. STOCKMANN. Am I allowed to speak?

ASLAKSEN (*ringing his bell*). Dr. Stockmann will address the meeting.

DR. STOCKMANN. I should like to have seen anyone, a few days ago, dare to attempt to silence me as has been done to-night! I would have defended my sacred rights as a man, like a lion! But now it is all one to me; I have something of even weightier importance to say to you.

(*The crowd presses nearer to him,* MORTEN KIIL *conspicuous among them.*)

DR. STOCKMANN (*continuing*). I have thought and pondered a great deal, these last few days—pondered over such a variety of things that in the end my head seemed too full to hold them——

PETER STOCKMANN (*with a cough*). Ahem!

DR. STOCKMANN. ——but I got them clear in my mind at last, and then I saw the whole situation lucidly. And that is why I am standing here to-night. I have a great revelation to make to you, my fellow-citizens! I will impart to you a discovery of a far wider scope than the trifling matter that our water-supply is poisoned and our medicinal Baths are standing on pestiferous soil.

A NUMBER OF VOICES (*shouting*). Don't talk about the Baths! We won't hear you! None of that!

DR. STOCKMANN. I have already told you that what I want to speak about is the great discovery I have made lately —the discovery that all the sources of our *moral* life are poisoned and that the whole fabric of our civic community is founded on the pestiferous soil of falsehood.

VOICES OF DISCONCERTED CITIZENS. What is that he says?

PETER STOCKMANN. Such an insinuation——!

ASLAKSEN (*with his hand on his bell*). I call upon the speaker to moderate his language.

DR. STOCKMANN. I have always loved my native town as a man only can love the home of his youthful days. I was not old when I went away from here; and exile, longing and memories cast as it were an additional halo over both the town and its inhabitants. (*Some clapping and applause.*) And there I stayed, for many years, in a horrible hole far away up north. When I came into contact with some of the people that lived scattered about among the rocks, I often thought it would of been more service to the poor half-starved creatures if a veterinary doctor had been sent up there, instead of a man like me. (*Murmurs among the crowd.*)

BILLING (*laying down his pen*). I'm damned if I have ever heard——!

HOVSTAD. It is an insult to a respectable population!

DR. STOCKMANN. Wait a bit! I do not think anyone will charge me with having forgotten my native town up there. I was like one of the eider-ducks brooding on its nest, and what I hatched was—the plans for these Baths. (*Applause and protests.*) And then when fate at last decreed for me the great happiness of coming home again—I assure you, gentlemen, I thought I had nothing more in the world to wish for. Or rather, there was one thing I wished for—eagerly, untiringly, ardently—and that was to be able to be of service to my native town and the good of the community.

PETER STOCKMANN (*looking at the ceiling*). You chose a strange way of doing it—ahem!

DR. STOCKMANN. And so, with my eyes blinded to the real facts, I revelled in happiness. But yesterday morning—no, to be precise, it was yesterday afternoon—the eyes of my mind were opened wide, and the first thing I realized was the colossal stupidity of the authorities——. (*Uproar, shouts and laughter.* MRS. STOCKMANN *coughs persistently.*)

PETER STOCKMANN. Mr. Chairman!

ASLAKSEN (*ringing his bell*). By virtue of my authority——!

DR. STOCKMANN. It is a petty thing to catch me up on a word, Mr. Aslaksen. What I mean is only that I got scent of the unbelievable piggishness our leading men had been responsible for down at the Baths. I can't stand leading men at any price!—I have had enough of such people in my time. They are like billy-goats in a young plantation; they do mischief everywhere. They stand in a free man's way, whichever way he turns, and what I should like best would be to see them exterminated like any other vermin——. (*Uproar*.)

PETER STOCKMANN. Mr. Chairman, can we allow such expressions to pass?

ASLAKSEN (*with his hand on his bell*). Doctor——!

DR. STOCKMANN. I cannot understand how it is that I have only now acquired a clear conception of what these gentry are, when I had almost daily before my eyes in this town such an excellent specimen of them—my brother Peter —slow-witted and hide-bound in prejudice——. (*Laughter, uproar and hisses.* MRS. STOCKMANN *sits coughing assiduously.* ASLAKSEN *rings his bell violently.*)

THE DRUNKEN MAN (*who has got in again*). Is it me he is talking about? My name's Petersen, all right—but devil take me if I——

ANGRY VOICES. Turn out that drunken man! Turn him out. (*He is turned out again.*)

PETER STOCKMANN. Who was that person?

1ST CITIZEN. I don't know who he is, Mr. Mayor.

2ND CITIZEN. He doesn't belong here.

3RD CITIZEN. I expect he is a navvy from over at (*the rest is inaudible*).

ASLAKSEN. He had obviously had too much beer.——Proceed, Doctor; but please strive to be moderate in your language.

DR. STOCKMANN. Very well, gentlemen, I will say no more about our leading men. And if anyone imagines, from what I have just said, that my object is to attack these people this evening, he is wrong—absolutely wide of the mark. For I cherish the comforting conviction that these parasites—all these venerable relics of a dying school of thought—are most admirably paving the way for their own extinction; they need no doctor's help to hasten their end. Nor is it folk of that kind who constitute the most pressing danger to the community. It is not they who are most instrumental in poisoning the sources of our moral life and infecting the ground on which we stand. It is not they who are the most dangerous enemies of truth and freedom amongst us.

SHOUTS FROM ALL SIDES. Who then? Who is it? Name! Name!

DR. STOCKMANN. You may depend upon it I shall name them! That is precisely the great discovery I made yesterday. (*Raises his voice.*) The most dangerous enemy of truth and freedom amongst us is the compact majority—yes, the damned compact Liberal majority—that is it! Now you know! (*Tremendous uproar. Most of the crowd are shouting, stamping and hissing. Some of the older men among them exchange stolen glances and seem to be enjoying themselves. MRS. STOCKMANN gets up, looking anxious. EJLIF and MORTEN advance threateningly upon some schoolboys who are playing pranks. ASLAKSEN rings his bell and begs for silence. HOVSTAD and BILLING both talk at once, but are inaudible. At last quiet is restored.*)

ASLAKSEN. As chairman, I call upon the speaker to withdraw the ill-considered expressions he has just used.

DR. STOCKMANN. Never, Mr. Aslaksen! It is the majority in our community that denies me my freedom and seeks to prevent my speaking the truth.

HOVSTAD. The majority always has right on its side.

BILLING. And truth too, by God!

DR. STOCKMANN. The majority *never* has right on its side. Never, I say! That is one of these social lies against which an independent, intelligent man must wage war. Who is it that constitute the majority of the population in a country? Is it the clever folk or the stupid? I don't imagine you will dispute the fact that at present the stupid people are in an absolutely overwhelming majority all the world over. But, good Lord!—you can never pretend that it is right that the stupid folk should govern the clever ones! (*Uproar and cries.*) Oh, yes—you can shout me down, I know! but you cannot answer me. The majority has *might* on its side—unfortunately; but *right* it has *not*. I am in the right—I and a few other scattered individuals. The minority is always in the right. (*Renewed uproar.*)

HOVSTAD. Aha!—so Dr. Stockmann has become an aristocrat since the day before yesterday!

DR. STOCKMANN. I have already said that I don't intend to waste a word on the puny, narrow-chested, short-winded crew whom we are leaving astern. Pulsating life no longer concerns itself with them. I am thinking of the few, the scattered few amongst us, who have absorbed new and vigorous truths. Such men stand, as it were, at the outposts, so far ahead that the compact majority has not yet been able to come up with them; and there they are fighting for truths that are too newly-born into the world of consciousness to have any considerable number of people on their side as yet.

HOVSTAD. So the Doctor is a revolutionary now!

DR. STOCKMANN. Good heavens—of course I am, Mr. Hovstad! I propose to raise a revolution against the lie that the majority has the monopoly of the truth. What sort of truths are they that the majority usually supports? They are truths that are of such advanced age that they are beginning to break up. And if a truth is as old as that, it is also in a fair way to become a lie, gentlemen. (*Laughter and mocking cries.*) Yes, believe me or not, as you like; but truths are by no means as long-lived as Methuselah—as some folk imagine. A normally constituted truth lives, let us say, as a rule seventeen or eighteen, or at most twenty years; seldom longer. But truths as aged as that are always worn frightfully thin, and nevertheless it is only then that the majority recognizes them and recommends them to the community as wholesome moral nourishment. There is no great nutritive value in that sort of fare, I can assure you; and, as a doctor, I ought to know. These "majority truths" are like last year's cured meat—like rancid, tainted ham; and they are the origin of the moral scurvy that is rampant in our communities.

ASLAKSEN. It appears to me that the speaker is wandering a long way from his subject.

PETER STOCKMANN. I quite agree with the Chairman.

DR. STOCKMANN. Have you gone clean out of your senses, Peter? I am sticking as closely to my subject as I can; for my subject is precisely this, that it is the masses, the majority —this infernal compact majority—that poisons the sources of our moral life and infects the ground we stand on.

HOVSTAD. And all this because the great, broad-minded majority of the people is prudent enough to show deference only to well-ascertained and well-approved truths?

DR. STOCKMANN. Ah, my good Mr. Hovstad, don't talk nonsense about well-ascertained truths! The truths of which the masses now approve are the very truths that the fighters at the outposts held to in the days of our grandfathers. We fighters at the outposts nowadays no longer approve of them; and I do not believe there is any other well-ascertained truth except this, that no community can live a healthy life if it is nourished only on such old marrowless truths.

HOVSTAD. But instead of standing there using vague generalities, it would be interesting if you would tell us what these old marrowless truths are, that we are nourished on.

(*Applause from many quarters.*)

DR. STOCKMANN. Oh, I could give you a whole string of such abominations; but to begin with I will confine myself to one well-approved truth, which at bottom is a foul lie, but upon which nevertheless Mr. Hovstad and the "People's Messenger" and all the "Messenger's" supporters are nourished.

HOVSTAD. And that is——?

DR. STOCKMANN. That is, the doctrine you have inherited from your forefathers and proclaim thoughtlessly far and wide—the doctrine that the public, the crowd, the masses, are the essential part of the population—that they constitute the People—that the common folk, the ignorant and incomplete element in the community, have the same right to pronounce judgment and to approve, to direct and to govern, as the isolated, intellectually superior personalities in it.

BILLING. Well, damn me if ever I——

HOVSTAD (*at the same time, shouting out*). Fellow-citizens, take good note of that!

A NUMBER OF VOICES (*angrily*). Oho!—we are not the People! Only the superior folk are to govern, are they!

A WORKMAN. Turn the fellow out, for talking such rubbish!

ANOTHER. Out with him!

ANOTHER (*calling out*). Blow your horn, Evensen!

(*A horn is blown loudly, amidst hisses and an angry uproar.*)

DR. STOCKMANN (*when the noise has somewhat abated*). Be reasonable! Can't you stand hearing the voice of truth for once? I don't in the least expect you to agree with me all at once; but I must say I did expect Mr. Hovstad to admit I was right, when he had recovered his composure a little. He claims to be a freethinker——

VOICES (*in murmurs of astonishment*). Freethinker, did he say? Is Hovstad a freethinker?

HOVSTAD (*shouting*). Prove it, Dr. Stockmann! When have I said so in print?

DR. STOCKMANN (*reflecting*). No, confound it, you are right!—you have never had the courage to. Well, I won't put you in a hole, Mr. Hovstad. Let us say it is I that am the freethinker, then. I am going to prove to you, scientifically, that the "People's Messenger" leads you by the nose in a shameful manner when it tells you that you—that the common people, the crowd, the masses, are the real essence of the People. That is only a newspaper lie, I tell you! The common people are nothing more than the raw material of which a People is made. (*Groans, laughter and uproar.*) Well, isn't that the case? Isn't there an enormous difference between a well-bred and an ill-bred strain of animals? Take, for instance, a common barn-door hen. What sort of eating do you get from a shrivelled up old scrag of a fowl like that? Not much, do you! And what sort of eggs does it lay? A fairly good crow or a raven can lay pretty nearly as good an egg. But take a well-bred Spanish or Japanese hen, or a good pheasant or a turkey—then you will see the difference. Or take the case of dogs, with whom we humans are on such intimate terms. Think first of an ordinary common cur—I mean one of the horrible, coarse-haired, low-bred curs that do nothing but run about the streets and befoul the walls of the houses. Compare one of these curs with a poodle whose sires for many generations have been bred in a gentleman's house, where they have had the best of food and had the opportunity of hearing soft voices and music. Do you not think that the poodle's brain is developed to quite a different degree from that of the cur? Of course it is. It is puppies of well-bred poodles like that, that showmen train to do incredibly clever tricks—things that a common cur could never learn to do even if it stood on its head. (*Uproar and mocking cries.*)

A CITIZEN (*calls out*). Are you going to make out we are dogs, now?

ANOTHER CITIZEN. We are not animals, Doctor!

DR. STOCKMANN. Yes, but, bless my soul, we *are*, my friend! It is true we are the finest animals anyone could wish for; but, even amongst us, exceptionally fine animals are rare. There is a tremendous difference between poodle-men and cur-men. And the amusing part of it is, that Mr. Hovstad quite agrees with me as long as it is a question of four-footed animals——

HOVSTAD. Yes, it is true enough as far as they are concerned.

DR. STOCKMANN. Very well. But as soon as I extend the principle and apply it to two-legged animals, Mr. Hovstad stops short. He no longer dares to think independently, or to pursue his ideas to their logical conclusion; so he turns the whole theory upside down and proclaims in the "People's Messenger" that it is the barn-door hens and street curs that are the finest specimens in the menagerie. But that is always the way, as long as a man retains the traces of common origin and has not worked his way up to intellectual distinction.

HOVSTAD. I lay no claim to any sort of distinction. I am the son of humble countryfolk, and I am proud that the stock I come from is rooted deep among the common people he insults!

VOICES. Bravo, Hovstad! Bravo! Bravo!

DR. STOCKMANN. The kind of common people I mean are not only to be found low down in the social scale; they crawl and swarm all around us—even in the highest social positions. You have only to look at your own fine, distinguished Mayor! My brother Peter is every bit as plebeian as anyone that walks in two shoes——(laughter and hisses).

PETER STOCKMANN. I protest against personal allusions of this kind.

DR. STOCKMANN (imperturbably). ——and that, not because he is, like myself, descended from some old rascal of a pirate from Pomerania or thereabouts—because that is who we are descended from——

PETER STOCKMANN. An absurd legend. I deny it!

DR. STOCKMANN. ——but because he thinks what his superiors think and holds the same opinions as they. People who do that are, intellectually speaking, common people; and that is why my magnificent brother Peter is in reality so very far from any distinction—and consequently also so far from being liberal-minded.

PETER STOCKMANN. Mr. Chairman——!

HOVSTAD. So it is only the distinguished men that are liberal-minded in this country? We are learning something quite new! (*Laughter.*)

DR. STOCKMANN. Yes, that is part of my new discovery too. And another part of it is that broad-mindedness is almost precisely the same thing as morality. That is why I maintain that it is absolutely inexcusable in the "People's Messenger" to proclaim, day in and day out, the false doctrine that it is the masses, the crowd, the compact majority, that have the monopoly of broad-mindedness and morality—and that vice and corruption and every kind of intellectual depravity are the result of culture, just as all the filth that is draining into our Baths is the result of the tanneries up at Mölledal! (*Uproar and interruptions.* DR. STOCKMANN *is undisturbed, and goes on, carried away by his ardor, with a smile.*) And yet this same "People's Messenger" can go on preaching that the masses ought to be elevated to higher conditions of life! But, bless my soul, if the "Messenger's" teaching is to be depended upon, this very raising up the masses would mean nothing more or less than setting them straightway upon the paths of depravity! Happily the theory that culture demoralizes is only an old falsehood that our forefathers believed in and we have inherited. No, it is ignorance, poverty, ugly conditions of life, that do the devil's work! In a house which does not get aired and swept every day—my wife Katherine maintains that the floor ought to be scrubbed as well, but that is a debatable question—in such a house, let me tell you, people will lose within two or three years the power of thinking or acting in a moral manner. Lack of oxygen weakens the conscience. And there must be a plentiful lack of oxygen in very many houses in this town, I should think, judging from the fact that the whole compact majority can be unconscientious enough to wish to build the town's prosperity on a quagmire of falsehood and deceit.

ASLAKSEN. We cannot allow such a grave accusation to be flung at a citizen community.

A CITIZEN. I move that the Chairman direct the speaker to sit down.

VOICES (*angrily*). Hear, hear! Quite right! Make him sit down!

DR. STOCKMANN (*losing his self-control*). Then I will go and shout the truth at every street corner! I will write it in other towns' newspapers! The whole country shall know what is going on here!

HOVSTAD. It almost seems as if Dr. Stockmann's intention were to ruin the town.

DR. STOCKMANN. Yes, my native town is so dear to me that I would rather ruin it than see it flourishing upon a lie.

ASLAKSEN. This is really serious. (*Uproar and cat-calls. MRS. STOCKMANN coughs, but to no purpose; her husband does not listen to her any longer.*)

HOVSTAD (*shouting above the din*). A man must be a public enemy to wish to ruin a whole community!

DR. STOCKMANN (*with growing fervor*). What does the destruction of a community matter, if it lives on lies! It ought to be razed to the ground, I tell you! All who live by lies ought to be exterminated like vermin! You will end by infecting the whole country; you will bring about such a state of things that the whole country will deserve to be ruined. And if things come to that pass, I shall say from the bottom of my heart: Let the whole country perish, let all these people be exterminated!

VOICES FROM THE CROWD. That is talking like an out-and-out enemy of the people!

BILLING. There sounded the voice of the people, by all that's holy!

THE WHOLE CROWD (*shouting*). Yes, yes! He is an enemy

of the people! He hates his country! He hates his own people!

ASLAKSEN. Both as a citizen and as an individual, I am profoundly disturbed by what we have had to listen to. Dr. Stockmann has shown himself in a light I should never have dreamed of. I am unhappily obliged to subscribe to the opinion which I have just heard my estimable fellow-citizens utter; and I propose that we should give expression to that opinion in a resolution. I propose a resolution as follows: "This meeting declares that it considers Dr. Thomas Stockmann, Medical Officer of the Baths, to be an enemy of the people." (*A storm of cheers and applause. A number of men surround the* DOCTOR *and hiss him.* MRS. STOCKMANN *and* PETRA *have got up from their seats.* MORTEN *and* EJLIF *are fighting the other schoolboys for hissing; some of their elders separate them.*)

DR. STOCKMANN (*to the men who are hissing him*). Oh, you fools! I tell you that——

ASLAKSEN (*ringing his bell*). We cannot hear you now, Doctor. A formal vote is about to be taken; but, out of regard for personal feelings, it shall be by ballot and not verbal. Have you any clean paper, Mr. Billing?

BILLING. I have both blue and white here.

ASLAKSEN (*going to him*). That will do nicely; we shall get on more quickly that way. Cut it up into small strips—yes, that's it. (*To the meeting.*) Blue means no; white means yes. I will come round myself and collect votes. (PETER STOCKMANN *leaves the hall.* ASLAKSEN *and one or two others go round the room with the slips of paper in their hats.*)

1ST CITIZEN (*to* HOVSTAD). I say, what has come to the Doctor? What are we to think of it?

HOVSTAD. Oh, you know how headstrong he is.

2ND CITIZEN (*to* BILLING). Billing, you go to their house —have you ever noticed if the fellow drinks?

BILLING. Well, I'm hanged if I know what to say. There are always spirits on the table when you go.

3RD CITIZEN. I rather think he goes quite off his head sometimes.

1ST CITIZEN. I wonder if there is any madness in his family?

BILLING. I shouldn't wonder if there were.

4TH CITIZEN. No, it is nothing more than sheer malice; he wants to get even with somebody for something or other.

BILLING. Well, certainly he suggested a rise in his salary on one occasion lately, and did not get it.

THE CITIZENS (*together*). Ah!—then it is easy to understand how it is!

THE DRUNKEN MAN (*who has got amongst the audience again*). I want a blue one, I do! And I want a white one too!

VOICES. It's that drunken chap again! Turn him out!

MORTEN KIIL (*going up to* DR. STOCKMANN). Well, Stockmann, do you see what these monkey tricks of yours lead to?

DR. STOCKMANN. I have done my duty.

MORTEN KIIL. What was that you said about the tanneries at Mölledal?

DR. STOCKMANN. You heard well enough. I said they were the source of all the filth.

MORTEN KIIL. My tannery too?

DR. STOCKMANN. Unfortunately your tannery is by far the worst.

MORTEN KIIL. Are you going to put that in the papers?

DR. STOCKMANN. I shall conceal nothing.

MORTEN KIIL. That may cost you dear, Stockmann. (*Goes out.*)

A STOUT MAN (*going up to* CAPTAIN HORSTER, *without taking any notice of the ladies*). Well, Captain, so you lend your house to enemies of the people?

HORSTER. I imagine I can do what I like with my own possessions, Mr. Vik.

THE STOUT MAN. Then you can have no objection to my doing the same with mine.

HORSTER. What do you mean, sir?

THE STOUT MAN. You shall hear from me in the morning. (*Turns his back on him and moves off.*)

PETRA. Was that not your owner, Captain Horster?

HORSTER. Yes, that was Mr. Vik the ship-owner.

ASLAKSEN (*with the voting-papers in his hands, gets up on to the platform and rings his bell*). Gentlemen, allow me to announce the result. By the votes of every one here except one person——

A YOUNG MAN. That is the drunk chap!

ASLAKSEN. By the votes of every one here except a tipsy man, this meeting of citizens declares Dr. Thomas Stockmann to be an enemy of the people. (*Shouts and applause.*) Three cheers for our ancient and honorable citizen community! (*Renewed applause.*) Three cheers for our able and energetic Mayor, who has so loyally suppressed the promptings of family feeling! (*Cheers.*) The meeting is dissolved. (*Gets down.*)

BILLING. Three cheers for the Chairman!

THE WHOLE CROWD. Three cheers for Aslaksen! Hurrah!

DR. STOCKMANN. My hat and coat, Petra! Captain, have you room on your ship for passengers to the New World?

HORSTER. For you and yours we will make room, Doctor.

DR. STOCKMANN (*as PETRA helps him into his coat*). Good. Come, Katherine! Come, boys!

MRS. STOCKMANN (*in an undertone*). Thomas, dear, let us go out by the back way.

DR. STOCKMANN. No back ways for me, Katherine. (*Raising his voice.*) You will hear more of this enemy of the people, before he shakes the dust off his shoes upon you! I am not so forgiving as a certain Person; I do not say: "I forgive you, for ye know not what ye do."

ASLAKSEN (*shouting*). That is a blasphemous comparison, Dr. Stockmann!

BILLING. It is, by God! It's dreadful for an earnest man to listen to.

A Coarse Voice. Threatens us now, does he!

Other Voices (*excitedly*). Let's go and break his windows! Duck him in the fjord!

Another Voice. Blow your horn, Evensen. Pip, pip!

(*Horn-blowing, hisses, and wild cries.* Dr. Stockmann *goes out through the hall with his family,* Horster *elbowing a way for them.*)

The Whole Crowd (*howling after them as they go*). Enemy of the People! Enemy of the People!

Billing (*as he puts his papers together*). Well, I'm damned if I go and drink toddy with the Stockmanns tonight!

(*The crowd press towards the exit. The uproar continues outside; shouts of "Enemy of the People!" are heard from without.*)

ACT V

(SCENE.—DR. STOCKMANN's *study. Bookcases, and cabinets containing specimens, line the walls. At the back is a door leading to the hall; in the foreground on the left, a door leading to the sitting-room. In the right-hand wall are two windows, of which all the panes are broken. The* DOCTOR's *desk, littered with books and papers, stands in the middle of the room, which is in disorder. It is morning.* DR. STOCKMANN *in dressing-gown, slippers and a smoking-cap, is bending down and raking with an umbrella under one of the cabinets. After a little while he rakes out a stone.*)

DR. STOCKMANN (*calling through the open sitting-room door*). Katherine, I have found another one.

MRS. STOCKMANN (*from the sitting-room*). Oh, you will find a lot more yet, I expect.

DR. STOCKMANN (*adding the stone to a heap of others on the table*). I shall treasure these stones as relics. Ejlif and Morten shall look at them every day, and when they are grown up they shall inherit them as heirlooms. (*Rakes about under a bookcase.*) Hasn't—what the deuce is her name?— the girl, you know—hasn't she been to fetch the glazier, yet?

MRS. STOCKMANN (*coming in*). Yes, but he said he didn't know if he would be able to come to-day.

DR. STOCKMANN. You will see he won't dare to come.

MRS. STOCKMANN. Well, that is just what Randine thought—that he didn't dare to, on account of the neighbors. (*Calls into the sitting-room.*) What is it you want, Randine? Give it to me. (*Goes in, and comes out again directly.*) Here is a letter for you, Thomas.

92

DR. STOCKMANN. Let me see it. (*Opens and reads it.*) Ah!—of course.

MRS. STOCKMANN. Who is it from?

DR. STOCKMANN. From the landlord. Notice to quit.

MRS. STOCKMANN. Is it possible? Such a nice man——

DR. STOCKMANN (*looking at the letter*). Does not dare do otherwise, he says. Doesn't like doing it, but dare not do otherwise—on account of his fellow-citizens—out of regard for public opinion. Is in a dependent position—dare not offend certain influential men——

MRS. STOCKMANN. There, you see, Thomas!

DR. STOCKMANN. Yes, yes, I see well enough; the whole lot of them in the town are cowards; not a man among them dares do anything for fear of the others. (*Throws the letter on to the table.*) But it doesn't matter to us, Katherine. We are going to sail away to the New World, and——

MRS. STOCKMANN. But, Thomas, are you sure we are well advised to take this step?

DR. STOCKMANN. Are you suggesting that I should stay here, where they have pilloried me as an enemy of the people —branded me—broken my windows! And just look here, Katherine—they have torn a great rent in my black trousers too!

MRS. STOCKMANN. Oh, dear!—and they are the best pair you have got!

DR. STOCKMANN. You should never wear your best trousers when you go out to fight for freedom and truth. It is not that I care so much about the trousers, you know; you can always sew them up again for me. But that the common herd should dare to make this attack on me, as if they were my equals—that is what I cannot, for the life of me, swallow!

MRS. STOCKMANN. There is no doubt they have behaved very ill to you, Thomas; but is that sufficient reason for our leaving our native country for good and all?

DR. STOCKMANN. If we went to another town, do you

suppose we should not find the common people just as insolent as they are here? Depend upon it, there is not much to choose between them. Oh, well, let the curs snap—that is not the worst part of it. The worst is that, from one end of this country to the other, every man is the slave of his Party. Although, as far as that goes, I dare say it is not much better in the free West either; the compact majority, and liberal public opinion, and all that infernal old bag of tricks are probably rampant there too. But there things are done on a larger scale, you see. They may kill you, but they won't put you to death by slow torture. They don't squeeze a free man's soul in a vise, as they do here. And, if need be, one can live in solitude. (*Walks up and down.*) If only I knew where there was a virgin forest or a small South Sea island for sale, cheap——

MRS. STOCKMANN. But think of the boys, Thomas.

DR. STOCKMANN (*standing still*). What a strange woman you are, Katherine! Would you prefer to have the boys grow up in a society like this? You saw for yourself last night that half the population are out of their minds; and if the other half have not lost their senses, it is because they are mere brutes, with no sense to lose.

MRS. STOCKMANN. But, Thomas dear, the imprudent things you said had something to do with it, you know.

DR. STOCKMANN. Well, isn't what I said perfectly true? Don't they turn every idea topsy-turvy? Don't they make a regular hotch-potch of right and wrong? Don't they say that the things I know are true, are lies? The craziest part of it all is the fact of these "liberals," men of full age, going about in crowds imagining that they are the broadminded party! Did you ever hear anything like it, Katherine!

MRS. STOCKMANN. Yes, yes, it's mad enough of them, certainly; but——(PETRA *comes in from the sitting-room*). Back from school already?

PETRA. Yes. I have been given notice of dismissal.

MRS. STOCKMANN. Dismissal?

DR. STOCKMANN. You too?

PETRA. Mrs. Busk gave me my notice; so I thought it was best to go at once.

DR. STOCKMANN. You were perfectly right, too!

MRS. STOCKMANN. Who would have thought Mrs. Busk was a woman like that!

PETRA. Mrs. Busk isn't a bit like that, mother; I saw quite plainly how it hurt her to do it. But she didn't dare do otherwise, she said; and so I got my notice.

DR. STOCKMANN (*laughing and rubbing his hands*). She didn't dare do otherwise, either! It's delicious!

MRS. STOCKMANN. Well, after the dreadful scenes last night——

PETRA. It was not only that. Just listen to this, father!

DR. STOCKMANN. Well?

PETRA. Mrs. Busk showed me no less than three letters she received this morning——

DR. STOCKMANN. Anonymous, I suppose?

PETRA. Yes.

DR. STOCKMANN. Yes, because they didn't dare to risk signing their names, Katherine!

PETRA. And two of them were to the effect that a man, who has been our guest here, was declaring last night at the Club that my views on various subjects are extremely emancipated——

DR. STOCKMANN. You did not deny that, I hope?

PETRA. No, you know I wouldn't. Mrs. Busk's own views are tolerably emancipated, when we are alone together; but now that this report about me is being spread, she dare not keep me on any longer.

MRS. STOCKMANN. And some one who had been a guest of ours! That shows you the return you get for your hospitality, Thomas!

DR. STOCKMANN. We won't live in such a disgusting hole

any longer. Pack up as quickly as you can, Katherine; the sooner we can get away, the better.

MRS. STOCKMANN. Be quiet—I think I hear some one in the hall. See who it is, Petra.

PETRA (*opening the door*). Oh, it's you, Captain Horster! Do come in.

HORSTER (*coming in*). Good morning. I thought I would just come in and see how you were.

DR. STOCKMANN (*shaking his hand*). Thanks—that is really kind of you.

MRS. STOCKMANN. And thank you, too, for helping us through the crowd, Captain Horster.

PETRA. How did you manage to get home again?

HORSTER. Oh, somehow or other. I am fairly strong, and there is more sound than fury about these folk.

DR. STOCKMANN. Yes, isn't their swinish cowardice astonishing? Look here, I will show you something! There are all the stones they have thrown through my windows. Just look at them! I'm hanged if there are more than two decently large bits of hardstone in the whole heap; the rest are nothing but gravel—wretched little things. And yet they stood out there bawling and swearing that they would do me some violence; but as for *doing* anything—you don't see much of that in this town.

HORSTER. Just as well for you this time, doctor!

DR. STOCKMANN. True enough. But it makes one angry all the same; because if some day it should be a question of a national fight in real earnest, you will see that public opinion will be in favor of taking to one's heels, and the compact majority will turn tail like a flock of sheep, Captain Horster. That is what is so mournful to think of; it gives me so much concern, that——. No, devil take it, it is ridiculous to care about it! They have called me an enemy of the people, so an enemy of the people let me be!

MRS. STOCKMANN. You will never be that, Thomas.

Dr. Stockmann. Don't swear to that, Katherine. To be called an ugly name may have the same effect as a pin-scratch in the lung. And that hateful name—I can't get quit of it. It is sticking here in the pit of my stomach, eating into me like a corrosive acid. And no magnesia will remove it.

Petra. Bah!—you should only laugh at them, father.

Horster. They will change their minds some day, Doctor.

Mrs. Stockmann. Yes, Thomas, as sure as you are standing here.

Dr. Stockmann. Perhaps, when it is too late. Much good may it do them! They may wallow in their filth then and rue the day when they drove a patriot into exile. When do you sail, Captain Horster?

Horster. Hm!—that was just what I had come to speak about——

Dr. Stockmann. Why, has anything gone wrong with the ship?

Horster. No; but what has happened is that I am not to sail in it.

Petra. Do you mean that you have been dismissed from your command?

Horster (*smiling*). Yes, that's just it.

Petra. You too.

Mrs. Stockmann. There, you see, Thomas!

Dr. Stockmann. And that for the truth's sake! Oh, if I had thought such a thing possible——

Horster. You mustn't take it to heart; I shall be sure to find a job with some ship-owner or other, elsewhere.

Dr. Stockmann. And that is this man Vik—a wealthy man, independent of every one and everything——! Shame on him!

Horster. He is quite an excellent fellow otherwise; he told me himself he would willingly have kept me on, if only he had dared——

Dr. Stockmann. But he didn't dare? No, of course not.

HORSTER. It is not such an easy matter, he said, for a party man——

DR. STOCKMANN. The worthy man spoke the truth. A party is like a sausage machine; it mashes up all sorts of heads together into the same mincemeat—fatheads and blockheads, all in one mash!

MRS. STOCKMANN. Come, come, Thomas dear!

PETRA (*to* HORSTER). If only you had not come home with us, things might not have come to this pass.

HORSTER. I do not regret it.

PETRA (*holding out her hand to him*). Thank you for that!

HORSTER (*to* DR. STOCKMANN). And so what I came to say was that if you are determined to go away, I have thought of another plan——

DR. STOCKMANN. That's splendid!—if only we can get away at once.

MRS. STOCKMANN. Hush!—wasn't that some one knocking?

PETRA. That is uncle, surely.

DR. STOCKMANN. Aha! (*Calls out.*) Come in!

MRS. STOCKMANN. Dear Thomas, promise me definitely——

(PETER STOCKMANN *comes in from the hall.*)

PETER STOCKMANN. Oh, you are engaged. In that case, I will——

DR. STOCKMANN. No, no, come in.

PETER STOCKMANN. But I wanted to speak to you alone.

MRS. STOCKMANN. We will go into the sitting-room in the meanwhile.

HORSTER. And I will look in again later.

DR. STOCKMANN. No, go in there with them, Captain Horster; I want to hear more about——

HORSTER. Very well, I will wait, then. (*He follows* MRS. STOCKMANN *and* PETRA *into the sitting-room.*)

DR. STOCKMANN. I daresay you find it rather draughty here to-day. Put your hat on.

PETER STOCKMANN. Thank you, if I may. (*Does so.*) I think I caught cold last night; I stood and shivered——

DR. STOCKMANN. Really? I found it warm enough.

PETER STOCKMANN. I regret that it was not in my power to prevent those excesses last night.

DR. STOCKMANN. Have you anything particular to say to me besides that?

PETER STOCKMANN (*taking a big letter from his pocket*). I have this document for you, from the Baths Committee.

DR. STOCKMANN. My dismissal?

PETER STOCKMANN. Yes, dating from to-day. (*Lays the letter on the table.*) It gives us pain to do it; but, to speak frankly, we dared not do otherwise on account of public opinion.

DR. STOCKMANN (*smiling*). Dared not? I seem to have heard that word before, to-day.

PETER STOCKMANN. I must beg you to understand your position clearly. For the future you must not count on any practice whatever in the town.

DR. STOCKMANN. Devil take the practice! But why are you so sure of that?

PETER STOCKMANN. The Householders' Association is circulating a list from house to house. All right-minded citizens are being called upon to give up employing you; and I can assure you that not a single head of a family will risk refusing his signature. They simply dare not.

DR. STOCKMANN. No, no; I don't doubt it. But what then?

PETER STOCKMANN. If I might advise you, it would be best to leave the place for a little while——

DR. STOCKMANN. Yes, the propriety of leaving the place *has* occurred to me.

PETER STOCKMANN. Good. And then, when you have had

six months to think things over, if, after mature consideration, you can persuade yourself to write a few words of regret, acknowledging your error——

DR. STOCKMANN. I might have my appointment restored to me, do you mean?

PETER STOCKMANN. Perhaps. It is not at all impossible.

DR. STOCKMANN. But what about public opinion, then? Surely you would not dare to do it on account of public feeling.

PETER STOCKMANN. Public opinion is an extremely mutable thing. And, to be quite candid with you, it is a matter of great importance to us to have some admission of that sort from you in writing.

DR. STOCKMANN. Oh, that's what you are after, is it! I will just trouble you to remember what I said to you lately about foxy tricks of that sort!

PETER STOCKMANN. Your position was quite different then. At that time you had reason to suppose you had the whole town at your back——

DR. STOCKMANN. Yes, and now I feel I have the whole town *on* my back—(*flaring up*). I would not do it if I had the devil and his dam on my back——! Never—never, I tell you!

PETER STOCKMANN. A man with a family has no right to behave as you do. You have no right to do it, Thomas.

DR. STOCKMANN. I have no right! There is only one single thing in the world a free man has no right to do. Do you know what that is?

PETER STOCKMANN. No.

DR. STOCKMANN. Of course you don't, but I will tell you. A free man has no right to soil himself with filth; he has no right to behave in a way that would justify his spitting in his own face.

PETER STOCKMANN. This sort of thing sounds extremely

plausible, of course; and if there were no other explanation for your obstinacy——. But as it happens that there is——

DR. STOCKMANN. What do you mean?

PETER STOCKMANN. You understand very well what I mean. But, as your brother and as a man of discretion, I advise you not to build too much upon expectations and prospects that may so very easily fail you.

DR. STOCKMANN. What in the world is all this about?

PETER STOCKMANN. Do you really ask me to believe that you are ignorant of the terms of Mr. Kiil's will?

DR. STOCKMANN. I know that the small amount he possesses is to go to an institution for indigent old workpeople. How does that concern me?

PETER STOCKMANN. In the first place, it is by no means a small amount that is in question. Mr. Kiil is a fairly wealthy man.

DR. STOCKMANN. I had no notion of that!

PETER STOCKMANN. Hm!—hadn't you really? Then I suppose you had no notion, either, that a considerable portion of his wealth will come to your children, you and your wife having a life-rent of the capital. Has he never told you so?

DR. STOCKMANN. Never, on my honor! Quite the reverse; he has consistently done nothing but fume at being so unconscionably heavily taxed. But are you perfectly certain of this, Peter?

PETER STOCKMANN. I have it from an absolutely reliable source.

DR. STOCKMANN. Then, thank God, Katherine is provided for—and the children too! I must tell her this at once—(calls out) Katherine, Katherine!

PETER STOCKMANN (restraining him). Hush, don't say a word yet!

MRS. STOCKMANN (opening the door). What is the matter?

DR. STOCKMANN. Oh, nothing, nothing; you can go back. (*She shuts the door.* DR. STOCKMANN *walks up and down in his excitement.*) Provided for!—Just think of it, we are all provided for. And for life! What a blessed feeling it is to know one is provided for!

PETER STOCKMANN. Yes, but that is just exactly what you are not. Mr. Kiil can alter his will any day he likes.

DR. STOCKMANN. But he won't do that, my dear Peter. The "Badger" is much too delighted at my attack on you and your wise friends.

PETER STOCKMANN (*starts and looks intently at him*). Ah, that throws a light on various things.

DR. STOCKMANN. What things?

PETER STOCKMANN. I see that the whole thing was a combined maneuver on your part and his. These violent, reckless attacks that you have made against the leading men of the town, under the pretence that it was in the name of truth——

DR. STOCKMANN. What about them?

PETER STOCKMANN. I see that they were nothing else than the stipulated price for that vindictive old man's will.

DR. STOCKMANN (*almost speechless*). Peter—you are the most disgusting plebeian I have ever met in all my life.

PETER STOCKMANN. All is over between us. Your dismissal is irrevocable—we have a weapon against you now. (*Goes out.*)

DR. STOCKMANN. For shame! For shame! (*Calls out.*) Katherine, you must have the floor scrubbed after him! Let—what's her name—devil take it, the girl who has always got soot on her nose——

MRS. STOCKMANN (*in the sitting-room*). Hush, Thomas, be quiet!

PETRA (*coming to the door*). Father, grandfather is here, asking if he may speak to you alone.

DR. STOCKMANN. Certainly he may. (*Going to the door.*) Come in, Mr. Kiil. (MORTEN KIIL *comes in.* DR. STOCKMANN *shuts the door after him.*) What can I do for you? Won't you sit down?

MORTEN KIIL. I won't sit. (*Looks around.*) You look very comfortable here to-day, Thomas.

DR. STOCKMANN. Yes, don't we!

MORTEN KIIL. Very comfortable—plenty of fresh air. I should think you have got enough to-day of that oxygen you were talking about yesterday. Your conscience must be in splendid order to-day, I should think.

DR. STOCKMANN. It is.

MORTEN KIIL. So I should think. (*Taps his chest.*) Do you know what I have got here?

DR. STOCKMANN. A good conscience, too, I hope.

MORTEN KIIL. Bah!—No, it is something better than that. (*He takes a thick pocket-book from his breast-pocket, opens it and displays a packet of papers.*)

DR. STOCKMANN (*looking at him in astonishment*). Shares in the Baths?

MORTEN KIIL. They were not difficult to get to-day.

DR. STOCKMANN. And you have been buying——?

MORTEN KIIL. As many as I could pay for.

DR. STOCKMANN. But, my dear Mr. Kiil—consider the state of the Baths' affairs!

MORTEN KIIL. If you behave like a reasonable man, you can soon set the Baths on their feet again.

DR. STOCKMANN. Well, you can see for yourself that I have done all I can, but——. They are all mad in this town!

MORTEN KIIL. You said yesterday that the worst of this pollution came from my tannery. If that is true, then my grandfather and my father before me, and I myself, for many years past, have been poisoning the town like three destroying angels. Do you think I am going to sit quiet under that reproach?

DR. STOCKMANN. Unfortunately I am afraid you will have to.

MORTEN KIIL. No, thank you. I am jealous of my name

and reputation. They call me "the Badger," I am told. A badger is a kind of pig, I believe; but I am not going to give them the right to call me that. I mean to live and die a clean man.

DR. STOCKMANN. And how are you going to set about it?

MORTEN KIIL. You shall cleanse me, Thomas.

DR. STOCKMANN. I!

MORTEN KIIL. Do you know what money I have bought these shares with? No, of course you can't know—but I will tell you. It is the money that Katherine and Petra and the boys will have when I am gone. Because I have been able to save a little bit after all, you know.

DR. STOCKMANN (*flaring up*). And you have gone and taken Katherine's money for *this*!

MORTEN KIIL. Yes, the whole of the money is invested in the Baths now. And now I just want to see whether you are quite stark, staring mad, Thomas! If you still make out that these animals and other nasty things of that sort come from my tannery, it will be exactly as if you were to flay broad strips of skin from Katherine's body, and Petra's, and the boys'; and no decent man would do that—unless he were mad.

DR. STOCKMANN (*walking up and down*). Yes, but I *am* mad; I *am* mad!

MORTEN KIIL. You cannot be so absurdly mad as all that, when it is a question of your wife and children.

DR. STOCKMANN (*standing still in front of him*). Why couldn't you consult me about it, before you went and bought all that trash?

MORTEN KIIL. What is done cannot be undone.

DR. STOCKMANN (*walks about uneasily*). If only I were not so certain about it——! But I am absolutely convinced that I am right.

MORTEN KIIL (*weighing the pocket-book in his hand*). If you stick to your mad idea, this won't be worth much, you know. (*Puts the pocket-book in his pocket.*)

DR. STOCKMANN. But, hang it all! it might be possible for science to discover some prophylactic, I should think—or some antidote of some kind——

MORTEN KIIL. To kill these animals, do you mean?

DR. STOCKMANN. Yes, or to make them innocuous.

MORTEN KIIL. Couldn't you try some rat's-bane?

DR. STOCKMANN. Don't talk nonsense! They all say it is only imagination, you know. Well, let it go at that! Let them have their own way about it! Haven't the ignorant, narrow-minded curs reviled me as an enemy of the people? —and haven't they been ready to tear the clothes off my back too?

MORTEN KIIL. And broken all your windows to pieces!

DR. STOCKMANN. And then there is my duty to my family. I must talk it over with Katherine; she is great on those things.

MORTEN KIIL. That is right; be guided by a reasonable woman's advice.

DR. STOCKMANN (*advancing towards him*). To think you could do such a preposterous thing! Risking Katherine's money in this way, and putting me in such a horribly painful dilemma! When I look at you, I think I see the devil himself——.

MORTEN KIIL. Then I had better go. But I must have an answer from you before two o'clock—yes or no. If it is no, the shares go to a charity, and that this very day.

DR. STOCKMANN. And what does Katherine get?

MORTEN KIIL. Not a halfpenny. (*The door leading to the hall opens and* HOVSTAD *and* ASLAKSEN *make their appearance.*) Look at those two!

DR. STOCKMANN (*staring at them*). What the devil!— have *you* actually the face to come into my house?

HOVSTAD. Certainly.

ASLAKSEN. We have something to say to you, you see.

MORTEN KIIL (*in a whisper*). Yes or no—before two o'clock.

ASLAKSEN (*glancing at* HOVSTAD). Aha! (MORTEN KIIL *goes out.*)

DR. STOCKMANN. Well, what do you want with me? Be brief.

HOVSTAD. I can quite understand that you are annoyed with us for our attitude at the meeting yesterday——

DR. STOCKMANN. Attitude, do you call it? Yes, it was a charming attitude! I call it weak, womanish—damnably shameful!

HOVSTAD. Call it what you like, we could not do otherwise.

DR. STOCKMANN. You *dared* not do otherwise—isn't that it?

HOVSTAD. Well, if you like to put it that way.

ASLAKSEN. But why did you not let us have word of it beforehand?—just a hint to Mr. Hovstad or to me?

DR. STOCKMANN. A hint? Of what?

ASLAKSEN. Of what was behind it all.

DR. STOCKMANN. I don't understand you in the least.

ASLAKSEN (*with a confidential nod*). Oh yes, you do, Dr. Stockmann.

HOVSTAD. It is no good making a mystery of it any longer.

DR. STOCKMANN (*looking first at one of them and then at the other*). What the devil do you both mean?

ASLAKSEN. May I ask if your father-in-law is not going round the town buying up all the shares in the Baths?

DR. STOCKMANN. Yes, he has been buying Bath shares to-day; but——

ASLAKSEN. It would have been more prudent to get some one else to do it—some one less nearly related to you.

HOVSTAD. And you should not have let your name appear in the affair. There was no need for anyone to know that the attack on the Baths came from you. You ought to have consulted me, Dr. Stockmann.

DR. STOCKMANN (*looks in front of him; then a light seems*

to dawn on him and he says in amazement:) Are such things conceivable? Are such things possible?

ASLAKSEN (*with a smile*). Evidently they are. But it is better to use a little *finesse*, you know.

HOVSTAD. And it is much better to have several persons in a thing of that sort; because the responsibility of each individual is lessened, when there are others with him.

DR. STOCKMANN (*composedly*). Come to the point, gentlemen. What do you want?

ASLAKSEN. Perhaps Mr. Hovstad had better——

HOVSTAD. No, you tell him, Aslaksen.

ASLAKSEN. Well, the fact is that, now we know the bearings of the whole affair, we think we might venture to put the "People's Messenger" at your disposal.

DR. STOCKMANN. Do you dare do that now? What about public opinion? Are you not afraid of a storm breaking upon our heads?

HOVSTAD. We will try to weather it.

ASLAKSEN. And you must be ready to go off quickly on a new tack, Doctor. As soon as your invective has done its work——

DR. STOCKMANN. Do you mean, as soon as my father-in-law and I have got hold of the shares at a low figure?

HOVSTAD. Your reasons for wishing to get the control of the Baths are mainly scientific, I take it.

DR. STOCKMANN. Of course; it was for scientific reasons that I persuaded the old "Badger" to stand in with me in the matter. So we will tinker at the conduit-pipes a little, and dig up a little bit of the shore, and it shan't cost the town a sixpence. That will be all right—eh?

HOVSTAD. I think so—if you have the "People's Messenger" behind you.

ASLAKSEN. The Press is a power in a free community, Doctor.

DR. STOCKMANN. Quite so. And so is public opinion.

And you, Mr. Aslaksen—I suppose you will be answerable for the Householders' Association?

ASLAKSEN. Yes, and for the Temperance Society. You may rely on that.

DR. STOCKMANN. But, gentlemen—I really am ashamed to ask the question—but, what return do you——?

HOVSTAD. We should prefer to help you without any return whatever, believe me. But the "People's Messenger" is in rather a shaky condition; it doesn't go really well; and I should be very unwilling to suspend the paper now, when there is so much work to do here in the political way.

DR. STOCKMANN. Quite so; that would be a great trial to such a friend of the people as you are. (*Flares up.*) But I am an enemy of the people, remember! (*Walks about the room.*) Where have I put my stick? Where the devil is my stick?

HOVSTAD. What's that?

ASLAKSEN. Surely you never mean——?

DR. STOCKMANN (*standing still*). And suppose I don't give you a single penny of all I get out of it? Money is not very easy to get out of us rich folk, please to remember!

HOVSTAD. And you please to remember that this affair of the shares can be represented in two ways!

DR. STOCKMANN. Yes, and you are just the man to do it. If I don't come to the rescue of the "People's Messenger," you will certainly take an evil view of the affair; you will hunt me down, I can well imagine—pursue me—try to throttle me as a dog does a hare.

HOVSTAD. It is a natural law; every animal must fight for its own livelihood.

ASLAKSEN. And get its food where it can, you know.

DR. STOCKMANN (*walking about the room*). Then you go and look for yours in the gutter; because I am going to show you which is the strongest animal of us three! (*Finds an umbrella and brandishes it above his head.*) Ah, now——!

HOVSTAD. You are surely not going to use violence!

ASLAKSEN. Take care what you are doing with that umbrella.

DR. STOCKMANN. Out of the window with you, Mr. Hovstad!

HOVSTAD (*edging to the door*). Are you quite mad!

DR. STOCKMANN. Out of the window, Mr. Aslaksen! Jump, I tell you! You will have to do it, sooner or later.

ASLAKSEN (*running round the writing-table*). Moderation, Doctor—I am a delicate man—I can stand so little—(*calls out*) help, help!

(MRS. STOCKMANN, PETRA *and* HORSTER *come in from the sitting-room.*)

MRS. STOCKMANN. Good gracious, Thomas! What is happening?

DR. STOCKMANN (*brandishing the umbrella*). Jump out, I tell you! Out into the gutter!

HOVSTAD. An assault on an unoffending man! I call you to witness, Captain Horster. (*Hurries out through the hall.*)

ASLAKSEN (*irresolutely*). If only I knew the way about here——. (*Steals out through the sitting-room.*)

MRS. STOCKMANN (*holding her husband back*). Control yourself, Thomas!

DR. STOCKMANN (*throwing down the umbrella*). Upon my soul, they have escaped after all.

MRS. STOCKMANN. What did they want you to do?

DR. STOCKMANN. I will tell you later on; I have something else to think about now. (*Goes to the table and writes something on a calling-card.*) Look there, Katherine; what is written there?

MRS. STOCKMANN. Three big No's; what does that mean?

DR. STOCKMANN. I will tell you that too, later on. (*Holds out the card to* PETRA.) There, Petra; tell sooty-face to run over to "the Badger's" with that, as quickly as she can. Hurry up! (PETRA *takes the card and goes out to the hall.*)

DR. STOCKMANN. Well, I think I have had a visit from every one of the devil's messengers to-day! But now I am going to sharpen my pen till they can feel its point; I shall dip it in venom and gall; I shall hurl my ink-pot at their heads!

MRS. STOCKMANN. Yes, but we are going away, you know, Thomas.

(PETRA *comes back.*)

DR. STOCKMANN. Well?

PETRA. She has gone with it.

DR. STOCKMANN. Good.—Going away, did you say? No, I'll be hanged if we are going away! We are going to stay where we are, Katherine!

PETRA. Stay here?

MRS. STOCKMANN. Here, in the town?

DR. STOCKMANN. Yes, here. This is the field of battle— this is where the fight will be. This is where I shall triumph! As soon as I have had my trousers sewn up I shall go out and look for another house. We must have a roof over our heads for the winter.

HORSTER. That you shall have in my house.

DR. STOCKMANN. Can I?

HORSTER. Yes, quite well. I have plenty of room, and I am almost never at home.

MRS. STOCKMANN. How good of you, Captain Horster!

PETRA. Thank you!

DR. STOCKMANN (*grasping his hand*). Thank you, thank you! That is one trouble over! Now I can set to work in earnest at once. There is an endless amount of things to look through here, Katherine! Luckily I shall have all my time at my disposal; because I have been dismissed from the Baths, you know.

MRS. STOCKMANN (*with a sigh*). Oh yes, I expected that.

DR. STOCKMANN. And they want to take my practice away from me too. Let them! I have got the poor people to fall back upon, anyway—those that don't pay anything; and, after all, they need me most, too. But, by Jove, they will have to listen to me; I shall preach to them in season and out of season, as it says somewhere.

MRS. STOCKMANN. But, dear Thomas, I should have thought events had showed you what use it is to preach.

DR. STOCKMANN. You are really ridiculous, Katherine. Do you want me to let myself be beaten off the field by public opinion and the compact majority and all that devilry? No, thank you! And what I want to do is so simple and clear and straightforward. I only want to drum into the heads of these curs the fact that the liberals are the most insidious enemies of freedom—that party programmes strangle every young and vigorous truth—that considerations of expediency turn morality and justice upside down—and that they will end by making life here unbearable. Don't you think, Captain Horster, that I ought to be able to make people understand that?

HORSTER. Very likely; I don't know much about such things myself.

DR. STOCKMANN. Well, look here—I will explain! It is the party leaders that must be exterminated. A party leader is like a wolf, you see—like a voracious wolf. He requires a certain number of smaller victims to prey upon every year, if he is to live. Just look at Hovstad and Aslaksen! How many smaller victims have they not put an end to—or at any rate maimed and mangled until they are fit for nothing except to be householders or subscribers to the "People's Messenger"! (Sits down on the edge of the table.) Come here, Katherine—look how beautifully the sun shines to-day! And this lovely spring air I am drinking in!

MRS. STOCKMANN. Yes, if only we could live on sunshine and spring air, Thomas.

DR. STOCKMANN. Oh, you will have to pinch and save a bit—then we shall get along. That gives me very little concern. What is much worse is, that I know of no one who is liberal-minded and high-minded enough to venture to take up my work after me.

PETRA. Don't think about that, father; you have plenty of time before you.—Hullo, here are the boys already!

(EJLIF *and* MORTEN *come in from the sitting-room.*)

MRS. STOCKMANN. Have you got a holiday?

MORTEN. No; but we were fighting with the other boys between lessons——

EJLIF. That isn't true; it was the other boys were fighting with us.

MORTEN. Well, and then Mr. Rörlund said we had better stay at home for a day or two.

DR. STOCKMANN (*snapping his fingers and getting up from the table*). I have it! I have it, by Jove! You shall never set foot in the school again!

THE BOYS. No more school!

MRS. STOCKMANN. But, Thomas——

DR. STOCKMANN. Never, I say. I will educate you myself; that is to say, you shan't learn a blessed thing——

MORTEN. Hooray!

DR. STOCKMANN. —but I will make liberal-minded and high-minded men of you. You must help me with that, Petra.

PETRA. Yes, father, you may be sure I will.

DR. STOCKMANN. And my school shall be in the room where they insulted me and called me an enemy of the people. But we are too few as we are; I must have at least twelve boys to begin with.

MRS. STOCKMANN. You will certainly never get them in this town.

DR. STOCKMANN. We shall. (*To the boys.*) Don't you know any street urchins—regular ragamuffins——?

MORTEN. Yes, father, I know lots!

DR. STOCKMANN. That's capital! Bring me some specimens of them. I am going to experiment with curs, just for once; there may be some exceptional heads amongst them.

MORTEN. And what are we going to do, when you have made liberal-minded and high-minded men of us?

DR. STOCKMANN. Then you shall drive all the wolves out of the country, my boys!

(EJLIF *looks rather doubtful about it;* MORTEN *jumps about crying* "Hurrah!")

MRS. STOCKMANN. Let us hope it won't be the wolves that will drive you out of the country, Thomas.

DR. STOCKMANN. Are you out of your mind, Katherine? Drive me out! Now—when I am the strongest man in the town!

MRS. STOCKMANN. The strongest—now?

DR. STOCKMANN. Yes, and I will go so far as to say that now I am the strongest man in the whole world.

MORTEN. I say!

DR. STOCKMANN (*lowering his voice*). Hush! You mustn't say anything about it yet; but I have made a great discovery.

MRS. STOCKMANN. Another one?

DR. STOCKMANN. Yes. (*Gathers them round him, and says confidentially:*) It is this, let me tell you—that the strongest man in the world is he who stands most alone.

MRS. STOCKMANN (*smiling and shaking her head*). Oh, Thomas, Thomas!

PETRA (*encouragingly, as she grasps her father's hands*). Father!

THE WILD DUCK

PLAY IN FIVE ACTS

CHARACTERS

WERLE, *a merchant, manufacturer, etc.*

GREGERS WERLE, *his son.*

OLD EKDAL.

HIALMAR EKDAL, *his son, a photographer.*

GINA EKDAL, *Hialmar's wife.*

HEDVIG, *their daughter, a girl of fourteen.*

MRS. SÖRBY, *Werle's housekeeper.*

RELLING, *a doctor.*

MOLVIK, *student of theology.*

GRÅBERG, *Werle's bookkeeper.*

PETTERSEN, *Werle's servant.*

JENSEN, *a hired waiter.*

A FLABBY GENTLEMAN.

A THIN-HAIRED GENTLEMAN.

A SHORT-SIGHTED GENTLEMAN.

SIX OTHER GENTLEMEN, *guests at Werle's dinner-party.*

SEVERAL HIRED WAITERS.

The first act passes in WERLE'S *house, the remaining acts at* HIALMAR EKDAL'S.

Pronunciation of Names: GREGERS WERLE = Grayghers Verlë; HIALMAR EKDAL = Yalmar Aykdal; GINA = Cheena; GRÅBERG = Groberg; JENSEN = Yensen.

ACT I

(*At* WERLE'S *house. A richly and comfortably furnished study; bookcases and upholstered furniture; a writing-table, with papers and documents, in the center of the room; lighted lamps with green shades, giving a subdued light. At the back, open folding-doors with curtains drawn back. Within is seen a large and handsome room, brilliantly lighted with lamps and branching candlesticks. In front, on the right (in the study), a small baize door leads into* WERLE'S *office. On the left, in front, a fire-place with a glowing coal fire, and farther back a double door leading into the dining-room.*)

(WERLE'S *servant,* PETTERSEN, *in livery and* JENSEN, *the hired waiter, in black, are putting the study in order. In the large room, two or three other hired waiters are moving about, arranging things and lighting more candles. From the dining-room, the hum of conversation and laughter of many voices are heard; a glass is tapped with a knife; silence follows, and a toast is proposed; shouts of "Bravo!" and then again a buzz of conversation.*)

PETTERSEN (*lights a lamp on the chimney-place and places a shade over it*). Hark to them, Jensen! now the old man's on his legs holding a long palaver about Mrs. Sörby.

JENSEN (*pushing forward an arm-chair*). Is it true, what folks say, that they're—very good friends, eh?

PETTERSEN. Lord knows.

JENSEN. I've heard tell as he's been a lively customer in his day.

PETTERSEN. May be.

JENSEN. And he's giving this spread in honor of his son, they say.

PETTERSEN. Yes. His son came home yesterday.

JENSEN. This is the first time I ever heard as Mr. Werle had a son.

PETTERSEN. Oh yes, he has a son, right enough. But he's a fixture, as you might say, up at the Höidal works. He's never once come to town all the years I've been in service here.

A WAITER (*in the doorway of the other room*). Pettersen, here's an old fellow wanting——

PETTERSEN (*mutters*). The devil—who's this now?

(OLD EKDAL *appears from the right, in the inner room. He is dressed in a threadbare overcoat with a high collar; he wears woollen mittens, and carries in his hand a stick and a fur cap. Under his arm, a brown paper parcel. Dirty red-brown wig and small gray moustache.*)

PETTERSEN (*goes towards him*). Good Lord—what do you want here?

EKDAL (*in the doorway*). Must get into the office, Pettersen.

PETTERSEN. The office was closed an hour ago, and——

EKDAL. So they told me at the front door. But Gråberg's in there still. Let me slip in this way, Pettersen; there's a good fellow. (*Points towards the baize door.*) It's not the first time I've come this way.

PETTERSEN. Well, you may pass. (*Opens the door.*) But mind you go out again the proper way, for we've got company.

EKDAL. I know, I know—h'm! Thanks, Pettersen, good old friend! Thanks! (*Mutters softly.*) Ass!

(*He goes into the office;* PETTERSEN *shuts the door after him.*)

JENSEN. Is he one of the office people?

PETTERSEN. No, he's only an outside hand that does odd jobs of copying. But he's been a tip-topper in his day, has old Ekdal.

JENSEN. You can see he's been through a lot.

PETTERSEN. Yes; he was an army officer, you know.

JENSEN. You don't say so?

PETTERSEN. No mistake about it. But then he went into the timber trade or something of the sort. They say he once played Mr. Werle a very nasty trick. They were partners in the Höidal works at the time. Oh, I know old Ekdal well, I do. Many a nip of bitters and bottle of ale we two have drunk at Madam Eriksen's.

JENSEN. He don't look as if he'd much to stand treat with.

PETTERSEN. Why, bless you, Jensen, it's me that stands treat. I always think there's no harm in being a bit civil to folks that have seen better days.

JENSEN. Did he go bankrupt then?

PETTERSEN. Worse than that. He went to prison.

JENSEN. To prison!

PETTERSEN. Or perhaps it was the Penitentiary. (*Listens.*) Sh! They're leaving the table.

(*The dining-room door is thrown open from within, by a couple of waiters.* MRS. SÖRBY *comes out conversing with two gentlemen. Gradually the whole company follows, amongst them* WERLE. *Last come* HIALMAR EKDAL *and* GREGERS WERLE.)

MRS. SÖRBY (*in passing, to the servant*). Tell them to serve the coffee in the music-room, Pettersen.

PETTERSEN. Very well, Madam.

(*She goes with the two Gentlemen into the inner room, and thence out to the right.* PETTERSEN *and* JENSEN *go out the same way.*)

A FLABBY GENTLEMAN (*to a* THIN-HAIRED GENTLE-MAN). Whew! What a dinner!—It was no joke to do it justice!

THE THIN-HAIRED GENTLEMAN. Oh, with a little good-will one can get through a lot in three hours.

THE FLABBY GENTLEMAN. Yes, but afterwards, after-wards, my dear Chamberlain!

A THIRD GENTLEMAN. I hear the coffee and maraschino are to be served in the music-room.

THE FLABBY GENTLEMAN. Bravo! Then perhaps Mrs. Sörby will play us something.

THE THIN-HAIRED GENTLEMAN (*in a low voice*). I hope Mrs. Sörby mayn't play us a tune we don't like, one of these days!

THE FLABBY GENTLEMAN. Oh, no, not she! Bertha will never turn against her old friends.

(*They laugh and pass into the inner room.*)

WERLE (*in a low voice, dejectedly*). I don't think any-body noticed it, Gregers.

GREGERS (*looks at him*). Noticed what?

WERLE. Did you not notice it either?

GREGERS. What do you mean?

WERLE. We were thirteen at table.

GREGERS. Indeed? Were there thirteen of us?

WERLE (*glances towards* HIALMAR EKDAL). Our usual party is twelve. (*To the others.*) This way, gentlemen!

(WERLE *and the others, all except* HIALMAR *and* GRE-GERS, *go out by the back, to the right.*)

HIALMAR (*who has overheard the conversation*). You ought not to have invited me, Gregers.

GREGERS. What! Not ask my best and only friend to a party supposed to be in my honor——?

HIALMAR. But I don't think your father likes it. You see I am quite outside his circle.

GREGERS. So I hear. But I wanted to see you and have a talk with you, and I certainly shan't be staying long.—Ah, we two old schoolfellows have drifted far apart from each other. It must be sixteen or seventeen years since we met.

HIALMAR. Is it so long?

GREGERS. It is indeed. Well, how goes it with you? You look well. You have put on flesh, and grown almost stout.

HIALMAR. Well, "stout" is scarcely the word; but I daresay I look a little more of a man than I used to.

GREGERS. Yes, you do; your outer man is in first-rate condition.

HIALMAR (*in a tone of gloom*). Ah, but the inner man! That is a very different matter, I can tell you! Of course you know of the terrible catastrophe that has befallen me and mine since last we met.

GREGERS (*more softly*). How are things going with your father now?

HIALMAR. Don't let us talk of it, old fellow. Of course my poor unhappy father lives with me. He hasn't another soul in the world to care for him. But you can understand that this is a miserable subject for me.—Tell me, rather, how you have been getting on up at the works.

GREGERS. I have had a delightfully lonely time of it— plenty of leisure to think and think about things. Come over here; we may as well make ourselves comfortable.

(*He seats himself in an arm-chair by the fire and draws* HIALMAR *down into another alongside of it.*)

HIALMAR (*sentimentally*). After all, Gregers, I thank you for inviting me to your father's table; for I take it as a sign that you have got over your feeling against me.

GREGERS (*surprised*). How could you imagine I had any feeling against you?

HIALMAR. You had at first, you know.

GREGERS. How at first?

HIALMAR. After the great misfortune. It was natural enough that you should. Your father was within an ace of being drawn into that—well, that terrible business.

GREGERS. Why should that give me any feeling against you? Who can have put that into your head?

HIALMAR. I know it did, Gregers; your father told me so himself.

GREGERS (*starts*). My father! Oh indeed. H'm.—Was that why you never let me hear from you?—not a single word.

HIALMAR. Yes.

GREGERS. Not even when you made up your mind to become a photographer?

HIALMAR. Your father said I had better not write to you at all, about anything.

GREGERS (*looking straight before him*). Well well, perhaps he was right.—But tell me now, Hialmar: are you pretty well satisfied with your present position?

HIALMAR (*with a little sigh*). Oh yes, I am; I have really no cause to complain. At first, as you may guess, I felt it a little strange. It was such a totally new state of things for me. But of course my whole circumstances were totally changed. Father's utter, irretrievable ruin,—the shame and disgrace of it, Gregers——

GREGERS (*affected*). Yes, yes; I understand.

HIALMAR. I couldn't think of remaining at college; there wasn't a shilling to spare; on the contrary, there were debts —mainly to your father I believe——

GREGERS. H'm——

HIALMAR. In short, I thought it best to break, once for all, with my old surroundings and associations. It was your father that specially urged me to it; and since he interested himself so much in me——

GREGERS. My father did?

HIALMAR. Yes, you surely knew that, didn't you? Where do you suppose I found the money to learn photography, and to furnish a studio and make a start? All that costs a pretty penny, I can tell you.

GREGERS. And my father provided the money?

HIALMAR. Yes, my dear fellow, didn't you know? I understood him to say he had written to you about it.

GREGERS. Not a word about his part in the business. He must have forgotten it. Our correspondence has always been purely a business one. So it was my father that——!

HIALMAR. Yes, certainly. He didn't wish it to be generally known; but he it was. And of course it was he, too, that put me in a position to marry. Don't you—don't you know about that either?

GREGERS. No, I haven't heard a word of it. (*Shakes him by the arm.*) But, my dear Hialmar, I can't tell you what pleasure all this gives me—pleasure, and self-reproach. I have perhaps done my father injustice after all—in some things. This proves that he has a heart. It shows a sort of compunction——

HIALMAR. Compunction——?

GREGERS. Yes, yes—whatever you like to call it. Oh, I can't tell you how glad I am to hear this of father.—So you are a married man, Hialmar! That is further than I shall ever get. Well, I hope you are happy in your married life?

HIALMAR. Yes, thoroughly happy. She is as good and capable a wife as any man could wish for. And she is by no means without culture.

GREGERS (*rather surprised*). No, of course not.

HIALMAR. You see, life is itself an education. Her daily intercourse with me—— And then we know one or two rather remarkable men, who come a good deal about us. I assure you, you would hardly know Gina again.

GREGERS. Gina?

HIALMAR. Yes; had you forgotten that her name was Gina?

GREGERS. Whose name? I haven't the slightest idea——

HIALMAR. Don't you remember that she used to be in service here?

GREGERS (*looks at him.*) Is it Gina Hansen——?

HIALMAR. Yes, of course it is Gina Hansen.

GREGERS. ——who kept house for us during the last year of my mother's illness?

HIALMAR. Yes, exactly. But, my dear friend, I'm quite sure your father told you that I was married.

GREGERS (*who has risen*). Oh yes, he mentioned it; but not that—— (*Walking about the room.*) Stay—perhaps he did—now that I think of it. My father always writes such short letters. (*Half seats himself on the arm of the chair.*) Now, tell me, Hialmar—this is interesting—how did you come to know Gina—your wife?

HIALMAR. The simplest thing in the world. You know Gina did not stay here long, everything was so much upset at that time, owing to your mother's illness and so forth, that Gina was not equal to it all; so she gave notice and left. That was the year before your mother died—or it may have been the same year.

GREGERS. It was the same year. I was up at the works then. But afterwards——?

HIALMAR. Well, Gina lived at home with her mother, Madam Hansen, an excellent hard-working woman, who kept a little eating-house. She had a room to let too; a very nice comfortable room.

GREGERS. And I suppose you were lucky enough to secure it?

HIALMAR. Yes; in fact, it was your father that recommended it to me. So it was there, you see, that I really came to know Gina.

GREGERS. And then you got engaged?

HIALMAR. Yes. It doesn't take young people long to fall in love——; h'm——

GREGERS (*rises and moves about a little*). Tell me: was it after your engagement—was it then that my father—I mean was it then that you began to take up photography?

HIALMAR. Yes, precisely. I wanted to make a start, and to set up house as soon as possible; and your father and I agreed that this photography business was the readiest way. Gina thought so too. Oh, and there was another thing in its favor, by-the-bye: it happened, luckily, that Gina had learned to retouch.

GREGERS. That chimed in marvellously.

HIALMAR (*pleased, rises*). Yes, didn't it? Don't you think it was a marvellous piece of luck?

GREGERS. Oh, unquestionably. My father seems to have been almost a kind of providence for you.

HIALMAR (*with emotion*). He did not forsake his old friend's son in the hour of his need. For he has a heart, you see.

MRS. SÖRBY (*enters, arm-in-arm with* WERLE). Nonsense, my dear Mr. Werle; you mustn't stop there any longer staring at all the lights. It's very bad for you.

WERLE (*lets go her arm and passes his hand over his eyes*). I daresay you are right.

(PETTERSEN *and* JENSEN *carry round refreshment trays.*)

MRS. SÖRBY (*to the Guests in the other room*). This way, if you please, gentlemen. Whoever wants a glass of punch must be so good as to come in here.

THE FLABBY GENTLEMAN (*comes up to* MRS. SÖRBY). Surely, it isn't possible that you have suspended our cherished right to smoke?

MRS. SÖRBY. Yes. No smoking here, in Mr. Werle's sanctum, Chamberlain.

THE THIN-HAIRED GENTLEMAN. When did you enact these stringent amendments on the cigar law, Mrs. Sörby?

MRS. SÖRBY. After the last dinner, Chamberlain, when certain persons permitted themselves to overstep the mark.

THE THIN-HAIRED GENTLEMAN. And may one never overstep the mark a little bit, Madame Bertha? Not the least little bit?

MRS. SÖRBY. Not in any respect whatsoever, Mr. Balle.

(*Most of the Guests have assembled in the study; servants hand round glasses of punch.*)

WERLE (*to* HIALMAR, *who is standing beside a table*). What are you studying so intently, Ekdal?

HIALMAR. Only an album, Mr. Werle.

THE THIN-HAIRED GENTLEMAN (*who is wandering about*). Ah, photographs! They are quite in your line of course.

THE FLABBY GENTLEMAN (*in an arm-chair*). Haven't you brought any of your own with you?

HIALMAR. No, I haven't.

THE FLABBY GENTLEMAN. You ought to have; it's very good for the digestion to sit and look at pictures.

THE THIN-HAIRED GENTLEMAN. And it contributes to the entertainment, you know.

THE SHORT-SIGHTED GENTLEMAN. And all contributions are thankfully received.

MRS. SÖRBY. The Chamberlains think that when one is invited out to dinner, one ought to exert oneself a little in return, Mr. Ekdal.

THE FLABBY GENTLEMAN. Where one dines so well, that duty becomes a pleasure.

THE THIN-HAIRED GENTLEMAN. And when it's a case of the struggle for existence, you know——

MRS. SÖRBY. I quite agree with you!

(*They continue the conversation, with laughter and joking.*)

GREGERS (*softly*). You must join in, Hialmar.

HIALMAR (*writhing*). What am I to talk about?

THE FLABBY GENTLEMAN. Don't you think, Mr. Werle, that Tokay may be considered one of the more wholesome sorts of wine?

WERLE (*by the fire*). I can answer for the Tokay you had to-day, at any rate; it's one of the very finest seasons. Of course you would notice that.

THE FLABBY GENTLEMAN. Yes, it had a remarkably delicate flavor.

HIALMAR (*shyly*). Is there any difference between the seasons?

THE FLABBY GENTLEMAN (*laughs*). Come! That's good!

WERLE (*smiles*). It really doesn't pay to set fine wine before you.

THE THIN-HAIRED GENTLEMAN. Tokay is like photographs, Mr. Ekdal: they both need sunshine. Am I not right?

HIALMAR. Yes, light is important no doubt.

MRS. SÖRBY. And it's exactly the same with Chamberlains—they, too, depend very much on sunshine,[1] as the saying is.

THE THIN-HAIRED GENTLEMAN. Oh fie! That's a very threadbare sarcasm!

THE SHORT-SIGHTED GENTLEMAN. Mrs. Sörby is coming out——

THE FLABBY GENTLEMAN. ——and at our expense, too. (*Holds up his finger reprovingly.*) Oh, Madame Bertha, Madame Bertha!

MRS. SÖRBY. Yes, and there's not the least doubt that the seasons differ greatly. The old vintages are the finest.

THE SHORT-SIGHTED GENTLEMAN. Do you reckon me among the old vintages?

MRS. SÖRBY. Oh, far from it.

THE THIN-HAIRED GENTLEMAN. There now! But me, dear Mrs. Sörby——?

THE FLABBY GENTLEMAN. Yes, and me? What vintage should you say that we belong to?

MRS. SÖRBY. Why, to the sweet vintages, gentlemen.

(*She sips a glass of punch. The gentlemen laugh and flirt with her.*)

WERLE. Mrs. Sörby can always find a loop-hole—when she wants to. Fill your glasses, gentlemen! Pettersen, will you see to it——! Gregers, suppose we have a glass together. (GREGERS *does not move.*) Won't you join us, Ekdal? I found no opportunity of drinking with you at table.

(GRÅBERG, *the Bookkeeper, looks in at the baize door.*)

[1] The "sunshine" of Court favor.

GRÅBERG. Excuse me, sir, but I can't get out.

WERLE. Have you been locked in again?

GRÅBERG. Yes, and Flakstad has carried off the keys.

WERLE. Well, you can pass out this way.

GRÅBERG. But there's some one else——

WERLE. All right; come through, both of you. Don't be afraid.

(GRÅBERG *and* OLD EKDAL *come out of the office.*)

WERLE (*involuntarily*). Ugh!

(*The laughter and talk among the Guests cease.* HIAL-
MAR *starts at the sight of his father, puts down his
glass, and turns towards the fireplace.*)

EKDAL (*does not look up, but makes little bows to both
sides as he passes, murmuring*). Beg pardon, come the wrong
way. Door locked—door locked. Beg pardon.

(*He and* GRÅBERG *go out by the back, to the right.*)

WERLE (*between his teeth*). That idiot Gråberg.

GREGERS (*open-mouthed and staring, to* HIALMAR). Why
surely that wasn't——!

THE FLABBY GENTLEMAN. What's the matter? Who was
it?

GREGERS. Oh, nobody, only the bookkeeper and some one
with him.

THE SHORT-SIGHTED GENTLEMAN (*to* HIALMAR). Did
you know that man?

HIALMAR. I don't know—I didn't notice——

THE FLABBY GENTLEMAN. What the deuce has come over
every one?

(*He joins another group who are talking softly*)

MRS. SÖRBY (*whispers to the Servant*). Give him something to take with him;—something good, mind.

PETTERSEN (*nods*). I'll see to it.

(*Goes out.*)

GREGERS (*softly and with emotion, to* HIALMAR). So that
was really he!

HIALMAR. Yes.

GREGERS. And you could stand there and deny that you knew him!

HIALMAR (*whispers vehemently*). But how could I——!

GREGERS. ——acknowledge your own father?

HIALMAR (*with pain*). Oh, if you were in my place——

(*The conversation amongst the Guests, which has been carried on in a low tone, now swells into constrained joviality.*)

THE THIN-HAIRED GENTLEMAN (*approaching* HIALMAR *and* GREGERS *in a friendly manner*). Aha! Reviving old college memories, eh? Don't you smoke, Mr. Ekdal? May I give you a light? Oh, by-the-bye, we mustn't——

HIALMAR. No, thank you, I won't——

THE FLABBY GENTLEMAN. Haven't you a nice little poem you could recite to us, Mr. Ekdal? You used to recite so charmingly.

HIALMAR. I am sorry I can't remember anything.

THE FLABBY GENTLEMAN. Oh, that's a pity. Well, what shall we do, Balle?

(*Both Gentlemen move away and pass into the other room.*)

HIALMAR (*gloomily*). Gregers—I am going! When a man has felt the crushing hand of Fate, you see—— Say good-bye to your father for me.

GREGERS. Yes, yes. Are you going straight home?

HIALMAR. Yes. Why?

GREGERS. Oh, because I may perhaps look in on you later.

HIALMAR. No, you mustn't do that. You must not come to my home. Mine is a melancholy abode, Gregers; especially after a splendid banquet like this. We can always arrange to meet somewhere in the town.

MRS. SÖRBY (*who has quietly approached*). Are you going, Ekdal?

HIALMAR. Yes.

MRS. SÖRBY. Remember me to Gina.

HIALMAR. Thanks.

MRS. SÖRBY. And say I am coming up to see her one of these days.

HIALMAR. Yes, thank you. (*To* GREGERS.) Stay here; I will slip out unobserved.

(*He saunters away, then into the other room, and so out to the right.*)

MRS. SÖRBY (*softly to the Servant, who has come back*). Well, did you give the old man something?

PETTERSEN. Yes; I sent him off with a bottle of cognac.

MRS. SÖRBY. Oh, you might have thought of something better than that.

PETTERSEN. Oh, no, Mrs. Sörby; cognac is what he likes best in the world.

THE FLABBY GENTLEMAN (*in the doorway with a sheet of music in his hand*). Shall we play a duet, Mrs. Sörby?

MRS. SÖRBY. Yes, suppose we do.

THE GUESTS. Bravo, bravo!

(*She goes with all the Guests through the back room, out to the right.* GREGERS *remains standing by the fire.* WERLE *is looking for something on the writing-table, and appears to wish that* GREGERS *would go; as* GREGERS *does not move,* WERLE *goes towards the door.*)

GREGERS. Father, won't you stay a moment?

WERLE (*stops*). What is it?

GREGERS. I must have a word with you.

WERLE. Can it not wait till we are alone?

GREGERS. No, it cannot; for perhaps we shall never be alone together.

WERLE (*drawing nearer*). What do you mean by that?

(*During what follows, the pianoforte is faintly heard from the distant music-room.*)

GREGERS. How has that family been allowed to go so miserably to the wall?

WERLE. You mean the Ekdals, I suppose.

GREGERS. Yes, I mean the Ekdals. Lieutenant Ekdal was once so closely associated with you.

WERLE. Much too closely; I have felt that to my cost for many a year. It is thanks to him that I—yes I—have had a kind of slur cast upon my reputation.

GREGERS (*softly*). Are you sure that he alone was to blame?

WERLE. Who else do you suppose——?

GREGERS. You and he acted together in that affair of the forests——

WERLE. But was it not Ekdal that drew the map of the tracts we had bought—that fraudulent map! It was he who felled all that timber illegally on Government ground. In fact, the whole management was in his hands. I was quite in the dark as to what Lieutenant Ekdal was doing.

GREGERS. Lieutenant Ekdal himself seems to have been very much in the dark as to what he was doing.

WERLE. That may be. But the fact remains that he was found guilty and I acquitted.

GREGERS. Yes, I know that nothing was proved against you.

WERLE. Acquittal is acquittal. Why do you rake up these old miseries that turned my hair grey before its time? Is that the sort of thing you have been brooding over up there, all these years? I can assure you, Gregers, here in the town the whole story has been forgotten long ago—so far as *I* am concerned.

GREGERS. But that unhappy Ekdal family——

WERLE. What would you have had me do for the people? When Ekdal came out of prison he was a broken-down being, past all help. There are people in the world who dive to the bottom the moment they get a couple of slugs in their body, and never come to the surface again. You may take my word for it, Gregers, I have done all I could without positively laying myself open to all sorts of suspicion and gossip——

GREGERS. Suspicion——? Oh, I see.

WERLE. I have given Ekdal copying to do for the office, and I pay him far, far more for it than his work is worth——

GREGERS (*without looking at him*). H'm; that I don't doubt.

WERLE. You laugh? Do you think I am not telling you the truth? Well, I certainly can't refer you to my books, for I never enter payments of that sort.

GREGERS (*smiles coldly*). No, there are certain payments it is best to keep no account of.

WERLE (*taken aback*). What do you mean by that?

GREGERS (*mustering up courage*). Have you entered what it cost you to have Hialmar Ekdal taught photography?

WERLE. I? How "entered" it?

GREGERS. I have learnt that it was you who paid for his training. And I have learnt, too, that it was you who enabled him to set up house so comfortably.

WERLE. Well, and yet you talk as though I had done nothing for the Ekdals! I can assure you these people have cost me enough in all conscience.

GREGERS. Have you entered any of these expenses in your books?

WERLE. Why do you ask?

GREGERS. Oh, I have my reasons. Now tell me: when you interested yourself so warmly in your old friend's son—it was just before his marriage, was it not?

WERLE. Why, deuce take it—after all these years, how can I——?

GREGERS. You wrote me a letter about that time—a business letter, of course; and in a postscript you mentioned—quite briefly—that Hialmar Ekdal had married a Miss Hansen.

WERLE. Yes, that was quite right. That was her name.

GREGERS. But you did not mention that this Miss Hansen was Gina Hansen—our former housekeeper.

WERLE (*with a forced laugh of derision*). No; to tell the truth, it didn't occur to me that you were so particularly interested in our former housekeeper.

GREGERS. No more I was. But (*lowers his voice*) there were others in this house who were particularly interested in her.

WERLE. What do you mean by that? (*Flaring up.*) You are not alluding to me, I hope?

GREGERS (*softly but firmly*). Yes, I am alluding to you.

WERLE. And you dare——! You presume to——! How can that ungrateful hound—that photographer fellow—how dare he go making such insinuations!

GREGERS. Hialmar has never breathed a word about this. I don't believe he has the faintest suspicion of such a thing.

WERLE. Then where have you got it from? Who can have put such notions in your head?

GREGERS. My poor unhappy mother told me; and that the very last time I saw her.

WERLE. Your mother! I might have known as much! You and she—you always held together. It was she who turned you against me, from the first.

GREGERS. No, it was all that she had to suffer and submit to, until she broke down and came to such a pitiful end.

WERLE. Oh, she had nothing to suffer or submit to; not more than most people, at all events. But there's no getting on with morbid, overstrained creatures—that I have learned to my cost.—And you could go on nursing such a suspicion—burrowing into all sorts of old rumors and slanders against your own father! I must say, Gregers, I really think that at your age you might find something more useful to do.

GREGERS. Yes, it is high time.

WERLE. Then perhaps your mind would be easier than it seems to be now. What can be your object in remaining up at the works, year out and year in, drudging away like a common clerk, and not drawing a farthing more than the ordinary monthly wage? It is downright folly.

GREGERS. Ah, if I were only sure of that.

WERLE. I understand you well enough. You want to be independent; you won't be beholden to me for anything. Well, now there happens to be an opportunity for you to become independent, your own master in everything.

GREGERS. Indeed? In what way——?

WERLE. When I wrote you insisting on your coming to town at once—h'm——

GREGERS. Yes, what is it you really want of me? I have been waiting all day to know.

WERLE. I want to propose that you should enter the firm, as partner.

GREGERS. I! Join your firm? As partner?

WERLE. Yes. It would not involve our being constantly together. You could take over the business here in town, and I should move up to the works.

GREGERS. You would?

WERLE. The fact is, I am not so fit for work as I once was. I am obliged to spare my eyes, Gregers; they have begun to trouble me.

GREGERS. They have always been weak.

WERLE. Not as they are now. And, besides, circumstances might possibly make it desirable for me to live up there—for a time, at any rate.

GREGERS. That is certainly quite a new idea to me.

WERLE. Listen, Gregers: there are many things that stand between us; but we are father and son after all. We ought surely to be able to come to some sort of understanding with each other.

GREGERS. Outwardly, you mean, of course?

WERLE. Well, even that would be something. Think it

over, Gregers. Don't you think it ought to be possible? Eh?

GREGERS (*looking at him coldly*). There is something behind all this.

WERLE. How so?

GREGERS. You want to make use of me in some way.

WERLE. In such a close relationship as ours, the one can always be useful to the other.

GREGERS. Yes, so people say.

WERLE. I want very much to have you at home with me for a time. I am a lonely man, Gregers; I have always felt lonely, all my life through; but most of all now that I am getting up in years. I feel the need of some one about me——

GREGERS. You have Mrs. Sörby.

WERLE. Yes, I have her; and she has become, I may say, almost indispensable to me. She is lively and even-tempered; she brightens up the house; and that is a very great thing for me.

GREGERS. Well, then, you have everything just as you wish it.

WERLE. Yes, but I am afraid it can't last. A woman so situated may easily find herself in a false position, in the eyes of the world. For that matter it does a man no good, either.

GREGERS. Oh, when a man gives such dinners as you give, he can risk a good deal.

WERLE. Yes, but how about the woman, Gregers? I fear she won't accept the situation much longer; and even if she did—even if, out of attachment to me, she were to take her chance of gossip and scandal and all that——? Do you think, Gregers—you with your strong sense of justice——

GREGERS (*interrupts him*). Tell me in one word: are you thinking of marrying her?

WERLE. Suppose I were thinking of it? What then?

GREGERS. That's what I say: what then?

WERLE. Should you be inflexibly opposed to it!

GREGERS. Not at all. Not by any means.

WERLE. I was not sure whether your devotion to your mother's memory——

GREGERS. I am not overstrained.

WERLE. Well, whatever you may or may not be, at all events you have lifted a great weight from my mind. I am extremely pleased that I can reckon on your concurrence in this matter.

GREGERS (looking intently at him). Now I see the use you want to put me to.

WERLE. Use to put you to? What an expression!

GREGERS. Oh, don't let us be nice in our choice of words—not when we are alone together, at any rate. (With a short laugh.) Well, well. So this is what made it absolutely essential that I should come to town in person. For the sake of Mrs. Sörby, we are to get up a pretence at family life in the house—a tableau of filial affection! That will be something new indeed.

WERLE. How dare you speak in that tone!

GREGERS. Was there ever any family life here? Never since I can remember. But now, forsooth, your plans demand something of the sort. No doubt it will have an excellent effect when it is reported that the son has hastened home, on the wings of filial piety, to the grey-haired father's wedding feast. What will then remain of all the rumors as to the wrongs the poor dead mother had to submit to? Not a vestige. Her son annihilates them at one stroke.

WERLE. Gregers—I believe there is no one in the world you detest as you do me.

GREGERS (softly). I have seen you at too close quarters.

WERLE. You have seen me with your mother's eyes. (Lowers his voice a little.) But you should remember that her eyes were—clouded now and then.

GREGERS (quivering). I see what you are hinting at. But who was to blame for mother's unfortunate weakness? Why you, and all those——! The last of them was this woman that you palmed off upon Hialmar Ekdal, when you were—— Ugh!

WERLE (*shrugs his shoulders*). Word for word as if it were your mother speaking!

GREGERS (*without heeding*). And there he is now, with his great, confiding, childlike mind, compassed about with all this treachery—living under the same roof with such a creature, and never dreaming that what he calls his home is built upon a lie! (*Comes a step nearer.*) When I look back upon your past, I seem to see a battle-field with shattered lives on every hand.

WERLE. I begin to think the chasm that divides us is too wide.

GREGERS (*bowing, with self-command*). So I have observed; and therefore I take my hat and go.

WERLE. You are going! Out of the house?

GREGERS. Yes. For at last I see my mission in life.

WERLE. What mission?

GREGERS. You would only laugh if I told you.

WERLE. A lonely man doesn't laugh so easily, Gregers.

GREGERS (*pointing towards the background*). Look, father,—the Chamberlains are playing blind-man's-buff with Mrs. Sörby.—Good-night and good-bye.

> (*He goes out by the back to the right. Sounds of laughter and merriment from the Company, who are now visible in the outer room.*)

WERLE (*muttering contemptuously after* GREGERS). Ha ——! Poor wretch—and he says he is not overstrained!

ACT II

(HIALMAR EKDAL'S *studio, a good-sized room, evidently in the top story of the building. On the right, a sloping roof of large panes of glass, half-covered by a blue curtain. In the right-hand corner, at the back, the entrance door; farther forward, on the same side, a door leading to the sitting-room. Two doors on the opposite side, and between them an iron stove. At the back, a wide double sliding-door. The studio is plainly but comfortably fitted up and furnished. Between the doors on the right, standing out a little from the wall, a sofa with a table and some chairs; on the table a lighted lamp with a shade; beside the stove an old arm-chair. Photographic instruments and apparatus of different kinds lying about the room. Against the back wall, to the left of the double door, stands a bookcase containing a few books, boxes, and bottles of chemicals, instruments, tools, and other objects. Photographs and small articles, such as camel's-hair pencils, paper, and so forth, lie on the table.*)

(GINA EKDAL *sits on a chair by the table, sewing.* HEDVIG *is sitting on the sofa, with her hands shading her eyes and her thumbs in her ears, reading a book.*)

GINA (*glances once or twice at* HEDVIG, *as if with secret anxiety; then says*): Hedvig!

(HEDVIG *does not hear.*)

GINA (*repeats more loudly*). Hedvig!

HEDVIG (*takes away her hands and looks up*). Yes, mother?

GINA. Hedvig dear, you mustn't sit reading any longer now.

138

HEDVIG. Oh mother, mayn't I read a little more? Just a little bit?

GINA. No, no, you must put away your book now. Father doesn't like it; he never reads hisself in the evening.

HEDVIG (*shuts the book*). No, father doesn't care much about reading.

GINA (*puts aside her sewing and takes up a lead pencil and a little account-book from the table*). Can you remember how much we paid for the butter to-day?

HEDVIG. It was one crown sixty-five.

GINA. That's right. (*Puts it down.*) It's terrible what a lot of butter we get through in this house. Then there was the smoked sausage, and the cheese—let me see—(*Writes*)—and the ham—(*Adds up.*) Yes, that makes just——

HEDVIG. And then the beer.

GINA. Yes, to be sure. (*Writes.*) How it do mount up! But we can't manage with no less.

HEDVIG. And then you and I didn't need anything hot for dinner, as father was out.

GINA. No; that was so much to the good. And then I took eight crowns fifty for the photographs.

HEDVIG. Really! So much as that?

GINA. Exactly eight crowns fifty.

(*Silence.* GINA *takes up her sewing again,* HEDVIG *takes paper and pencil and begins to draw, shading her eyes with her left hand.*)

HEDVIG. Isn't it jolly to think that father is at Mr. Werle's big dinner-party?

GINA. You know he's not really Mr. Werle's guest. It was the son invited him. (*After a pause.*) We have nothing to do with that Mr. Werle.

HEDVIG. I'm longing for father to come home. He promised to ask Mrs. Sörby for something nice for me.

GINA. Yes, there's plenty of good things going in that house, I can tell you.

HEDVIG (*goes on drawing*). And I believe I'm a little hungry too.

(OLD EKDAL, *with the paper parcel under his arm and another parcel in his coat pocket, comes in by the entrance door.*)

GINA. How late you are to-day, grandfather!

EKDAL. They had locked the office door. Had to wait in Gråberg's room. And then they let me through—h'm.

HEDVIG. Did you get some more copying to do, grandfather?

EKDAL. This whole packet. Just look.

GINA. That's capital.

HEDVIG. And you have another parcel in your pocket.

EKDAL. Eh? Oh never mind, that's nothing. (*Puts his stick away in a corner.*) This work will keep me going a long time, Gina. (*Opens one of the sliding-doors in the back wall a little.*) Hush! (*Peeps into the room for a moment, then pushes the door carefully to again.*) Hee-hee! They're fast asleep, all the lot of them. And she's gone into the basket herself. Hee-hee!

HEDVIG. Are you sure she isn't cold in that basket, grandfather?

EKDAL. Not a bit of it! Cold? With all that straw? (*Goes towards the farther door on the left.*) There are matches in here, I suppose.

GINA. The matches is on the drawers.

(EKDAL *goes into his room.*)

HEDVIG. It's nice that grandfather has got all that copying.

GINA. Yes, poor old father; it means a bit of pocket-money for him.

HEDVIG. And he won't be able to sit the whole forenoon down at that horrid Madam Eriksen's.

GINA. No more he won't.

(*Short silence.*)

HEDVIG. Do you suppose they are still at the dinner-table?

GINA. Goodness knows; as like as not.

HEDVIG. Think of all the delicious things father is having to eat! I'm certain he'll be in splendid spirits when he comes. Don't you think so, mother?

GINA. Yes; and if only we could tell him that we'd got the room let——

HEDVIG. But we don't need that this evening.

GINA. Oh, we'd be none the worst of it, I can tell you. It's no use to us as it is.

HEDVIG. I mean we don't need it this evening, for father will be in a good humor at any rate. It is best to keep the letting of the room for another time.

GINA (*looks across at her*). You like having some good news to tell father when he comes home in the evening?

HEDVIG. Yes; for then things are pleasanter somehow.

GINA (*thinking to herself*). Yes, yes, there's something in that.

(OLD EKDAL *comes in again and is going out by the foremost door to the left.*)

GINA (*half turning in her chair*). Do you want something out of the kitchen, grandfather?

EKDAL. Yes, yes, I do. Don't you trouble. (*Goes out.*)

GINA. He's not poking away at the fire, is he? (*Waits a moment.*) Hedvig, go and see what he's about.

(EKDAL *comes in again with a small jug of steaming hot water.*)

HEDVIG. Have you been getting some hot water, grandfather?

EKDAL. Yes, hot water. Want it for something. Want to write, and the ink has got as thick as porridge—h'm.

GINA. But you'd best have your supper, first, grandfather. It's laid in there.

EKDAL. Can't be bothered with supper, Gina. Very busy, I tell you. No one's to come to my room. No one—h'm.

(*He goes into his room;* GINA *and* HEDVIG *look at each other.*)

GINA (*softly*). Can you imagine where he's got money from?

HEDVIG. From Gråberg, perhaps.

GINA. Not a bit of it. Gråberg always sends the money to me.

HEDVIG. Then he must have got a bottle on credit somewhere.

GINA. Poor grandfather, who'd give him credit?

(HIALMAR EKDAL, *in an overcoat and grey felt hat, comes in from the right.*)

GINA (*throws down her sewing and rises*). Why, Ekdal, is that you already?

HEDVIG (*at the same time jumping up*). Fancy your coming so soon, father!

HIALMAR (*taking off his hat*). Yes, most of the people were coming away.

HEDVIG. So early?

HIALMAR. Yes, it was a dinner-party, you know.
(*Is taking off his overcoat.*)

GINA. Let me help you.

HEDVIG. Me too.

(*They draw off his coat;* GINA *hangs it up on the back wall.*)

HEDVIG. Were there many people there, father?

HIALMAR. Oh no, not many. We were about twelve or fourteen at table.

GINA. And you had some talk with them all?

HIALMAR. Oh yes, a little; but Gregers took me up most of the time.

GINA. Is Gregers as ugly as ever?

HIALMAR. Well, he's not very much to look at. Hasn't the old man come home?

HEDVIG. Yes, grandfather is in his room, writing.

HIALMAR. Did he say anything?

GINA. No, what should he say?

HIALMAR. Didn't he say anything about——? I heard something about his having been with Gråberg. I'll go in and see him for a moment.

GINA. No, no, better not.

HIALMAR. Why not? Did he say he didn't want me to go in?

GINA. I don't think he wants to see nobody this evening——

HEDVIG (*making signs*). H'm—h'm!

GINA (*not noticing*). ——he has been in to fetch hot water——

HIALMAR. Aha! Then he's——

GINA. Yes, I suppose so.

HIALMAR. Oh God! my poor old white-haired father!— Well, well; there let him sit and get all the enjoyment he can.

(OLD EKDAL, *in an indoor coat and with a lighted pipe, comes from his room.*)

EKDAL. Got home? Thought it was you I heard talking.

HIALMAR. Yes, I have just come.

EKDAL. You didn't see me, did you?

HIALMAR. No, but they told me you had passed through —so I thought I would follow you.

EKDAL. H'm, good of you, Hialmar.—Who were they, all those fellows?

HIALMAR. Oh, all sorts of people. There was Chamberlain Flor, and Chamberlain Balle, and Chamberlain Kaspersen, and Chamberlain—this, that, and the other—I don't know who all——

EKDAL (*nodding*). Hear that, Gina! Chamberlains every one of them!

GINA. Yes, I hear as they're terrible genteel in that house nowadays.

HEDVIG. Did the Chamberlains sing, father? Or did they read aloud?

HIALMAR. No, they only talked nonsense. They wanted

me to recite something for them; but I knew better than that.

EKDAL. You weren't to be persuaded, eh?

GINA. Oh, you might have done it.

HIALMAR. No; one mustn't be at everybody's beck and call. (*Walks about the room.*) That's not my way, at any rate.

EKDAL. No, no; Hialmar's not to be had for the asking, he isn't.

HIALMAR. I don't see why *I* should bother myself to entertain people on the rare occasions when I go into society. Let the others exert themselves. These fellows go from one great dinner-table to the next and gorge and guzzle day out and day in. It's for them to bestir themselves and do something in return for all the good feeding they get.

GINA. But you didn't say that?

HIALMAR (*humming*). Ho-ho-ho——; faith, I gave them a bit of my mind.

EKDAL. Not the Chamberlains?

HIALMAR. Oh, why not? (*Lightly.*) After that, we had a little discussion about Tokay.

EKDAL. Tokay! There's a fine wine for you!

HIALMAR (*comes to a standstill*). It may be a fine wine. But of course you know the vintages differ; it all depends on how much sunshine the grapes have had.

GINA. Why, you know everything, Ekdal.

EKDAL. And did they dispute that?

HIALMAR. They tried to; but they were requested to observe that it was just the same with Chamberlains—that with them, too, different batches were of different qualities.

GINA. What things you do think of!

EKDAL. Hee-hee! So they got that in their pipes too?

HIALMAR. Right in their teeth.

EKDAL. Do you hear that, Gina? He said it right in the very teeth of all the Chamberlains.

GINA. Fancy——! Right in their teeth!

HIALMAR. Yes, but I don't want it talked about. One doesn't speak of such things. The whole affair passed off quite amicably of course. They were nice, genial fellows; I didn't want to wound them—not I!

EKDAL. Right in their teeth, though——!

HEDVIG (*caressingly*). How nice it is to see you in a dress-coat! It suits you so well, father.

HIALMAR. Yes, don't you think so? And this one really sits to perfection. It fits almost as if it had been made for me;—a little tight in the arm-holes perhaps;—help me, Hedvig (*takes off the coat*). I think I'll put on my jacket. Where is my jacket, Gina?

GINA. Here it is. (*Brings the jacket and helps him.*)

HIALMAR. That's it! Don't forget to send the coat back to Molvik first thing to-morrow morning.

GINA (*laying it away*). I'll be sure and see to it.

HIALMAR (*stretching himself*). After all, there's a more homely feeling about this. A free-and-easy indoor costume suits my whole personality better. Don't you think so, Hedvig?

HEDVIG. Yes, father.

HIALMAR. When I loosen my necktie into a pair of flowing ends—like this—eh?

HEDVIG. Yes, that goes so well with your moustache and the sweep of your curls.

HIALMAR. I should not call them curls exactly; I should rather say locks.

HEDVIG. Yes, they are too big for curls.

HIALMAR. Locks describes them better.

HEDVIG (*after a pause, twitching his jacket*). Father!

HIALMAR. Well, what is it?

HEDVIG. Oh, you know very well.

HIALMAR. No, really I don't——

HEDVIG (*half laughing, half whispering*). Oh, yes, father; now don't tease me any longer!

HIALMAR. Why, what do you mean?

HEDVIG (*shaking him*). Oh what nonsense; come, where are they, father? All the good things you promised me, you know?

HIALMAR. Oh—if I haven't forgotten all about them!

HEDVIG. Now you're only teasing me, father! Oh, it's too bad of you! Where have you put them?

HIALMAR. No, I positively forgot to get anything. But wait a little! I have something else for you, Hedvig.

(*Goes and searches in the pockets of the coat.*)

HEDVIG (*skipping and clapping her hands*). Oh mother, mother!

GINA. There, you see; if you only give him time——

HIALMAR (*with a paper*). Look, here it is.

HEDVIG. That? Why, that's only a paper.

HIALMAR. That is the bill of fare, my dear; the whole bill of fare. Here you see: "Menu"—that means bill of fare.

HEDVIG. Haven't you anything else?

HIALMAR. I forgot the other things, I tell you. But you may take my word for it, these dainties are very unsatisfying. Sit down at the table and read the bill of fare, and then I'll describe to you how the dishes taste. Here you are, Hedvig.

HEDVIG (*gulping down her tears*). Thank you. (*She seats herself, but does not read; GINA makes signs to her; HIALMAR notices it.*)

HIALMAR (*pacing up and down the room*). It's monstrous what absurd things the father of a family is expected to think of; and if he forgets the smallest trifle, he is treated to sour faces at once. Well, well, one gets used to that too. (*Stops near the stove, by the old man's chair.*) Have you peeped in there this evening, father?

EKDAL. Yes, to be sure I have. She's gone into the basket.

HIALMAR. Ah, she has gone into the basket. Then she's beginning to get used to it.

EKDAL. Yes; just as I prophesied. But you know there are still a few little things——

HIALMAR. A few improvements, yes.

EKDAL. They've got to be made, you know.

HIALMAR. Yes, let us have a talk about the improvements, father. Come, let us sit on the sofa.

EKDAL. All right. H'm—think I'll just fill my pipe first. Must clean it out, too. H'm.

(*He goes into his room.*)

GINA (*smiling to* HIALMAR). His pipe!

HIALMAR. Oh yes yes, Gina; let him alone—the poor shipwrecked old man.—Yes, these improvements—we had better get them out of hand to-morrow.

GINA. You'll hardly have time to-morrow, Ekdal.

HEDVIG (*interposing*). Oh yes he will, mother!

GINA. ——for remember them prints that has to be re-touched; they've sent for them time after time.

HIALMAR. There now! those prints again! I shall get them finished all right! Have any new orders come in?

GINA. No, worse luck; to-morrow I have nothing but those two sittings, you know.

HIALMAR. Nothing else? Oh no, if people won't set about things with a will——

GINA. But what more can I do? Don't I advertise in the papers as much as we can afford?

HIALMAR. Yes, the papers, the papers; you see how much good they do. And I suppose no one has been to look at the room either?

GINA. No, not yet.

HIALMAR. That was only to be expected. If people won't keep their eyes open——. Nothing can be done without a real effort, Gina!

HEDVIG (*going towards him*). Shall I fetch you the flute, father?

HIALMAR. No; no flute for me; *I* want no pleasures in this world. (*Pacing about.*) Yes, indeed I will work to-morrow; you shall see if I don't. You may be sure I shall work as long as my strength holds out.

GINA. But my dear good Ekdal, I didn't mean it in that way.

HEDVIG. Father, mayn't I bring in a bottle of beer?

HIALMAR. No, certainly not. I require nothing, nothing—— (*Comes to a standstill.*) Beer? Was it beer you were talking about?

HEDVIG (*cheerfully*). Yes, father; beautiful fresh beer.

HIALMAR. Well—since you insist upon it, you may bring in a bottle.

GINA. Yes, do; and we'll be nice and cosy.

(HEDVIG *runs towards the kitchen door.*)

HIALMAR (*by the stove, stops her, looks at her, puts his arm round her neck and presses her to him*). Hedvig, Hedvig!

HEDVIG (*with tears of joy*). My dear, kind father!

HIALMAR. No, don't call me that. Here have I been feasting at the rich man's table,—battening at the groaning board——! And I couldn't even——!

GINA (*sitting at the table*). Oh, nonsense, nonsense, Ekdal.

HIALMAR. It's not nonsense! And yet you mustn't be too hard upon me. You know that I love you for all that.

HEDVIG (*throwing her arms round him*). And we love you, oh, so dearly, father!

HIALMAR. And if I am unreasonable once in a while,— why then—you must remember that I am a man beset by a host of cares. There, there! (*Dries his eyes.*) No beer at such a moment as this. Give me the flute.

(HEDVIG *runs to the bookcase and fetches it.*)

HIALMAR. Thanks! That's right. With my flute in my hand and you two at my side—ah——!

(HEDVIG *seats herself at the table near* GINA; HIALMAR *paces backwards and forwards, pipes up vigorously, and plays a Bohemian peasant dance, but in a slow plaintive tempo, and with sentimental expression.*)

HIALMAR (*breaking off the melody, holds out his left hand*

to GINA, *and says with emotion*): Our roof may be poor and humble, Gina; but it is home. And with all my heart I say: here dwells my happiness.

> (*He begins to play again; almost immediately after, a knocking is heard at the entrance door.*)

GINA (*rising*). Hush, Ekdal—I think there's some one at the door.

HIALMAR (*laying the flute on the bookcase*). There! Again!

> (GINA *goes and opens the door.*)

GREGERS WERLE (*in the passage*). Excuse me——

GINA (*starting back slightly*). Oh!

GREGERS. ——does not Mr. Ekdal, the photographer, live here?

GINA. Yes, he does.

HIALMAR (*going towards the door*). Gregers! You here after all? Well, come in then.

GREGERS (*coming in*). I told you I would come and look you up.

HIALMAR. But this evening——? Have you left the party?

GREGERS. I have left both the party and my father's house.—Good evening, Mrs. Ekdal. I don't know whether you recognize me?

GINA. Oh yes; it's not difficult to know young Mr. Werle again.

GREGERS. No, I am like my mother; and no doubt you remember her.

HIALMAR. Left your father's house, did you say?

GREGERS. Yes, I have gone to a hotel.

HIALMAR. Indeed. Well, since you're here, take off your coat and sit down.

GREGERS. Thanks.

> (*He takes off his overcoat. He is now dressed in a plain grey suit of a countrified cut.*)

HIALMAR. Here, on the sofa. Make yourself comfortable.

(GREGERS *seats himself on the sofa;* HIALMAR *takes a chair at the table.*)

GREGERS (*looking around him*). So these are your quarters, Hialmar—this is your home.

HIALMAR. This is the studio, as you see—

GINA. But it's the largest of our rooms, so we generally sit here.

HIALMAR. We used to live in a better place; but this flat has one great advantage: there are such capital outer rooms——

GINA. And we have a room on the other side of the passage that we can let.

GREGERS (*to* HIALMAR). Ah—so you have lodgers too?

HIALMAR. No, not yet. They're not so easy to find, you see; you have to keep your eyes open. (*To* HEDVIG.) What about that beer, eh?

(HEDVIG *nods and goes out into the kitchen.*)

GREGERS. So that is your daughter?

HIALMAR. Yes, that is Hedvig.

GREGERS. And she is your only child?

HIALMAR. Yes, the only one. She is the joy of our lives, and—(*lowering his voice*)—at the same time our deepest sorrow, Gregers.

GREGERS. What do you mean?

HIALMAR. She is in serious danger of losing her eyesight.

GREGERS. Becoming blind?

HIALMAR. Yes. Only the first symptoms have appeared as yet, and she may not feel it much for some time. But the doctor has warned us. It is coming, inexorably.

GREGERS. What a terrible misfortune! How do you account for it?

HIALMAR (*sighs*). Hereditary, no doubt.

GREGERS (*starting*). Hereditary?

GINA. Ekdal's mother had weak eyes.

HIALMAR. Yes, so my father says; I can't remember her.

GREGERS. Poor child! And how does she take it?

HIALMAR. Oh, you can imagine we haven't the heart to tell her of it. She dreams of no danger. Gay and careless and chirping like a little bird, she flutters onward into a life of endless night. (*Overcome.*) Oh, it is cruelly hard on me, Gregers.

(HEDVIG *brings a tray with beer and glasses, which she sets upon the table.*)

HIALMAR (*stroking her hair*). Thanks, thanks, Hedvig.

(HEDVIG *puts her arm round his neck and whispers in his ear.*)

HIALMAR. No, no bread and butter just now. (*Looks up*). But perhaps you would like some, Gregers.

GREGERS (*with a gesture of refusal*). No, no, thank you.

HIALMAR (*still melancholy*). Well, you can bring in a little all the same. If you have a crust, that is all I want. And plenty of butter on it, mind.

(HEDVIG *nods gaily and goes out into the kitchen again.*)

GREGERS (*who has been following her with his eyes*). She seems quite strong and healthy otherwise.

GINA. Yes. In other ways there's nothing amiss with her, thank goodness.

GREGERS. She promises to be very like you, Mrs. Ekdal. How old is she now?

GINA. Hedvig is close on fourteen; her birthday is the day after to-morrow.

GREGERS. She is pretty tall for her age, then.

GINA. Yes, she's shot up wonderful this last year.

GREGERS. It makes one realize one's own age to see these young people growing up.—How long is it now since you were married?

GINA. We've been married—let me see—just on fifteen years.

GREGERS. Is it so long as that?

GINA (*becomes attentive; looks at him*). Yes, it is indeed.

HIALMAR. Yes, so it is. Fifteen years all but a few months.

(*Changing his tone.*) They must have been long years for you, up at the works, Gregers.

GREGERS. They seemed long while I was living them; now they are over, I hardly know how the time has gone.

(OLD EKDAL *comes from his room without his pipe, but with his old-fashioned uniform cap on his head; his gait is somewhat unsteady.*)

EKDAL. Come now, Hialmar, let's sit down and have a good talk about this—h'm—what was it again?

HIALMAR (*going towards him*). Father, we have a visitor here—Gregers Werle.—I don't know if you remember him.

EKDAL (*looking at* GREGERS, *who has risen*). Werle? Is that the son? What does he want with me?

HIALMAR. Nothing; it's me he has come to see.

EKDAL. Oh! Then there's nothing wrong?

HIALMAR. No, no, of course not.

EKDAL (*with a large gesture*). Not that I'm afraid, you know; but——

GREGERS (*goes over to him*). I bring you a greeting from your old hunting-grounds, Lieutenant Ekdal.

EKDAL. Hunting-grounds?

GREGERS. Yes, up in Höidal, about the works, you know.

EKDAL. Oh, up there. Yes, I knew all those places well in the old days.

GREGERS. You were a great sportsman then.

EKDAL. So I was, I don't deny it. You're looking at my uniform cap. I don't ask anybody's leave to wear it in the house. So long as I don't go out in the streets with it——

(HEDVIG *brings a plate of bread and butter, which she puts upon the table.*)

HIALMAR. Sit down, father, and have a glass of beer. Help yourself, Gregers.

(EKDAL *mutters and stumbles over to the sofa.* GREGERS *seats himself on the chair nearest to him,* HIALMAR *on the other side of* GREGERS. GINA *sits a little way from the table, sewing;* HEDVIG *stands beside her father.)*

GREGERS. Can you remember, Lieutenant Ekdal, how Hialmar and I used to come up and visit you in the summer and at Christmas?

EKDAL. Did you? No, no, no; I don't remember it. But sure enough I've been a tidy bit of a sportsman in my day. I've shot bears too. I've shot nine of 'em, no less.

GREGERS (*looking sympathetically at him*). And now you never get any shooting?

EKDAL. Can't just say that, sir. Get a shot now and then perhaps. Of course not in the old way. For the woods you see—the woods, the woods——! (*Drinks.*) Are the woods fine up there now?

GREGERS. Not so fine as in your time. They have been thinned a good deal.

EKDAL. Thinned? (*More softly, and as if afraid.*) It's dangerous work that. Bad things come of it. The woods revenge themselves.

HIALMAR (*filling up his glass*). Come—a little more, father.

GREGERS. How can a man like you—such a man for the open air—live in the midst of a stuffy town, boxed within four walls?

EKDAL (*laughs quietly and glances at* HIALMAR). Oh, it's not so bad here. Not at all so bad.

GREGERS. But don't you miss all the things that used to be a part of your very being—the cool sweeping breezes, the free life in the woods and on the uplands, among beasts and birds——?

EKDAL (*smiling*). Hialmar, shall we let him see it?

HIALMAR (*hastily and a little embarrassed*). Oh, no no, father; not this evening.

GREGERS. What does he want to show me?

HIALMAR. Oh, it's only something—you can see it another time.

GREGERS (*continues, to the old man*). You see I have been thinking, Lieutenant Ekdal, that you should come up with me to the works; I am sure to be going back soon. No doubt you could get some copying there too. And here, you have nothing on earth to interest you—nothing to liven you up.

EKDAL (*stares in astonishment at him*). Have *I* nothing on earth to——!

GREGERS. Of course you have Hialmar; but then he has his own family. And a man like you, who has always had such a passion for what is free and wild——

EKDAL (*thumps the table*). Hialmar, he shall see it!

HIALMAR. Oh, do you think it's worth while, father? It's all dark.

EKDAL. Nonsense; it's moonlight. (*Rises*). He shall see it, I tell you. Let me pass! Come and help me, Hialmar.

HEDVIG. Oh yes, do, father.

HIALMAR (*rising*). Very well then.

GREGERS (*to* GINA). What is it?

GINA. Oh, nothing so very wonderful, after all.

(EKDAL *and* HIALMAR *have gone to the back wall and are each pushing back a side of the sliding door;* HEDVIG *helps the old man;* GREGERS *remains standing by the sofa;* GINA *sits still and sews. Through the open doorway a large, deep irregular garret is seen with odd nooks and corners; a couple of stove-pipes running through it, from rooms below. There are skylights through which clear moonbeams shine in on some parts of the great room; others lie in deep shadow.*)

EKDAL (*to* GREGERS). You may come close up if you like.

GREGERS (*going over to them*). Why, what is it?

EKDAL. Look for yourself. H'm.

HIALMAR (*somewhat embarrassed*). This belongs to father, you understand.

GREGERS (*at the door, looks into the garret*). Why, you keep poultry, Lieutenant Ekdal.

EKDAL. Should think we did keep poultry. They've gone to roost now. But you should just see our fowls by daylight, sir!

HEDVIG. And there's a——

EKDAL. Sh—sh! don't say anything about it yet.

GREGERS. And you have pigeons too, I see.

EKDAL. Oh yes, haven't we just got pigeons! They have their nest-boxes up there under the roof-tree; for pigeons like to roost high, you see.

HIALMAR. They aren't all common pigeons.

EKDAL. Common! Should think not indeed! We have tumblers, and a pair of pouters, too. But come here! Can you see that hutch down there by the wall?

GREGERS. Yes; what do you use it for?

EKDAL. That's where the rabbits sleep, sir.

GREGERS. Dear me; so you have rabbits too?

EKDAL. Yes, you may take my word for it, we have rabbits! He wants to know if we have rabbits, Hialmar! H'm! But now comes the thing, let me tell you! Here we have it! Move away, Hedvig. Stand here; that's right,—and now look down there.—Don't you see a basket with straw in it?

GREGERS. Yes. And I can see a fowl lying in the basket.

EKDAL. H'm—"a fowl"——

GREGERS. Isn't it a duck?

EKDAL (*hurt*). Why, of course it's a duck.

HIALMAR. But what kind of duck, do you think?

HEDVIG. It's not just a common duck——

EKDAL. Sh!

GREGERS. And it's not a Muscovy duck either.

EKDAL. No, Mr.—Werle; it's not a Muscovy duck; for it's a wild duck!

GREGERS. Is it really? A wild duck?

EKDAL. Yes, that's what it is. That "fowl" as you call it —is the wild duck. It's our wild duck, sir.

HEDVIG. My wild duck. It belongs to me.

GREGERS. And can it live up here in the garret? Does it thrive?

EKDAL. Of course it has a trough of water to splash about in, you know.

HIALMAR. Fresh water every other day.

GINA (*turning towards* HIALMAR). But my dear Ekdal, it's getting icy cold here.

EKDAL. H'm, we had better shut up then. It's as well not to disturb their night's rest, too. Close up, Hedvig.

(HIALMAR *and* HEDVIG *push the garret doors together*.)

EKDAL. Another time you shall see her properly. (*Seats himself in the arm-chair by the stove*.) Oh, they're curious things, these wild ducks, I can tell you.

GREGERS. How did you manage to catch it, Lieutenant Ekdal?

EKDAL. *I* didn't catch it. There's a certain man in this town whom we have to thank for it.

GREGERS (*starts slightly*). That man was not my father, was he?

EKDAL. You've hit it. Your father and no one else. H'm.

HIALMAR. Strange that you should guess that, Gregers.

GREGERS. You were telling me that you owed so many things to my father; and so I thought perhaps——

GINA. But we didn't get the duck from Mr. Werle him-self——

EKDAL. It's Håkon Werle we have to thank for her, all the same, Gina. (*To* GREGERS.) He was shooting from a boat, you see, and he brought her down. But your father's sight is not very good now. H'm; she was only wounded.

GREGERS. Ah! She got a couple of slugs in her body, I suppose.

HIALMAR. Yes, two or three.

HEDVIG. She was hit under the wing, so that she couldn't fly.

GREGERS. And I suppose she dived to the bottom, eh?

EKDAL (*sleepily, in a thick voice*). Of course. Always do that, wild ducks do. They shoot to the bottom as deep as they can get, sir—and bite themselves fast in the tangle and seaweed—and all the devil's. own mess that grows down there. And they never come up again.

GREGERS. But your wild duck came up again, Lieutenant Ekdal.

EKDAL. He had such an amazingly clever dog, your father had. And that dog—he dived in after the duck and fetched her up again.

GREGERS (*who has turned to* HIALMAR). And then she was sent to you here?

HIALMAR. Not at once; at first your father took her home. But she wouldn't thrive there; so Pettersen was told to put an end to her——

EKDAL (*half asleep*). H'm—yes—Pettersen—that ass——

HIALMAR (*speaking more softly*). That was how we got her, you see; for father knows Pettersen a little; and when he heard about the wild duck he got him to hand her over to us.

GREGERS. And now she thrives as well as possible in the garret there?

HIALMAR. Yes, wonderfully well. She has got fat. You see, she has lived in there so long now that she has forgotten her natural wild life; and it all depends on that.

GREGERS. You are right there, Hialmar. Be sure you never let her get a glimpse of the sky and the sea——. But I mustn't stay any longer; I think your father is asleep.

HIALMAR. Oh, as for that——

GREGERS. But, by-the-bye—you said you had a room to let—a spare room?

HIALMAR. Yes; what then? Do you know of anybody——?

GREGERS. Can *I* have that room?

HIALMAR. You?

GINA. Oh no, Mr. Werle, you——

GREGERS. May I have the room? If so, I'll take possession first thing to-morrow morning.

HIALMAR. Yes, with the greatest pleasure——

GINA. But, Mr. Werle, I'm sure it's not at all the sort of room for you.

HIALMAR. Why, Gina! how can you say that?

GINA. Why, because the room's neither large enough nor light enough, and——

GREGERS. That really doesn't matter, Mrs. Ekdal.

HIALMAR. I call it quite a nice room, and not at all badly furnished either.

GINA. But remember the pair of them underneath.

GREGERS. What pair?

GINA. Well, there's one as has been a tutor——

HIALMAR. That's Molvik—Mr. Molvik, B.A.

GINA. And then there's a doctor, by the name of Relling.

GREGERS. Relling? I know him a little; he practised for a time up in Höidal.

GINA. They're a regular rackety pair, they are. As often as not, they're out on the loose in the evenings; and then they come home at all hours, and they're not always just——

GREGERS. One soon gets used to that sort of thing. I daresay I shall be like the wild duck——

GINA. H'm; I think you ought to sleep upon it first, anyway.

GREGERS. You seem very unwilling to have me in the house, Mrs. Ekdal.

GINA. Oh, no! What makes you think that?

HIALMAR. Well, you really behave strangely about it,

GINA. (*To* GREGERS.) Then I suppose you intend to remain in the town for the present?

GREGERS (*putting on his overcoat*). Yes, now I intend to remain here.

HIALMAR. And yet not at your father's? What do you propose to do, then?

GREGERS. Ah, if I only knew that, Hialmar, I shouldn't be so badly off! But when one has the misfortune to be called Gregers—! "Gregers"—and then "Werle" after it; did you ever hear anything so hideous?

HIALMAR. Oh, I don't think so at all.

GREGERS. Ugh! Bah! I feel I should like to spit upon the fellow that answers to such a name. But when a man is once for all doomed to be Gregers—Werle in this world, as I am——

HIALMAR (*laughs*). Ha, ha! If you weren't Gregers Werle, what would you like to be?

GREGERS. If I should choose, I should like best to be a clever dog.

GINA. A dog!

HEDVIG (*involuntarily*). Oh, no!

GREGERS. Yes, an amazingly clever dog; one that goes to the bottom after wild ducks when they dive and bite themselves fast in tangle and sea-weed, down among the ooze.

HIALMAR. Upon my word now, Gregers—I don't in the least know what you're driving at.

GREGERS. Oh, well, you might not be much the wiser if you did. It's understood, then, that I move in early to-morrow morning. (*To* GINA.) I won't give you any trouble; I do everything for myself. (*To* HIALMAR.) We can talk about the rest to-morrow.—Good-night, Mrs. Ekdal. (*Nods to* HEDVIG.) Good-night.

GINA. Good-night, Mr. Werle.

HEDVIG. Good-night.

HIALMAR (*who has lighted a candle*). Wait a moment; I must show you a light; the stairs are sure to be dark.

(GREGERS *and* HIALMAR *go out by the passage door*.)

GINA (*looking straight before her, with her sewing in her lap*). Wasn't that queer-like talk about wanting to be a dog?

HEDVIG. Do you know, mother—I believe he meant something quite different by that.

GINA. Why, what should he mean?

HEDVIG. Oh, I don't know; but it seemed to me he meant something different from what he said—all the time.

GINA. Do you think so? Yes, it was sort of queer.

HIALMAR (*comes back*). The lamp was still burning. (*Puts out the candle and sets it down*). Ah, now one can get a mouthful of food at last. (*Begins to eat the bread and butter*.) Well, you see, Gina—if only you keep your eyes open——

GINA. How, keep your eyes open——?

HIALMAR. Why, haven't we at last had the luck to get the room let? And just think—to a person like Gregers—a good old friend.

GINA. Well, I don't know what to say about it.

HEDVIG. Oh, mother, you'll see; it'll be such fun!

HIALMAR. You're very strange. You were so bent upon getting the room let before; and now you don't like it.

GINA. Yes I do, Ekdal; if it had only been to some one else—— But what do you suppose Mr. Werle will say?

HIALMAR. Old Werle? It doesn't concern him.

GINA. But surely you can see that there's something amiss between them again, or the young man wouldn't be leaving home. You know very well those two can't get on with each other.

HIALMAR. Very likely not, but——

GINA. And now Mr. Werle may fancy it's you that has egged him on——

HIALMAR. Let him fancy so, then! Mr. Werle has done a

great deal for me; far be it from me to deny it. But that doesn't make me everlastingly dependent upon him.

GINA. But, my dear Ekdal, maybe grandfather'll suffer for it. He may lose the little bit of work he gets from Gråberg.

HIALMAR. I could almost say: so much the better! Is it not humiliating for a man like me to see his grey-haired father treated as a pariah? But now I believe the fulness of time is at hand. (*Takes a fresh piece of bread and butter.*) As sure as I have a mission in life, I mean to fulfil it now!

HEDVIG. Oh, yes, father, do!

GINA. Hush! Don't wake him!

HIALMAR (*more softly*). I will fulfil it, I say. The day shall come when—— And that is why I say it's a good thing we have let the room; for that makes me more independent. The man who has a mission in life must be independent. (*By the arm-chair, with emotion.*) Poor old white-haired father! Rely on your Hialmar. He has broad shoulders— strong shoulders, at any rate. You shall yet wake up some fine day and—— (*To* GINA.) Do you not believe it?

GINA (*rising*). Yes, of course I do; but in the meantime suppose we see about getting him to bed.

HIALMAR. Yes, come.

(*They take hold of the old man carefully.*)

ACT III

(HIALMAR EKDAL'S *studio. It is morning: the daylight shines through the large window in the slanting roof; the curtain is drawn back.*)

(HIALMAR *is sitting at the table, busy retouching a photograph; several others lie before him. Presently* GINA, *wearing her hat and cloak, enters by the passage door; she has a covered basket on her arm.*)

HIALMAR. Back already, Gina?

GINA. Oh, yes, one can't let the grass grow under one's feet.

(*Sets her basket on a chair, and takes off her things.*)

HIALMAR. Did you look in at Greger's room?

GINA. Yes, that I did. It's a rare sight, I can tell you; he's made a pretty mess to start off with.

HIALMAR. How so?

GINA. He was determined to do everything for himself, he said; so he sets to work to light the stove, and what must he do but screw down the damper till the whole room is full of smoke. Ugh! There was a smell fit to——

HIALMAR. Well, really!

GINA. But that's not the worst of it; for then he thinks he'll put out the fire, and goes and empties his water-jug into the stove, and so makes the whole floor one filthy puddle.

HIALMAR. How annoying!

GINA. I've got the porter's wife to clear up after him, pig that he is! But the room won't be fit to live in till the afternoon.

HIALMAR. What's he doing with himself in the meantime?

GINA. He said he was going out for a little while.

HIALMAR. I looked in upon him, too, for a moment—after you had gone.

GINA. So I heard. You've asked him to lunch.

HIALMAR. Just to a little bit of early lunch, you know. It's his first day—we can hardly do less. You've got something in the house, I suppose?

GINA. I shall have to find something or other.

HIALMAR. And don't cut it too fine, for I fancy Relling and Molvik are coming up, too. I just happened to meet Relling on the stairs, you see; so I had to——

GINA. Oh, are we to have those two as well?

HIALMAR. Good Lord—a couple more or less can't make any difference.

OLD EKDAL (*opens his door and looks in*). I say, Hialmar—— (*Sees* GINA.) Oh!

GINA. Do you want anything, grandfather?

EKDAL. Oh, no, it doesn't matter. H'm!
                    (*Retires again.*)

GINA (*takes up the basket*). Be sure you see that he doesn't go out.

HIALMAR. All right, all right. And, Gina, a little herring-salad wouldn't be a bad idea; Relling and Molvik were out on the loose again last night.

GINA. If only they don't come before I'm ready for them——

HIALMAR. No, of course they won't; take your own time.

GINA. Very well; and meanwhile you can be working a bit.

HIALMAR. Well, I am working! I am working as hard as I can!

GINA. Then you'll have that job off your hands, you see.
  (*She goes out to the kitchen with her basket.* HIALMAR
    *sits for a time pencilling away at the photograph, in
    an indolent and listless manner.*)

EKDAL (*peeps in, looks round the studio, and says softly*):
Are you busy?

HIALMAR. Yes, I'm toiling at these wretched pictures——

EKDAL. Well, well, never mind,—since you're so busy—
h'm!

(*He goes out again; the door stands open.*)

HIALMAR (*continues for some time in silence; then he lays
down his brush and goes over to the door*). Are you busy,
father?

EKDAL (*in a grumbling tone, within*). If you're busy, I'm
busy, too. H'm.

HIALMAR. Oh, very well, then.

(*Goes to his work again.*)

EKDAL (*presently, coming to the door again*). H'm; I
say, Hialmar, I'm not so very busy, you know.

HIALMAR. I thought you were writing.

EKDAL. Oh, devil take it! can't Gråberg wait a day or
two? After all, it's not a matter of life and death.

HIALMAR. No; and you're not his slave either.

EKDAL. And about that other business in there——

HIALMAR. Just what I was thinking of. Do you want to
go in? Shall I open the door for you?

EKDAL. Well, it wouldn't be a bad notion.

HIALMAR (*rises*). Then we'd have that off our hands.

EKDAL. Yes, exactly. It's got to be ready first thing to-
morrow. It is to-morrow, isn't it? H'm?

HIALMAR. Yes, of course it's to-morrow.

(HIALMAR *and* EKDAL *push aside each his half of the
sliding door. The morning sun is shining in through
the skylights; some doves are flying about; others sit
cooing, upon the perches; the hens are heard clucking
now and then, further back in the garret.*)

HIALMAR. There; now you can get to work, father.

EKDAL (*goes in*). Aren't you coming, too?

HIALMAR. Well, really, do you know——; I almost

think——— (*Sees* GINA *at the kitchen door.*) I? No; I haven't time; I must work.—But now for our new contrivance———

> (*He pulls a cord, a curtain slips down inside, the lower part consisting of a piece of old sailcloth, the upper part of a stretched fishing net. The floor of the garret is thus no longer visible.*)

HIALMAR (*goes to the table*). So! Now, perhaps I can sit in peace for a little while.

GINA. Is he rampaging in there again?

HIALMAR. Would you rather have had him slip down to Madam Eriksen's? (*Seats himself.*) Do you want anything? You know you said———

GINA. I only wanted to ask if you think we can lay the table for lunch here?

HIALMAR. Yes; we have no early appointment, I suppose?

GINA. No, I expect no one to-day except those two sweethearts that are to be taken together.

HIALMAR. Why the deuce couldn't they be taken together another day!

GINA. Don't you know, I told them to come in the afternoon, when you are having your nap.

HIALMAR. Oh, that's capital. Very well, let us have lunch here then.

GINA. All right; but there's no hurry about laying the cloth; you can have the table for a good while yet.

HIALMAR. Do you think I am not sticking at my work? I'm at it as hard as I can!

GINA. Then you'll be free later on, you know.

> (*Goes out into the kitchen again. Short pause.*)

EKDAL (*in the garret doorway, behind the net*). Hialmar!

HIALMAR. Well?

EKDAL. Afraid we shall have to move the water-trough, after all.

HIALMAR. What else have I been saying all along?

EKDAL. H'm—h'm—h'm.

(*Goes away from the door again.* HIALMAR *goes on working a little; glances towards the garret and half rises.* HEDVIG *comes in from the kitchen.*)

HIALMAR. (*sits down again hurriedly*). What do you want?

HEDVIG. I only wanted to come in beside you, father.

HIALMAR (*after a pause*). What makes you go prying around like that? Perhaps you are told off to watch me?

HEDVIG. No, no.

HIALMAR. What is your mother doing out there?

HEDVIG. Oh, mother's in the middle of making the herring-salad. (*Goes to the table.*) Isn't there any little thing I could help you with, father?

HIALMAR. Oh, no. It is right that I should bear the whole burden—so long as my strength holds out. Set your mind at rest, Hedvig; if only your father keeps his health——

HEDVIG. Oh, no, father! You mustn't talk in that horrid way.

(*She wanders about a little, stops by the doorway and looks into the garret.*)

HIALMAR. Tell me, what is he doing?

HEDVIG. I think he's making a new path to the water-trough.

HIALMAR. He can never manage that by himself! And here am I doomed to sit——!

HEDVIG (*goes to him*). Let me take the brush, father; I can do it, quite well.

HIALMAR. Oh, nonsense; you will only hurt your eyes.

HEDVIG. Not a bit. Give me the brush.

HIALMAR (*rising*). Well, it won't take more than a minute or two.

HEDVIG. Pooh, what harm can it do then? (*Takes the brush.*) There! (*Seats herself.*) I can begin upon this one.

HIALMAR. But mind you don't hurt your eyes! Do you hear? *I* won't be answerable; you do it on your own responsibility—understand that.

HEDVIG (*retouching*). Yes, yes, I understand.

HIALMAR. You are quite clever at it, Hedvig. Only a minute or two, you know.

(*He slips through by the edge of the curtain into the garret.* HEDVIG *sits at her work.* HIALMAR *and* EKDAL *are heard disputing inside.*)

HIALMAR (*appears behind the net*). I say, Hedvig—give me those pincers that are lying on the shelf. And the chisel. (*Turns away inside.*) Now you shall see, father. Just let me show you first what I mean!

(HEDVIG *has fetched the required tools from the shelf, and hands them to him through the net.*)

HIALMAR. Ah, thanks. I didn't come a moment too soon.

(*Goes back from the curtain again; they are heard carpentering and talking inside.* HEDVIG *stands looking in at them. A moment later there is a knock at the passage door; she does not notice it.*)

GREGERS WERLE (*bareheaded, in indoor dress, enters and stops near the door*). H'm——!

HEDVIG (*turns and goes towards him*). Good morning. Please come in.

GREGERS. Thank you. (*Looking towards the garret.*) You seem to have workpeople in the house.

HEDVIG. No, it is only father and grandfather. I'll tell them you are here.

GREGERS. No, no, don't do that; I would rather wait a little.

(*Seats himself on the sofa.*)

HEDVIG. It looks so untidy here——

(*Begins to clear away the photographs.*)

GREGERS. Oh, don't take them away. Are those prints that have to be finished off?

HEDVIG. Yes, they are a few I was helping father with.

GREGERS. Please don't let me disturb you.

HEDVIG. Oh, no.

(*She gathers the things to her and sits down to work;*
GREGERS *looks at her, meanwhile, in silence.*)

GREGERS. Did the wild duck sleep well last night?

HEDVIG. Yes, I think so, thanks.

GREGERS (*turning towards the garret*). It looks quite different by day from what it did last night in the moonlight.

HEDVIG. Yes, it changes ever so much. It looks different in the morning and in the afternoon; and it's different on rainy days from what it is in fine weather.

GREGERS. Have you noticed that?

HEDVIG. Yes, how could I help it?

GREGERS. Are you, too, fond of being in there with the wild duck?

HEDVIG. Yes, when I can manage it——

GREGERS. But I suppose you haven't much spare time; you go to school, no doubt.

HEDVIG. No, not now; father is afraid of my hurting my eyes.

GREGERS. Oh; then he reads with you himself?

HEDVIG. Father has promised to read with me; but he has never had time yet.

GREGERS. Then is there nobody else to give you a little help?

HEDVIG. Yes, there is Mr. Molvik; but he is not always exactly—quite——

GREGERS. Sober?

HEDVIG. Yes, I suppose that's it!

GREGERS. Why, then you must have any amount of time on your hands. And in there I suppose it is a sort of world by itself?

HEDVIG. Oh, yes, quite. And there are such lots of wonderful things.

GREGERS. Indeed?

HEDVIG. Yes, there are big cupboards full of books; and a great many of the books have pictures in them.

GREGERS. Aha!

HEDVIG. And there's an old bureau with drawers and flaps, and a big clock with figures that go out and in. But the clock isn't going now.

GREGERS. So time has come to a standstill in there—in the wild duck's domain.

HEDVIG. Yes. And then there's an old paint-box and things of that sort; and all the books.

GREGERS. And you read the books, I suppose?

HEDVIG. Oh, yes, when I get the chance. Most of them are English though, and I don't understand English. But then I look at the pictures.—There is one great big book called "Harrison's History of London."[1] It must be a hundred years old; and there are such heaps of pictures in it. At the beginning there is Death with an hour-glass and a woman. I think that is horrid. But then there are all the other pictures of churches, and castles, and streets, and great ships sailing on the sea.

GREGERS. But tell me, where did all those wonderful things come from?

HEDVIG. Oh, an old sea captain once lived here, and he brought them home with him. They used to call him "The Flying Dutchman." That was curious, because he wasn't a Dutchman at all.

GREGERS. Was he not?

HEDVIG. No. But at last he was drowned at sea; and so he left all those things behind him.

GREGERS. Tell me now—when you are sitting in there looking at the pictures, don't you wish you could travel and see the real world for yourself?

HEDVIG. Oh, no! I mean always to stay at home and help father and mother.

[1] *A New and Universal History of the Cities of London and Westminster,* by Walter Harrison. London, 1775, folio.

GREGERS. To retouch photographs?

HEDVIG. No, not only that. I should love above every-thing to learn to engrave pictures like those in the English books.

GREGERS. H'm. What does your father say to that?

HEDVIG. I don't think father likes it; father is strange about such things. Only think, he talks of my learning basket-making, and straw-plaiting! But I don't think that would be much good.

GREGERS. Oh, no, I don't think so either.

HEDVIG. But father was right in saying that if I had learned basket-making I could have made the new basket for the wild duck.

GREGERS. So you could; and it was you that ought to have done it, wasn't it?

HEDVIG. Yes, for it's my wild duck.

GREGERS. Of course it is.

HEDVIG. Yes, it belongs to me. But I lend it to father and grandfather as often as they please.

GREGERS. Indeed? What do they do with it?

HEDVIG. Oh, they look after it, and build places for it, and so on.

GREGERS. I see; for no doubt the wild duck is by far the most distinguished inhabitant of the garret?

HEDVIG. Yes, indeed she is; for she is a real wild fowl, you know. And then she is so much to be pitied; she has no one to care for, poor thing.

GREGERS. She has no family, as the rabbits have——

HEDVIG. No. The hens too, many of them, were chick-ens together; but she has been taken right away from all her friends. And then there is so much that is strange about the wild duck. Nobody knows her, and nobody knows where she came from either.

GREGERS. And she has been down in the depths of the sea.

HEDVIG (*with a quick glance at him, represses a smile and asks*): Why do you say "depths of the sea"?

GREGERS. What else should I say?

HEDVIG. You could say "the bottom of the sea."[1]

GREGERS. Oh, mayn't I just as well say the depths of the sea?

HEDVIG. Yes; but it sounds so strange to me when other people speak of the depths of the sea.

GREGERS. Why so? Tell me why?

HEDVIG. No, I won't; it's so stupid.

GREGERS. Oh, no, I am sure it's not. Do tell me why you smiled.

HEDVIG. Well, this is the reason: whenever I come to realize suddenly—in a flash—what is in there, it always seems to me that the whole room and everything in it should be called "the depths of the sea."—But that is so stupid.

GREGERS. You mustn't say that.

HEDVIG. Oh, yes, for you know it is only a garret.

GREGERS (*looks fixedly at her*). Are you so sure of that?

HEDVIG (*astonished*). That it's a garret?

GREGERS. Are you quite certain of it?

(HEDVIG *is silent, and looks at him open-mouthed.* GINA *comes in from the kitchen with the table things.*)

GREGERS (*rising*). I have come in upon you too early.

GINA. Oh, you must be somewhere; and we're nearly ready now, anyway. Clear the table, Hedvig.

(HEDVIG *clears away her things; she and* GINA *lay the cloth during what follows.* GREGERS *seats himself in the arm-chair, and turns over an album.*)

GREGERS. I hear you can retouch, Mrs. Ekdal.

GINA (*with a side glance*). Yes, I can.

GREGERS. That was exceedingly lucky.

[1] Gregers here uses the old-fashioned expression "havsens bund," while Hedvig would have him use the more commonplace "havets bund" or "havbunden."

GINA. How—lucky?

GREGERS. Since Ekdal took to photography, I mean.

HEDVIG. Mother can take photographs, too.

GINA. Oh, yes; I was bound to learn that.

GREGERS. So it is really you that carry on the business, I suppose?

GINA. Yes, when Ekdal hasn't time himself—

GREGERS. He is a great deal taken up with his old father, I daresay.

GINA. Yes; and then you can't expect a man like Ekdal to do nothing but take car-de-visits of Dick, Tom and Harry.

GREGERS. I quite agree with you; but having once gone in for the thing——

GINA. You can surely understand, Mr. Werle, that Ekdal's not like one of your common photographers.

GREGERS. Of course not; but still——

(*A shot is fired within the garret.*)

GREGERS (*starting up*). What's that?

GINA. Ugh! now they're firing again!

GREGERS. Have they firearms in there?

HEDVIG. They are out shooting.

GREGERS. What! (*At the door of the garret.*) Are you shooting, Hialmar?

HIALMAR (*inside the net*). Are you there? I didn't know; I was so taken up—— (*To* HEDVIG.) Why did you not let us know?

(*Comes into the studio.*)

GREGERS. Do you go shooting in the garret?

HIALMAR (*showing a double-barrelled pistol*). Oh, only with this thing.

GINA. Yes, you and grandfather will do yourselves a mischief some day with that there pigstol.

HIALMAR (*with irritation*). I believe I have told you that this kind of firearm is called a pistol.

GINA. Oh, that doesn't make it much better, that I can see.

GREGERS. So you have become a sportsman, too, Hialmar?

HIALMAR. Only a little rabbit-shooting now and then. Mostly to please father, you understand.

GINA. Men are strange beings; they must always have something to pervert theirselves with.

HIALMAR (*snappishly*). Just so; we must always have something to divert ourselves with.

GINA. Yes, that's just what I say.

HIALMAR. H'm. (*To* GREGERS). You see the garret is fortunately so situated that no one can hear us shooting. (*Lays the pistol on the top shelf of the bookcase.*) Don't touch the pistol, Hedvig! One of the barrels is loaded; remember that.

GREGERS (*looking through the net*). You have a fowling-piece too, I see.

HIALMAR. That is father's old gun. It's of no use now; something has gone wrong with the lock. But it's fun to have it all the same; for we can take it to pieces now and then, and clean and grease it, and screw it together again.—Of course, it's mostly father that fiddle-faddles with all that sort of thing.

HEDVIG (*beside* GREGERS). Now you can see the wild duck properly.

GREGERS. I was just looking at her. One of her wings seems to me to droop a bit.

HEDVIG. Well, no wonder; her wing was broken, you know.

GREGERS. And she trails one foot a little. Isn't that so?

HIALMAR. Perhaps a very little bit.

HEDVIG. Yes, it was by that foot the dog took hold of her.

HIALMAR. But otherwise she hasn't the least thing the matter with her; and that is simply marvelous for a creature that has a charge of shot in her body, and has been between a dog's teeth——

GREGERS (*with a glance at* HEDVIG)——and that has lain in the depths of the sea—so long.

HEDVIG (*smiling*). Yes.

GINA (*laying the table*). That blessèd wild duck! What a lot of fuss you do make over her.

HIALMAR. H'm;—will lunch soon be ready?

GINA. Yes, directly. Hedvig, you must come and help me now.

(GINA *and* HEDVIG *go out into the kitchen.*)

HIALMAR (*in a low voice*). I think you had better not stand there looking in at father; he doesn't like it. (GREGERS *moves away from the garret door.*) Besides, I may as well shut up before the others come. (*Claps his hands to drive the fowls back.*) Shh—shh, in with you! (*Draws up the curtain and pulls the doors together.*) All the contrivances are my own invention. It's really quite amusing to have things of this sort to potter with, and to put to rights when they get out of order. And it's absolutely necessary, too; for Gina objects to having rabbits and fowls in the studio.

GREGERS. To be sure; and I suppose the studio is your wife's special department?

HIALMAR. As a rule, I leave the everyday details of business to her; for then I can take refuge in the parlor and give my mind to more important things.

GREGERS. What things may they be, Hialmar?

HIALMAR. I wonder you have not asked that question sooner. But perhaps you haven't heard of the invention?

GREGERS. The invention? No.

HIALMAR. Really? Have you not? Oh, no, out there in the wilds——

GREGERS. So you have invented something, have you?

HIALMAR. It is not quite completed yet; but I am working at it. You can easily imagine that when I resolved to devote myself to photography, it wasn't simply with the idea of taking likenesses of all sorts of commonplace people.

GREGERS. No; your wife was saying the same thing just now.

HIALMAR. I swore that if I consecrated my powers to this handicraft, I would so exalt it that it should become both an art and a science. And to that end I determined to make this great invention.

GREGERS. And what is the nature of the invention? What purpose does it serve?

HIALMAR. Oh, my dear fellow, you mustn't ask for details yet. It takes time, you see. And you must not think that my motive is vanity. It is not for my own sake that I am working. Oh, no; it is my life's mission that stands before me night and day.

GREGERS. What is your life's mission?

HIALMAR. Do you forget the old man with the silver hair?

GREGERS. Your poor father? Well, but what can you do for him?

HIALMAR. I can raise up his self-respect from the dead, by restoring the name of Ekdal to honor and dignity.

GREGERS. Then that is your life's mission?

HIALMAR. Yes. I will rescue the shipwrecked man. For shipwrecked he was, by the very first blast of the storm. Even while those terrible investigations were going on, he was no longer himself. That pistol there—the one we use to shoot rabbits with—has played its part in the tragedy of the house of Ekdal.

GREGERS. The pistol? Indeed?

HIALMAR. When the sentence of imprisonment was passed —he had the pistol in his hand——

GREGERS. Had he——?

HIALMAR. Yes; but he dared not use it. His courage failed him. So broken, so demoralized was he even then! Oh, can you understand it? He, a soldier; he, who had shot nine bears, and who was descended from two lieutenant-colonels—one after the other, of course. Can you understand it, Gregers?

GREGERS. Yes, I understand it well enough.

HIALMAR. I cannot. And once more the pistol played a

part in the history of our house. When he had put on the gray clothes and was under lock and key—oh, that was a terrible time for me, I can tell you. I kept the blinds drawn down over both my windows. When I peeped out, I saw the sun shining as if nothing had happened. I could not understand it. I saw people going along the street, laughing and talking about indifferent things. I could not understand it. It seemed to me that the whole of existence must be at a standstill—as if under an eclipse.

GREGERS. I felt that, too, when my mother died.

HIALMAR. It was in such an hour that Hialmar Ekdal pointed the pistol at his own breast.

GREGERS. You, too, thought of——!

HIALMAR. Yes.

GREGERS. But you did not fire?

HIALMAR. No. At the decisive moment I won the victory over myself. I remained in life. But I can assure you it takes some courage to choose life under circumstances like those.

GREGERS. Well, that depends on how you look at it.

HIALMAR. Yes, indeed, it takes courage. But I am glad I was firm: for now I shall soon perfect my invention; and Dr. Relling thinks, as I do myself, that father may be allowed to wear his uniform again. I will demand that as my sole reward.

GREGERS. So that is what he meant about his uniform——?

HIALMAR. Yes, that is what he most yearns for. You can't think how my heart bleeds for him. Every time we celebrate any little family festival—Gina's and my wedding-day, or whatever it may be—in comes the old man in the lieutenant's uniform of happier days. But if he only hears a knock at the door—for he daren't show himself to strangers, you know—he hurries back to his room again as fast as his old legs can carry him. Oh, it's heart-rending for a son to see such things!

GREGERS. How long do you think it will take you to finish your invention?

HIALMAR. Come now, you mustn't expect me to enter into particulars like that. An invention is not a thing completely under one's own control. It depends largely on inspiration—on intuition—and it is almost impossible to predict when the inspiration may come.

GREGERS. But it's advancing?

HIALMAR. Yes, certainly, it is advancing. I turn it over in my mind every day; I am full of it. Every afternoon, when I have had my dinner, I shut myself up in the parlor, where I can ponder undisturbed. But I can't be goaded to it; it's not a bit of good; Relling says so, too.

GREGERS. And you don't think that all that business in the garret draws you off and distracts you too much?

HIALMAR. No, no, no; quite the contrary. You mustn't say that. I cannot be everlastingly absorbed in the same laborious train of thought. I must have something alongside of it to fill up the time of waiting. The inspiration, the intuition, you see—when it comes, it comes, and there's an end of it.

GREGERS. My dear Hialmar, I almost think you have something of the wild duck in you.

HIALMAR. Something of the wild duck? How do you mean?

GREGERS. You have dived down and bitten yourself fast in the undergrowth.

HIALMAR. Are you alluding to the well-nigh fatal shot that has broken my father's wing—and mine, too?

GREGERS. Not exactly to that. I don't say that your wing has been broken; but you have strayed into a poisonous marsh, Hialmar; an insidious disease has taken hold of you, and you have sunk down to die in the dark.

HIALMAR. I? To die in the dark? Look here, Gregers, you must really leave off talking such nonsense.

GREGERS. Don't be afraid; I shall find a way to help you up again. I, too, have a mission in life now; I found it yesterday.

HIALMAR. That's all very well; but you will please leave me out of it. I can assure you that—apart from my very natural melancholy, of course—I am as contented as any one can wish to be.

GREGERS. Your contentment is an effect of the marsh poison.

HIALMAR. Now, my dear Gregers, pray do not go on about disease and poison; I am not used to that sort of talk. In my house nobody ever speaks to me about unpleasant things.

GREGERS. Ah, that I can easily believe.

HIALMAR. It's not good for me, you see. And there are no marsh poisons here, as you express it. The poor photographer's roof is lowly, I know—and my circumstances are narrow. But I am an inventor, and I am the bread-winner of a family. That exalts me above my mean surroundings.— Ah, here comes lunch!

(GINA *and* HEDVIG *bring bottles of ale, a decanter of brandy, glasses, etc. At the same time,* RELLING *and* MOLVIK *enter from the passage; they are both without hat or overcoat.* MOLVIK *is dressed in black.*)

GINA (*placing the things upon the table*). Ah, you two have come in the nick of time.

RELLING. Molvik got it into his head that he could smell herring-salad, and then there was no holding him.—Good morning again, Ekdal.

HIALMAR. Gregers, let me introduce you to Mr. Molvik. Doctor—— Oh, you know Relling, don't you?

GREGERS. Yes, slightly.

RELLING. Oh, Mr. Werle, junior! Yes, we two have had one or two little skirmishes up at the Höidal works. You've just moved in?

GREGERS. I moved in this morning.

RELLING. Molvik and I live right under you; so you haven't far to go for the doctor and the clergyman, if you should need anything in that line.

GREGERS. Thanks, it's not quite unlikely; for yesterday we were thirteen at table.

HIALMAR. Oh, come now, don't let us get upon unpleasant subjects again!

RELLING. You may make your mind easy, Ekdal; I'll be hanged if the finger of fate points to you.

HIALMAR. I should hope not, for the sake of my family. But let us sit down now, and eat and drink and be merry.

GREGERS. Shall we not wait for your father?

HIALMAR. No, his lunch will be taken in to him later. Come along!

(*The men seat themselves at table, and eat and drink.* GINA *and* HEDVIG *go in and out and wait upon them.*)

RELLING. Molvik was frightfully screwed yesterday, Mrs. Ekdal.

GINA. Really? Yesterday again?

RELLING. Didn't you hear him when I brought him home last night?

GINA. No, I can't say I did.

RELLING. That was a good thing, for Molvik was disgusting last night.

GINA. Is that true, Molvik?

MOLVIK. Let us draw a veil over last night's proceedings. That sort of thing is totally foreign to my better self.

RELLING (*to* GREGERS). It comes over him like a sort of possession, and then I have to go out on the loose with him. Mr. Molvik is dæmonic, you see.

GREGERS. Dæmonic?

RELLING. Molvik is dæmonic, yes.

GREGERS. H'm.

RELLING. And dæmonic natures are not made to walk straight through the world; they must meander a little now and then.—Well, so you still stick up there at those horrible grimy works?

GREGERS. I have stuck there until now.

RELLING. And did you ever manage to collect that claim you went about presenting?

GREGERS. Claim? (*Understands him.*) Ah, I see.

HIALMAR. Have you been presenting claims, Gregers?

GREGERS. Oh, nonsense.

RELLING. Faith, but he has, though! He went round to all the cottars' cabins presenting something he called "the claim of the ideal."

GREGERS. I was young then.

RELLING. You're right; you were very young. And as for the claim of the ideal—you never got it honored while *I* was up there.

GREGERS. Nor since either.

RELLING. Ah, then you've learned to knock a little discount off, I expect.

GREGERS. Never, when I have a true man to deal with.

HIALMAR. No, I should think not, indeed. A little butter, Gina.

RELLING. And a slice of bacon for Molvik.

MOLVIK. Ugh; not bacon!

(*A knock at the garret door.*)

HIALMAR.   Open the door, Hedvig; father wants to come out.

(HEDVIG *goes over and opens the door a little way;*
    EKDAL *enters with a fresh rabbit-skin; she closes the door after him.*)

EKDAL. Good morning, gentlemen! Good sport to-day. Shot a big one.

HIALMAR. And you've gone and skinned it without waiting for me——!

EKDAL. Salted it, too. It's good tender meat, is rabbit; it's sweet; it tastes like sugar. Good appetite to you, gentlemen!

(*Goes into his room.*)

MOLVIK (*rising.*) Excuse me——; I can't——; I must get downstairs immediately——

RELLING. Drink some soda water, man!

MOLVIK (*hurrying away*). Ugh—ugh!

 (*Goes out by the passage door.*)

RELLING (*to* HIALMAR). Let us drain a glass to the old hunter.

HIALMAR (*clinks glasses with him*). To the undaunted sportsman who has looked death in the face!

RELLING. To the grey-haired—— (*Drinks.*) By-the-bye, is his hair grey or white?

HIALMAR. Something between the two, I fancy; for that matter, he has very few hairs left of any color.

RELLING. Well, well, one can get through the world with a wig. After all, you are a happy man, Ekdal; you have your noble mission to labor for——

HIALMAR. And I do labor, I can tell you.

RELLING. And then you have your excellent wife, shuffling quietly in and out in her felt slippers, with that see-saw walk of hers, and making everything cozy and comfortable about you.

HIALMAR. Yes, Gina—(*nods to her*)—you were a good helpmate on the path of life.

GINA. Oh, don't sit there cricketising me.

RELLING. And your Hedvig, too, Ekdal!

HIALMAR (*affected*). The child, yes! The child before everything! Hedvig, come here to me. (*Strokes her hair.*) What day is it to-morrow, eh?

HEDVIG (*shaking him*). Oh, no, you're not to say anything, father.

HIALMAR. It cuts me to the heart when I think what a poor affair it will be; only a little festivity in the garret——

HEDVIG. Oh, but that's just what I like!

RELLING. Just you wait till the wonderful invention sees the light, Hedvig!

HIALMAR. Yes, indeed—then you shall see——! Hedvig, I have resolved to make your future secure. You shall live

in comfort all your days. I will demand—something or other
—on your behalf. That shall be the poor inventor's sole reward.

HEDVIG (*whispering, with her arms round his neck*). Oh,
you dear, kind father!

RELLING (*to* GREGERS). Come now, don't you find it
pleasant, for once in a way, to sit at a well-spread table in
a happy family circle?

HIALMAR. Ah, yes, I really prize these social hours.

GREGERS. For my part, I don't thrive in marsh vapors.

RELLING. Marsh vapors?

HIALMAR. Oh, don't begin with that stuff again!

GINA. Goodness knows there's no vapors in this house,
Mr. Werle; I give the place a good airing every blessed day.

GREGERS (*leaves the table*). No airing you can give will
drive out the taint I mean.

HIALMAR. Taint!

GINA. Yes, what do you say to that, Ekdal!

RELLING. Excuse me—may it not be you yourself that
have brought the taint from those mines up there?

GREGERS. It is like you to call what I bring into this house
a taint.

RELLING (*goes up to him*). Look here, Mr. Werle, junior:
I have a strong suspicion that you are still carrying about
that "claim of the ideal" large as life, in your coat-tail pocket.

GREGERS. I carry it in my breast.

RELLING. Well, wherever you carry it, I advise you not to
come dunning us with it here, so long as *I* am on the prem-
ises.

GREGERS. And if I do so none the less?

RELLING. Then you'll go head-foremost down the stairs;
now I've warned you.

HIALMAR (*rising*). Oh, but Relling——!

GREGERS. Yes, you may turn me out——

GINA (*interposing between them*). We can't have that,

Relling. But I must say, Mr. Werle, it ill becomes you to talk about vapors and taints, after all the mess you made with your stove.

(*A knock at the passage door.*)

HEDVIG. Mother, there's somebody knocking.

HIALMAR. There now, we're going to have a whole lot of people!

GINA. I'll go—— (*Goes over and opens the door, starts, and draws back.*) Oh—oh, dear!

(WERLE, *in a fur coat, advances one step into the room.*)

WERLE. Excuse me; but I think my son is staying here.

GINA (*with a gulp*). Yes.

HIALMAR (*approaching him*). Won't you do us the honor to——?

WERLE. Thank you, I merely wish to speak to my son.

GREGERS. What is it? Here I am.

WERLE. I want a few words with you, in your room.

GREGERS. In my room? Very well——

(*About to go.*)

GINA. No, no, your room's not in a fit state——

WERLE. Well then, out in the passage here; I want to have a few words with you alone.

HIALMAR. You can have them here, sir. Come into the parlor, Relling.

(HIALMAR *and* RELLING *go off to the right.* GINA *takes* HEDVIG *with her into the kitchen.*)

GREGERS (*after a short pause*). Well, now we are alone.

WERLE. From something you let fall last evening, and from your coming to lodge with the Ekdals, I can't help inferring that you intend to make yourself unpleasant to me, in one way or another.

GREGERS. I intend to open Hialmar Ekdal's eyes. He shall see his position as it really is—that is all.

WERLE. Is that the mission in life you spoke of yesterday?

GREGERS. Yes. You have left me no other.

WERLE. Is it I, then, that have crippled your mind, Gregers?

GREGERS. You have crippled my whole life. I am not thinking of all that about mother—— But it's thanks to you that I am continually haunted and harassed by a guilty conscience.

WERLE. Indeed! It is your conscience that troubles you, is it?

GREGERS. I ought to have taken a stand against you when the trap was set for Lieutenant Ekdal. I ought to have cautioned him; for I had a misgiving as to what was in the wind.

WERLE. Yes, that was the time to have spoken.

GREGERS. I did not dare to, I was so cowed and spiritless. I was mortally afraid of you—not only then, but long afterwards.

WERLE. You have got over that fear now, it appears.

GREGERS. Yes, fortunately. The wrong done to old Ekdal, both by me and by—others, can never be undone; but Hialmar I can rescue from all the falsehood and deception that are bringing him to ruin.

WERLE. Do you think that will be doing him a kindness?

GREGERS. I have not the least doubt of it.

WERLE. You think our worthy photographer is the sort of man to appreciate such friendly offices?

GREGERS. Yes, I do.

WERLE. H'm—we shall see.

GREGERS. Besides, if I am to go on living, I must try to find some cure for my sick conscience.

WERLE. It will never be sound. Your conscience has been sickly from childhood. That is a legacy from your mother, Gregers—the only one she left you.

GREGERS (*with a scornful half-smile*). Have you not yet forgiven her for the mistake you made in supposing she would bring you a fortune?

WERLE. Don't let us wander from the point.—Then you hold to your purpose of setting young Ekdal upon what you imagine to be the right scent?

GREGERS. Yes, that is my fixed resolve.

WERLE. Well, in that case I might have spared myself this visit; for, of course, it is useless to ask whether you will return home with me?

GREGERS. Quite useless.

WERLE. And I suppose you won't enter the firm either?

GREGERS. No.

WERLE. Very good. But as I am thinking of marrying again, your share in the property will fall to you at once.[1]

GREGERS (*quickly*). No, I do not want that.

WERLE. You don't want it?

GREGERS. No, I dare not take it, for conscience' sake.

WERLE (*after a pause*). Are you going up to the works again?

GREGERS. No; I consider myself released from your service.

WERLE. But what are you going to do?

GREGERS. Only to fulfil my mission; nothing more.

WERLE. Well, but afterwards? What are you going to live upon?

GREGERS. I have laid by a little out of my salary.

WERLE. How long will that last?

GREGERS. I think it will last my time.

WERLE. What do you mean?

GREGERS. I shall answer no more questions.

WERLE. Good-bye then, Gregers.

GREGERS. Good-bye.

(WERLE *goes.*)

HIALMAR (*peeping in*). He's gone, isn't he?

GREGERS. Yes.

---

[1] By Norwegian law, before a widower can marry again, a certain proportion of his property must be settled on his children by his former marriage.

(HIALMAR *and* RELLING *enter; also* GINA *and* HEDVIG *from the kitchen.*)

RELLING. That luncheon-party was a failure.

GREGERS. Put on your coat, Hialmar; I want you to come for a long walk with me.

HIALMAR. With pleasure. What was it your father wanted? Had it anything to do with me?

GREGERS. Come along. We must have a talk. I'll go and put on my overcoat.

(*Goes out by the passage door.*)

GINA. You shouldn't go out with him, Ekdal.

RELLING. No, don't you do it. Stay where you are.

HIALMAR (*gets his hat and overcoat*). Oh, nonsense! When a friend of my youth feels impelled to open his mind to me in private——

RELLING. But devil take it—don't you see that the fellow's mad, cracked, demented!

GINA. There, what did I tell you! His mother before him had crazy fits like that sometimes.

HIALMAR. The more need for a friend's watchful eye. (*To* GINA.) Be sure you have dinner ready in good time. Good-bye for the present.

(*Goes out by the passage door.*)

RELLING. It's a thousand pities the fellow didn't go to hell through one of the Höidal mines.

GINA. Good Lord! what makes you say that?

RELLING (*muttering*). Oh, I have my own reasons.

GINA. Do you think young Werle is really mad?

RELLING. No, worse luck; he's no madder than most other people. But one disease he has certainly got in his system.

GINA. What is it that's the matter with him?

RELLING. Well, I'll tell you, Mrs. Ekdal. He is suffering from an acute attack of integrity.

GINA. Integrity?

HEDVIG. Is that a kind of disease?

RELLING. Yes, it's a national disease; but it only appears sporadically. (*Nods to* GINA.) Thanks for your hospitality. (*He goes out by the passage door.*)

GINA (*moving restlessly to and fro*). Ugh, that Gregers Werle—he was always a wretched creature.

HEDVIG (*standing by the table, and looking searchingly at her*). I think all this is very strange.

ACT IV

(HIALMAR EKDAL'S *studio. A photograph has just been taken; a camera with the cloth over it, a pedestal, two chairs, a folding table, etc., are standing out in the room. Afternoon light; the sun is going down; a little later it begins to grow dusk.*)

(GINA *stands in the passage doorway, with a little box and a wet glass plate in her hand, and is speaking to somebody outside.*)

GINA. Yes, certainly. When I make a promise I keep it. The first dozen shall be ready on Monday. Good afternoon.

(*Someone is heard going downstairs.* GINA *shuts the door, slips the plate into the box, and puts it into the covered camera.*)

HEDVIG (*comes in from the kitchen*). Are they gone?

GINA (*tidying up*). Yes, thank goodness, I've got rid of them at last.

HEDVIG. But can you imagine why father hasn't come home yet?

GINA. Are you sure he's not down in Relling's room?

HEDVIG. No, he's not; I ran down the kitchen stair just now and asked.

GINA. And his dinner standing and getting cold, too.

HEDVIG. Yes, I can't understand it. Father's always so careful to be home to dinner!

GINA. Oh, he'll be here directly, you'll see.

HEDVIG. I wish he would come; everything seems so queer to-day.

GINA (*calls out*). There he is!

(HIALMAR EKDAL *comes in at the passage door.*)

HEDVIG (*going to him*). Father! Oh, what a time we've been waiting for you!

GINA (*glancing sidelong at him*). You've been out a long time, Ekdal.

HIALMAR (*without looking at her*). Rather long, yes.

(*He takes off his overcoat; GINA and HEDVIG go to help him; he motions them away.*)

GINA. Perhaps you've had dinner with Werle?

HIALMAR (*hanging up his coat*). No.

GINA (*going towards the kitchen door*). Then I'll bring some in for you.

HIALMAR. No; let the dinner alone. I want nothing to eat.

HEDVIG (*going nearer to him*). Are you not well, father?

HIALMAR. Well? Oh, yes, well enough. We have had a tiring walk, Gregers and I.

GINA. You didn't ought to have gone so far, Ekdal; you're not used to it.

HIALMAR. H'm; there's many a thing a man must get used to in this world. (*Wanders about the room.*) Has any one been here whilst I was out?

GINA. Nobody but the two sweethearts.

HIALMAR. No new orders?

GINA. No, not to-day.

HEDVIG. There will be some to-morrow, father, you'll see.

HIALMAR. I hope there will; for to-morrow I am going to set to work in real earnest.

HEDVIG. To-morrow! Don't you remember what day it is to-morrow?

HIALMAR. Oh, yes, by-the-bye——. Well, the day after, then. Henceforth I mean to do everything myself; I shall take all the work into my own hands.

GINA. Why, what can be the good of that, Ekdal? It'll only make your life a burden to you. I can manage the photography all right; and you can go on working at your invention.

HEDVIG. And think of the wild duck, father,—and all the hens and rabbits and——!

HIALMAR. Don't talk to me of all that trash! From to-morrow I will never set foot in the garret again.

HEDVIG. Oh, but father, you promised that we should have a little party——

HIALMAR. H'm, true. Well, then, from the day after to-morrow. I should almost like to wring that cursed wild duck's neck!

HEDVIG (*shrieks*). The wild duck!

GINA. Well, I never!

HEDVIG (*shaking him*). Oh, no, father; you know it's my wild duck!

HIALMAR. That is why I don't do it. I haven't the heart to—for your sake, Hedvig. But in my inmost soul I feel that I ought to do it. I ought not to tolerate under my roof a creature that has been through those hands.

GINA. Why, good gracious, even if grandfather did get it from that poor creature, Pettersen——

HIALMAR (*wandering about*). There are certain claims—what shall I call them?—let me say claims of the ideal—certain obligations, which a man cannot disregard without injury to his soul.

HEDVIG (*going after him*). But think of the wild duck, —the poor wild duck!

HIALMAR (*stops*). I tell you I will spare it—for your sake. Not a hair of its head shall be—I mean, it shall be spared. There are greater problems than that to be dealt with. But you should go out a little now, Hedvig, as usual; it is getting dusk enough for you now.

HEDVIG. No, I don't care about going out now.

HIALMAR. Yes, do; it seems to me your eyes are blinking a great deal; all these vapors in here are bad for you. The air is heavy under this roof.

HEDVIG. Very well, then, I'll run down the kitchen stair and go for a little walk. My cloak and hat?—oh, they're in my own room. Father—be sure you don't do the wild duck any harm whilst I'm out.

HIALMAR. Not a feather of its head shall be touched. (*Draws her to him.*) You and I, Hedvig—we two——! Well, go along.

(HEDVIG *nods to her parents and goes out through the kitchen.*)

HIALMAR (*walks about without looking up*). Gina.

GINA. Yes?

HIALMAR. From to-morrow—or, say, from the day after to-morrow—I should like to keep the household account-book myself.

GINA. Do you want to keep the accounts too, now?

HIALMAR. Yes; or to check the receipts at any rate.

GINA. Lord help us! that's soon done.

HIALMAR. One would hardly think so; at any rate you seem to make the money go a very long way. (*Stops and looks at her.*) How do you manage it?

GINA. It's because me and Hedvig, we need so little.

HIALMAR. Is it the case that father is very liberally paid for the copying he does for Mr. Werle?

GINA. I don't know as he gets anything out of the way. I don't know the rates for that sort of work.

HIALMAR. Well, what does he get, about? Let me hear!

GINA. Oh, it varies; I daresay it'll come to about as much as he costs us, with a little pocket-money over.

HIALMAR. As much as he costs us! And you have never told me this before!

GINA. No, how could I tell you? It pleased you so much to think he got everything from you.

HIALMAR. And he gets it from Mr. Werle.

GINA. Oh, well, he has plenty and to spare, he has.

HIALMAR. Light the lamp for me, please!

GINA (*lighting the lamp*). And, of course, we don't know as it's Mr. Werle himself; it may be Gråberg——

HIALMAR. Why attempt such an evasion?

GINA. I don't know; I only thought——

HIALMAR. H'm!

GINA. It wasn't me that got grandfather that copying. It was Bertha, when she used to come about us.

HIALMAR. It seems to me your voice is trembling.

GINA (*putting the lamp-shade on*). Is it?

HIALMAR. And your hands are shaking, are they not?

GINA (*firmly*). Come right out with it, Ekdal. What has he been saying about me?

HIALMAR. Is it true—can it be true that—that there was an—an understanding between you and Mr. Werle, while you were in service there?

GINA. That's not true. Not at that time. Mr. Werle did come after me, that's a fact. And his wife thought there was something in it, and then she made such a hocus-pocus and hurly-burly, and she hustled me and bustled me about so that I left her service.

HIALMAR. But afterwards, then?

GINA. Well, then I went home. And mother—well, she wasn't the woman you took her for, Ekdal; she kept on worrying and worrying at me about one thing and another— for Mr. Werle was a widower by that time.

HIALMAR. Well, and then?

GINA. I suppose you've got to know it. He gave me no peace until he'd had his way.

HIALMAR (*striking his hands together*). And this is the mother of my child! How could you hide this from me?

GINA. Yes, it was wrong of me; I ought certainly to have told you long ago.

HIALMAR. You should have told me at the very first;— then I should have known the sort of woman you were.

GINA. But would you have married me all the same?

HIALMAR. How can you dream that I would?

GINA. That's just why I didn't dare tell you anything,

then. For I'd come to care for you so much, you see; and I couldn't go and make myself utterly miserable——

HIALMAR (*walks about*). And this is my Hedvig's mother. And to know that all I see before me—(*kicks at a chair*)—all that I call my home—I owe to a favored predecessor! Oh, that scoundrel Werle!

GINA. Do you repent of the fourteen—the fifteen years we've lived together?

HIALMAR (*placing himself in front of her*). Have you not every day, every hour, repented of the spider's-web of deceit you have spun around me? Answer me that! How could you help writhing with penitence and remorse?

GINA. Oh, my dear Ekdal, I've had all I could do to look after the house and get through the day's work——

HIALMAR. Then you never think of reviewing your past?

GINA. No; Heaven knows I'd almost forgotten those old stories.

HIALMAR. Oh, this dull, callous contentment! To me there is something revolting about it. Think of it—never so much as a twinge of remorse!

GINA. But tell me, Ekdal—what would have become of you if you hadn't had a wife like me?

HIALMAR. Like you——!

GINA. Yes; for you know I've always been a bit more practical and wide-awake than you. Of course I'm a year or two older.

HIALMAR. What would have become of me!

GINA. You'd got into all sorts of bad ways when first you met me; that you can't deny.

HIALMAR. "Bad ways" do you call them? Little do you know what a man goes through when he is in grief and despair—especially a man of my fiery temperament.

GINA. Well, well, that may be so. And I've no reason to crow over you, neither; for you turned a moral of a husband, that you did, as soon as ever you had a house and

home of your own.—And now we'd got everything so nice
and cozy about us; and me and Hedvig was just thinking
we'd soon be able to let ourselves go a bit, in the way of
both food and clothes.

HIALMAR. In the swamp of deceit, yes.

GINA. I wish to goodness that detestable thing had never
set his foot inside our doors!

HIALMAR. And I, too, thought my home such a pleasant
one. That was a delusion. Where shall I now find the
elasticity of spirit to bring my invention into the world of
reality? Perhaps it will die with me; and then it will be your
past, Gina, that will have killed it.

GINA (*nearly crying*). You mustn't say such things,
Ekdal. Me, that has only wanted to do the best I could for
you, all my days!

HIALMAR. I ask you, what becomes of the breadwinner's
dream? When I used to lie in there on the sofa and brood
over my invention, I had a clear enough presentiment that
it would sap my vitality to the last drop. I felt even then
that the day when I held the patent in my hand—that day—
would bring my—release. And then it was my dream that
you should live on after me, the dead inventor's well-to-do
widow.

GINA (*drying her tears*). No, you mustn't talk like that,
Ekdal. May the Lord never let me see the day I am left a
widow!

HIALMAR. Oh, the whole dream has vanished. It is all
over now. All over!

(GREGERS WERLE *opens the passage door cautiously and
looks in.*)

GREGERS. May I come in?

HIALMAR. Yes, come in.

GREGERS (*comes forward, his face beaming with satisfaction, and holds out both his hands to them*). Well, dear
friends——! (*Looks from one to the other, and whispers
to* HIALMAR.) Have you not done it yet?

HIALMAR (*aloud*). It is done.

GREGERS. It is?

HIALMAR. I have passed through the bitterest moments of my life.

GREGERS. But also, I trust, the most ennobling.

HIALMAR. Well, at any rate, we have got through it for the present.

GINA. God forgive you, Mr. Werle.

GREGERS (*in great surprise*). But I don't understand this.

HIALMAR. What don't you understand?

GREGERS. After so great a crisis—a crisis that is to be the starting-point of an entirely new life—of a communion founded on truth, and free from all taint of deception——

HIALMAR. Yes, yes, I know; I know that quite well.

GREGERS. I confidently expected, when I entered the room, to find the light of transfiguration shining upon me from both husband and wife. And now I see nothing but dullness, oppression, gloom——

GINA. Oh, is that it?

(*Takes off the lamp-shade.*)

GREGERS. You will not understand me, Mrs. Ekdal. Ah, well, you, I suppose, need time to——. But you, Hialmar? Surely you feel a new consecration after the great crisis.

HIALMAR. Yes, of course I do. That is—in a sort of way.

GREGERS. For surely nothing in the world can compare with the joy of forgiving one who has erred, and raising her up to oneself in love.

HIALMAR. Do you think a man can so easily throw off the bitter cup I have drained?

GREGERS. No, not a common man, perhaps. But a man like you——!

HIALMAR. Good God! I know that well enough. But you must keep me up to it, Gregers. It takes time, you know.

GREGERS. You have much of the wild duck in you, Hialmar.

(RELLING *has come in at the passage door.*)

RELLING. Oho! is the wild duck to the fore again?

HIALMAR. Yes; Mr. Werle's wing-broken victim.

RELLING. Mr. Werle's——? So it's him you are talking about?

HIALMAR. Him and—ourselves.

RELLING (*in an undertone to* GREGERS). May the devil fly away with you!

HIALMAR. What is that you are saying?

RELLING. Only uttering a heartfelt wish that this quack-salver would take himself off. If he stays here, he is quite equal to making an utter mess of life, for both of you.

GREGERS. These two will not make a mess of life, Mr. Relling. Of course I won't speak of Hialmar—him we know. But she, too, in her innermost heart, has certainly something loyal and sincere——

GINA (*almost crying*). You might have let me alone for what I was, then.

RELLING (*to* GREGERS). Is it rude to ask what you really want in this house?

GREGERS. To lay the foundations of a true marriage.

RELLING. So you don't think Ekdal's marriage is good enough as it is?

GREGERS. No doubt it is as good a marriage as most others, worse luck. But a true marriage it has yet to become.

HIALMAR. You have never had eyes for the claims of the ideal, Relling.

RELLING. Rubbish, my boy!—but excuse me, Mr. Werle: how many—in round numbers—how many true marriages have you seen in the course of your life?

GREGERS. Scarcely a single one.

RELLING. Nor I either.

GREGERS. But I have seen innumerable marriages of the opposite kind. And it has been my fate to see at close quarters what ruin such a marriage can work in two human souls.

HIALMAR. A man's whole moral basis may give away beneath his feet; that is the terrible part of it.

RELLING. Well, I can't say I've ever been exactly married, so I don't pretend to speak with authority. But this I know, that the child enters into the marriage problem. And you must leave the child in peace.

HIALMAR. Oh—Hedvig! my poor Hedvig!

RELLING. Yes, you must be good enough to keep Hedvig outside of all this. You two are grown-up people; you are free, in God's name, to make what mess and muddle you please of your life. But you must deal cautiously with Hedvig, I tell you; else you may do her a great injury.

HIALMAR. An injury!

RELLING. Yes, or she may do herself an injury—and perhaps others, too.

GINA. How can you know that, Relling?

HIALMAR. Her sight is in no immediate danger, is it?

RELLING. I am not talking about her sight. Hedvig is at a critical age. She may be getting all sorts of mischief into her head.

GINA. That's true—I've noticed it already! She's taken to carrying on with the fire, out in the kitchen. She calls it playing at house-on-fire. I'm often scared for fear she really sets fire to the house.

RELLING. You see; I thought as much.

GREGERS (to RELLING). But how do you account for that?

RELLING (sullenly). Her constitution's changing, sir.

HIALMAR. So long as the child has me——! So long as I am above ground——!

(A knock at the door.)

GINA. Hush, Ekdal; there's some one in the passage. (Calls out.) Come in!

(MRS. SÖRBY, in walking dress, comes in.)

MRS. SÖRBY. Good evening.

GINA (going towards her). Is it really you, Bertha?

MRS. SÖRBY. Yes, of course it is. But I'm disturbing you, I'm afraid?

HIALMAR. No, not at all; an emissary from that house——

MRS. SÖRBY (*to* GINA). To tell the truth, I hoped your men-folk would be out at this time. I just ran up to have a little chat with you, and to say good-bye.

GINA. Good-bye? Are you going away, then?

MRS. SÖRBY. Yes, to-morrow morning,—up to Höidal. Mr. Werle started this afternoon. (*Lightly to* GREGERS.) He asked me to say good-bye for him.

GINA. Only fancy——!

HIALMAR. So Mr. Werle has gone? And now you are going after him?

MRS. SÖRBY. Yes, what do you say to that, Ekdal?

HIALMAR. I say: beware!

GREGERS. I must explain the situation. My father and Mrs. Sörby are going to be married.

HIALMAR. Going to be married!

GINA. Oh, Bertha! So it's come to that at last!

RELLING (*his voice quivering a little*). This is surely not true?

MRS. SÖRBY. Yes, my dear Relling, it's true enough.

RELLING. You are going to marry again?

MRS. SÖRBY. Yes, it looks like it. Werle has got a special license, and we are going to be married quite quietly, up at the works.

GREGERS. Then I must wish you all happiness, like a dutiful stepson.

MRS. SÖRBY. Thank you very much—if you mean what you say. I certainly hope it will lead to happiness, both for Werle and for me.

RELLING. You have every reason to hope that. Mr. Werle never gets drunk—so far as I know; and I don't suppose he's in the habit of thrashing his wives, like the late lamented horse-doctor.

MRS. SÖRBY. Come now, let Sörby rest in peace. He had his good points, too.

RELLING. Mr. Werle has better ones, I have no doubt.

Mrs. Sörby. He hasn't frittered away all that was good in him, at any rate. The man who does that must take the consequences.

Relling. I shall go out with Molvik this evening.

Mrs. Sörby. You mustn't do that, Relling. Don't do it— for my sake.

Relling. There's nothing else for it. (*To* Hialmar.) If you're going with us, come along.

Gina. No, thank you. Ekdal doesn't go in for that sort of dissertation.

Hialmar (*half aloud, in vexation*). Oh, do hold your tongue!

Relling. Good-bye, Mrs.—Werle.

  (*Goes out through the passage door.*)

Gregers (*to* Mrs. Sörby). You seem to know Dr. Relling pretty intimately.

Mrs. Sörby. Yes, we have known each other for many years. At one time it seemed as if things might have gone further between us.

Gregers. It was surely lucky for you that they did not.

Mrs. Sörby. You may well say that. But I have always been wary of acting on impulse. A woman can't afford absolutely to throw herself away.

Gregers. Are you not in the least afraid that I may let my father know about this old friendship?

Mrs. Sörby. Why, of course, I have told him all about it myself.

Gregers. Indeed?

Mrs. Sörby. Your father knows every single thing that can, with any truth, be said about me. I have told him all; it was the first thing I did when I saw what was in his mind.

Gregers. Then you have been franker than most people, I think.

Mrs. Sörby. I have always been frank. We women find that the best policy.

HIALMAR. What do you say to that, Gina?

GINA. Oh, we're not all alike, us women aren't. Some are made one way, some another.

MRS. SÖRBY. Well, for my part, Gina, I believe it's wisest to do as I've done. And Werle has no secrets either, on his side. That's really the great bond between us, you see. Now he can talk to me as openly as a child. He has never had the chance to do that before. Fancy a man like him, full of health and vigor, passing his whole youth and the best years of his life in listening to nothing but penitential sermons! And very often the sermons had for their text the most imaginary offences—at least so I understand.

GINA. That's true enough.

GREGERS. If you ladies are going to follow up this topic, I had better withdraw.

MRS. SÖRBY. You can stay as far as that's concerned. I shan't say a word more. But I wanted you to know that I had done nothing secretly or in an underhand way. I may seem to have come in for a great piece of luck; and so I have, in a sense. But after all, I don't think I am getting any more than I am giving. I shall stand by him always, and I can tend and care for him as no one else can, now that he is getting helpless.

HIALMAR. Getting helpless?

GREGERS (*to* MRS. SÖRBY). Hush, don't speak of that here.

MRS. SÖRBY. There is no disguising it any longer, however much he would like to. He is going blind.

HIALMAR (*starts*). Going blind? That's strange. He, too, going blind!

GINA. Lots of people do.

MRS. SÖRBY. And you can imagine what that means to a business man. Well, I shall try as well as I can to make my eyes take the place of his. But I mustn't stay any longer; I have heaps of things to do.—Oh, by-the-bye, Ekdal, I was to tell you that if there is anything Werle can do for you, you must just apply to Gråberg.

GREGERS. That offer I am sure Hialmar Ekdal will decline with thanks.

MRS. SÖRBY. Indeed? I don't think he used to be so——

GINA. No, Bertha, Ekdal doesn't need anything from Mr. Werle now.

HIALMAR (*slowly, and with emphasis*). Will you present my compliments to your future husband, and say that I intend very shortly to call upon Mr. Gråberg——

GREGERS. What! You don't really mean that?

HIALMAR. To call upon Mr. Gråberg, I say, and obtain an account of the sum I owe his principal. I will pay that debt of honor—ha ha ha! a debt of honor, let us call it! In any case, I will pay the whole with five per cent interest.

GINA. But, my dear Ekdal, God knows we haven't got the money to do it.

HIALMAR. Be good enough to tell your future husband that I am working assiduously at my invention. Please tell him that what sustains me in this laborious task is the wish to free myself from a torturing burden of debt. That is my reason for proceeding with the invention. The entire profits shall be devoted to releasing me from my pecuniary obligations to your future husband.

MRS. SÖRBY. Something has happened here.

HIALMAR. Yes, you are right.

MRS. SÖRBY. Well, good-bye. I had something else to speak to you about, Gina; but it must keep till another time. Good-bye.

(HIALMAR *and* GREGERS *bow silently.* GINA *follows* MRS. SÖRBY *to the door.*)

HIALMAR. Not beyond the threshold, Gina!

(MRS. SÖRBY *goes;* GINA *shuts the door after her.*)

HIALMAR. There now, Gregers; I have got that burden of debt off my mind.

GREGERS. You soon will, at all events.

HIALMAR. I think my attitude may be called correct.

GREGERS. You are the man I have always taken you for.

HIALMAR. In certain cases, it is impossible to disregard the claim of the ideal. Yet, as the breadwinner of a family, I cannot but writhe and groan under it. I can tell you it is no joke for a man without capital to attempt the repayment of a long-standing obligation, over which, so to speak, the dust of oblivion had gathered. But it cannot be helped: the Man in me demands his rights.

GREGERS (laying his hand on HIALMAR'S shoulder). My dear Hialmar—was it not a good thing I came?

HIALMAR. Yes.

GREGERS. Are you not glad to have had your true position made clear to you?

HIALMAR (somewhat impatiently). Yes, of course I am. But there is one thing that is revolting to my sense of justice.

GREGERS. And what is that?

HIALMAR. It is that—but I don't know whether I ought to express myself so unreservedly about your father.

GREGERS. Say what you please, so far as I am concerned.

HIALMAR. Well, then, is it not exasperating to think that it is not I, but he, who will realize the true marriage?

GREGERS. How can you say such a thing?

HIALMAR. Because it is clearly the case. Isn't the marriage between your father and Mrs. Sörby founded upon complete confidence, upon entire and unreserved candor on both sides? They hide nothing from each other, they keep no secrets in the background; their relation is based, if I may put it so, on mutual confession and absolution.

GREGERS. Well, what then?

HIALMAR. Well, is not that the whole thing? Did you not yourself say that this was precisely the difficulty that had to be overcome in order to found a true marriage?

GREGERS. But this is a totally different matter, Hialmar.

You surely don't compare either yourself or your wife with those two——? Oh, you understand me well enough.

HIALMAR. Say what you like, there is something in all this that hurts and offends my sense of justice. It really looks as if there were no just providence to rule the world.

GINA. Oh, no, Ekdal; for God's sake don't say such things.

GREGERS. H'm; don't let us get upon those questions.

HIALMAR. And yet, after all, I cannot but recognize the guiding finger of fate. He is going blind.

GINA. Oh, you can't be sure of that.

HIALMAR. There is no doubt about it. At all events there ought not to be; for in that very fact lies the righteous retribution. He has hoodwinked a confiding fellow creature in days gone by——

GREGERS. I fear he has hoodwinked many.

HIALMAR. And now comes inexorable, mysterious Fate, and demands Werle's own eyes.

GINA. Oh, how dare you say such dreadful things! You make me quite scared.

HIALMAR. It is profitable, now and then, to plunge deep into the night side of existence.

(HEDVIG, *in her hat and cloak, comes in by the passage door. She is pleasurably excited and out of breath.*)

GINA. Are you back already?

HEDVIG. Yes, I didn't care to go any farther. It was a good thing, too; for I've just met some one at the door.

HIALMAR. It must have been that Mrs. Sörby.

HEDVIG. Yes.

HIALMAR (*walks up and down*). I hope you have seen her for the last time.

(*Silence.* HEDVIG, *discouraged, looks first at one and then at the other, trying to divine their frame of mind.*)

HEDVIG (*approaching, coaxingly*). Father.

HIALMAR. Well—what is it, Hedvig?

HEDVIG. Mrs. Sörby had something with her for me.

HIALMAR (*stops*). For you?

HEDVIG. Yes. Something for to-morrow.

GINA. Bertha has always given you some little thing on your birthday.

HIALMAR. What is it?

HEDVIG. Oh, you mustn't see it now. Mother is to give it to me to-morrow morning before I'm up.

HIALMAR. What is all this hocus-pocus that I am to be in the dark about!

HEDVIG (*quickly*). Oh, no, you may see it if you like. It's a big letter.

(*Takes the letter out of her cloak pocket.*)

HIALMAR. A letter, too?

HEDVIG. Yes, it is only a letter. The rest will come afterwards, I suppose. But fancy—a letter! I've never had a letter before. And there's "Miss" written upon it. (*Reads.*) "Miss Hedvig Ekdal." Only fancy—that's me!

HIALMAR. Let me see that letter.

HEDVIG (*hands it to him*). There it is.

HIALMAR. That is Mr. Werle's hand.

GINA. Are you sure of that, Ekdal?

HIALMAR. Look for yourself.

GINA. Oh, what do I know about such-like things?

HIALMAR. Hedvig, may I open the letter—and read it?

HEDVIG. Yes, of course you may, if you want to.

GINA. No, not to-night, Ekdal; it's to be kept till to-morrow.

HEDVIG (*softly*). Oh, can't you let him read it! It's sure to be something good; and then father will be glad, and everything will be nice again.

HIALMAR. I may open it then?

HEDVIG. Yes, do, father. I'm so anxious to know what it is.

HIALMAR. Well and good. (*Opens the letter, takes out a paper, reads it through, and appears bewildered.*) What is this——!

GINA. What does it say?

HEDVIG. Oh, yes, father—tell us!

HIALMAR. Be quiet. (*Reads it through again; he has turned pale, but says with self-control*:) It is a deed of gift, Hedvig.

HEDVIG. Is it? What sort of gift am I to have?

HIALMAR. Read for yourself.

(HEDVIG *goes over and reads for a time by the lamp.*)

HIALMAR (*half-aloud, clenching his hands*). The eyes! The eyes—and then that letter!

HEDVIG (*leaves off reading*). Yes, but it seems to me that it's grandfather that's to have it.

HIALMAR (*takes letter from her*). Gina—can you understand this?

GINA. I know nothing whatever about it; tell me what's the matter.

HIALMAR. Mr. Werle writes to Hedvig that her old grandfather need not trouble himself any longer with the copying, but that he can henceforth draw on the office for a hundred crowns a month——

GREGERS. Aha!

HEDVIG. A hundred crowns, mother! I read that.

GINA. What a good thing for grandfather!

HIALMAR. ——a hundred crowns a month so long as he needs it—that means, of course, so long as he lives.

GINA. Well, so he's provided for, poor dear.

HIALMAR. But there is more to come. You didn't read that, Hedvig. Afterwards this gift is to pass on to you.

HEDVIG. To me! The whole of it?

HIALMAR. He says that the same amount is assured to you for the whole of your life. Do you hear that, Gina?

GINA. Yes, I hear.

HEDVIG. Fancy—all that money for me! (*Shakes him.*) Father, father, aren't you glad——?

HIALMAR (*eluding her*). Glad! (*Walks about.*) Oh what vistas—what perspectives open up before me! It is Hedvig, Hedvig that he showers these benefactions upon!

GINA. Yes, because it's Hedvig's birthday——

HEDVIG. And you'll get it all the same, father! You know quite well I shall give all the money to you and mother.

HIALMAR. To mother, yes! There we have it.

GREGERS. Hialmar, this is a trap he is setting for you.

HIALMAR. Do you think it's another trap?

GREGERS. When he was here this morning he said: Hialmar Ekdal is not the man you imagine him to be.

HIALMAR. Not the man——!

GREGERS. That you shall see, he said.

HIALMAR. He meant you should see that I would let myself be bought off——!

HEDVIG. Oh mother, what does all this mean?

GINA. Go and take off your things.

(HEDVIG *goes out by the kitchen door, half-crying.*)

GREGERS. Yes, Hialmar—now is the time to show who was right, he or I.

HIALMAR (*slowly tears the paper across, lays both pieces on the table, and says*): Here is my answer.

GREGERS. Just what I expected.

HIALMAR (*goes over to* GINA, *who stands by the stove, and says in a low voice*): Now please make a clean breast of it. If the connection between you and him was quite over when you—came to care for me, as you call it—why did he place us in a position to marry?

GINA. I suppose he thought as he could come and go in our house.

HIALMAR. Only that? Was not he afraid of a possible contingency?

GINA. I don't know what you mean.

HIALMAR. I want to know whether—your child has the right to live under my roof.

GINA (*draws herself up; her eyes flash*). You ask that!

HIALMAR. You shall answer me this one question: Does Hedvig belong to me—or——? Well!

GINA (*looking at him with cold defiance*). I don't know.

HIALMAR (*quivering a little*). You don't know!

GINA. How should I know. A creature like me——

HIALMAR (*quietly turning away from her*). Then I have nothing more to do in this house.

GREGERS. Take care, Hialmar! Think what you are doing!

HIALMAR (*puts on his overcoat*). In this case, there is nothing for a man like me to think twice about.

GREGERS. Yes indeed, there are endless things to be considered. You three must be together if you are to attain the true frame of mind for self-sacrifice and forgiveness.

HIALMAR. I don't want to attain it. Never, never! My hat! (*Takes his hat.*) My home has fallen in ruins about me. (*Bursts into tears.*) Gregers, I have no child!

HEDVIG (*who has opened the kitchen door*). What is that you're saying? (*Coming to him.*) Father, father!

GINA. There, you see!

HIALMAR. Don't come near me, Hedvig! Keep far away. I cannot bear to see you. Oh! those eyes——! Good-bye.

(*Makes for the door.*)

HEDVIG (*clinging close to him and screaming loudly*). No! no! Don't leave me!

GINA (*cries out*). Look at the child, Ekdal! Look at the child!

HIALMAR. I will not! I cannot! I must get out—away from all this!

(*He tears himself away from* HEDVIG, *and goes out by the passage door.*)

HEDVIG (*with despairing eyes*). He is going away from us, mother! He is going away from us! He will never come back again!

GINA. Don't cry, Hedvig. Father's sure to come back again.

HEDVIG (*throws herself sobbing on the sofa*). No, no, he'll never come home to us any more.

GREGERS. Do you believe I meant all for the best, Mrs. Ekdal?

GINA. Yes, I daresay you did; but God forgive you, all the same.

HEDVIG (*lying on the sofa*). Oh, this will kill me! What have I done to him? Mother, you must fetch him home again!

GINA. Yes yes yes; only be quiet, and I'll go out and look for him. (*Puts on her outdoor things.*) Perhaps he's gone in to Relling's. But you mustn't lie there and cry. Promise me!

HEDVIG (*weeping convulsively*). Yes, I'll stop, I'll stop; if only father comes back!

GREGERS (*to* GINA, *who is going*). After all, had you not better leave him to fight out his bitter fight to the end?

GINA. Oh, he can do that afterwards. First of all, we must get the child quieted. (*Goes out by the passage door.*)

HEDVIG (*sits up and dries her tears*). Now you must tell me what all this means. Why doesn't father want me any more?

GREGERS. You mustn't ask that till you are a big girl— quite grown-up.

HEDVIG (*sobs*). But I can't go on being as miserable as this till I'm grown-up.—I think I know what it is.—Perhaps I'm not really father's child.

GREGERS (*uneasily*). How could that be?

HEDVIG. Mother might have found me. And perhaps father has just got to know it; I've read of such things.

GREGERS. Well, but if it were so——

HEDVIG. I think he might be just as fond of me for all that. Yes, fonder almost. We got the wild duck in a present, you know, and I love it so dearly all the same.

GREGERS (*turning the conversation*). Ah, the wild duck, by-the-bye! Let us talk about the wild duck a little, Hedvig.

HEDVIG. The poor wild duck! He doesn't want to see it

any more either. Only think, he wanted to wring its neck!

GREGERS. Oh, he won't do that.

HEDVIG. No; but he said he would like to. And I think it was horrid of father to say it; for I pray for the wild duck every night, and ask that it may be preserved from death and all that is evil.

GREGERS (*looking at her*). Do you say your prayers every night?

HEDVIG. Yes.

GREGERS. Who taught you to do that?

HEDVIG. I myself; one time when father was very ill, and had leeches on his neck, and said that death was staring him in the face.

GREGERS. Well?

HEDVIG. Then I prayed for him as I lay in bed; and since then I have always kept it up.

GREGERS. And now you pray for the wild duck too?

HEDVIG. I thought it was best to bring in the wild duck; for she was so weakly at first.

GREGERS. Do you pray in the morning, too?

HEDVIG. No, of course not.

GREGERS. Why not in the morning as well?

HEDVIG. In the morning it's light, you know, and there's nothing in particular to be afraid of.

GREGERS. And your father was going to wring the neck of the wild duck that you love so dearly?

HEDVIG. No; he said he ought to wring its neck, but he would spare it for my sake; and that was kind of father.

GREGERS (*coming a little nearer*). But suppose you were to sacrifice the wild duck of your own free will for his sake.

HEDVIG (*rising*). The wild duck!

GREGERS. Suppose you were to make a free-will offering, for his sake, of the dearest treasure you have in the world!

HEDVIG. Do you think that would do any good?

GREGERS. Try it, Hedvig.

HEDVIG (*softly, with flashing eyes*). Yes, I will try it.

GREGERS. Have you really the courage for it, do you think?

HEDVIG. I'll ask grandfather to shoot the wild duck for me.

GREGERS. Yes, do. But not a word to your mother about it.

HEDVIG. Why not?

GREGERS. She doesn't understand us.

HEDVIG. The wild duck! I'll try it to-morrow morning.

(GINA *comes in by the passage door.*)

HEDVIG (*going towards her*). Did you find him, mother?

GINA. No, but I heard as he had called and taken Relling with him.

GREGERS. Are you sure of that?

GINA. Yes, the porter's wife said so. Molvik went with them too, she said.

GREGERS. This evening, when his mind so sorely needs to wrestle in solitude——!

GINA (*takes off her things*). Yes, men are strange creatures, so they are. The Lord only knows where Relling has dragged him to! I ran over to Madam Eriksen's, but they weren't there.

HEDVIG (*struggling to keep back her tears*). Oh, if he should never come home any more!

GREGERS. He will come home again. I shall have news to give him to-morrow; and then you shall see how he comes home. You may rely upon that, Hedvig, and sleep in peace. Good-night.

(*He goes out by the passage door.*)

HEDVIG (*throws herself sobbing on* GINA's *neck*). Mother, mother!

GINA (*pats her shoulder and sighs*). Ah yes; Relling was right, he was. That's what comes of it when crazy creatures go about presenting the claims of the—what-you-may-call-it.

ACT V

(HIALMAR EKDAL's *studio. Cold, gray morning light. Wet
snow lies upon the large panes of the sloping roof-
window.*)

(GINA *comes from the kitchen with an apron and bib on, and
carrying a dusting-brush and a duster; she goes towards
the sitting-room door. At the same moment* HEDVIG
comes hurriedly in from the passage.)

GINA (*stops*). Well?

HEDVIG. Oh, mother, I almost think he's down at Relling's——

GINA. There, you see!

HEDVIG. ——because the porter's wife says she could
hear that Relling had two people with him when he came
home last night.

GINA. That's just what I thought.

HEDVIG. But it's no use his being there, if he won't come
up to us.

GINA. I'll go down and speak to him at all events.

(OLD EKDAL, *in dressing-gown and slippers, and with a
lighted pipe, appears at the door of his room.*)

EKDAL. Hialmar—— Isn't Hialmar at home?

GINA. No, he's gone out.

EKDAL. So early? And in such a tearing snowstorm? Well
well; just as he pleases; I can take my morning walk alone.

(*He slides the garret door aside;* HEDVIG *helps him; he
goes in; she closes it after him.*)

HEDVIG (*in an undertone*). Only think, mother, when
poor grandfather hears that father is going to leave us.

GINA. Oh, nonsense; grandfather mustn't hear anything

about it. It was a heaven's mercy he wasn't at home yesterday in all that hurly-burly.

HEDVIG. Yes, but——

(GREGERS *comes in by the passage door.*)

GREGERS. Well, have you any news of him?

GINA. They say he's down at Relling's.

GREGERS. At Relling's! Has he really been out with those
creatures?

GINA. Yes, like enough.

GREGERS. When he ought to have been yearning for solitude, to collect and clear his thoughts——

GINA. Yes, you may well say so.

(RELLING *enters from the passage.*)

HEDVIG (*going to him*). Is father in your room?

GINA (*at the same time*). Is he there?

RELLING. Yes, to be sure he is.

HEDVIG. And you never let us know!

RELLING. Yes; I'm a brute. But in the first place I had
to look after the other brute; I mean our dæmonic friend, of
course; and then I fell so dead asleep that——

GINA. What does Ekdal say to-day?

RELLING. He says nothing whatever.

HEDVIG. Doesn't he speak?

RELLING. Not a blessed word.

GREGERS. No no; I can understand that very well.

GINA. But what's he doing then?

RELLING. He's lying on the sofa, snoring.

GINA. Oh is he? Yes, Ekdal's a rare one to snore.

HEDVIG. Asleep? Can he sleep?

RELLING. Well, it certainly looks like it.

GREGERS. No wonder, after the spiritual conflict that has
rent him——

GINA. And then he's never been used to gadding about
out of doors at night.

HEDVIG. Perhaps it's a good thing that he's getting sleep, mother.

GINA. Of course it is; and we must take care we don't wake him up too early. Thank you, Relling. I must get the house cleaned up a bit now, and then—— Come and help me, Hedvig.

(GINA *and* HEDVIG *go into the sitting-room.*)

GREGERS (*turning to* RELLING). What is your explanation of the spiritual tumult that is now going on in Hialmar Ekdal?

RELLING. Devil a bit of a spiritual tumult have *I* noticed in him.

GREGERS. What! Not at such a crisis, when his whole life has been placed on a new foundation——? How can you think that such an individuality as Hialmar's——?

RELLING. Oh, individuality—he! If he ever had any tendency to the abnormal developments you call individuality, I can assure you it was rooted out of him while he was still in his teens.

GREGERS. That would be strange indeed,—considering the loving care with which he was brought up.

RELLING. By those two high-flown, hysterical maiden aunts, you mean?

GREGERS. Let me tell you that they were women who never forgot the claim of the ideal—but of course you will only jeer at me again.

RELLING. No, I'm in no humor for that. I know all about those ladies; for he has ladled out no end of rhetoric on the subject of his "two soul-mothers." But I don't think he has much to thank them for. Ekdal's misfortune is that in his own circle he has always been looked upon as a shining light——

GREGERS. Not without reason, surely. Look at the depth of his mind!

RELLING. *I* have never discovered it. That his father believed in it I don't so much wonder; the old lieutenant has been an ass all his days.

GREGERS. He has had a child-like mind all his days; that is what you cannot understand.

RELLING. Well, so be it. But then, when our dear, sweet Hialmar went to college, he at once passed for the great light of the future amongst his comrades too! He was handsome, the rascal—red and white—a shop-girl's dream of manly beauty; and with his superficially emotional temperament, and his sympathetic voice, and his talent for declaiming other people's verses and other people's thoughts——

GREGERS (*indignantly*). Is it Hialmar Ekdal you are talking about in this strain?

RELLING. Yes, with your permission; I am simply giving you an inside view of the idol you are groveling before.

GREGERS. I should hardly have thought I was quite stone blind.

RELLING. Yes you are—or not far from it. You are a sick man, too, you see.

GREGERS. You are right there.

RELLING. Yes. Yours is a complicated case. First of all there is that plaguy integrity-fever; and then—what's worse —you are always in a delirium of hero-worship; you must always have something to adore, outside yourself.

GREGERS. Yes, I must certainly seek it outside myself.

RELLING. But you make such shocking mistakes about every new phœnix you think you have discovered. Here again you have come to a cotter's cabin with your claim of the ideal; and the people of the house are insolvent.

GREGERS. If you don't think better than that of Hialmar Ekdal, what pleasure can you find in being everlastingly with him?

RELLING. Well, you see, I'm supposed to be a sort of a

doctor—save the mark! I can't but give a hand to the poor sick folk who live under the same roof with me.

GREGERS. Oh, indeed! Hialmar Ekdal is sick too, is he!

RELLING. Most people are, worse luck.

GREGERS. And what remedy are you applying in Hialmar's case?

RELLING. My usual one. I am cultivating the life-illusion[1] in him.

GREGERS. Life—illusion? I didn't catch what you said.

RELLING. Yes, I said illusion. For illusion, you know, is the stimulating principle.

GREGERS. May I ask with what illusion Hialmar is inoculated?

RELLING. No, thank you; I don't betray professional secrets to quacksalvers. You would probably go and muddle his case still more than you have already. But my method is infallible. I have applied it to Molvik as well. I have made him "dæmonic." That's the blister I have to put on his neck.

GREGERS. Is he not really dæmonic then?

RELLING. What the devil do you mean by dæmonic! It's only a piece of gibberish I've invented to keep up a spark of life in him. But for that, the poor harmless creature would have succumbed to self-contempt and despair many a long year ago. And then the old lieutenant! But he has hit upon his own cure, you see.

GREGERS. Lieutenant Ekdal? What of him?

RELLING. Just think of the old bear-hunter shutting himself up in that dark garret to shoot rabbits! I tell you there is not a happier sportsman in the world than that old man pottering about in there among all that rubbish. The four or five withered Christmas-trees he has saved up are the same to him as the whole great fresh Höidal forest; the cock and the hens are big game-birds in the fir-tops; and the rabbits that

[1] "Livslögnen," literally "the life-lie."

flop about the garret floor are the bears he has to battle with
—the mighty hunter of the mountains!

GREGERS. Poor unfortunate old man! Yes; he has indeed
had to narrow the ideals of his youth.

RELLING. While I think of it, Mr. Werle, junior—don't
use that foreign word: ideals. We have the excellent native
word: lies.

GREGERS. Do you think the two things are related?

RELLING. Yes, just about as closely as typhus and putrid
fever.

GREGERS. Dr. Relling, I shall not give up the struggle
until I have rescued Hialmar from your clutches!

RELLING. So much the worse for him. Rob the average
man of his life-illusion, and you rob him of his happiness at
the same stroke. (*To* HEDVIG, *who comes in from the sitting-
room.*) Well, little wild-duck-mother, I'm just going down
to see whether papa is still lying meditating upon that wonderful invention of his. (*Goes out by passage door.*)

GREGERS (*approaches* HEDVIG.) I can see by your face
that you have not yet done it.

HEDVIG. What? Oh, that about the wild duck! No.

GREGERS. I suppose your courage failed when the time
came.

HEDVIG. No, that wasn't it. But when I awoke this morning and remembered what we had been talking about, it
seemed so strange.

GREGERS. Strange?

HEDVIG. Yes, I don't know—— Yesterday evening, at
the moment, I thought there was something so delightful
about it; but since I have slept and thought of it again, it
somehow doesn't seem worth while.

GREGERS. Ah, I thought you could not have grown up
quite unharmed in this house.

HEDVIG. I don't care about that, if only father would
come up——

GREGERS. Oh, if only your eyes had been opened to that which gives life its value—if you possessed the true, joyous, fearless spirit of sacrifice, you would soon see how he would come up to you.—But I believe in you still, Hedvig.

(*He goes out by the passage door.* HEDVIG *wanders about the room for a time; she is on the point of going into the kitchen when a knock is heard at the garret door.* HEDVIG *goes over and opens it a little;* OLD EKDAL *comes out; she pushes the door to again.*)

EKDAL. H'm it's not much fun to take one's morning walk alone.

HEDVIG. Wouldn't you like to go shooting, grandfather?

EKDAL. It's not the weather for it to-day. It's so dark there, you can scarcely see where you're going.

HEDVIG. Do you never want to shoot anything besides the rabbits?

EKDAL. Do you think the rabbits aren't good enough?

HEDVIG. Yes, but what about the wild duck?

EKDAL. Ho-ho! are you afraid I shall shoot your wild duck? Never in the world. Never.

HEDVIG. No, I suppose you couldn't; they say it's very difficult to shoot wild ducks.

EKDAL. Couldn't! Should rather think I could.

HEDVIG. How would you set about it, grandfather?—I don't mean with my wild duck, but with others?

EKDAL. I should take care to shoot them in the breast, you know; that's the surest place. And then you must shoot against the feathers, you see—not the way of the feathers.

HEDVIG. Do they die then, grandfather?

EKDAL. Yes, they die right enough—when you shoot properly. Well, I must go and brush up a bit. H'm—understand—h'm.

(*Goes into his room.*)

(HEDVIG *waits a little, glances towards the sitting-room door, goes over to the book-case, stands on tip-toe, takes the double-barreled pistol down from the shelf, and looks at it. GINA, with brush and duster, comes from the sitting-room. HEDVIG hastily lays down the pistol, unobserved.*)

GINA. Don't stand raking amongst father's things, Hedvig.

HEDVIG (*goes away from the bookcase*). I was only going to tidy up a little.

GINA. You'd better go into the kitchen, and see if the coffee's keeping hot; I'll take his breakfast on a tray, when I go down to him.

(HEDVIG *goes out.* GINA *begins to sweep and clean up the studio. Presently the passage door is opened with hesitation, and* HIALMAR EKDAL *looks in. He has on his overcoat, but not his hat; he is unwashed, and his hair is disheveled and unkempt. His eyes are dull and heavy.*)

GINA (*standing with the brush in her hand, and looking at him*). Oh, there now, Ekdal—so you've come after all?

HIALMAR (*comes in and answers in a toneless voice*). I come—only to depart again immediately.

GINA. Yes, yes, I suppose so. But, Lord help us! what a sight you are!

HIALMAR. A sight?

GINA. And your nice winter coat too! Well, that's done for.

HEDVIG (*at the kitchen door*). Mother, hadn't I better——? (*Sees* HIALMAR, *gives a loud scream of joy, and runs to him.*) Oh, father, father!

HIALMAR (*turns away and makes a gesture of repulsion*). Away, away, away! (*To* GINA.) Keep her away from me, I say!

GINA (*in a low tone*). Go into the sitting-room, Hedvig.
(HEDVIG *does so without a word.*)

HIALMAR (*fussily pulls out the table-drawer*). I must have my books with me. Where are my books?

GINA. Which books?

HIALMAR. My scientific books, of course; the technical magazines I require for my invention.

GINA. (*searches in the bookcase*). Is it these here paper-covered ones?

HIALMAR. Yes, of course.

GINA (*lays a heap of magazines on the table*). Shan't I get Hedvig to cut them for you?

HIALMAR. I don't require to have them cut for me.
(*Short silence.*)

GINA. Then you're still set on leaving us, Ekdal?

HIALMAR (*rummaging amongst the books*). Yes, that is a matter of course, I should think.

GINA. Well, well.

HIALMAR (*vehemently*). How can I live here, to be stabbed to the heart every hour of the day?

GINA. God forgive you for thinking such vile things of me.

HIALMAR. Prove——!

GINA. I think it's you as has got to prove.

HIALMAR. After a past like yours? There are certain claims—I may almost call them claims of the ideal——

GINA. But what about grandfather? What's to become of him, poor dear?

HIALMAR. I know my duty; my helpless father will come with me. I am going out into the town to make arrangements—— H'm—(*hesitatingly*)—has any one found my hat on the stairs?

GINA. No. Have you lost your hat?

HIALMAR. Of course I had it on when I came in last night; there's no doubt about that; but I couldn't find it this morning.

GINA. Lord help us! where have you been to with those two ne'er-do-weels?

HIALMAR. Oh, don't bother me about trifles. Do you suppose I am in the mood to remember details?

GINA. If only you haven't caught cold, Ekdal——
(*Goes out into the kitchen.*)

HIALMAR (*talks to himself in a low tone of irritation, whilst he empties the table-drawer*). You're a scoundrel, Relling!—You're a low fellow!—Ah, you shameless tempter! —I wish I could get some one to stick a knife into you!

(*He lays some old letters on one side, finds the torn document of yesterday, takes it up and looks at the pieces; puts it down hurriedly as* GINA *enters.*)

GINA (*sets a tray with coffee, etc., on the table*). Here's a drop of something hot, if you'd fancy it. And there's some bread and butter and a snack of salt meat.

HIALMAR (*glancing at the tray*). Salt meat? Never under this roof! It's true I have not had a mouthful of solid food for nearly twenty-four hours; but no matter.—My memoranda! The commencement of my autobiography! What has become of my diary, and all my important papers? (*Opens the sitting-room door but draws back.*) She is there too!

GINA. Good Lord! the child must be somewhere!

HIALMAR. Come out.

(*He makes room,* HEDVIG *comes, scared, into the studio.*)

HIALMAR (*with his hand upon the door-handle, says to* GINA): In these, the last moments I spend in my former home, I wish to be spared from interlopers——
(*Goes into the room.*)

HEDVIG (*with a bound towards her mother, asks softly, trembling*). Does that mean me?

GINA. Stay out in the kitchen, Hedvig; or, no—you'd best go into your own room. (*Speaks to* HIALMAR *as she goes in to him.*) Wait a bit, Ekdal; don't rummage so in the drawers; I know where everything is.

HEDVIG (*stands a moment immovable, in terror and per-*

plexity, biting her lips to keep back the tears; then she clenches her hands convulsively, and says softly): The wild duck.

> *(She steals over and takes the pistol from the shelf, opens the garret door a little way, creeps in, and draws the door to after her.)*

> *(HIALMAR and GINA can be heard disputing in the sitting-room.)*

HIALMAR *(comes in with some manuscript books and old loose papers, which he lays upon the table)*. That portmanteau is of no use! There are a thousand and one things I must drag with me.

GINA *(following with the portmanteau)*. Why not leave all the rest for the present, and only take a shirt and a pair of woolen drawers with you?

HIALMAR. Whew!—all these exhausting preparations——!

> *(Pulls off his overcoat and throws it upon the sofa.)*

GINA. And there's the coffee getting cold.

HIALMAR. H'm.

> *(Drinks a mouthful without thinking of it, and then another.)*

GINA *(dusting the backs of the chairs)*. A nice job you'll have to find such another big garret for the rabbits.

HIALMAR. What! Am I to drag all those rabbits with me too?

GINA. You don't suppose grandfather can get on without his rabbits.

HIALMAR. He must just get used to doing without them. Have not I to sacrifice very much greater things than rabbits?

GINA *(dusting the bookcase)*. Shall I put the flute in the portmanteau for you?

HIALMAR. No. No flute for me. But give me the pistol!

GINA. Do you want to take the pigstol with you?

HIALMAR. Yes. My loaded pistol.

GINA (*searching for it*). It's gone. He must have taken it in with him.

HIALMAR. Is he in the garret?

GINA. Yes, of course he's in the garret.

HIALMAR. H'm—poor lonely old man.

(*He takes a piece of bread and butter, eats it, and finishes his cup of coffee.*)

GINA. If we hadn't have let that room, you could have moved in there.

HIALMAR. And continued to live under the same roof with——! Never,—never!

GINA. But couldn't you put up with the sitting-room for a day or two? You could have it all to yourself.

HIALMAR. Never within these walls!

GINA. Well then, down with Relling and Molvik.

HIALMAR. Don't mention those wretches' names to me! The very thought of them almost takes away my appetite.— Oh no, I must go out into the storm and the snow-drift,— go from house to house and seek shelter for my father and myself.

GINA. But you've got no hat, Ekdal! You've been and lost your hat, you know.

HIALMAR. Oh those two brutes, those slaves of all the vices! A hat must be procured. (*Takes another piece of bread and butter.*) Some arrangements must be made. For I have no mind to throw away my life, either.

(*Looks for something on the tray.*)

GINA. What are you looking for?

HIALMAR. Butter.

GINA. I'll get some at once. (*Goes out into the kitchen.*)

HIALMAR (*calls after her*). Oh it doesn't matter; dry bread is good enough for me.

GINA (*brings a dish of butter*). Look here; this is fresh churned.

(*She pours out another cup of coffee for him; he seats*

himself on the sofa, spreads more butter on the already buttered bread, and eats and drinks awhile in silence.)

HIALMAR. Could I, without being subject to intrusion—intrusion of any sort—could I live in the sitting-room there for a day or two?

GINA. Yes, to be sure you could, if you only would.

HIALMAR. For I see no possibility of getting all father's things out in such a hurry.

GINA. And, besides, you've surely got to tell him first as you don't mean to live with us others no more.

HIALMAR (*pushes away his coffee cup*). Yes, there is that too; I shall have to lay bare the whole tangled story to him—— I must turn matters over; I must have breathing-time; I cannot take all these burdens on my shoulders in a single day.

GINA. No, especially in such horrible weather as it is outside.

HIALMAR (*touching* WERLE's *letter*). I see that paper is still lying about here.

GINA. Yes, *I* haven't touched it.

HIALMAR. So far as I am concerned it is mere waste paper——

GINA. Well, *I* have certainly no notion of making any use of it.

HIALMAR. ——but we had better not let it get lost all the same;—in all the upset when I move, it might easily——

GINA. I'll take good care of it, Ekdal.

HIALMAR. The donation is in the first instance made to father, and it rests with him to accept or decline it.

GINA (*sighs*). Yes, poor old father——

HIALMAR. To make quite safe—— Where shall I find some gum?

GINA (*goes to the bookcase*). Here's the gum-pot.

HIALMAR. And a brush?

GINA. The brush is here too.

(*Brings him the things.*)

HIALMAR (*takes a pair of scissors*). Just a strip of paper at the back——(*Clips and gums.*) Far be it from me to lay hands upon what is not my own—and least of all upon what belongs to a destitute old man—and to—the other as well.— There now. Let it lie there for a time; and when it is dry, take it away. I wish never to see that document again. Never!

(GREGERS WERLE *enters from the passage.*)

GREGERS (*somewhat surprised*). What,—are you sitting here, Hialmar?

HIALMAR (*rises hurriedly*). I had sunk down from fatigue.

GREGERS. You have been having breakfast, I see.

HIALMAR. The body sometimes makes its claims felt too.

GREGERS. What have you decided to do?

HIALMAR. For a man like me, there is only one course possible. I am just putting my most important things together. But it takes time, you know.

GINA (*with a touch of impatience*). Am I to get the room ready for you, or am I to pack your portmanteau?

HIALMAR (*after a glance of annoyance at* GREGERS). Pack —and get the room ready!

GINA (*takes the portmanteau*). Very well; then I'll put in the shirt and the other things.

(*Goes into the sitting-room and draws the door to after her.*)

GREGERS (*after a short silence*). I never dreamed that this would be the end of it. Do you really feel it a necessity to leave house and home?

HIALMAR (*wanders about restlessly*). What would you have me do?—I am not fitted to bear unhappiness, Gregers. I must feel secure and at peace in my surroundings.

GREGERS. But can you not feel that here? Just try it. I should have thought you had firm ground to build upon now—if only you start afresh. And, remember, you have your invention to live for.

HIALMAR. Oh don't talk about my invention. It's perhaps still in the dim distance.

GREGERS. Indeed!

HIALMAR. Why, great heavens, what would you have me invent? Other people have invented almost everything already. It becomes more and more difficult every day——

GREGERS. And you have devoted so much labor to it.

HIALMAR. It was that blackguard Relling that urged me to it.

GREGERS. Relling?

HIALMAR. Yes, it was he that first made me realize my aptitude for making some notable discovery in photography.

GREGER. Aha—it was Relling!

HIALMAR. Oh, I have been so truly happy over it! Not so much for the sake of the invention itself, as because Hedvig believed in it—believed in it with a child's whole eagerness of faith.—At least, I have been fool enough to go and imagine that she believed in it.

GREGERS. Can you really think Hedvig has been false towards you?

HIALMAR. I can think anything now. It is Hedvig that stands in my way. She will blot out the sunlight from my whole life.

GREGERS. Hedvig! Is it Hedvig you are talking of? How should she blot out your sunlight?

HIALMAR (*without answering*). How unutterably I have loved that child! How unutterably happy I have felt every time I came home to my humble room, and she flew to meet me, with her sweet little blinking eyes. Oh, confiding fool that I have been! I loved her unutterably;—and I yielded myself up to the dream, the delusion, that she loved me unutterably in return.

GREGERS. Do you call that a delusion?

HIALMAR. How should I know? I can get nothing out of Gina; and besides, she is totally blind to the ideal side of these complications. But to you I feel impelled to open my mind, Gregers. I cannot shake off this frightful doubt—perhaps Hedvig has never really and honestly loved me.

GREGERS. What would you say if she were to give you a proof of her love? (*Listens.*) What's that? I thought I heard the wild duck——

HIALMAR. It's the wild duck quacking. Father's in the garret.

GREGERS. Is he? (*His face lights up with joy.*) I say you may yet have proof that your poor misunderstood Hedvig loves you!

HIALMAR. Oh, what proof can she give me? I dare not believe in any assurance from that quarter.

GREGERS. Hedvig does not know what deceit means.

HIALMAR. Oh Gregers, that is just what I cannot be sure of. Who knows what Gina and that Mrs. Sörby may many a time have sat here whispering and tattling about? And Hedvig usually has her ears open, I can tell you. Perhaps the deed of gift was not such a surprise to her, after all. In fact, I'm not sure but that I noticed something of the sort.

GREGERS. What spirit is this that has taken possession of you?

HIALMAR. I have had my eyes opened. Just you notice; —you'll see, the deed of gift is only a beginning. Mrs. Sörby has always been a good deal taken up with Hedvig; and now she has the power to do whatever she likes for the child. They can take her from me whenever they please.

GREGERS. Hedvig will never, never leave you.

HIALMAR. Don't be so sure of that. If only they beckon to her and throw out a golden bait——! And oh! I have loved her so unspeakably! I would have counted it my highest happiness to take her tenderly by the hand and lead her, as one leads a timid child through a great dark empty room!—I am cruelly certain now that the poor photographer in his humble attic has never really and truly been anything to her. She has only cunningly contrived to keep on a good footing with him until the time came.

GREGERS. You don't believe that yourself, Hialmar.

HIALMAR. That is just the terrible part of it—I don't know what to believe,—I never can know it. But can you really doubt that it must be as I say? Ho-ho, you have far too much faith in the claim of the ideal, my good Gregers! If those others came, with the glamor of wealth about them, and called to the child:—"Leave him: come to us: here life awaits you——!"

GREGERS (*quickly*). Well, what then?

HIALMAR. If I then asked her: Hedvig, are you willing to renounce that life for me? (*Laughs scornfully.*) No thank you! You would soon hear what answer I should get.

(*A pistol shot is heard from within the garret.*)

GREGERS (*loudly and joyfully*). Hialmar!

HIALMAR. There now; he must needs go shooting too.

GINA (*comes in*). Oh Ekdal, I can hear grandfather blazing away in the garret by hisself.

HIALMAR. I'll look in——

GREGERS (*eagerly, with emotion*). Wait a moment! Do you know what that was?

HIALMAR. Yes, of course I know.

GREGERS. No you don't know. But *I* do. That was the proof!

HIALMAR. What proof?

GREGERS. It was a child's free-will offering. She has got your father to shoot the wild duck.

HIALMAR. To shoot the wild duck!

GINA. Oh, think of that——!

HIALMAR. What was that for?

GREGERS. She wanted to sacrifice to you her most cherished possession; for then she thought you would surely come to love her again.

HIALMAR (*tenderly, with emotion*). Oh, poor child!

GINA. What things she does think of!

GREGERS. She only wanted your love again, Hialmar. She could not live without it.

GINA (*struggling with her tears*). There, you can see for yourself, Ekdal.

HIALMAR. Gina, where is she?

GINA (*sniffs*). Poor dear, she's sitting out in the kitchen, I dare say.

HIALMAR (*goes over, tears open the kitchen door, and says*): Hedvig, come, come in to me! (*Looks around.*) No, she's not here.

GINA. Then she must be in her own little room.

HIALMAR (*without*). No, she's not here either. (*Comes in.*) She must have gone out.

GINA. Yes, you wouldn't have her anywheres in the house.

HIALMAR. Oh, if she would only come home quickly, so that I can tell her—— Everything will come right now, Gregers; now I believe we can begin life afresh.

GREGERS (*quietly*). I knew it; I knew the child would make amends.

(OLD EKDAL *appears at the door of his room; he is in full uniform, and is busy buckling on his sword.*)

HIALMAR (*astonished*). Father! Are you there?

GINA. Have you been firing in your room?

EKDAL (*resentfully, approaching*). So you go shooting alone, do you, Hialmar?

HIALMAR (*excited and confused*). Then it wasn't you that fired that shot in the garret?

EKDAL. Me that fired? H'm.

GREGERS (*calls out to* HIALMAR). She has shot the wild duck herself!

HIALMAR. What can it mean? (*Hastens to the garret door, tears it aside, looks in and calls loudly*): Hedvig!

GINA (*runs to the door*). Good God, what's that!

HIALMAR (*goes in*). She's lying on the floor!

GREGERS. Hedvig! lying on the floor!

(*Goes in to* HIALMAR.)

GINA (*at the same time*). Hedvig! (*Inside the garret.*) No, no, no!

EKDAL. Ho-ho! does she go shooting, too, now?

(HIALMAR, GINA *and* GREGERS *carry* HEDVIG *into the studio; in her dangling right hand she holds the pistol fast clasped in her fingers.*)

HIALMAR (*distracted*). The pistol has gone off. She has wounded herself. Call for help! Help!

GINA (*runs into the passage and calls down*). Relling! Relling! Doctor Relling; come up as quick as you can!

(HIALMAR *and* GREGERS *lay* HEDVIG *down on the sofa.*)

EKDAL (*quietly*). The woods avenge themselves.

HIALMAR (*on his knees beside* HEDVIG). She'll soon come to now. She's coming to——; yes, yes, yes.

GINA (*who has come in again*). Where has she hurt herself? I can't see anything——

(RELLING *comes hurriedly, and immediately after him* MOLVIK; *the latter without his waistcoat and necktie, and with his coat open.*)

RELLING. What's the matter here?

GINA. They say Hedvig has shot herself.

HIALMAR. Come and help us!

RELLING. Shot herself!

(*He pushes the table aside and begins to examine her.*)

HIALMAR (*kneeling and looking anxiously up at him*). It can't be dangerous? Speak, Relling! She is scarcely bleeding at all. It can't be dangerous?

RELLING. How did it happen?

HIALMAR. Oh, we don't know——

GINA. She wanted to shoot the wild duck.

RELLING. The wild duck?

HIALMAR. The pistol must have gone off.

RELLING. H'm. Indeed.

EKDAL. The wood avenge themselves. But I'm not afraid, all the same.

(*Goes into the garret and closes the door after him.*)

HIALMAR. Well, Relling,—why don't you say something?

RELLING. The ball has entered the breast.

HIALMAR. Yes, but she's coming to!

RELLING. Surely you can see that Hedvig is dead.

GINA (*bursts into tears*). Oh my child, my child——

GREGERS (*huskily*). In the depths of the sea——

HIALMAR (*jumps up*). No, no, she must live! Oh, for God's sake, Relling—only a moment—only just till I can tell her how unspeakably I loved her all the time!

RELLING. The bullet has gone through her heart. Internal hemorrhage. Death must have been instantaneous.

HIALMAR. And I! I hunted her from me like an animal! And she crept terrified into the garret and died for love of me! (*Sobbing.*) I can never atone to her! I can never tell her——! (*Clenches his hands and cries, upwards.*) O thou above——! If thou be indeed! Why hast thou done this thing to me?

GINA. Hush, hush, you mustn't go on that awful way. We had no right to keep her, I suppose.

MOLVIK. The child is not dead, but sleepeth.

RELLING. Bosh.

HIALMAR (*becomes calm, goes over to the sofa, folds his arms, and looks at* HEDVIG). There she lies so stiff and still.

RELLING (*tries to loosen the pistol*). She's holding it so tight, so tight.

GINA. No, no, Relling, don't break her fingers; let the pigstol be.

HIALMAR. She shall take it with her.

GINA. Yes, let her. But the child mustn't lie here for a show. She shall go to her own room, so she shall. Help me, Ekdal.

(HIALMAR *and* GINA *take* HEDVIG *between them.*)

HIALMAR (*as they are carrying her*). Oh, Gina, Gina, can you survive this!

GINA. We must help each other to bear it. For now at least she belongs to both of us.

MOLVIK (*stretches out his arms and mumbles*). Blessed be the Lord; to earth thou shalt return; to earth thou shalt return——

RELLING (*whispers*). Hold your tongue, you fool; you're drunk.

> (HIALMAR *and* GINA *carry the body out through the kitchen door.* RELLING *shuts it after them.* MOLVIK *slinks out into the passage.*)

RELLING (*goes over to* GREGERS *and says*): No one shall ever convince me that the pistol went off by accident.

GREGERS (*who has stood terrified, with convulsive twitchings*). Who can say how the dreadful thing happened?

RELLING. The powder has burnt the body of her dress. She must have pressed the pistol right against her breast and fired.

GREGERS. Hedvig has not died in vain. Did you not see how sorrow set free what is noble in him?

RELLING. Most people are ennobled by the actual presence of death. But how long do you suppose this nobility will last in him?

GREGERS. Why should it not endure and increase throughout his life?

RELLING. Before a year is over, little Hedvig will be nothing to him but a pretty theme for declamation.

GREGERS. How dare you say that of Hialmar Ekdal?

RELLING. We will talk of this again, when the grass has first withered on her grave. Then you'll hear him spouting about "the child too early torn from her father's heart;" then you'll see him steep himself in a syrup of sentiment and self-admiration and self-pity. Just you wait!

GREGERS. If you are right and I am wrong, then life is not worth living.

RELLING. Oh, life would be quite tolerable, after all, if only we could be rid of the confounded duns that keep on pestering us, in our poverty, with the claim of the ideal.

GREGERS (*looking straight before him*). In that case, I am glad that my destiny is what it is.

RELLING. May I inquire,—what is your destiny?

GREGERS (*going*). To be the thirteenth at table.

RELLING. The devil it is.

HEDDA GABLER
(1890)

PLAY IN THREE ACTS

CAST OF CHARACTERS

GEORGE TESMAN.[1]

HEDDA TESMAN, *his wife.*

MISS JULIANA TESMAN, *his aunt.*

MRS. ELVSTED.

JUDGE[2] BRACK.

EILERT LÖVBORG.

BERTA, *servant at the Tesmans*.

The scene of the action is Tesman's villa, in the west end of Christiania.

[1] Tesman, whose Christian name in the original is "Jörgen," is described as "stipendiat i kulturhistorie"—that is to say, the holder of a scholarship for purposes of research into the History of Civilization.
[2] In the original "Assessor."

ACT I

(*A spacious, handsome, and tastefully furnished drawing-room, decorated in dark colors. In the back, a wide doorway with curtains drawn back, leading into a smaller room decorated in the same style as the drawing-room. In the right-hand wall of the front room, a folding door leading out to the hall. In the opposite wall, on the left, a glass door, also with curtains drawn back. Through the panes can be seen part of a veranda outside, and trees covered with autumn foliage. An oval table, with a cover on it, and surrounded by chairs, stands well forward. In front, by the wall on the right, a wide stove of dark porcelain, a high-backed arm-chair, a cushioned foot-rest, and two foot-stools. A settee, with a small round table in front of it, fills the upper right-hand corner. In front, on the left, a little way from the wall, a sofa. Further back than the glass door, a piano. On either side of the doorway at the back a whatnot with terra-cotta and majolica ornaments.—Against the back wall of the inner room a sofa, with a table, and one or two chairs. Over the sofa hangs the portrait of a handsome elderly man in a General's uniform. Over the table a hanging lamp, with an opal glass shade.—A number of bouquets are arranged about the drawing-room, in vases and glasses. Others lie upon the tables. The floors in both rooms are covered with thick carpets.—Morning light. The sun shines in through the glass door.*)

MISS JULIANA TESMAN, *with her bonnet on and carrying a parasol, comes in from the hall, followed by* BERTA, *who carries a bouquet wrapped in paper.* MISS TESMAN *is a comely and pleasant-looking lady of about sixty-five. She is nicely but simply dressed in a gray walking-costume.* BERTA *is a middle-aged woman of plain and rather countrified appearance.*)

MISS TESMAN (*stops close to the door, listens, and says softly*). Upon my word, I don't believe they are stirring yet!

BERTA (*also softly*). I told you so, Miss. Remember how late the steamboat got in last night. And then, when they got home!—good Lord, what a lot the young mistress had to unpack before she could get to bed.

MISS TESMAN. Well, well—let them have their sleep out. But let us see that they get a good breath of the fresh morning air when they do appear. (*She goes to the glass door and throws it open.*)

BERTA (*beside the table, at a loss what to do with the bouquet in her hand*). I declare there isn't a bit of room left. I think I'll put it down here, Miss. (*She places it on the piano.*)

MISS TESMAN. So you've got a new mistress now, my dear Berta. Heaven knows it was a wrench to me to part with you.

BERTA (*on the point of weeping*). And do you think it wasn't hard for me too, Miss? After all the blessed years I've been with you and Miss Rina.[1]

MISS TESMAN. We must make the best of it, Berta. There was nothing else to be done. George can't do without you, you see—he absolutely can't. He has had you to look after him ever since he was a little boy.

BERTA. Ah but, Miss Julia, I can't help thinking of Miss Rina lying helpless at home there, poor thing. And with only that new girl too! She'll never learn to take proper care of an invalid.

MISS TESMAN. Oh, I shall manage to train her. And of course, you know, I shall take most of it upon myself. You needn't be uneasy about my poor sister, my dear Berta.

[1] Pronounce *Reena.*

BERTA. Well, but there's another thing, Miss. I'm so mortally afraid I shan't be able to suit the young mistress.

MISS TESMAN. Oh well—just at first there may be one or two things——

BERTA. Most like she'll be terrible grand in her ways.

MISS TESMAN. Well, you can't wonder at that—General Gabler's daughter! Think of the sort of life she was accustomed to in her father's time. Don't you remember how we used to see her riding down the road along with the General? In that long black habit—and with feathers in her hat?

BERTA. Yes, indeed—I remember well enough——! But good Lord, I should never have dreamt in those days that she and Master George would make a match of it.

MISS TESMAN. Nor I.—But, by-the-bye, Berta—while I think of it: in future you mustn't say Master George. You must say Dr. Tesman.

BERTA. Yes, the young mistress spoke of that too—last night—the moment they set foot in the house. Is it true then, Miss?

MISS TESMAN. Yes, indeed it is. Only think, Berta—some foreign university has made him a doctor—while he has been abroad, you understand. I hadn't heard a word about it, until he told me himself upon the pier.

BERTA. Well, well, he's clever enough for anything, he is. But I didn't think he'd have gone in for doctoring people too.

MISS TESMAN. No, no, it's not that sort of doctor he is. (*Nods significantly.*) But let me tell you, we may have to call him something still grander before long.

BERTA. You don't say so! What can that be, Miss?

MISS TESMAN (*smiling*). H'm—wouldn't you like to know! (*With emotion.*) Ah, dear, dear—if my poor brother could only look up from his grave now, and see what his little boy has grown into! (*Looks around.*) But bless me, Berta—why have you done this? Taken the chintz covers off all the furniture?

BERTA. The mistress told me to. She can't abide covers on the chairs, she says.

MISS TESMAN. Are they going to make this their every-day sitting-room then?

BERTA. Yes, that's what I understood—from the mistress. Master George—the doctor—he said nothing.

(GEORGE TESMAN *comes from the right into the inner room, humming to himself, and carrying an un-strapped empty portmanteau. He is a middle-sized, young-looking man of thirty-three, rather stout, with a round, open, cheerful face, fair hair and beard. He wears spectacles, and is somewhat carelessly dressed in comfortable indoor clothes.*)

MISS TESMAN. Good morning, good morning, George.

TESMAN (*in the doorway between the rooms*). Aunt Julia! Dear Aunt Julia! (*Goes up to her and shakes hands warmly.*) Come all this way—so early! Eh?

MISS TESMAN. Why, of course I had to come and see how you were getting on.

TESMAN. In spite of your having had no proper night's rest?

MISS TESMAN. Oh, that makes no difference to me.

TESMAN. Well, I suppose you got home all right from the pier? Eh?

MISS TESMAN. Yes, quite safely, thank goodness. Judge Brack was good enough to see me right to my door.

TESMAN. We were so sorry we couldn't give you a seat in the carriage. But you saw what a pile of boxes Hedda had to bring with her.

MISS TESMAN. Yes, she had certainly plenty of boxes.

BERTA (*to Tesman*). Shall I go in and see if there's any-thing I can do for the mistress?

TESMAN. No, thank you, Berta—you needn't. She said she would ring if she wanted anything.

BERTA (*going towards the right*). Very well.

TESMAN. But look here—take this portmanteau with you.

BERTA (*taking it*). I'll put it in the attic. (*She goes out by the hall door.*)

TESMAN. Fancy, Auntie—I had the whole of that portmanteau chock full of copies of documents. You wouldn't believe how much I have picked up from all the archives I have been examining—curious old details that no one has had any idea of——

MISS TESMAN. Yes, you don't seem to have wasted your time on your wedding trip, George.

TESMAN. No, that I haven't. But do take off your bonnet, Auntie. Look here! Let me untie the strings—eh?

MISS TESMAN (*while he does so*). Well, well—this is just as if you were still at home with us.

TESMAN (*with the bonnet in his hand, looks at it from all sides*). Why, what a gorgeous bonnet you've been investing in!

MISS TESMAN. I bought it on Hedda's account.

TESMAN. On Hedda's account? Eh?

MISS TESMAN. Yes, so that Hedda needn't be ashamed of me if we happened to go out together.

TESMAN (*patting her cheek*). You always think of everything, Aunt Julia. (*Lays the bonnet on a chair beside the table.*) And now, look here—suppose we sit comfortably on the sofa and have a little chat, till Hedda comes. (*They seat themselves. She places her parasol in the corner of the sofa.*)

MISS TESMAN (*takes both his hands and looks at him*). What a delight it is to have you again, as large as life, before my very eyes, George! My George—my poor brother's own boy!

TESMAN. And it's a delight for me, too, to see you again, Aunt Julia! You, who have been father and mother in one to me.

MISS TESMAN. Oh, yes, I know you will always keep a place in your heart for your old aunts.

TESMAN. And what about Aunt Rina? No improvement —eh?

MISS TESMAN. Oh, no—we can scarcely look for any improvement in her case, poor thing. There she lies, helpless, as she has lain for all these years. But heaven grant I may not lose her yet awhile! For if I did, I don't know what I should make of my life, George—especially now that I haven't you to look after any more.

TESMAN (*patting her back*). There, there, there——!

MISS TESMAN (*suddenly changing her tone*). And to think that here are you a married man, George!—And that you should be the one to carry off Hedda Gabler—the beautiful Hedda Gabler! Only think of it—she, that was so beset with admirers!

TESMAN (*hums a little and smiles complacently*). Yes, I fancy I have several good friends about town who would like to stand in my shoes—eh?

MISS TESMAN. And then this fine long wedding-tour you have had! More than five—nearly six months——

TESMAN. Well, for me it has been a sort of tour of research as well. I have had to do so much grubbing among old records—and to read no end of books too, Auntie.

MISS TESMAN. Oh, yes, I suppose so. (*More confidentially, and lowering her voice a little.*) But listen now, George—have you nothing—nothing special to tell me?

TESMAN. As to our journey?

MISS TESMAN. Yes.

TESMAN. No, I don't know of anything except what I have told you in my letters. I had a doctor's degree conferred on me—but that I told you yesterday.

MISS TESMAN. Yes, yes, you did. But what I mean is— haven't you any—any—expectations——?

TESMAN. Expectations?

MISS TESMAN. Why, you know, George—I'm your old auntie!

TESMAN. Why, of course I have expectations.

MISS TESMAN. Ah!

TESMAN. I have every expectation of being a professor one of these days.

MISS TESMAN. Oh, yes, a professor——

TESMAN. Indeed, I may say I am certain of it. But my dear Auntie—you know all about that already!

MISS TESMAN (*laughing to herself*). Yes, of course I do. You are quite right there. (*Changing the subject.*) But we were talking about your journey. It must have cost a great deal of money, George?

TESMAN. Well, you see—my handsome traveling-scholarship went a good way.

MISS TESMAN. But I can't understand how you can have made it go far enough for two.

TESMAN. No, that's not so easy to understand—eh?

MISS TESMAN. And especially traveling with a lady—they tell me that makes it ever so much more expensive.

TESMAN. Yes, of course—it makes it a little more expensive. But Hedda had to have this trip, Auntie! She really had to. Nothing else would have done.

MISS TESMAN. No, no, I suppose not. A wedding-tour seems to be quite indispensable nowadays.——But tell me now—have you gone thoroughly over the house yet?

TESMAN. Yes, you may be sure I have. I have been afoot ever since daylight.

MISS TESMAN. And what do you think of it all?

TESMAN. I'm delighted! Quite delighted! Only I can't think what we are to do with the two empty rooms between this inner parlor and Hedda's bedroom.

MISS TESMAN (*laughing*). Oh, my dear George, I daresay you may find some use for them—in the course of time.

TESMAN. Why, of course you are quite right, Aunt Julia! You mean as my library increases—eh?

MISS TESMAN. Yes, quite so, my dear boy. It was your library I was thinking of.

TESMAN. I am specially pleased on Hedda's account.

Often and often, before we were engaged, she said that she would never care to live anywhere but in Secretary Falk's villa.[1]

Miss Tesman. Yes, it was lucky that this very house should come into the market, just after you had started.

Tesman. Yes, Aunt Julia, the luck was on our side, wasn't it—eh?

Miss Tesman. But the expense, my dear George! You will find it very expensive, all this.

Tesman (*looks at her, a little cast down*). Yes, I suppose I shall, Auntie!

Miss Tesman. Oh, frightfully!

Tesman. How much do you think? In round numbers? —Eh?

Miss Tesman. Oh, I can't even guess until all the accounts come in.

Tesman. Well, fortunately, Judge Brack has secured the most favorable terms for me,—so he said in a letter to Hedda.

Miss Tesman. Yes, don't be uneasy, my dear boy.—Besides, I have given security for the furniture and all the carpets.

Tesman. Security? You? My dear Aunt Julia—what sort of security could you give?

Miss Tesman. I have given a mortgage on our annuity.

Tesman (*jumps up*). What! On your—and Aunt Rina's annuity!

Miss Tesman. Yes, I knew of no other plan, you see.

Tesman (*placing himself before her*). Have you gone out of your senses, Auntie! Your annuity—it's all that you and Aunt Rina have to live upon.

Miss Tesman. Well, well, don't get so excited about it. It's only a matter of form you know—Judge Brack assured me of that. It was he that was kind enough to arrange the whole affair for me. A mere matter of form, he said.

---

[1] In the original, "Statsradinde Falks villa"—showing that it had belonged to the widow of a cabinet minister.

TESMAN. Yes, that may be all very well. But nevertheless——

MISS TESMAN. You will have your own salary to depend upon now. And, good heavens, even if we did have to pay up a little——! To eke things out a bit at the start——! Why, it would be nothing but a pleasure to us.

TESMAN. Oh, Auntie—will you never be tired of making sacrifices for me!

MISS TESMAN (*rises and lays her hands on his shoulders*). Have I any other happiness in this world except to smooth your way for you, my dear boy? You, who have had neither father nor mother to depend on. And now we have reached the goal, George! Things have looked black enough for us, sometimes; but, thank heaven, now you have nothing to fear.

TESMAN. Yes, it is really marvelous how everything has turned out for the best.

MISS TESMAN. And the people who opposed you—who wanted to bar the way for you—now you have them at your feet. They have fallen, George. Your most dangerous rival —his fall was the worst.—And now he has to lie on the bed he has made for himself—poor misguided creature.

TESMAN. Have you heard anything of Eilert? Since I went away, I mean.

MISS TESMAN. Only that he is said to have published a new book.

TESMAN. What! Eilert Lövborg! Recently—eh?

MISS TESMAN. Yes, so they say. Heaven knows whether it can be worth anything! Ah, when your new book appears —that will be another story, George! What is it to be about?

TESMAN. It will deal with the domestic industries of Brabant during the Middle Ages.

MISS TESMAN. Fancy—to be able to write on such a subject as that!

TESMAN. However, it may be some time before the book is ready. I have all these collections to arrange first, you see.

MISS TESMAN. Yes, collecting and arranging—no one can

beat you at that. There you are my poor brother's own son.

TESMAN. I am looking forward eagerly to setting to work at it; especially now that I have my own delightful home to work in.

MISS TESMAN. And, most of all, now that you have got the wife of your heart, my dear George.

TESMAN (*embracing her*). Oh, yes, yes, Aunt Julia. Hedda—she is the best part of it all! (*Looks towards the doorway.*) I believe I hear her coming—eh?

(HEDDA *enters from the left through the inner room. She is a woman of nine-and-twenty. Her face and figure show refinement and distinction. Her complexion is pale and opaque. Her steel-gray eyes express a cold, unruffled repose. Her hair is of an agreeable medium brown, but not particularly abundant. She is dressed in a tasteful, somewhat loose-fitting morning gown.*)

MISS TESMAN (*going to meet* HEDDA). Good morning, my dear Hedda! Good morning, and a hearty welcome.

HEDDA (*holds out her hand*). Good morning, dear Miss Tesman! So early a call! That is kind of you.

MISS TESMAN (*with some embarrassment*). Well—has the bride slept well in her new home?

HEDDA. Oh yes, thanks. Passably.

TESMAN (*laughing*). Passably! Come, that's good, Hedda! You were sleeping like a stone when I got up.

HEDDA. Fortunately. Of course one has always to accustom one's self to new surroundings, Miss Tesman—little by little. (*Looking towards the left.*) Oh—there the servant has gone and opened the veranda door, and let in a whole flood of sunshine.

MISS TESMAN (*going towards the door*). Well, then, we will shut it.

HEDDA. No, no, not that! Tesman, please draw the curtains. That will give a softer light.

TESMAN (*at the door*). All right—all right. There now, Hedda, now you have both shade and fresh air.

HEDDA. Yes, fresh air we certainly must have, with all these stacks of flowers—— But—won't you sit down, Miss Tesman?

MISS TESMAN. No, thank you. Now that I have seen that everything is all right here—thank heaven!—I must be getting home again. My sister is lying longing for me, poor thing.

TESMAN. Give her my very best love, Auntie; and say I shall look in and see her later in the day.

MISS TESMAN. Yes, yes, I'll be sure to tell her. But by-the-bye, George (*feeling in her dress pocket*)—I had almost forgotten—I have something for you here.

TESMAN. What is it, Auntie? Eh?

MISS TESMAN (*produces a flat parcel wrapped in newspaper and hands it to him*). Look here, my dear boy.

TESMAN (*opening the parcel*). Well, I declare!—Have you really saved them for me, Aunt Julia! Hedda! isn't this touching—eh?

HEDDA (*beside the whatnot on the right*). Well, what is it?

TESMAN. My old morning-shoes! My slippers.

HEDDA. Indeed. I remember you often spoke of them while we were abroad.

TESMAN. Yes, I missed them terribly. (*Goes up to her.*) Now you shall see them, Hedda!

HEDDA (*going towards the stove*). Thanks, I really don't care about it.

TESMAN (*following her*). Only think—ill as she was, Aunt Rina embroidered these for me. Oh you can't think how many associations cling to them.

HEDDA (*at the table*). Scarcely for me.

MISS TESMAN. Of course not for Hedda, George.

TESMAN. Well, but now that she belongs to the family, I thought——

HEDDA (*interrupting*). We shall never get on with this servant, Tesman.

MISS TESMAN. Not get on with Berta?

TESMAN. Why, dear, what puts that in your head? Eh?

HEDDA (*pointing*). Look there! She has left her old bonnet lying about on a chair.

TESMAN (*in consternation, drops the slippers on the floor.*) Why, Hedda——

HEDDA. Just fancy, if any one should come in and see it!

TESMAN. But Hedda—that's Aunt Julia's bonnet.

HEDDA. Is it?

MISS TESMAN (*taking up the bonnet.*) Yes, indeed it's mine. And, what's more, it's not old, Madam Hedda.

HEDDA. I really did not look closely at it, Miss Tesman.

MISS TESMAN (*trying on the bonnet*). Let me tell you it's the first time I have worn it—the very first time.

TESMAN. And a very nice bonnet it is too—quite a beauty!

MISS TESMAN. Oh, it's no such great things, George. (*Looks around her.*) My parasol——? Ah, here. (*Takes it.*) For this is mine too (*mutters*)—not Berta's.

TESMAN. A new bonnet and a new parasol! Only think, Hedda!

HEDDA. Very handsome indeed.

TESMAN. Yes, isn't it? Eh? But Auntie, take a good look at Hedda before you go! See how handsome she is!

MISS TESMAN. Oh, my dear boy, there's nothing new in that. Hedda was always lovely. (*She nods and goes towards the right.*)

TESMAN (*following*). Yes, but have you noticed what splendid condition she is in? How she has filled out on the journey?

HEDDA (*crossing the room*). Oh, do be quiet——!

MISS TESMAN (*who has stopped and turned*). Filled out?

TESMAN. Of course you don't notice it so much now that she has that dress on. But I, who can see——

HEDDA (*at the glass door, impatiently.*) Oh, you can't see anything.

TESMAN. It must be the mountain air in the Tyrol——

HEDDA (*curtly, interrupting.*) I am exactly as I was when I started.

TESMAN. So you insist; but I'm quite certain you are not. Don't you agree with me, Auntie?

MISS TESMAN (*who has been gazing at her with folded hands.*) Hedda is lovely—lovely—lovely. (*Goes up to her, takes her head between both hands, draws it downwards, and kisses her hair.*) God bless and preserve Hedda Tesman— for George's sake.

HEDDA (*gently freeing herself*). Oh—! Let me go.

MISS TESMAN (*in quiet emotion*). I shall not let a day pass without coming to see you.

TESMAN. No, you won't, will you, Auntie? Eh?

MISS TESMAN. Good-bye—good-bye!

(*She goes out by the hall door.* TESMAN *accompanies her. The door remains half open.* TESMAN *can be heard repeating his message to Aunt Rina and his thanks for the slippers.*)

(*In the meantime,* HEDDA *walks about the room, raising her arms and clenching her hands as if in desperation. Then she flings back the curtains from the glass door, and stands there looking out.*)

(*Presently* TESMAN *returns and closes the door behind him.*)

TESMAN (*picks up the slippers from the floor*). What are you looking at, Hedda?

HEDDA (*once more calm and mistress of herself*). I am only looking at the leaves. They are so yellow—so withered.

TESMAN (*wraps up the slippers and lays them on the table*). Well, you see, we are well into September now.

HEDDA (*again restless*). Yes, to think of it!—Already in —in September.

TESMAN. Don't you think Aunt Julia's manner was strange, dear? Almost solemn? Can you imagine what was the matter with her? Eh?

HEDDA. I scarcely know her, you see. Is she not often like that?

TESMAN. No, not as she was to-day.

HEDDA (*leaving the glass door*). Do you think she was annoyed about the bonnet?

TESMAN. Oh, scarcely at all. Perhaps a little, just at the moment——

HEDDA. But what an idea, to pitch her bonnet about in the drawing-room! No one does that sort of thing.

TESMAN. Well, you may be sure Aunt Julia won't do it again.

HEDDA. In any case, I shall manage to make my peace with her.

TESMAN. Yes, my dear, good Hedda, if you only would.

HEDDA. When you call this afternoon, you might invite her to spend the evening here.

TESMAN. Yes, that I will. And there's one thing more you could do that would delight her heart.

HEDDA. What is it?

TESMAN. If you could only prevail on yourself to say *du*[1] to her. For my sake, Hedda? Eh?

HEDDA. No, no, Tesman—you really mustn't ask that of me. I have told you so already. I shall try to call her "Aunt"; and you must be satisfied with that.

TESMAN. Well, well. Only I think now that you belong to the family, you——

HEDDA. H'm—I can't in the least see why——

(*She goes up towards the middle doorway.*)

TESMAN (*after a pause*). Is there anything the matter with you, Hedda? Eh?

[1] Du = thou; Tesman means, "If you could persuade yourself to *tutoyer* her."

HEDDA. I'm only looking at my old piano. It doesn't go at all well with all the other things.

TESMAN. The first time I draw my salary, we'll see about exchanging it.

HEDDA. No, no—no exchanging. I don't want to part with it. Suppose we put it there in the inner room, and then get another here in its place. When it's convenient, I mean.

TESMAN (*a little taken aback*). Yes—of course we could do that.

HEDDA (*takes up the bouquet from the piano*). These flowers were not here last night when we arrived.

TESMAN. Aunt Julia must have brought them for you.

HEDDA (*examining the bouquet*). A visiting-card. (*Takes it out and reads:*) "Shall return later in the day." Can you guess whose card it is?

TESMAN. No. Whose? Eh?

HEDDA. The name is "Mrs. Elvsted."

TESMAN. Is it really? Sheriff Elvsted's wife? Miss Rysing that was.

HEDDA. Exactly. The girl with the irritating hair, that she was always showing off. An old flame of yours I've been told.

TESMAN (*laughing*). Oh, that didn't last long; and it was before I knew you, Hedda. But fancy her being in town!

HEDDA. It's odd that she should call upon us. I have scarcely seen her since we left school.

TESMAN. I haven't seen her either for—heaven knows how long. I wonder how she can endure to live in such an out-of-the-way hole—eh?

HEDDA (*after a moment's thought says suddenly*). Tell me, Tesman—isn't it somewhere near there that he—that—Eilert Lövborg is living?

TESMAN. Yes, he is somewhere in that part of the country.

(BERTA *enters by the hall door.*)

BERTA. That lady, ma'am, that brought some flowers a little while ago, is here again. (*Pointing.*) The flowers you have in your hand, ma'am.

HEDDA. Ah, is she? Well, please show her in.

(BERTA *opens the door for* MRS. ELVSTED, *and goes out herself.*—MRS. ELVSTED *is a woman of fragile figure, with pretty, soft features. Her eyes are light blue, large, round, and somewhat prominent, with a startled, inquiring expression. Her hair is remarkably light, almost flaxen, and unusually abundant and wavy. She is a couple of years younger than* HEDDA. *She wears a dark visiting dress, tasteful, but not quite in the latest fashion.*)

HEDDA (*receives her warmly*). How do you do, my dear Mrs. Elvsted? It's delightful to see you again.

MRS. ELVSTED (*nervously, struggling for self-control*). Yes, it's a very long time since we met.

TESMAN (*gives her his hand*). And we too—eh?

HEDDA. Thanks for your lovely flowers——

MRS. ELVSTED. Oh, not at all—— I would have come straight here yesterday afternoon; but I heard that you were away——

TESMAN. Have you just come to town? Eh?

MRS. ELVSTED. I arrived yesterday, about midday. Oh, I was quite in despair when I heard that you were not at home.

HEDDA. In despair! How so?

TESMAN. Why, my dear Mrs. Rysing—I mean Mrs. Elvsted——

HEDDA. I hope that you are not in any trouble?

MRS. ELVSTED. Yes, I am. And I don't know another living creature here that I can turn to.

HEDDA (*laying the bouquet on the table*). Come—let us sit here on the sofa——

MRS. ELVSTED. Oh, I am too restless to sit down.

HEDDA. Oh no, you're not. Come here. (*She draws* MRS.
ELVSTED *down upon the sofa and sits at her side.*)

TESMAN. Well? What is it, Mrs. Elvsted?

HEDDA. Has anything particular happened to you at
home?

MRS. ELVSTED. Yes—and no. Oh—I am so anxious you
should not misunderstand me——

HEDDA. Then your best plan is to tell us the whole story,
Mrs. Elvsted.

TESMAN. I suppose that's what you have come for—eh?

MRS. ELVSTED. Yes, yes—of course it is. Well then, I must
tell you—if you don't already know—that Eilert Lövborg is
in town, too.

HEDDA. Lövborg——!

TESMAN. What! Has Eilert Lövborg come back? Fancy
that, Hedda!

HEDDA. Well, well—I hear it.

MRS. ELVSTED. He has been here a week already. Just
fancy—a whole week! In this terrible town, alone! With so
many temptations on all sides.

HEDDA. But my dear Mrs. Elvsted—how does he concern
you so much?

MRS. ELVSTED. (*Looks at her with a startled air, and says
rapidly.*) He was the children's tutor.

HEDDA. Your children's?

MRS. ELVSTED. My husband's. I have none.

HEDDA. Your step-children's, then?

MRS. ELVSTED. Yes.

TESMAN (*somewhat hesitatingly*). Then was he—I don't
know how to express it—was he—regular enough in his habits
to be fit for the post? Eh?

MRS. ELVSTED. For the last two years his conduct has been
irreproachable.

TESMAN. Has it indeed? Fancy that, Hedda!

HEDDA. I hear it.

MRS. ELVSTED. Perfectly irreproachable, I assure you! In every respect. But all the same—now that I know he is here—in this great town—and with a large sum of money in his hands—I can't help being in mortal fear for him.

TESMAN. Why did he not remain where he was? With you and your husband? Eh?

MRS. ELVSTED. After his book was published he was too restless and unsettled to remain with us.

TESMAN. Yes, by-the-bye, Aunt Julia told me he had published a new book.

MRS. ELVSTED. Yes, a big book, dealing with the march of civilization—in broad outline, as it were. It came out about a fortnight ago. And since it has sold so well, and been so much read—and made such a sensation——

TESMAN. Has it indeed? It must be something he has had lying by since his better days.

MRS. ELVSTED. Long ago, you mean?

TESMAN. Yes.

MRS. ELVSTED. No, he has written it all since he has been with us—within the last year.

TESMAN. Isn't that good news, Hedda? Think of that.

MRS. ELVSTED. Ah, yes, if only it would last!

HEDDA. Have you seen him here in town?

MRS. ELVSTED. No, not yet. I have had the greatest difficulty in finding out his address. But this morning I discovered it at last.

HEDDA (*looks searchingly at her*). Do you know, it seems to me a little odd of your husband—h'm——

MRS. ELVSTED (*starting nervously*). Of my husband! What?

HEDDA. That he should send you to town on such an errand—that he does not come himself and look after his friend.

MRS. ELVSTED. Oh no, no—my husband has no time. And besides, I—I had some shopping to do.

HEDDA (*with a slight smile*). Ah, that is a different matter.

MRS. ELVSTED (*rising quickly and uneasily*). And now I beg and implore you, Mr. Tesman—receive Eilert Lövborg kindly if he comes to you! And that he is sure to do. You see you were such great friends in the old days. And then you are interested in the same studies—the same branch of science—so far as I can understand.

TESMAN. We used to be, at any rate.

MRS. ELVSTED. That is why I beg so earnestly that you— you too—will keep a sharp eye upon him. Oh, you will promise me that, Mr. Tesman—won't you?

TESMAN. With the greatest of pleasure, Mrs. Rysing——

HEDDA. Elvsted.

TESMAN. I assure you I shall do all I possibly can for Eilert. You may rely upon me.

MRS. ELVSTED. Oh, how very, very kind of you! (*Presses his hands.*) Thanks, thanks, thanks! (*Frightened.*) You see, my husband is so very fond of him!

HEDDA (*rising*). You ought to write to him, Tesman. Perhaps he may not care to come to you of his own accord.

TESMAN. Well, perhaps it would be the right thing to do, Hedda. Eh?

HEDDA. And the sooner the better. Why not at once?

MRS. ELVSTED (*imploringly*). Oh, if you only would!

TESMAN. I'll write this moment. Have you his address, Mrs.—Mrs. Elvsted?

MRS. ELVSTED. Yes. (*Takes a slip of paper from her pocket, and hands it to him.*) Here it is.

TESMAN. Good, good. Then I'll go in—— (*Looks about him.*) By-the-bye,—my slippers? Oh, here. (*Takes the packet, and is about to go.*)

HEDDA. Be sure you write him a cordial, friendly letter. And a good long one too.

TESMAN. Yes, I will.

MRS. ELVSTED. But please, please don't say a word to show that I have suggested it.

TESMAN. No, how could you think I would? Eh? (*He goes out to the right, through the inner room.*)

HEDDA (*goes up to* MRS. ELVSTED, *smiles, and says in a low voice.*) There! We have killed two birds with one stone.

MRS. ELVSTED. What do you mean?

HEDDA. Could you not see that I wanted him to go?

MRS. ELVSTED. Yes, to write the letter——

HEDDA. And that I might speak to you alone.

MRS. ELVSTED (*confused*). About the same thing?

HEDDA. Precisely.

MRS. ELVSTED (*apprehensively*). But there is nothing more, Mrs. Tesman! Absolutely nothing!

HEDDA. Oh, yes, but there is. There is a great deal more— I can see that. Sit here—and we'll have a cozy, confidential chat. (*She forces* MRS. ELVSTED *to sit in the easy-chair beside the stove, and seats herself on one of the footstools.*)

MRS. ELVSTED (*anxiously, looking at her watch*). But, my dear Mrs. Tesman—I was really on the point of going.

HEDDA. Oh, you can't be in such a hurry.—Well? Now tell me something about your life at home.

MRS. ELVSTED. Oh, that is just what I care least to speak about.

HEDDA. But to me, dear——? Why, weren't we school-fellows?

MRS. ELVSTED. Yes, but you were in the class above me. Oh, how dreadfully afraid of you I was then!

HEDDA. Afraid of me?

MRS. ELVSTED. Yes, dreadfully. For when we met on the stairs you used always to pull my hair.

HEDDA. Did I, really?

MRS. ELVSTED. Yes, and once you said you would burn it off my head.

HEDDA. Oh, that was all nonsense, of course.

MRS. ELVSTED. Yes, but I was so silly in those days.—And since then, too—we have drifted so far—far apart from each other. Our circles have been so entirely different.

HEDDA. Well then, we must try to drift together again. Now listen! At school we said *du* to each other; and we called each other by our Christian names——

MRS. ELVSTED. No, I am sure you must be mistaken.

HEDDA. No, not at all! I can remember quite distinctly. So now we are going to renew our old friendship. (*Draws the footstool closer to* MRS. ELVSTED.) There now! (*Kisses her cheek.*) You must say *du* to me and call me Hedda.

MRS. ELVSTED (*presses and pats her hands*). Oh, how good and kind you are! I am not used to such kindness.

HEDDA. There, there, there! And I shall say *du* to you, as in the old days, and call you my dear Thora.[1]

MRS. ELVSTED. My name is Thea.[1]

HEDDA. Why, of course! I meant Thea. (*Looks at her compassionately.*) So you are not accustomed to goodness and kindness, Thea? Not in your own home?

MRS. ELVSTED. Oh, if I only had a home! But I haven't any; I have never had a home.

HEDDA (*looks at her for a moment*). I almost suspected as much.

MRS. ELVSTED (*gazing helplessly before her*). Yes—yes—yes.

HEDDA. I don't quite remember—was it not as house-keeper that you first went to Mr. Elvsted's?

MRS. ELVSTED. I really went as governess. But his wife—his late wife—was an invalid,—and rarely left her room. So I had to look after the housekeeping as well.

HEDDA. And then—at last—you became mistress of the house.

MRS. ELVSTED (*sadly*). Yes, I did.

HEDDA. Let me see—about how long ago was that?

[1] Pronounce *Tora* and *Taya*.

Mrs. Elvsted. My marriage?

Hedda. Yes.

Mrs. Elvsted. Five years ago.

Hedda. To be sure; it must be that.

Mrs. Elvsted. Oh, those five years——! Or at all events the last two or three of them! Oh, if you[1] could only imagine——

Hedda (*giving her a little slap on the hand*). De? Fie, Thea!

Mrs. Elvsted. Yes, yes, I will try—— Well, if—you could only imagine and understand——

Hedda (*lightly*). Eilert Lövborg has been in your neighborhood about three years, hasn't he?

Mrs. Elvsted (*looks at her doubtfully*). Eilert Lövborg? Yes—he has.

Hedda. Had you known him before, in town here?

Mrs. Elvsted. Scarcely at all. I mean—I knew him by name of course.

Hedda. But you saw a good deal of him in the country?

Mrs. Elvsted. Yes, he came to us every day. You see, he gave the children lessons; for in the long run I couldn't manage it all myself.

Hedda. No, that's clear.—And your husband——? I suppose he is often away from home?

Mrs. Elvsted. Yes. Being sheriff, you know, he has to travel about a good deal in his district.

Hedda (*leaning against the arm of the chair.*) Thea—my poor, sweet Thea—now you must tell me everything—exactly as it stands.

Mrs. Elvsted. Well then, you must question me.

Hedda. What sort of man is your husband, Thea? I mean—you know—in everyday life. Is he kind to you?

_____
[1] Mrs. Elvsted here uses the formal pronoun *De,* whereupon Hedda rebukes her. In her next speech Mrs. Elvsted says *du.*

MRS. ELVSTED (*evasively*). I am sure he means well in everything.

HEDDA. I should think he must be altogether too old for you. There is at least twenty years' difference between you, is there not?

MRS. ELVSTED (*irritably*). Yes, that is true, too. Everything about him is repellent to me! We have not a thought in common. We have no single point of sympathy—he and I.

HEDDA. But is he not fond of you all the same? In his own way?

MRS. ELVSTED. Oh, I really don't know. I think he regards me simply as a useful property. And then it doesn't cost much to keep me. I am not expensive.

HEDDA. That is stupid of you.

MRS. ELVSTED (*shakes her head*). It cannot be otherwise—not with him. I don't think he really cares for any one but himself—and perhaps a little for the children.

HEDDA. And for Eilert Lövborg, Thea.

MRS. ELVSTED (*looking at her*). For Eilert Lövborg? What puts that into your head?

HEDDA. Well, my dear—I should say, when he sends you after him all the way to town—— (*Smiling almost imperceptibly.*) And besides, you said so yourself, to Tesman.

MRS. ELVSTED (*with a little nervous twitch*). Did I? Yes, I suppose I did. (*Vehemently, but not loudly.*) No—I may just as well make a clean breast of it at once! For it must all come out in any case.

HEDDA. Why, my dear Thea——?

MRS. ELVSTED. Well, to make a long story short: My husband did not know that I was coming.

HEDDA. What! Your husband didn't know it!

MRS. ELVSTED. No, of course not. For that matter, he was away from home himself—he was traveling. Oh, I could bear it no longer, Hedda! I couldn't indeed—so utterly alone as I should have been in future.

HEDDA. Well? And then?

MRS. ELVSTED. So I put together some of my things—what I needed most—as quietly as possible. And then I left the house.

HEDDA. Without a word?

MRS. ELVSTED. Yes—and took the train straight to town.

HEDDA. Why, my dear, good Thea—to think of you daring to do it!

MRS. ELVSTED (*rises and moves about the room*). What else could I possibly do?

HEDDA. But what do you think your husband will say when you go home again?

MRS. ELVSTED (*at the table, looks at her*). Back to him?

HEDDA. Of course.

MRS. ELVSTED. I shall never go back to him again.

HEDDA (*rising and going towards her*). Then you have left your home—for good and all?

MRS. ELVSTED. Yes. There was nothing else to be done.

HEDDA. But then—to take flight so openly.

MRS. ELVSTED. Oh, it's impossible to keep things of that sort secret.

HEDDA. But what do you think people will say of you, Thea?

MRS. ELVSTED. They may say what they like, for aught I care. (*Seats herself wearily and sadly on the sofa.*) I have done nothing but what I had to do.

HEDDA (*after a short silence*). And what are your plans now? What do you think of doing?

MRS. ELVSTED. I don't know yet. I only know this, that I must live here, where Eilert Lövborg is—if I am to live at all.

HEDDA (*takes a chair from the table, seats herself beside her, and strokes her hands*). My dear Thea—how did this— this friendship—between you and Eilert Lövborg come about?

MRS. ELVSTED. Oh, it grew up gradually. I gained a sort of influence over him.

HEDDA. Indeed?

MRS. ELVSTED. He gave up his old habits. Not because I asked him to, for I never dared do that. But of course he saw how repulsive they were to me; and so he dropped them.

HEDDA (*concealing an involuntary smile of scorn*). Then you have reclaimed him—as the saying goes—my little Thea.

MRS. ELVSTED. So he says himself, at any rate. And he, on his side, has made a real human being of me—taught me to think, and to understand so many things.

HEDDA. Did he give you lessons too, then?

MRS. ELVSTED. No, not exactly lessons. But he talked to me—talked about such an infinity of things. And then came the lovely, happy time when I began to share in his work—when he allowed me to help him!

HEDDA. Oh, he did, did he?

MRS. ELVSTED. Yes! He never wrote anything without my assistance.

HEDDA. You were two good comrades, in fact?

MRS. ELVSTED (*eagerly*). Comrades! Yes, fancy, Hedda —that is the very word he used!—Oh, I ought to feel perfectly happy; and yet I cannot; for I don't know how long it will last.

HEDDA. Are you no surer of him than that?

MRS. ELVSTED (*gloomily*). A woman's shadow stands between Eilert Lövborg and me.

HEDDA (*looks at her anxiously*). Who can that be?

MRS. ELVSTED. I don't know. Some one he knew in his— in his past. Some one he has never been able wholly to forget.

HEDDA. What has he told you—about this?

MRS. ELVSTED. He has only once—quite vaguely—alluded to it.

HEDDA. Well! And what did he say?

MRS. ELVSTED. He said that when they parted, she threatened to shoot him with a pistol.

HEDDA (*with cold composure*). Oh, nonsense! No one does that sort of thing here.

MRS. ELVSTED. No. And this is why I think it must have been that red-haired singing-woman whom he once——

HEDDA. Yes, very likely.

MRS. ELVSTED. For I remember they used to say of her that she carried loaded firearms.

HEDDA. Oh—then of course it must have been she.

MRS. ELVSTED (*wringing her hands*). And now just fancy, Hedda—I hear that this singing-woman—that she is in town again! Oh, I don't know what to do——

HEDDA (*glancing towards the inner room*). Hush! Here comes Tesman. (*Rises and whispers.*) Thea—all this must remain between you and me.

MRS. ELVSTED (*springing up*). Oh, yes, yes! for heaven's sake——!

(GEORGE TESMAN, *with a letter in his hand, comes from the right through the inner room.*)

TESMAN. There now—the epistle is finished.

HEDDA. That's right. And now Mrs. Elvsted is just going. Wait a moment—I'll go with you to the garden gate.

TESMAN. Do you think Berta could post the letter, Hedda dear?

HEDDA (*takes it*). I will tell her to.

(BERTA *enters from the hall.*)

BERTA. Judge Brack wishes to know if Mrs. Tesman will receive him.

HEDDA. Yes, ask Judge Brack to come in. And look here—put this letter in the post.

BERTA (*taking the letter*). Yes, ma'am.

(*She opens the door for* JUDGE BRACK *and goes out herself.* BRACK *is a man of forty-five; thick-set, but well-built and elastic in his movements. His face is*

*roundish with an aristocratic profile. His hair is short,
still almost black, and carefully dressed. His eyes are
lively and sparkling. His eyebrows thick. His mous-
taches are also thick, with short-cut ends. He wears
a well-cut walking-suit, a little too youthful for his
age. He uses an eye-glass, which he now and then lets
drop.)*

JUDGE BRACK (*with his hat in his hand, bowing*). May
one venture to call so early in the day?

HEDDA. Of course one may.

TESMAN (*presses his hand*). You are welcome at any time.
(*Introducing him.*) Judge Brack——Miss Rysing——

HEDDA. Oh——!

BRACK (*bowing*). Ah——delighted——

HEDDA (*looks at him and laughs*). It's nice to have a look
at you by daylight, Judge!

BRACK. Do you find me——altered?

HEDDA. A little younger, I think.

BRACK. Thank you so much.

TESMAN. But what do you think of Hedda——eh? Doesn't
she look flourishing? She has actually——

HEDDA. Oh, do leave me alone. You haven't thanked
Judge Brack for all the trouble he has taken——

BRACK. Oh, nonsense——it was a pleasure to me——

HEDDA. Yes, you are a friend indeed. But here stands
Thea all impatience to be off——so *au revoir* Judge. I shall be
back again presently. (*Mutual salutations.* MRS. ELVSTED *and*
HEDDA *go out by the hall door.*)

BRACK. Well,——is your wife tolerably satisfied——

TESMAN. Yes, we can't thank you sufficiently. Of course
she talks of a little re-arrangement here and there; and one
or two things are still wanting. We shall have to buy some
additional trifles.

BRACK. Indeed!

TESMAN. But we won't trouble you about these things.

Hedda says she herself will look after what is wanting.—
Shan't we sit down? Eh?

BRACK. Thanks, for a moment. (*Seats himself beside the
table.*) There is something I wanted to speak to you about,
my dear Tesman.

TESMAN. Indeed? Ah, I understand! (*Seating himself.*)
I suppose it's the serious part of the frolic that is coming now.
Eh?

BRACK. Oh, the money question is not so very pressing;
though, for that matter, I wish we had gone a little more
economically to work.

TESMAN. But that would never have done, you know!
Think of Hedda, my dear fellow! You, who know her so
well——. I couldn't possibly ask her to put up with a shabby
style of living!

BRACK. No, no—that is just the difficulty.

TESMAN. And then—fortunately—it can't be long before
I receive my appointment.

BRACK. Well, you see—such things are often apt to hang
fire for a time.

TESMAN. Have you heard anything definite? Eh?

BRACK. Nothing exactly definite—— (*Interrupting himself.*) But, by-the-bye—I have one piece of news for you.

TESMAN. Well?

BRACK. Your old friend, Eilert Lövborg, has returned to
town.

TESMAN. I know that already.

BRACK. Indeed! How did you learn it?

TESMAN. From that lady who went out with Hedda.

BRACK. Really? What was her name? I didn't quite
catch it.

TESMAN. Mrs. Elvsted.

BRACK. Aha—Sheriff Elvsted's wife? Of course—he has
been living up in their regions.

TESMAN. And fancy—I'm delighted to hear that he is
quite a reformed character!

BRACK. So they say.

TESMAN. And then he has published a new book—eh?

BRACK. Yes, indeed he has.

TESMAN. And I hear it has made some sensation!

BRACK. Quite an unusual sensation.

TESMAN. Fancy—isn't that good news! A man of such extraordinary talents——. I felt so grieved to think that he had gone irretrievably to ruin.

BRACK. That was what everybody thought.

TESMAN. But I cannot imagine what he will take to now! How in the world will he be able to make his living? Eh?

(*During the last words,* HEDDA *has entered by the hall door.*)

HEDDA (*to* BRACK, *laughing with a touch of scorn*). Tesman is forever worrying about how people are to make their living.

TESMAN. Well, you see, dear—we were talking about poor Eilert Lövborg.

HEDDA (*glancing at him rapidly*). Oh, indeed? (*Seats herself in the arm-chair beside the stove and asks indifferently:*) What is the matter with him?

TESMAN. Well—no doubt he has run through all his property long ago; and he can scarcely write a new book every year—eh? So I really can't see what is to become of him.

BRACK. Perhaps I can give you some information on that point.

TESMAN. Indeed!

BRACK. You must remember that his relations have a good deal of influence.

TESMAN. Oh, his relations, unfortunately, have entirely washed their hands of him.

BRACK. At one time they called him the hope of the family.

TESMAN. At one time, yes! But he has put an end to all that.

HEDDA. Who knows? (*With a slight smile.*) I hear they have reclaimed him up at Sheriff Elvsted's——

BRACK. And then this book that he has published——

TESMAN. Well, well, I hope to goodness they may find something for him to do. I have just written to him. I asked him to come and see us this evening, Hedda dear.

BRACK. But, my dear fellow, you are booked for my bachelors' party this evening. You promised on the pier last night.

HEDDA. Had you forgotten, Tesman?

TESMAN. Yes, I had utterly forgotten.

BRACK. But it doesn't matter, for you may be sure he won't come.

TESMAN. What makes you think that? Eh?

BRACK (*with a little hesitation, rising and resting his hands on the back of his chair*). My dear Tesman—and you too, Mrs. Tesman—I think I ought not to keep you in the dark about something that—that——

TESMAN. That concerns Eilert——?

BRACK. Both you and him.

TESMAN. Well, my dear Judge, out with it.

BRACK. You must be prepared to find your appointment deferred longer than you desired or expected.

TESMAN (*jumping up uneasily*). Is there some hitch about it? Eh?

BRACK. The nomination may perhaps be made conditional on the result of a competition——

TESMAN. Competition! Think of that, Hedda!

HEDDA (*leans farther back in the chair*). Aha—aah!

TESMAN. But who can my competitor be? Surely not——?

BRACK. Yes, precisely—Eilert Lövborg.

TESMAN (*clasping his hands*). No, no—it's quite inconceivable! Quite impossible! Eh?

BRACK. H'm—that is what it may come to, all the same.

TESMAN. Well, but, Judge Brack—it would show the most

incredible lack of consideration for me. (*Gesticulates with his arms.*) For—just think—I'm a married man! We have married on the strength of these prospects, Hedda and I; and run deep into debt; and borrowed money from Aunt Julia too. Good heavens, they had as good as promised me the appointment. Eh?

BRACK. Well, well, well—no doubt you will get it in the end; only after a contest.

HEDDA (*immovable in her arm-chair.*) Fancy, Tesman, there will be a sort of sporting interest in that.

TESMAN. Why, my dearest Hedda, how can you be so indifferent about it.

HEDDA (*as before*). I am not at all indifferent. I am most eager to see who wins.

BRACK. In any case, Mrs. Tesman, it is best that you should know how matters stand. I mean—before you set about the little purchases I hear you are threatening.

HEDDA. This can make no difference.

BRACK. Indeed! Then I have no more to say. Good-bye! (*To* TESMAN.) I shall look in on my way back from my afternoon walk, and take you home with me.

TESMAN. Oh yes, yes—your news has quite upset me.

HEDDA (*reclining, holds out her hand*). Good-bye, Judge; and be sure you call in the afternoon.

BRACK. Many thanks. Good-bye, good-bye!

TESMAN (*accompanying him to the door*). Good-bye, my dear Judge! You must really excuse me—— (JUDGE BRACK *goes out by the hall door.*)

TESMAN (*crosses the room*). Oh, Hedda—one should never rush into adventures. Eh?

HEDDA (*looks at him, smiling*). Do you do that?

TESMAN. Yes, dear—there is no denying—it was adventurous to go and marry and set up house upon mere expectations.

HEDDA. Perhaps you are right there.

TESMAN. Well—at all events, we have our delightful home, Hedda! Fancy, the home we both dreamed of—the home we were in love with, I may almost say. Eh?

HEDDA (*rising slowly and wearily*). It was part of our compact that we were to go into society—to keep open house.

TESMAN. Yes, if you only knew how I had been looking forward to it! Fancy—to see you as hostess—in a select circle! Eh? Well, well, well—for the present we shall have to get on without society, Hedda—only to invite Aunt Julia now and then.—Oh, I intended you to lead such an utterly different life, dear——!

HEDDA. Of course I cannot have my man in livery just yet.

TESMAN. Oh no, unfortunately. It would be out of the question for us to keep a footman, you know.

HEDDA. And the saddle-horse I was to have had——

TESMAN (*aghast*). The saddle-horse!

HEDDA. ——I suppose I must not think of that now.

TESMAN. Good heavens, no!—that's as clear as daylight.

HEDDA (*goes up the room*). Well, I shall have one thing at least to kill time with in the meanwhile.

TESMAN (*beaming*). Oh, thank heaven for that! What is it, Hedda? Eh?

HEDDA (*in the middle doorway, looks at him with covert scorn*). My pistols, George.

TESMAN (*in alarm*). Your pistols!

HEDDA (*with cold eyes*). General Gabler's pistols. (*She goes out through the inner room, to the left.*)

TESMAN (*rushes up to the middle doorway and calls after her:*) No, for heaven's sake, Hedda darling—don't touch those dangerous things! For my sake, Hedda! Eh?

ACT II

(*The room at the* TESMANS' *as in the first Act, except that the piano has been removed, and an elegant little writing-table with book-shelves put in its place. A smaller table stands near the sofa on the left. Most of the bouquets have been taken away.* MRS. ELVSTED'S *bouquet is upon the large table in front.—It is afternoon.*)

(HEDDA, *dressed to receive callers, is alone in the room. She stands by the open glass door, loading a revolver. The fellow to it lies in an open pistol-case on the writing-table.*)

HEDDA (*looks down the garden, and calls:*) So you are here again, Judge!

BRACK (*is heard calling from a distance*). As you see, Mrs. Tesman!

HEDDA (*raises the pistol and points*). Now I'll shoot you, Judge Brack!

BRACK (*calling unseen*). No, no, no! Don't stand aiming at me!

HEDDA. This is what comes of sneaking in by the back way.[1] (*She fires.*)

BRACK (*nearer*). Are you out of your senses——!

HEDDA. Dear me—did I happen to hit you?

BRACK (*still outside*). I wish you would let these pranks alone!

HEDDA. Come in then, Judge.

(JUDGE BRACK, *dressed as though for a men's party, enters by the glass door. He carries a light overcoat over his arm.*)

BRACK. What the deuce—haven't you tired of that sport, yet? What are you shooting at?

[1] "Bagveje" means both "back ways" and "underhand courses."

HEDDA. Oh, I am only firing in the air.

BRACK (*gently takes the pistol out of her hand*). Allow me, madam! (*Looks at it.*) Ah—I know this pistol well! (*Looks around.*) Where is the case? Ah, here it is. (*Lays the pistol in it, and shuts it.*) Now we won't play at that game any more to-day.

HEDDA. Then what in heaven's name would you have me do with myself?

BRACK. Have you had no visitors?

HEDDA (*closing the glass door*). Not one. I suppose all our set are still out of town.

BRACK. And is Tesman not at home either?

HEDDA (*at the writing-table, putting the pistol-case in a drawer which she shuts*). No. He rushed off to his aunt's directly after lunch; he didn't expect you so early.

BRACK. H'm—how stupid of me not to have thought of that!

HEDDA (*turning her head to look at him*). Why stupid?

BRACK. Because if I had thought of it I should have come a little—earlier.

HEDDA (*crossing the room*). Then you would have found no one to receive you; for I have been in my room changing my dress ever since lunch.

BRACK. And is there no sort of little chink that we could hold a parley through?

HEDDA. You have forgotten to arrange one.

BRACK. That was another piece of stupidity.

HEDDA. Well, we must just settle down here—and wait. Tesman is not likely to be back for some time yet.

BRACK. Never mind; I shall not be impatient.

(HEDDA *seats herself in the corner of the sofa.* BRACK *lays his overcoat over the back of the nearest chair, and sits down, but keeps his hat in his hand. A short silence. They look at each other.*)

HEDDA. Well?

BRACK (*in the same tone*). Well?

HEDDA. I spoke first.

BRACK (*bending a little forward*). Come, let us have a cozy little chat, Mrs. Hedda.[1]

HEDDA (*leaning further back in the sofa*). Does it not seem like a whole eternity since our last talk? Of course I don't count those few words yesterday evening and this morning.

BRACK. You mean since our last confidential talk. Our last *tête-à-tête*?

HEDDA. Well, yes—since you put it so.

BRACK. Not a day has passed but I have wished that you were home again.

HEDDA. And I have done nothing but wish the same thing.

BRACK. You? Really, Mrs. Hedda? And I thought you had been enjoying your tour so much!

HEDDA. Oh, yes, you may be sure of that!

BRACK. But Tesman's letters spoke of nothing but happiness.

HEDDA. Oh, Tesman! You see, he thinks nothing so delightful as grubbing in libraries and making copies of old parchments, or whatever you call them.

BRACK (*with a spice of malice*). Well, that is his vocation in life—or part of it at any rate.

HEDDA. Yes, of course; and no doubt when it's your vocation—— But *I*! Oh, my dear Mr. Brack, how mortally bored I have been.

BRACK (*sympathetically*). Do you really say so? In downright earnest?

HEDDA. Yes, you can surely understand it——! To go for six whole months without meeting a soul that knew any-

---

[1] As this form of address is contrary to English usage, and as the note of familiarity would be lacking in "Mrs. Tesman," Brack may, in stage presentation, say "Miss Hedda," thus ignoring her marriage and reverting to the form of address no doubt customary between them of old.

thing of our circle, or could talk about the things we are interested in.

BRACK. Yes, yes—I too should feel that a deprivation.

HEDDA. And then, what I found most intolerable of all——

BRACK. Well?

HEDDA. ——was being everlastingly in the company of—one and the same person——

BRACK (*with a nod of assent*). Morning, noon, and night, yes—at all possible times and seasons.

HEDDA. I said "everlastingly."

BRACK. Just so. But I should have thought, with our excellent Tesman, one could——

HEDDA. Tesman is—a specialist, my dear Judge.

BRACK. Undeniably.

HEDDA. And specialists are not at all amusing to travel with. Not in the long run at any rate.

BRACK. Not even—the specialist one happens to love?

HEDDA. Faugh—don't use that sickening word!

BRACK (*taken aback*). What do you say, Mrs. Hedda?

HEDDA (*half laughing, half irritated*). You should just try it! To hear of nothing but the history of civilization, morning, noon, and night——

BRACK. Everlastingly.

HEDDA. Yes, yes, yes! And then all this about the domestic industry of the middle ages——! That's the most disgusting part of it!

BRACK (*looks searchingly at her*). But tell me—in that case, how am I to understand your——? H'm——

HEDDA. My accepting George Tesman, you mean?

BRACK. Well, let us put it so.

HEDDA. Good heavens, do you see anything so wonderful in that?

BRACK. Yes and no—Mrs. Hedda.

HEDDA. I had positively danced myself tired, my dear

Judge. My day was done—— (*With a slight shudder.*) Oh no—I won't say that; nor think it either!

BRACK. You have assuredly no reason to.

HEDDA. Oh, reasons—— (*Watching him closely.*) And George Tesman—after all, you must admit that he is correctness itself.

BRACK. His correctness and respectability are beyond all question.

HEDDA. And I don't see anything absolutely ridiculous about him.—Do you?

BRACK. Ridiculous? N—no—I shouldn't exactly say so——

HEDDA. Well—and his powers of research, at all events, are untiring.—I see no reason why he should not one day come to the front, after all.

BRACK (*looks at her hesitatingly*). I thought that you, like every one else, expected him to attain the highest distinction.

HEDDA (*with an expression of fatigue*). Yes, so I did.— And then, since he was bent, at all hazards, on being allowed to provide for me—I really don't know why I should not have accepted his offer?

BRACK. No—if you look at it in that light——

HEDDA. It was more than my other adorers were prepared to do for me, my dear Judge.

BRACK (*laughing*). Well, I can't answer for all the rest; but as for myself, you know quite well that I have always entertained a—a certain respect for the marriage tie—for marriage as an institution, Mrs. Hedda.

HEDDA (*jestingly*). Oh, I assure you I have never cherished any hopes with respect to you.

BRACK. All I require is a pleasant and intimate interior, where I can make myself useful in every way, and am free to come and go as—as a trusted friend——

HEDDA. Of the master of the house, do you mean?

BRACK (*bowing*). Frankly—of the mistress first of all; but of course of the master, too, in the second place. Such a triangular friendship—if I may call it so—is really a great convenience for all parties, let me tell you.

HEDDA. Yes, I have many a time longed for some one to make a third on our travels. Oh—those railway-carriage *tête-à-têtes*——!

BRACK. Fortunately your wedding journey is over now.

HEDDA. (*shaking her head*). Not by a long—long way. I have only arrived at a station on the line.

BRACK. Well, then the passengers jump out and move about a little, Mrs. Hedda.

HEDDA. I never jump out.

BRACK. Really?

HEDDA. No—because there is always some one standing by to——

BRACK (*laughing*). To look at your ankles, do you mean?

HEDDA. Precisely.

BRACK. Well, but, dear me——

HEDDA (*with a gesture of repulsion*). I won't have it. I would rather keep my seat where I happen to be—and continue the *tête-à-tête*.

BRACK. But suppose a third person were to jump in and join the couple.

HEDDA. Ah—that is quite another matter!

BRACK. A trusted, sympathetic friend——

HEDDA. ——with a fund of conversation on all sorts of lively topics——

BRACK. ——and not the least bit of a specialist!

HEDDA (*with an audible sigh*). Yes, that would be a relief indeed.

BRACK (*hears the front door open, and glances in that direction*). The triangle is completed.

HEDDA (*half aloud*). And on goes the train.

GEORGE TESMAN, *in a gray walking-suit, with a soft felt*

*hat, enters from the hall. He has a number of un-
bound books under his arm and in his pockets.*)

TESMAN (*goes up to the table beside the corner settee*).
Ouf—what a load for a warm day—all these books. (*Lays
them on the table.*) I'm positively perspiring, Hedda. Hallo
—are you there already, my dear Judge? Eh? Berta didn't
tell me.

BRACK (*rising*). I came in through the garden.

HEDDA. What books have you got there?

TESMAN (*stands looking them through*). Some new books
on my special subjects—quite indispensable to me.

HEDDA. Your special subjects?

BRACK. Yes, books on his special subjects, Mrs. Tesman.
(BRACK *and* HEDDA *exchange a confidential smile.*)

HEDDA. Do you need still more books on your special subjects?

TESMAN. Yes, my dear Hedda, one can never have too
many of them. Of course one must keep up with all that is
written and published.

HEDDA. Yes, I suppose one must.

TESMAN (*searching among his books*). And look here—
I have got hold of Eilert Lövborg's new book too. (*Offering
it to her.*) Perhaps you would like to glance through it,
Hedda? Eh?

HEDDA. No, thank you. Or rather—afterwards perhaps.

TESMAN. I looked into it a little on the way home.

BRACK. Well, what do you think of it—as a specialist?

TESMAN. I think it shows quite remarkable soundness of
judgment. He never wrote like that before. (*Putting the
books together.*) Now I shall take all these into my study.
I'm longing to cut the leaves——! And then I must change
my clothes. (*To* BRACK.) I suppose we needn't start just
yet? Eh?

BRACK. Oh, dear no—there is not the slightest hurry.

TESMAN. Well then, I will take my time. (*Is going with*

his books, but stops in the doorway and turns.) By-the-bye, Hedda—Aunt Julia is not coming this evening.

HEDDA. Not coming? Is it that affair of the bonnet that keeps her away?

TESMAN. Oh, not at all. How could you think such a thing of Aunt Julia? Just fancy——! The fact is, Aunt Rina is very ill.

HEDDA. She always is.

TESMAN. Yes, but to-day she is much worse than usual, poor dear.

HEDDA. Oh, then it's only natural that her sister should remain with her. I must bear my disappointment.

TESMAN. And you can't imagine, dear, how delighted Aunt Julia seemed to be—because you had come home looking so flourishing!

HEDDA (*half aloud, rising*). Oh, those everlasting aunts!

TESMAN. What?

HEDDA (*going to the glass door*). Nothing.

TESMAN. Oh, all right. (*He goes through the inner room, out to the right.*)

BRACK. What bonnet were you talking about?

HEDDA. Oh, it was a little episode with Miss Tesman this morning. She had laid down her bonnet on the chair there— (*looks at him and smiles.*)—And I pretended to think it was the servant's.

BRACK (*shaking his head*). Now my dear Mrs. Hedda, how could you do such a thing? To that excellent old lady, too!

HEDDA (*nervously crossing the room*). Well, you see— these impulses come over me all of a sudden; and I cannot resist them. (*Throws herself down in the easy-chair by the stove.*) Oh, I don't know how to explain it.

BRACK (*behind the easy-chair*). You are not really happy —that is at the bottom of it.

HEDDA (*looking straight before her*). I know of no reason why I should be—happy. Perhaps you can give me one?

BRACK. Well—amongst other things, because you have got exactly the home you had set your heart on.

HEDDA (*looks up at him and laughs*). Do you too believe in that legend?

BRACK. Is there nothing in it, then?

HEDDA. Oh, yes, there is something in it.

BRACK. Well?

HEDDA. There is this in it, that I made use of Tesman to see me home from evening parties last summer——

BRACK. I, unfortunately, had to go quite a different way.

HEDDA. That's true. I know you were going a different way last summer.

BRACK (*laughing*). Oh fie, Mrs. Hedda! Well, then—you and Tesman——?

HEDDA. Well, we happened to pass here one evening; Tesman, poor fellow, was writhing in the agony of having to find conversation; so I took pity on the learned man——

BRACK (*smiles doubtfully*). You took pity? H'm——

HEDDA. Yes, I really did. And so—to help him out of his torment—I happened to say, in pure thoughtlessness, that I should like to live in this villa.

BRACK. No more than that?

HEDDA. Not that evening.

BRACK. But afterwards?

HEDDA. Yes, my thoughtlessness had consequences, my dear Judge.

BRACK. Unfortunately that too often happens, Mrs. Hedda.

HEDDA. Thanks! So you see it was this enthusiasm for Secretary Falk's villa that first constituted a bond of sympathy between George Tesman and me. From that came our engagement and our marriage, and our wedding journey, and all the rest of it. Well, well, my dear Judge—as you make your bed so you must lie, I could almost say.

BRACK. This is exquisite! And you really cared not a rap about it all the time?

HEDDA. No, heaven knows I didn't.

BRACK. But now? Now that we have made it so homelike for you?

HEDDA. Uh—the rooms all seem to smell of lavender and dried rose-leaves.—But perhaps it's Aunt Julia that has brought that scent with her.

BRACK (*laughing*). No, I think it must be a legacy from the late Mrs. Secretary Falk.

HEDDA. Yes, there is an odor of mortality about it. It reminds me of a bouquet—the day after the ball. (*Clasps her hands behind her head, leans back in her chair and looks at him.*) Oh, my dear Judge—you cannot imagine how horribly I shall bore myself here.

BRACK. Why should not you, too, find some sort of vocation in life, Mrs. Hedda?

HEDDA. A vocation—that should attract me?

BRACK. If possible, of course.

HEDDA. Heaven knows what sort of vocation that could be. I often wonder whether—— (*Breaking off.*) But that would never do either.

BRACK. Who can tell? Let me hear what it is.

HEDDA. Whether I might not get Tesman to go into politics, I mean.

BRACK (*laughing*). Tesman? No, really now, political life is not the thing for him—not at all in his line.

HEDDA. No, I daresay not.—But if I could get him into it all the same?

BRACK. Why—what satisfaction could you find in that? If he is not fitted for that sort of thing, why should you want to drive him into it?

HEDDA. Because I am bored, I tell you! (*After a pause.*) So you think it quite out of the question that Tesman should ever get into the ministry?

BRACK. H'm—you see, my dear Mrs. Hedda—to get into the ministry, he would have to be a tolerably rich man.

HEDDA (*rising impatiently*). Yes, there we have it! It is this genteel poverty I have managed to drop into——!

(*Crosses the room.*) That is what makes life so pitiable! So utterly ludicrous!—For that's what it is.

BRACK. Now *I* should say the fault lay elsewhere.

HEDDA. Where, then?

BRACK. You have never gone through any really stimulating experience.

HEDDA. Anything serious, you mean?

BRACK. Yes, you may call it so. But now you may perhaps have one in store.

HEDDA (*tossing her head*). Oh, you're thinking of the annoyances about this wretched professorship! But that must be Tesman's own affair. I assure you I shall not waste a thought upon it.

BRACK. No, no, I daresay not. But suppose now that what people call—in elegant language—a solemn responsibility were to come upon you? (*Smiling.*) A new responsibility, Mrs. Hedda?

HEDDA (*angrily*). Be quiet! Nothing of that sort will ever happen!

BRACK (*warily*). We will speak of this again a year hence —at the very outside.

HEDDA (*curtly*). I have no turn for anything of the sort, Judge Brack. No responsibilities for me!

BRACK. Are you so unlike the generality of women as to have no turn for duties which——?

HEDDA (*beside the glass door*). Oh, be quiet, I tell you! —I often think there is only one thing in the world I have any turn for.

BRACK (*drawing near to her*). And what is that, if I may ask?

HEDDA (*stands looking out*). Boring myself to death. Now you know it. (*Turns, looks towards the inner room, and laughs.*) Yes, as I thought! Here comes the Professor.

BRACK (*softly, in a tone of warning*). Come, come, come, Mrs. Hedda!

GEORGE TESMAN, *dressed for the party, with his gloves*

and hat in his hand, enters from the right through the inner room.)

TESMAN. Hedda, has no message come from Eilert Lövborg? Eh?

HEDDA. No.

TESMAN. Then you'll see he'll be here presently.

BRACK. Do you really think he will come?

TESMAN. Yes, I am almost sure of it. For what you were telling us this morning must have been a mere floating rumor.

BRACK. You think so?

TESMAN. At any rate, Aunt Julia said she did not believe for a moment that he would ever stand in my way again. Fancy that!

BRACK. Well then, that's all right.

TESMAN (*placing his hat and gloves on a chair on the right.*) Yes, but you must really let me wait for him as long as possible.

BRACK. We have plenty of time yet. None of my guests will arrive before seven or half-past.

TESMAN. Then meanwhile we can keep Hedda company, and see what happens. Eh?

HEDDA (*placing* BRACK's *hat and overcoat upon the corner settee.*) And at the worst Mr. Lövborg can remain here with me.

BRACK (*offering to take his things*). Oh, allow me, Mrs. Tesman!—What do you mean by "At the worst"?

HEDDA. If he won't go with you and Tesman.

TESMAN (*looks dubiously at her*). But, Hedda dear—do you think it would quite do for him to remain with you? Eh? Remember, Aunt Julia can't come.

HEDDA. No, but Mrs. Elvsted is coming. We three can have a cup of tea together.

TESMAN. Oh, yes, that will be all right.

BRACK (*smiling*). And that would perhaps be the safest plan for him.

HEDDA. Why so?

BRACK. Well, you know, Mrs. Tesman, how you used to gird at my little bachelor parties. You declared they were adapted only for men of the strictest principles.

HEDDA. But no doubt Mr. Lövborg's principles are strict enough now. A converted sinner——

(BERTA *appears at the hall door.*)

BERTA. There's a gentleman asking if you are at home, ma'am——

HEDDA. Well, show him in.

TESMAN (*softly*). I'm sure it is he! Fancy that!

(EILERT LÖVBORG *enters from the hall. He is slim and lean; of the same age as* TESMAN, *but looks older and somewhat worn-out. His hair and beard are of a blackish brown, his face long and pale, but with patches of color on the cheek-bones. He is dressed in a well-cut black visiting suit, quite new. He has dark gloves and a silk hat. He stops near the door, and makes a rapid bow, seeming somewhat embarrassed.*)

TESMAN (*goes up to him and shakes him warmly by the hand*). Well, my dear Eilert—so at last we meet again!

EILERT LÖVBORG (*speaks in a subdued voice*). Thanks for your letter, Tesman. (*Approaching* HEDDA.) Will you too shake hands with me, Mrs. Tesman?

HEDDA (*taking his hand*). I am glad to see you, Mr. Lövborg. (*With a motion of her hand.*) I don't know whether you two gentlemen——?

LÖVBORG (*bowing slightly*). Judge Brack, I think.

BRACK (*doing likewise*). Oh yes,—in the old days——

TESMAN (*to* LÖVBORG, *with his hands on his shoulders*). And now you must make yourself entirely at home, Eilert! Mustn't he, Hedda?—For I hear you are going to settle in town again? Eh?

LÖVBORG. Yes, I am.

TESMAN. Quite right, quite right. Let me tell you, I have

got hold of your new book; but I haven't had time to read it yet.

LÖVBORG. You may spare yourself the trouble.

TESMAN. Why so?

LÖVBORG. Because there is very little in it.

TESMAN. Just fancy—how can you say so?

BRACK. But it has been very much praised, I hear.

LÖVBORG. That was what I wanted; so I put nothing into the book but what every one would agree with.

BRACK. Very wise of you.

TESMAN. Well, but, my dear Eilert——!

LÖVBORG. For now I mean to win myself a position again —to make a fresh start.

TESMAN (*a little embarrassed*). Ah, that is what you wish to do? Eh?

LÖVBORG (*smiling, lays down his hat, and draws a packet, wrapped in paper, from his coat pocket*). But when this one appears, George Tesman, you will have to read it. For this is the real book—the book I have put my true self into.

TESMAN. Indeed? And what is it?

LÖVBORG. It is the continuation.

TESMAN. The continuation? Of what?

LÖVBORG. Of the book.

TESMAN. Of the new book?

LÖVBORG. Of course.

TESMAN. Why, my dear Eilert—does it not come down to our own days?

LÖVBORG. Yes, it does; and this one deals with the future.

TESMAN. With the future! But, good heavens, we know nothing of the future!

LÖVBORG. No; but there is a thing or two to be said about it all the same. (*Opens the packet.*) Look here——

TESMAN. Why, that's not your handwriting.

LÖVBORG. I dictated it. (*Turning over the pages.*) It falls into two sections. The first deals with the civilizing forces of the future. And here is the second—(*running through the pages towards the end*)—forecasting the probable line of development.

TESMAN. How odd now! I should never have thought of writing anything of that sort.

HEDDA (*at the glass door, drumming on the pane*). H'm —I daresay not.

LÖVBORG (*replacing the manuscript in its paper and laying the packet on the table*). I brought it, thinking I might read you a little of it this evening.

TESMAN. That was very good of you, Eilert. But this evening——? (*Looking at* BRACK.) I don't quite see how we can manage it——

LÖVBORG. Well then, some other time. There is no hurry.

BRACK. I must tell you, Mr. Lövborg—there is a little gathering at my house this evening—mainly in honor of Tesman, you know——

LÖVBORG (*looking for his hat*). Oh—then I won't detain you——

BRACK. No, but listen—will you not do me the favor of joining us?

LÖVBORG (*curtly and decidedly*). No, I can't—thank you very much.

BRACK. Oh, nonsense—do! We shall be quite a select little circle. And I assure you we shall have a "lively time," as Mrs. Hed—as Mrs. Tesman says.

LÖVBORG. I have no doubt of it. But nevertheless——

BRACK. And then you might bring your manuscript with you, and read it to Tesman at my house. I could give you a room to yourselves.

TESMAN. Yes, think of that, Eilert,—why shouldn't you? Eh?

HEDDA (*interposing*). But, Tesman, if Mr. Lövborg would really rather not! I am sure Mr. Lövborg is much more inclined to remain here and have supper with me.

LÖVBORG (*looking at her*). With you, Mrs. Tesman?

HEDDA. And with Mrs. Elvsted.

LÖVBORG. Ah—— (*Lightly.*) I saw her for a moment this morning.

HEDDA. Did you? Well, she is coming this evening. So you see you are almost bound to remain, Mr. Lövborg, or she will have no one to see her home.

LÖVBORG. That's true. Many thanks, Mrs. Tesman—in that case I will remain.

HEDDA. Then I have one or two orders to give the servant —— (*She goes to the hall door and rings.* BERTA *enters.* HEDDA *talks to her in a whisper, and points towards the inner room.* BERTA *nods and goes out again.*)

TESMAN (*at the same time, to* LÖVBORG). Tell me, Eilert —is it this new subject—the future—that you are going to lecture about?

LÖVBORG. Yes.

TESMAN. They told me at the bookseller's that you are going to deliver a course of lectures this autumn.

LÖVBORG. That is my intention. I hope you won't take it ill, Tesman.

TESMAN. Oh no, not in the least! But——?

LÖVBORG. I can quite understand that it must be disagreeable to you.

TESMAN (*cast down*). Oh, I can't expect you, out of consideration for me, to——

LÖVBORG. But I shall wait till you have received your appointment.

TESMAN. Will you wait? Yes, but—yes, but—are you not going to compete with me? Eh?

LÖVBORG. No; it is only the moral victory I care for.

TESMAN. Why, bless me—then Aunt Julia was right after all! Oh yes—I knew it! Hedda! Just fancy—Eilert Lövborg is not going to stand in our way!

HEDDA (*curtly*). Our way? Pray leave me out of the

question. (*She goes up towards the inner room, where* BERTA *is placing a tray with decanters and glasses on the table.* HEDDA *nods approval, and comes forward again.* BERTA *goes out.*)

TESMAN (*at the same time*). And you, Judge Brack—what do you say to this? Eh?

BRACK. Well, I say that a moral victory—h'm—may be all very fine——

TESMAN. Yes, certainly. But all the same——

HEDDA (*looking at* TESMAN *with a cold smile.*) You stand there looking as if you were thunderstruck——

TESMAN. Yes—so I am—I almost think——

BRACK. Don't you see, Mrs. Tesman, a thunderstorm has just passed over?

HEDDA (*pointing towards the inner room*). Will you not take a glass of cold punch, gentlemen?

BRACK (*looking at his watch*). A stirrup-cup? Yes, it wouldn't come amiss.

TESMAN. A capital idea, Hedda! Just the thing! Now that the weight has been taken off my mind——

HEDDA. Will you not join them, Mr. Lövborg?

LÖVBORG (*with a gesture of refusal*). No, thank you. Nothing for me.

BRACK. Why, bless me—cold punch is surely not poison.

LÖVBORG. Perhaps not for every one.

HEDDA. I will keep Mr. Lövborg company in the meantime.

TESMAN. Yes, yes, Hedda dear, do. (*He and* BRACK *go into the inner room, seat themselves, drink punch, smoke cigarettes, and carry on a lively conversation during what follows.* EILERT LÖVBORG *remains standing beside the stove.* HEDDA *goes to the writing-table.*)

HEDDA (*raising her voice a little*). Do you care to look at some photographs, Mr. Lövborg? You know Tesman and I made a tour in the Tyrol on our way home? (*She takes*

*up an album, and places it on the table beside the sofa, in the
further corner of which she seats herself.* EILERT LÖVBORG
*approaches, stops, and looks at her. Then he takes a chair
and seats himself to her left, with his back towards the inner
room.*

HEDDA (*opening the album*). Do you see this range of
mountains, Mr. Lövborg? It's the Ortler group. Tesman has
written the name underneath. Here it is: "The Ortler group
near Meran."

LÖVBORG (*who has never taken his eyes off her, says softly
and slowly:*) Hedda—Gabler!

HEDDA (*glancing hastily at him*). Ah! Hush!

LÖVBORG (*repeats softly*). Hedda Gabler!

HEDDA (*looking at the album*). That was my name in
the old days—when we two knew each other.

LÖVBORG. And I must teach myself never to say Hedda
Gabler again—never, as long as I live.

HEDDA (*still turning over the pages*). Yes, you must.
And I think you ought to practice in time. The sooner the
better, I should say.

LÖVBORG (*in a tone of indignation*). Hedda Gabler married? And married to—George Tesman!

HEDDA. Yes—so the world goes.

LÖVBORG. Oh, Hedda, Hedda—how could you[1] throw
yourself away!

HEDDA (*looks sharply at him*). What? I can't allow this!

LÖVBORG. What do you mean? (TESMAN *comes into the
room and goes towards the sofa.*)

HEDDA (*hears him coming and says in an indifferent tone*).
And this is a view from the Val d'Ampezzo, Mr. Lövborg.
Just look at these peaks! (*Looks affectionately up at* TES-
MAN.) What's the name of these curious peaks, dear?

TESMAN. Let me see. Oh, those are the Dolomites.

[1] He uses the familiar *du.*

HEDDA. Yes, that's it!—Those are the Dolomites, Mr. Lövborg.

TESMAN. Hedda dear,—I only wanted to ask whether I shouldn't bring you a little punch after all? For yourself at any rate—eh?

HEDDA. Yes, do, please; and perhaps a few biscuits.

TESMAN. No cigarettes?

HEDDA. No.

TESMAN. Very well. (*He goes into the inner room and out to the right.* BRACK *sits in the inner room, and keeps an eye from time to time on* HEDDA *and* LÖVBORG.

LÖVBORG (*softly, as before*). Answer me, Hedda—how could you go and do this?

HEDDA (*apparently absorbed in the album*). If you continue to say *du* to me I won't talk to you.

LÖVBORG. May I not say *du* when we are alone?

HEDDA. No. You may think it; but you mustn't say it.

LÖVBORG. Ah, I understand. It is an offense against George Tesman, whom you[1]—love.

HEDDA (*glances at him and smiles.*) Love? What an idea!

LÖVBORG. You don't love him then!

HEDDA. But I won't hear of any sort of unfaithfulness! Remember that.

LÖVBORG. Hedda—answer me one thing—

HEDDA. Hush! (TESMAN *enters with a small tray from the inner room.*)

TESMAN. Here you are! Isn't this tempting? (*He puts the tray on the table.*)

HEDDA. Why do you bring it yourself?

TESMAN (*filling the glasses*). Because I think it's such fun to wait upon you, Hedda.

HEDDA. But you have poured out two glasses. Mr. Lövborg said he wouldn't have any——

---

[1] From this point onward Lövborg uses the formal *De.*

TESMAN. No, but Mrs. Elvsted will soon be here, won't she?

HEDDA. Yes, by-the-bye—Mrs. Elvsted——

TESMAN. Had you forgotten her? Eh?

HEDDA. We were so absorbed in these photographs. (*Shows him a picture.*) Do you remember this little village?

TESMAN. Oh, it's that one just below the Brenner Pass. It was there we passed the night——

HEDDA. —and met that lively party of tourists.

TESMAN. Yes, that was the place. Fancy—if we could only have had you with us, Eilert! Eh? (*He returns to the inner room and sits beside* BRACK.)

LÖVBORG. Answer me this one thing, Hedda——

HEDDA. Well?

LÖVBORG. Was there no love in your friendship for me either? Not a spark—not a tinge of love in it?

HEDDA. I wonder if there was? To me it seems as though we were two good comrades—two thoroughly intimate friends. (*Smilingly.*) You especially were frankness itself.

LÖVBORG. It was you that made me so.

HEDDA. As I look back upon it all, I think there was really something beautiful, something fascinating—something daring—in—in that secret intimacy—that comradeship which no living creature so much as dreamed of.

LÖVBORG. Yes, yes, Hedda! Was there not?—When I used to come to your father's in the afternoon—and the General sat over at the window reading his papers—with his back towards us——

HEDDA. And we two on the corner sofa——

LÖVBORG. Always with the same illustrated paper before us——

HEDDA. For want of an album, yes.

LÖVBORG. Yes, Hedda, and when I made my confessions to you—told you about myself, things that at that time no one else knew! There I would sit and tell you of my escapades—my days and nights of devilment. Oh, Hedda—what was the power in you that forced me to confess these things?

HEDDA. Do you think it was any power in me?

LÖVBORG. How else can I explain it? And all those—those roundabout questions you used to put to me——

HEDDA. Which you understood so particularly well——

LÖVBORG. How could you sit and question me like that? Question me quite frankly——

HEDDA. In roundabout terms, please observe.

LÖVBORG. Yes, but frankly nevertheless. Cross-question me about—all that sort of thing?

HEDDA. And how could you answer, Mr. Lövborg?

LÖVBORG. Yes, that is just what I can't understand—in looking back upon it. But tell me now, Hedda—was there not love at the bottom of our friendship? On your side, did you not feel as though you might purge my stains away—if I made you my confessor? Was it not so?

HEDDA. No, not quite.

LÖVBORG. What was your motive, then?

HEDDA. Do you think it quite incomprehensible that a young girl—when it can be done—without any one knowing——

LÖVBORG. Well?

HEDDA. —should be glad to have a peep, now and then, into a world which—

LÖVBORG. Which——?

HEDDA. —which she is forbidden to know anything about?

LÖVBORG. So that was it?

HEDDA. Partly. Partly—I almost think.

LÖVBORG. Comradeship in the thirst for life. But why should not that, at any rate, have continued?

HEDDA. The fault was yours.

LÖVBORG. It was you that broke with me.

HEDDA. Yes, when our friendship threatened to develop into something more serious. Shame upon you, Eilert Lövborg! How could you think of wronging your—your frank comrade?

LÖVBORG (*clenching his hands*). Oh, why did you not carry out your threat? Why did you not shoot me down?

HEDDA. Because I have such a dread of scandal.

LÖVBORG. Yes, Hedda, you are a coward at heart.

HEDDA. A terrible coward. (*Changing her tone.*) But it was a lucky thing for you. And now you have found ample consolation at the Elvsteds'.

LÖVBORG. I know what Thea has confided to you.

HEDDA. And perhaps you have confided to her some thing about us?

LÖVBORG. Not a word. She is too stupid to understand anything of that sort.

HEDDA. Stupid?

LÖVBORG. She is stupid about matters of that sort.

HEDDA. And I am cowardly. (*Bends over towards him, without looking him in the face, and says more softly:*) But now I will confide something to you.

LÖVBORG (*eagerly*). Well?

HEDDA. The fact that I dared not shoot you down—

LÖVBORG. Yes!

HEDDA. —that was not my most arrant cowardice—that evening.

LÖVBORG (*looks at her a moment, understands, and whispers passionately*). Oh, Hedda! Hedda Gabler! Now I begin to see a hidden reason beneath our comradeship! You[1] and I——! After all, then, it was your craving for life——

HEDDA (*softly, with a sharp glance*). Take care! Believe nothing of the sort!

(*Twilight has begun to fall. The hall door is opened from without by* BERTA.)

[1] In this speech he once more says *du*. Hedda addresses him throughout as *De*.

HEDDA. (*Closes the album with a bang and calls smilingly:*) Ah, at last! My darling Thea,—come along!

MRS. ELVSTED *enters from the hall. She is in evening dress. The door is closed behind her.*

HEDDA. (*on the sofa, stretches out her arms towards her.*) My sweet Thea—you can't think how I have been longing for you!

(MRS. ELVSTED, *in passing, exchanges slight salutations with the gentlemen in the inner room, then goes up to the table and gives* HEDDA *her hand.* EILERT LÖVBORG *has risen. He and* MRS. ELVSTED *greet each other with a silent nod.*)

MRS. ELVSTED. Ought I to go in and talk to your husband for a moment?

HEDDA. Oh, not at all. Leave those two alone. They will soon be going.

MRS. ELVSTED. Are they going out?

HEDDA. Yes, to a supper-party.

MRS. ELVSTED (*quickly, to* LÖVBORG.) Not you?

LÖVBORG. No.

HEDDA. Mr. Lövborg remains with us.

MRS. ELVSTED (*Takes a chair and is about to seat herself at his side.*) Oh, how nice it is here!

HEDDA. No, thank you, my little Thea! Not there! You'll be good enough to come over here to me. I will sit between you.

MRS. ELVSTED. Yes, just as you please.

(*She goes round the table and seats herself on the sofa on* HEDDA's *right.* LÖVBORG *re-seats himself on his chair.*)

LÖVBORG (*after a short pause, to* HEDDA.) Is not she lovely to look at?

HEDDA (*lightly stroking her hair.*) Only to look at?

LÖVBORG. Yes. For we two—she and I—we are two real comrades. We have absolute faith in each other; so we can sit and talk with perfect frankness——

HEDDA. Not round about, Mr. Lövborg?

Lövborg. Well——

Mrs. Elvsted (*softly clinging close to* Hedda). Oh, how happy I am, Hedda; for, only think, he says I have inspired him too.

Hedda. (*Looks at her with a smile.*) Ah! Does he say that, dear?

Lövborg. And then she is so brave, Mrs. Tesman!

Mrs. Elvsted. Good heavens—am I brave?

Lövborg. Exceedingly—where your comrade is concerned.

Hedda. Ah yes—courage! If one only had that!

Lövborg. What then? What do you mean?

Hedda. Then life would perhaps be liveable, after all. (*With a sudden change of tone.*) But now, my dearest Thea, you really must have a glass of cold punch.

Mrs. Elvsted. No, thanks—I never take anything of that kind.

Hedda. Well then, you, Mr. Lövborg.

Lövborg. Nor I, thank you.

Mrs. Elvsted. No, he doesn't either.

Hedda. (*Looks fixedly at him.*) But if I say you shall?

Lövborg. It would be no use.

Hedda (*laughing*). Then I, poor creature, have no sort of power over you?

Lövborg. Not in that respect.

Hedda. But seriously, I think you ought to—for your own sake.

Mrs. Elvsted. Why, Hedda——!

Lövborg. How so?

Hedda. Or rather on account of other people.

Lövborg. Indeed?

Hedda. Otherwise people might be apt to suspect that—in your heart of hearts—you did not feel quite secure—quite confident in yourself.

Mrs. Elvsted (*softly*). Oh please, Hedda——.

LÖVBORG. People may suspect what they like—for the present.

MRS. ELVSTED (*joyfully*). Yes, let them!

HEDDA. I saw it plainly in Judge Brack's face a moment ago.

LÖVBORG. What did you see?

HEDDA. His contemptuous smile, when you dared not go with them into the inner room.

LÖVBORG. Dared not? Of course I preferred to stop here and talk to you.

MRS. ELVSTED. What could be more natural, Hedda?

HEDDA. But the Judge could not guess that. And I saw, too, the way he smiled and glanced at Tesman when you dared not accept his invitation to this wretched little supper-party of his.

LÖVBORG. Dared not! Do you say I dared not?

HEDDA. *I* don't say so. But that was how Judge Brack understood it.

LÖVBORG. Well, let him.

HEDDA. Then you are not going with them?

LÖVBORG. I will stay here with you and Thea.

MRS. ELVSTED. Yes, Hedda—how can you doubt that?

HEDDA (*smiles and nods approvingly to* LÖVBORG). Firm as a rock! Faithful to your principles, now and forever! Ah, that is how a man should be! (*Turns to* MRS. ELVSTED *and caresses her.*) Well now, what did I tell you, when you came to us this morning in such a state of distraction——

LÖVBORG (*surprised.*) Distraction!

MRS. ELVSTED (*terrified.*) Hedda—oh Hedda——!

HEDDA. You can see for yourself; you haven't the slightest reason to be in such mortal terror——(*Interrupting herself.*) There! Now we can all three enjoy ourselves!

LÖVBORG (*who has given a start.*) Ah—what is all this, Mrs. Tesman?

MRS. ELVSTED. Oh, my God, Hedda! What are you saying? What are you doing?

HEDDA. Don't get excited! That horrid Judge Brack is sitting watching you.

LÖVBORG. So she was in mortal terror! On my account!

MRS. ELVSTED (*softly and piteously.*) Oh, Hedda—now you have ruined everything!

LÖVBORG. (*Looks fixedly at her for a moment. His face is distorted.*) So that was my comrade's frank confidence in me?

MRS. ELVSTED (*imploringly.*) Oh, my dearest friend—only let me tell you——

LÖVBORG. (*Takes one of the glasses of punch, raises it to his lips, and says in a low, husky voice.*) Your health, Thea! (*He empties the glass, puts it down, and takes the second.*)

MRS. ELVSTED (*softly*). Oh, Hedda, Hedda—how could you do this?

HEDDA. *I* do it? I? Are you crazy?

LÖVBORG. Here's to your health too, Mrs. Tesman. Thanks for the truth. Hurrah for the truth!

(*He empties the glass and is about to re-fill it.*)

HEDDA. (*Lays her hand on his arm.*) Come, come—no more for the present. Remember you are going out to supper.

MRS. ELVSTED. No, no, no!

HEDDA. Hush! They are sitting watching you.

LÖVBORG (*putting down the glass.*) Now, Thea—tell me the truth——

MRS. ELVSTED. Yes.

LÖVBORG. Did your husband know that you had come after me?

MRS. ELVSTED (*wringing her hands.*) Oh, Hedda—do you hear what he is asking?

LÖVBORG. Was it arranged between you and him that you were to come to town and look after me? Perhaps it was the Sheriff himself that urged you to come? Aha, my dear

—no doubt he wanted my help in his office! Or was it at the card-table that he missed me?

MRS. ELVSTED (*softly, in agony*). Oh, Lövborg, Lövborg——!

LÖVBORG. (*Seizes a glass and is on the point of filling it.*) Here's a glass for the old Sheriff too!

HEDDA. (*preventing him.*) No more just now. Remember you have to read your manuscript to Tesman.

LÖVBORG (*calmly, putting down the glass*). It was stupid of me all this, Thea—to take it in this way, I mean. Don't be angry with me, my dear, dear comrade. You shall see—both you and the others—that if I was fallen once—now I have risen again! Thanks to you, Thea.

MRS. ELVSTED (*radiant with joy*). Oh, heaven be praised——!

(BRACK *has in the meantime looked at his watch. He and* TESMAN *rise and come into the drawing-room.*)

BRACK. (*Takes his hat and overcoat.*) Well, Mrs. Tesman, our time has come.

HEDDA. I suppose it has.

LÖVBORG (*rising*). Mine too, Judge Brack.

MRS. ELVSTED (*softly and imploringly*). Oh, Lövborg, don't do it!

HEDDA (*pinching her arm*). They can hear you!

MRS. ELVSTED (*with a suppressed shriek*). Ow!

LÖVBORG (*to* BRACK). You were good enough to invite me.

BRACK. Well, are you coming after all?

LÖVBORG. Yes, many thanks.

BRACK. I'm delighted——

LÖVBORG (*to* TESMAN, *putting the parcel of MS. in his pocket*). I should like to show you one or two things before I send it to the printers.

TESMAN. Fancy—that will be delightful. But, Hedda dear, how is Mrs. Elvsted to get home? Eh?

HEDDA. Oh, that can be managed somehow.

LÖVBORG (*looking towards the ladies*). Mrs. Elvsted? Of course, I'll come again and fetch her. (*Approaching.*) At ten or thereabouts, Mrs. Tesman? Will that do?

HEDDA. Certainly. That will do capitally.

TESMAN. Well, then, that's all right. But you must not expect me so early, Hedda.

HEDDA.—Oh, you may stop as long—as long as ever you please.

MRS. ELVSTED (*trying to conceal her anxiety*). Well then, Mr. Lövborg—I shall remain here until you come.

LÖVBORG (*with his hat in his hand*). Pray do, Mrs. Elvsted.

BRACK. And now off goes the excursion train, gentlemen! I hope we shall have a lively time, as a certain fair lady puts it.

HEDDA. Ah, if only the fair lady could be present unseen——!

BRACK. Why unseen?

HEDDA. In order to hear a little of your liveliness at first hand, Judge Brack.

BRACK (*laughing*). I should not advise the fair lady to try it.

TESMAN (*also laughing*). Come, you're a nice one Hedda! Fancy that!

BRACK. Well, good-bye, good-bye, ladies.

LÖVBORG (*bowing*). About ten o'clock, then.

(BRACK, LÖVBORG, *and* TESMAN *go out by the hall door. At the same time,* BERTA *enters from the inner room with a lighted lamp, which she places on the dining-room table; she goes out by the way she came.*)

MRS. ELVSTED (*who has risen and is wandering restlessly about the room*). Hedda—Hedda—what will come of all this?

HEDDA. At ten o'clock—he will be here. I can see him

already—with vine-leaves in his hair—flushed and fearless—

MRS. ELVSTED. Oh, I hope he may.

HEDDA. And then, you see—then he will have regained control over himself. Then he will be a free man for all his days.

MRS. ELVSTED. Oh God!—if he would only come as you see him now!

HEDDA. He will come as I see him—so, and not otherwise! (*Rises and approaches* THEA.) You may doubt him as long as you please; *I* believe in him. And now we will try——

MRS. ELVSTED. You have some hidden motive in this, Hedda!

HEDDA. Yes, I have. I want for once in my life to have power to mold a human destiny.

MRS. ELVSTED. Have you not the power?

HEDDA. I have not—and have never had it.

MRS. ELVSTED. Not your husband's?

HEDDA. Do you think that is worth the trouble? Oh, if you could only understand how poor I am. And fate has made you so rich! (*Clasps her passionately in her arms.*) I think I must burn your hair off, after all.

MRS. ELVSTED. Let me go! Let me go! I am afraid of you, Hedda!

BERTA (*in the middle doorway*). Tea is laid in the dining-room, ma'am.

HEDDA. Very well. We are coming.

MRS. ELVSTED. No, no, no! I would rather go home alone! At once!

HEDDA. Nonsense! First you shall have a cup of tea, you little stupid. And then—at ten o'clock—Eilert Lövborg will be here—with vine-leaves in his hair.

(*She drags* MRS. ELVSTED *almost by force towards the middle doorway.*)

ACT III

(*The room at the* TESMANS'. *The curtains are drawn over
the middle doorway, and also over the glass door. The
lamp, half turned down, and with a shade over it, is
burning on the table. In the stove, the door of which
stands open, there has been a fire, which is now nearly
burnt out.*)

(MRS. ELVSTED, *wrapped in a large shawl, and with her
feet upon a foot-rest, sits close to the stove, sunk back
in the arm-chair.* HEDDA, *fully dressed, lies sleeping
upon the sofa, with a sofa-blanket over her.*)

MRS. ELVSTED (*after a pause, suddenly sits up in her chair,
and listens eagerly. Then she sinks back again wearily, moan-
ing to herself*). Not yet!—Oh God—oh God—not yet!

(BERTA *slips cautiously in by the hall door. She has a
letter in her hand.*)

MRS. ELVSTED. (*Turns and whispers eagerly.*) Well—has
any one come?

BERTA (*softly*). Yes, a girl has brought this letter.

MRS. ELVSTED (*quickly, holding out her hand*). A letter!
Give it to me!

BERTA. No, it's for Dr. Tesman, ma'am.

MRS. ELVSTED. Oh, indeed.

BERTA. It was Miss Tesman's servant that brought it. I'll
lay it here on the table.

MRS. ELVSTED. Yes, do.

BERTA (*laying down the letter*). I think I had better put
out the lamp. It's smoking.

MRS. ELVSTED. Yes, put it out. It must soon be daylight
now.

BERTA (*putting out the lamp*). It is daylight already, ma'am.

MRS. ELVSTED. Yes, broad day! And no one come back yet——!

BERTA. Lord bless you, ma'am—I guessed how it would be.

MRS. ELVSTED. You guessed?

BERTA. Yes, when I saw that a certain person had come back to town—and that he went off with them. For we've heard enough about that gentleman before now.

MRS. ELVSTED. Don't speak so loud. You will waken Mrs. Tesman.

BERTA (*looks towards the sofa and sighs*). No, no—let her sleep, poor thing. Shan't I put some wood on the fire?

MRS. ELVSTED. Thanks, not for me.

BERTA. Oh, very well. (*She goes softly out by the hall door.*)

HEDDA (*is awakened by the shutting of the door, and looks up*). What's that——?

MRS. ELVSTED. It was only the servant——

HEDDA (*looking about her*). Oh, we're here——! Yes, now I remember. (*Sits erect upon the sofa, stretches herself, and rubs her eyes.*) What o'clock is it, Thea?

MRS. ELVSTED. (*Looks at her watch.*) It's past seven.

HEDDA. When did Tesman come home?

MRS. ELVSTED. He has not come.

HEDDA. Not come home yet?

MRS. ELVSTED (*rising*). No one has come.

HEDDA. Think of our watching and waiting here till four in the morning——

MRS. ELVSTED (*wringing her hands*). And how I watched and waited for him!

HEDDA. (*Yawns, and says with her hand before her mouth.*) Well well—we might have spared ourselves the trouble.

MRS. ELVSTED. Did you get a little sleep?

HEDDA. Oh yes; I believe I have slept pretty well. Have you not?

MRS. ELVSTED. Not for a moment. I couldn't, Hedda!—not to save my life.

HEDDA. (*Rises and goes towards her.*) There there there! There's nothing to be so alarmed about. I understand quite well what has happened.

MRS. ELVSTED. Well, what do you think? Won't you tell me?

HEDDA. Why, of course it has been a very late affair at Judge Brack's——

MRS. ELVSTED. Yes, yes, that is clear enough. But all the same——

HEDDA. And then, you see, Tesman hasn't cared to come home and ring us up in the middle of the night. (*Laughing.*) Perhaps he wasn't inclined to show himself either—immediately after a jollification.

MRS. ELVSTED. But in that case—where can he have gone?

HEDDA. Of course he has gone to his aunts' and slept there. They have his old room ready for him.

MRS. ELVSTED. No, he can't be with them; for a letter has just come for him from Miss Tesman. There it lies.

HEDDA. Indeed? (*Looks at the address.*) Why yes, it's addressed in Aunt Julia's own hand. Well then, he has remained at Judge Brack's. And as for Eilert Lövborg—he is sitting, with vine leaves in his hair, reading his manuscript.

MRS. ELVSTED. Oh Hedda, you are just saying things you don't believe a bit.

HEDDA. You really are a little blockhead, Thea.

MRS. ELVSTED. Oh yes, I suppose I am.

HEDDA. And how mortally tired you look.

MRS. ELVSTED. Yes, I am morally tired.

HEDDA. Well then, you must do as I tell you. You must go into my room and lie down for a little while.

MRS. ELVSTED. Oh no, no—I shouldn't be able to sleep.

HEDDA. I am sure you would.

MRS. ELVSTED. Well, but your husband is certain to come soon now; and then I want to know at once——

HEDDA. I shall take care to let you know when he comes.

MRS. ELVSTED. Do you promise me, Hedda?

HEDDA. Yes, rely upon me. Just you go in and have a sleep in the meantime.

MRS. ELVSTED. Thanks; then I'll try to. (*She goes off through the inner room.*)

> (HEDDA *goes up to the glass door and draws back the curtains. The broad daylight streams into the room. Then she takes a little hand-glass from the writing-table, looks at herself in it, and arranges her hair. Next she goes to the hall door and presses the bell-button.*)

> (BERTA *presently appears at the hall door.*)

BERTA. Did you want anything, ma'am?

HEDDA. Yes; you must put some more wood in the stove. I am shivering.

BERTA. Bless me—I'll make up the fire at once. (*She rakes the embers together and lays a piece of wood upon them; then stops and listens.*) That was a ring at the front door, ma'am.

HEDDA. Then go to the door. I will look after the fire.

BERTA. It'll soon burn up. (*She goes out by the hall door.*)

> (HEDDA *kneels on the foot-rest and lays some more pieces of wood in the stove.*)

> (*After a short pause,* GEORGE TESMAN *enters from the hall. He looks tired and rather serious. He steals on tiptoe towards the middle doorway and is about to slip through the curtains.*)

HEDDA. (*At the stove, without looking up.*) Good morning.

TESMAN. (*Turns.*) Hedda! (*Approaching her.*) Good heavens—are you up so early? Eh?

HEDDA. Yes, I am up very early this morning.

TESMAN. And I never doubted you were still sound asleep! Fancy that, Hedda!

HEDDA. Don't speak so loud. Mrs. Elvsted is resting in my room.

TESMAN. Has Mrs. Elvsted been here all night?

HEDDA. Yes, since no one came to fetch her.

TESMAN. Ah, to be sure.

HEDDA. (*Closes the door of the stove and rises.*) Well, did you enjoy yourselves at Judge Brack's?

TESMAN. Have you been anxious about me? Eh?

HEDDA. No, I should never think of being anxious. But I asked if you had enjoyed yourself.

TESMAN. Oh yes,—for once in a way. Especially the beginning of the evening; for then Eilert read me part of his book. We arrived more than an hour too early—fancy that! And Brack had all sorts of arrangements to make—so Eilert read to me.

HEDDA (*seating herself by the table on the right*). Well? Tell me, then——

TESMAN (*sitting on a footstool near the stove*). Oh Hedda, you can't conceive what a book that is going to be! I believe it is one of the most remarkable things that have ever been written. Fancy that!

HEDDA. Yes, yes; I don't care about that——

TESMAN. I must make a confession to you, Hedda. When he had finished reading—a horrid feeling came over me.

HEDDA. A horrid feeling?

TESMAN. I felt jealous of Eilert for having had it in him to write such a book. Only think, Hedda!

HEDDA. Yes, yes, I am thinking!

TESMAN. And then how pitiful to think that he—with all his gifts—should be irreclaimable, after all.

HEDDA. I suppose you mean that he has more courage than the rest?

TESMAN. No, not at all—I mean that he is incapable of taking his pleasures in moderation.

HEDDA. And what came of it all—in the end?

TESMAN. Well, to tell the truth, I think it might best be described as an orgie, Hedda.

HEDDA. Had he vine-leaves in his hair?

TESMAN. Vine-leaves? No, I saw nothing of the sort. But he made a long, rambling speech in honor of the woman who had inspired him in his work—that was the phrase he used.

HEDDA. Did he name her?

TESMAN. No, he didn't; but I can't help thinking he meant Mrs. Elvsted. You may be sure he did.

HEDDA. Well—where did you part from him?

TESMAN. On the way to town. We broke up—the last of us at any rate—all together; and Brack came with us to get a breath of fresh air. And then, you see, we agreed to take Eilert home; for he had had far more than was good for him.

HEDDA. I daresay.

TESMAN. But now comes the strange part of it, Hedda; or, I should rather say, the melancholy part of it. I declare I am almost ashamed—on Eilert's account—to tell you——

HEDDA. Oh, go on——

TESMAN. Well, as we were getting near town, you see, I happened to drop a little behind the others. Only for a minute or two—fancy that!

HEDDA. Yes, yes, yes, but——?

TESMAN. And then, as I hurried after them—what do you think I found by the wayside? Eh?

HEDDA. Oh, how should I know!

TESMAN. You mustn't speak of it to a soul, Hedda! Do you hear! Promise me, for Eilert's sake. (*Draws a parcel, wrapped in paper, from his coat pocket.*) Fancy, dear—I found this.

HEDDA. Is not that the parcel he had with him yesterday?

TESMAN. Yes, it is the whole of his precious, irreplaceable manuscript! And he had gone and lost it, and knew nothing about it. Only fancy, Hedda! So deplorably——

HEDDA. But why did you not give him back the parcel at once?

TESMAN. I didn't dare to—in the state he was then in——

HEDDA. Did you not tell any of the others that you had found it?

TESMAN. Oh, far from it! You can surely understand that, for Eilert's sake, I wouldn't do that.

HEDDA. So no one knows that Eilert Lövborg's manuscript is in your possession?

TESMAN. No. And no one must know it.

HEDDA. Then what did you say to him afterwards?

TESMAN. I didn't talk to him again at all; for when we got in among the streets, he and two or three of the others gave us the slip and disappeared. Fancy that!

HEDDA. Indeed! They must have taken him home then.

TESMAN. Yes, so it would appear. And Brack, too, left us.

HEDDA. And what have you been doing with yourself since?

TESMAN. Well, I and some of the others went home with one of the party, a jolly fellow, and took our morning coffee with him; or perhaps I should rather call it our night coffee —eh? But now, when I have rested a little, and given Eilert, poor fellow, time to have his sleep out, I must take this back to him.

HEDDA. (*Holds out her hand for the packet.*) No—don't give it to him! Not in such a hurry, I mean. Let me read it first.

TESMAN. No, my dearest Hedda, I mustn't, I really mustn't.

HEDDA. You must not?

TESMAN. No—for you can imagine what a state of despair he will be in when he awakens and misses the manuscript. He has no copy of it, you must know! He told me so.

HEDDA (*looking searchingly at him*). Can such a thing not be reproduced? Written over again?

TESMAN. No, I don't think that would be possible. For the inspiration, you see——

HEDDA. Yes, yes—I suppose it depends on that. (*Lightly.*) But, by-the-bye—here is a letter for you.

TESMAN. Fancy——!

HEDDA (*handing it to him*). It came early this morning.

TESMAN. It's from Aunt Julia! What can it be? (*He lays the packet on the other footstool, opens the letter, runs his eye through it, and jumps up.*) Oh, Hedda—she says that poor Aunt Rina is dying!

HEDDA. Well, we were prepared for that.

TESMAN. And that if I want to see her again, I must make haste. I'll run in to them at once.

HEDDA (*suppressing a smile*). Will you run?

TESMAN. Oh, dearest Hedda—if you could only make up your mind to come with me! Just think!

HEDDA. (*Rises and says wearily, repelling the idea.*) No, no, don't ask me. I will not look upon sickness and death. I loath all sort of ugliness.

TESMAN. Well, well, then——! (*Bustling around.*) My hat—— My overcoat——? Oh, in the hall—— I do hope I mayn't come too late, Hedda! Eh?

HEDDA. Oh, if you run——

(BERTA *appears at the hall door.*)

BERTA. Judge Brack is at the door, and wishes to know if he may come in.

TESMAN. At this time! No, I can't possibly see him.

HEDDA. But I can. (*To* BERTA.) Ask Judge Brack to come in. (BERTA *goes out.*)

HEDDA (*quickly, whispering*). The parcel, Tesman! (*She snatches it up from the stool.*)

TESMAN. Yes, give it to me!

HEDDA. No, no, I will keep it till you come back.

(*She goes to the writing-table and places it in the bookcase. TESMAN stands in a flurry of haste, and cannot get his gloves on.*)

(JUDGE BRACK *enters from the hall.*)

HEDDA (*nodding to him*). You are an early bird, I must say.

BRACK. Yes, don't you think so? (*To TESMAN.*) Are you on the move, too?

TESMAN. Yes, I must rush off to my aunts'. Fancy— the invalid one is lying at death's door, poor creature.

BRACK. Dear me, is she indeed? Then on no account let me detain you. At such a critical moment——

TESMAN. Yes, I must really rush—— Good-bye! Good-bye! (*He hastens out by the hall door.*)

HEDDA (*approaching*). You seem to have made a particularly lively night of it at your rooms, Judge Brack.

BRACK. I assure you I have not had my clothes off, Mrs. Hedda.

HEDDA. Not you, either?

BRACK. No, as you may see. But what has Tesman been telling you of the night's adventures?

HEDDA. Oh, some tiresome story. Only that they went and had coffee somewhere or other.

BRACK. I have heard about that coffee party already. Eilert Lövborg was not with them, I fancy?

HEDDA. No, they had taken him home before that.

BRACK. Tesman, too?

HEDDA. No, but some of the others, he said.

BRACK (*smiling*). George Tesman is really an ingenuous creature, Mrs. Hedda.

HEDDA. Yes, heaven knows he is. Then is there something behind all this?

BRACK. Yes, perhaps there may be.

HEDDA. Well then, sit down, my dear Judge, and tell your story in comfort.

(*She seats herself to the left of the table.* BRACK *sits near her, at the long side of the table.*)

HEDDA. Now then?

BRACK. I had special reasons for keeping track of my guests—or rather of some of my guests—last night.

HEDDA. Of Eilert Lövborg among the rest, perhaps?

BRACK. Frankly, yes.

HEDDA. Now you make me really curious——

BRACK. Do you know where he and one or two of the others finished the night, Mrs. Hedda?

HEDDA. If it is not quite unmentionable, tell me.

BRACK. Oh no, it's not at all unmentionable. Well, they put in an appearance at a particularly animated soirée.

HEDDA. Of the lively kind?

BRACK. Of the very liveliest——

HEDDA. Tell me more of this, Judge Brack——

BRACK. Lövborg, as well as the others, had been invited in advance. I knew all about it. But he had declined the invitation; for now, as you know, he has become a new man.

HEDDA. Up at the Elvsteds', yes. But he went after all, then?

BRACK. Well, you see, Mrs. Hedda—unhappily the spirit moved him at my rooms last evening——

HEDDA. Yes, I hear he found inspiration.

BRACK. Pretty violent inspiration. Well, I fancy that altered his purpose; for we men folk are unfortunately not always so firm in our principles as we ought to be.

HEDDA. Oh, I am sure you are an exception, Judge Brack. But as to Lövborg——?

BRACK. To make a long story short—he landed at last in Mademoiselle Diana's rooms.

HEDDA. Mademoiselle Diana's?

BRACK. It was Mademoiselle Diana that was giving the soirée, to a select circle of her admirers and her lady friends.

HEDDA. Is she a red-haired woman?

BRACK. Precisely.

HEDDA. A sort of a—singer?

BRACK. Oh yes—in her leisure moments. And moreover a mighty huntress—of men—Mrs. Hedda. You have no doubt heard of her. Eilert Lövborg was one of her most enthusiastic protectors—in the days of his glory.

HEDDA. And how did all this end?

BRACK. Far from amicably, it appears. After a most tender meeting, they seem to have come to blows——

HEDDA. Lövborg and she?

BRACK. Yes. He accused her or her friends of having robbed him. He declared that his pocket-book had disappeared—and other things as well. In short, he seems to have made a furious disturbance.

HEDDA. And what came of it all?

BRACK. It came to a general scrimmage, in which the ladies as well as the gentlemen took part. Fortunately the police at last appeared on the scene.

HEDDA. The police, too?

BRACK. Yes. I fancy it will prove a costly frolic for Eilert Lövborg, crazy being that he is.

HEDDA. How so?

BRACK. He seems to have made a violent resistance—to have hit one of the constables on the head and torn the coat off his back. So they had to march him off to the police-station with the rest.

HEDDA. How have you learned all this?

BRACK. From the police themselves.

HEDDA (*gazing straight before her*). So that is what happened. Then he had no vine-leaves in his hair.

BRACK. Vine-leaves, Mrs. Hedda?

HEDDA (*changing her tone*). But tell me now, Judge—what is your real reason for tracking out Eilert Lövborg's movements so carefully?

BRACK. In the first place, it could not be entirely indifferent to me if it should appear in the police court that he came straight from my house.

HEDDA. Will the matter come into court then?

BRACK. Of course. However, I should scarcely have troubled so much about that. But I thought that, as a friend of the family, it was my duty to supply you and Tesman with a full account of his nocturnal exploits.

HEDDA. Why so, Judge Brack?

BRACK. Why, because I have a shrewd suspicion that he intends to use you as a sort of blind.

HEDDA. Oh, how can you think such a thing!

BRACK. Good heavens, Mrs. Hedda—we have eyes in our head. Mark my words! This Mrs. Elvsted will be in no hurry to leave town again.

HEDDA. Well, even if there should be anything between them, I suppose there are plenty of other places where they could meet.

BRACK. Not a single home. Henceforth, as before, every respectable house will be closed against Eilert Lövborg.

HEDDA. And so ought mine to be, you mean?

BRACK. Yes. I confess it would be more than painful to me if this personage were to be made free of your house. How superfluous, how intrusive, he would be, if he were to force his way into——

HEDDA. —into the triangle?

BRACK. Precisely. It would simply mean that I should find myself homeless.

HEDDA. (*Looks at him with a smile.*) So you want to be the one cock in the basket[1]—that is your aim.

BRACK (*nods slowly and lowers his voice.*) Yes, that is

[1] "Eneste hane i kurven"—a proverbial saying.

my aim. And for that I will fight—with every weapon I can command.

HEDDA (*her smile vanishing*). I see you are a dangerous person—when it comes to the point.

BRACK. Do you think so?

HEDDA. I am beginning to think so. And I am exceedingly glad to think—that you have no sort of hold over me.

BRACK (*laughing equivocally*). Well, well, Mrs. Hedda—perhaps you are right there. If I had, who knows what I might be capable of?

HEDDA. Come, come now, Judge Brack! That sounds almost like a threat.

BRACK (*rising*). Oh, not at all! The triangle, you know, ought, if possible, to be spontaneously constructed.

HEDDA. There I agree with you.

BRACK. Well, now I have said all I had to say; and I had better be getting back to town. Good-bye, Mrs. Hedda. (*He goes towards the glass door.*)

HEDDA (*rising*). Are you going through the garden?

BRACK. Yes, it's a short cut for me.

HEDDA. And then it is a back way, too.

BRACK. Quite so. I have no objection to back ways. They may be piquant enough at times.

HEDDA. When there is ball practice going on, you mean?

BRACK (*in the doorway, laughing to her*). Oh, people don't shoot their tame poultry, I fancy.

HEDDA (*also laughing*). Oh no, when there is only one cock in the basket——

(*They exchange laughing nods of farewell. He goes. She closes the door behind him.*)

(HEDDA, *who has become quite serious, stands for a moment looking out. Presently she goes and peeps through the curtain over the middle doorway. Then she goes to the writing-table, takes* LÖVBORG's *packet out of the bookcase, and is on the point of looking*

through its contents. BERTA *is heard speaking loudly
in the hall.* HEDDA *turns and listens. Then she
hastily locks up the packet in the drawer, and lays
the key on the inkstand.*)

(EILERT LÖVBORG, *with his greatcoat on and his hat in
his hand, tears open the hall door. He looks somewhat confused and irritated.*)

LÖVBORG (*looking towards the hall*). And I tell you I
must and will come in! There!

(*He closes the door, turns, sees* HEDDA, *at once regains
his self-control, and bows.*)

HEDDA (*at the writing-table*). Well, Mr. Lövborg, this
is rather a late hour to call for Thea.

LÖVBORG. You mean rather an early hour to call on you.
Pray pardon me.

HEDDA. How do you know that she is still here?

LÖVBORG. They told me at her lodgings that she had
been out all night.

HEDDA (*going to the oval table*). Did you notice anything about the people of the house when they said that?

LÖVBORG. (*Looks inquiringly at her.*) Notice anything
about them?

HEDDA. I mean, did they seem to think it odd?

LÖVBORG (*suddenly understanding*). Oh yes, of course!
I am dragging her down with me! However, I didn't notice
anything. I suppose Tesman is not up yet?

HEDDA. No—I think not——

LÖVBORG. When did he come home?

HEDDA. Very late.

LÖVBORG. Did he tell you anything?

HEDDA. Yes, I gathered that you had had an exceedingly
jolly evening at Judge Brack's.

LÖVBORG. Nothing more?

HEDDA. I don't think so. However, I was so dreadfully
sleepy——

(MRS. ELVSTED *enters through the curtains of the middle doorway.*)

MRS. ELVSTED (*going towards him*). Ah, Lövborg! At last——!

LÖVBORG. Yes, at last. And too late!

MRS. ELVSTED (*Looks anxiously at him.*) What is too late?

LÖVBORG. Everything is too late now. It is all over with me.

MRS. ELVSTED. Oh no, no—don't say that!

LÖVBORG. You will say the same when you hear——

MRS. ELVSTED. I won't hear anything!

HEDDA. Perhaps you would prefer to talk to her alone! If so, I will leave you.

LÖVBORG. No, stay—you too. I beg you to stay.

MRS. ELVSTED. Yes, but I won't hear anything, I tell you.

LÖVBORG. It is not last night's adventures that I want to talk about.

MRS. ELVSTED. What is it then——?

LÖVBORG. I want to say that now our ways must part.

MRS. ELVSTED. Part!

HEDDA (*involuntarily*). I knew it!

LÖVBORG. You can be of no more service to me, Thea.

MRS. ELVSTED. How can you stand there and say that! No more service to you! Am I not to help you now, as before? Are we not to go on working together?

LÖVBORG. Henceforward I shall do no work.

MRS. ELVSTED (*despairingly*). Then what am I to do with my life?

LÖVBORG. You must try to live your life as if you had never known me.

MRS. ELVSTED. But you know I cannot do that!

LÖVBORG. Try if you cannot, Thea. You must go home again——

MRS. ELVSTED (*in vehement protest*). Never in this

world! Where you are, there will I be also! I will not let myself be driven away like this! I will remain here! I will be with you when the book appears.

HEDDA (*half aloud, in suspense*). Ah yes—the book!

LÖVBORG. (*Looks at her.*) My book and Thea's; for that is what it is.

MRS. ELVSTED. Yes, I feel that it is. And that is why I have a right to be with you when it appears! I will see with my own eyes how respect and honor pour in upon you afresh. And the happiness—the happiness—oh, I must share it with you!

LÖVBORG. Thea—our book will never appear.

HEDDA. Ah!

MRS. ELVSTED. Never appear!

LÖVBORG. Can never appear.

MRS. ELVSTED (*in agonized foreboding*). Lövborg—what have you done with the manuscript?

HEDDA. (*Looks anxiously at him.*) Yes, the manuscript——?

MRS. ELVSTED. Where is it?

LÖVBORG. Oh, Thea—don't ask me about it!

MRS. ELVSTED. Yes, yes, I will know. I demand to be told at once.

LÖVBORG. The manuscript—— Well then—I have torn the manuscript into a thousand pieces.

MRS. ELVSTED. (*Shrieks.*) Oh no, no——!

HEDDA (*involuntarily*). But that's not——

LÖVBORG. (*Looks at her.*) Not true, you think?

HEDDA (*collecting herself*). Oh well, of course—since you say so. But it sounded so improbable——

LÖVBORG. It is true, all the same.

MRS. ELVSTED (*wringing her hands*). Oh God—oh God, Hedda—torn his own work to pieces!

LÖVBORG. I have torn my own life to pieces. So why should I not tear my life-work too——?

MRS. ELVSTED. And you did this last night?

LÖVBORG. Yes, I tell you! Tore it into a thousand pieces and scattered them on the fiord—far out. There there is cool sea-water at any rate—let them drift upon it—drift with the current and the wind. And then presently they will sink—deeper and deeper—as I shall, Thea.

MRS. ELVSTED. Do you know, Lövborg, that what you have done with the book—I shall think of it to my dying day as though you had killed a little child.

LÖVBORG. Yes, you are right. It is a sort of child-murder.

MRS. ELVSTED. How could you, then—! Did not the child belong to me too?

HEDDA (*almost inaudibly*). Ah, the child——

MRS. ELVSTED (*breathing heavily*). It is all over then. Well, well, now I will go, Hedda.

HEDDA. But you are not going away from town?

MRS. ELVSTED. Oh, I don't know what I shall do. I see nothing but darkness before me. (*She goes out by the hall door.*)

HEDDA. (*Stands waiting for a moment.*) So you are not going to see her home, Mr. Lövborg?

LÖVBORG. I? Through the streets? Would you have people see her walking with me?

HEDDA. Of course I don't know what else may have happened last night. But is it so utterly irretrievable?

LÖVBORG. It will not end with last night—I know that perfectly well. And the thing is that now I have no taste for that sort of life either. I won't begin it anew. She has broken my courage and my power of braving life out.

HEDDA (*looking straight before her*). So that pretty little fool has had her fingers in a man's destiny. (*Looks at him.*) But all the same, how could you treat her so heartlessly?

LÖVBORG. Oh, don't say that it was heartless!

HEDDA. To go and destroy what has filled her whole soul for months and years! You do not call that heartless!

LÖVBORG. To you I can tell the truth, Hedda.

HEDDA. The truth?

LÖVBORG. First promise me—give me your word—that what I now confide to you Thea shall never know.

HEDDA. I give you my word.

LÖVBORG. Good. Then let me tell you that what I said just now was untrue.

HEDDA. About the manuscript?

LÖVBORG. Yes. I have not torn it to pieces—nor thrown it into the fiord.

HEDDA. No, n— But—where is it then?

LÖVBORG. I have destroyed it none the less—utterly destroyed it, Hedda!

HEDDA. I don't understand.

LÖVBORG. Thea said that what I had done seemed to her like a child-murder.

HEDDA. Yes, so she said.

LÖVBORG. But to kill this child—that is not the worst thing a father can do to it.

HEDDA. Not the worst?

LÖVBORG. No. I wanted to spare Thea from hearing the worst.

HEDDA. Then what is the worst?

LÖVBORG. Suppose now, Hedda, that a man—in the small hours of the morning—came home to his child's mother after a night of riot and debauchery, and said: "Listen—I have been here and there—in this place and in that. And I have taken our child with me—to this place and to that. And I have lost the child—utterly lost it. The devil knows into what hands it may have fallen—who may have had their clutches on it."

HEDDA. Well—but when all is said and done, you know —this was only a book——

LÖVBORG. Thea's pure soul was in that book.

HEDDA. Yes, so I understand.

LÖVBORG. And you can understand, too, that for her and me together no future is possible.

HEDDA. What path do you mean to take then?

LÖVBORG. None. I will only try to make an end of it all —the sooner the better.

HEDDA (*a step nearer him*). Eilert Lövborg—listen to me. Will you not try to—to do it beautifully?

LÖVBORG. Beautifully? (*Smiling.*) With vine--leaves in my hair, as you used to dream in the old days——?

HEDDA. No, no. I have lost my faith in the vine-leaves. But beautifully nevertheless! For once in a way!—Good-bye! You must go now—and do not come here any more.

LÖVBORG. Good-bye, Mrs. Tesman. And give George Tesman my love. (*He is on the point of going.*)

HEDDA. No, wait! I must give you a memento to take with you.

(*She goes to the writing-table and opens the drawer and the pistol-case; then returns to* LÖVBORG *with one of the pistols.*)

LÖVBORG (*looks at her*). This? Is this the memento?

HEDDA (*nodding slowly*). Do you recognize it? It was aimed at you once.

LÖVBORG. You should have used it then.

HEDDA. Take it—and do you use it now.

LÖVBORG (*puts the pistol in his breast pocket*). Thanks!

HEDDA. And beautifully, Eilert Lövborg. Promise me that!

LÖVBORG. Good-bye, Hedda Gabler. (*He goes out by the hall door.*)

(*HEDDA listens for a moment at the door. Then she goes up to the writing-table, takes out the packet of man-uscript, peeps under the cover, draws a few of the sheets half out, and looks at them. Next she goes over and seats herself in the arm-chair beside the stove, with the packet in her lap. Presently she opens the stove door, and then the packet.*)

HEDDA (*throws one of the quires into the fire and whispers to herself*). Now I am burning your child, Thea!— Burning it, curly-locks! (*Throwing one or two more quires into the stove.*) Your child and Eilert Lövborg's. (*Throws the rest in.*) I am burning—I am burning your child.

ACT IV

(*The same rooms at the* TESMANS'. *It is evening. The
drawing-room is in darkness. The back room is lighted
by the hanging lamp over the table. The curtains over
the glass door are drawn close.*)

(HEDDA, *dressed in black, walks to and fro in the dark
room. Then she goes into the back room and disap-
pears for a moment to the left. She is heard to strike a
few chords on the piano. Presently she comes in sight
again, and returns to the drawing-room.*)

(BERTA *enters from the right, through the inner room, with
a lighted lamp, which she places on the table in front of
the corner settee in the drawing-room. Her eyes are
red with weeping, and she has black ribbons in her cap.
She goes quietly and circumspectly out to the right.*)

(HEDDA *goes up to the glass door, lifts the curtain a little
aside, and looks out into the darkness.*)

(*Shortly afterwards,* MISS TESMAN, *in mourning, with a
bonnet and veil on, comes in from the hall.* HEDDA *goes
towards her and holds out her hand.*)

MISS TESMAN. Yes, Hedda, here I am, in mourning and
forlorn; for now my poor sister has at last found peace.

HEDDA. I have heard the news already, as you see. Tesman sent me a card.

MISS TESMAN. Yes, he promised me he would. But nevertheless I thought that to Hedda—here in the house of life—
I ought myself to bring the tidings of death.

HEDDA. That was very kind of you.

MISS TESMAN. Ah, Rina ought not to have left us just
now. This is not the time for Hedda's house to be a house of
mourning.

316

HEDDA (*changing the subject*). She died quite peacefully, did she not, Miss Tesman?

MISS TESMAN. Oh, her end was so calm, so beautiful. And then she had the unspeakable happiness of seeing George once more—and bidding him good-bye.—Has he come home yet?

HEDDA. No. He wrote that he might be detained. But won't you sit down?

MISS TESMAN. No thank you, my dear, dear Hedda. I should like to, but I have so much to do. I must prepare my dear one for her rest as well as I can. She shall go to her grave looking her best.

HEDDA. Can I not help you in any way?

MISS TESMAN. Oh, you must not think of it! Hedda Tesman must have no hand in such mournful work. Nor let her thoughts dwell on it either—not at this time.

HEDDA. One is not always mistress of one's thoughts——

MISS TESMAN (*continuing*). Ah yes, it is the way of the world. At home we shall be sewing a shroud; and here there will soon be sewing too, I suppose—but of another sort, thank God!

(GEORGE TESMAN *enters by the hall door.*)

HEDDA. Ah, you have come at last!

TESMAN. You here, Aunt Julia? With Hedda? Fancy that!

MISS TESMAN. I was just going, my dear boy. Well, have you done all you promised?

TESMAN. No; I'm really afraid I have forgotten half of it. I must come to you again to-morrow. To-day my brain is all in a whirl. I can't keep my thoughts together.

MISS TESMAN. Why, my dear George, you mustn't take it in this way.

TESMAN. Mustn't——? How do you mean?

MISS TESMAN. Even in your sorrow you must rejoice, as I do—rejoice that she is at rest.

TESMAN. Oh yes, yes—you are thinking of Aunt Rina.

HEDDA. You will feel lonely now, Miss Tesman.

MISS TESMAN. Just at first, yes. But that will not last very long, I hope. I daresay I shall soon find an occupant for poor Rina's little room.

TESMAN. Indeed? Who do you think will take it? Eh?

MISS TESMAN. Oh, there's always some poor invalid or other in want of nursing, unfortunately.

HEDDA. Would you really take such a burden upon you again?

MISS TESMAN. A burden! Heaven forgive you, child—it has been no burden to me.

HEDDA. But suppose you had a total stranger on your hands——

MISS TESMAN. Oh, one soon makes friends with sick folk; and it's such an absolute necessity for me to have some one to live for. Well, heaven be praised, there may soon be something in this house, too, to keep an old aunt busy.

HEDDA. Oh, don't trouble about anything here.

TESMAN. Yes, just fancy what a nice time we three might have together, if——?

HEDDA. If——?

TESMAN (*uneasily*). Oh, nothing. It will all come right. Let us hope so—eh?

MISS TESMAN. Well, well, I daresay you two want to talk to each other. (*Smiling.*) And perhaps Hedda may have something to tell you too, George. Good-bye! I must go home to Rina. (*Turning at the door.*) How strange it is to think that now Rina is with me and with my poor brother as well!

TESMAN. Yes, fancy that, Aunt Julia! Eh? (MISS TESMAN *goes out by the hall door.*)

HEDDA (*follows* TESMAN *coldly and searchingly with her eyes*). I almost believe your Aunt Rina's death affects you more than it does your Aunt Julia.

TESMAN. Oh, it's not that alone. It's Eilert I am so terribly uneasy about.

HEDDA (*quickly*). Is there anything new about him?

TESMAN. I looked in at his rooms this afternoon, intending to tell him the manuscript was in safe keeping.

HEDDA. Well, did you not find him?

TESMAN. No. He wasn't at home. But afterwards I met Mrs. Elvsted, and she told me that he had been here early this morning.

HEDDA. Yes, directly after you had gone.

TESMAN. And he said that he had torn his manuscript to pieces—eh?

HEDDA. Yes, so he declared.

TESMAN. Why, good heavens, he must have been completely out of his mind! And I suppose you thought it best not to give it back to him, Hedda?

HEDDA. No, he did not get it.

TESMAN. But of course you told him that we had it?

HEDDA. No. (*Quickly.*) Did you tell Mrs. Elvsted?

TESMAN. No; I thought I had better not. But you ought to have told him. Fancy, if, in desperation, he should go and do himself some injury! Let me have the manuscript, Hedda! I will take it to him at once. Where is it?

HEDDA (*cold and immovable, leaning on the arm-chair*). I have not got it.

TESMAN. Have not got it? What in the world do you mean?

HEDDA. I have burnt it—every line of it.

TESMAN (*with a violent movement of terror*). Burnt! Burnt Eilert's manuscript!

HEDDA. Don't scream so. The servant might hear you.

TESMAN. Burnt! Why, good God——! No, no, no! It's impossible!

HEDDA. It is so, nevertheless.

TESMAN. Do you know what you have done, Hedda? It's unlawful appropriation of lost property. Fancy that! Just ask Judge Brack, and he'll tell you what it is.

HEDDA. I advise you not to speak of it—either to Judge Brack, or to any one else.

TESMAN. But how could you do anything so unheard-of? What put it into your head? What possessed you? Answer me that—eh?

HEDDA (*suppressing an almost inperceptible smile*). I did it for your sake, George.

TESMAN. For my sake!

HEDDA. This morning, when you told me about what he had read to you——

TESMAN. Yes, yes—what then?

HEDDA. You acknowledged that you envied him his work.

TESMAN. Oh, of course I didn't mean that literally.

HEDDA. No matter—I could not bear the idea that any one should throw you into the shade.

TESMAN (*in an outburst of mingled doubt and joy*). Hedda! Oh, is this true? But—but—I never knew you to show your love like that before. Fancy that!

HEDDA. Well, I may as well tell you that—just at this time—— (*Impatiently, breaking off.*) No, no; you can ask Aunt Julia. She will tell you, fast enough.

TESMAN. Oh, I almost think I understand you, Hedda! (*Clasps his hands together.*) Great heavens! do you really mean it! Eh?

HEDDA. Don't shout so. The servant might hear.

TESMAN. (*laughing in irrepressible glee.*) The servant! Why, how absurd you are, Hedda. It's only my old Berta! Why, I'll tell Berta myself.

HEDDA (*clenching her hands together in desperation*). Oh, it is killing me,—it is killing me, all this!

TESMAN. What is, Hedda? Eh?

HEDDA (*coldly, controlling herself*). All this—absurdity— George.

TESMAN. Absurdity! Do you see anything absurd in my being overjoyed at the news! But after all—perhaps I had better not say anything to Berta.

HEDDA. Oh—why not that too?

TESMAN. No, no, not yet! But I must certainly tell Aunt Julia. And then that you have begun to call me George too! Fancy that! Oh, Aunt Julia will be so happy—so happy.

HEDDA. When she hears that I have burnt Eilert Lövborg's manuscript—for your sake?

TESMAN. No, by-the-bye—that affair of the manuscript —of course nobody must know about that. But that you love me so much,[1] Hedda—Aunt Julia must really share my joy in that! I wonder, now, whether this sort of thing is usual in young wives? Eh?

HEDDA. I think you had better ask Aunt Julia that question too.

TESMAN. I will indeed, some time or other. (*Looks uneasy and downcast again.*) And yet the manuscript—the manuscript! Good God! it is terrible to think what will become of poor Eilert now.

MRS. ELVSTED, *dressed as in the first Act, with hat and cloak, enters by the hall door.*)

MRS. ELVSTED (*greets them hurriedly, and says in evident agitation*). Oh, dear Hedda, forgive my coming again.

HEDDA. What is the matter with you, Thea?

TESMAN. Something about Eilert Lövborg again—eh?

MRS. ELVSTED. Yes! I am dreadfully afraid some misfortune has happened to him.

HEDDA (*seizes her arm*). Ah,—do you think so?

TESMAN. Why, good Lord—what makes you think that, Mrs. Elvsted?

MRS. ELVSTED. I heard them talking of him at my boarding-house—just as I came in. Oh, the most incredible rumors are afloat about him to-day.

TESMAN. Yes, fancy, so I heard too! And I can bear wit-

---

[1] Literally, "That you burn for me."

ness that he went straight home to bed last night. Fancy that!

HEDDA. Well, what did they say at the boarding-house?

MRS. ELVSTED. Oh, I couldn't make out anything clearly. Either they knew nothing definite, or else—— They stopped talking when they saw me; and I did not dare to ask.

TESMAN (*moving about uneasily*). We must hope—we must hope that you misunderstood them, Mrs. Elvsted.

MRS. ELVSTED. No, no; I am sure it was of him they were talking. And I heard something about the hospital or——

TESMAN. The hospital?

HEDDA. No—surely that cannot be!

MRS. ELVSTED. Oh, I was in such mortal terror! I went to his lodgings and asked for him there.

HEDDA. You could make up your mind to that, Thea!

MRS. ELVSTED. What else could I do? I really could bear the suspense no longer.

TESMAN. But you didn't find him either—eh?

MRS. ELVSTED. No. And the people knew nothing about him. He hadn't been home since yesterday afternoon, they said.

TESMAN. Yesterday! Fancy, how could they say that?

MRS. ELVSTED. Oh, I am sure something terrible must have happened to him.

TESMAN. Hedda dear—how would it be if I were to go and make inquiries——?

HEDDA. No, no—don't you mix yourself up in this affair.

(JUDGE BRACK, *with his hat in his hand, enters by the hall door, which* BERTA *opens, and closes behind him. He looks grave and bows in silence.*)

TESMAN. Oh, is that you, my dear Judge? Eh?

BRACK. Yes. It was imperative I should see you this evening.

TESMAN. I can see you have heard the news about Aunt Rina?

BRACK. Yes, that among other things.

TESMAN. Isn't it sad—eh?

BRACK. Well, my dear Tesman, that depends on how you look at it.

TESMAN (*looks doubtfully at him*). Has anything else happened?

BRACK. Yes.

HEDDA (*in suspense*). Anything sad, Judge Brack?

BRACK. That, too, depends on how you look at it, Mrs. Tesman.

MRS. ELVSTED (*unable to restrain her anxiety*). Oh! it is something about Eilert Lövborg!

BRACK (*with a glance at her*). What makes you think that, Madam? Perhaps you have already heard something——?

MRS. ELVSTED (*in confusion*). No, nothing at all, but——

TESMAN. Oh, for heaven's sake, tell us!

BRACK (*shrugging his shoulders*). Well, I regret to say Eilert Lövborg has been taken to the hospital. He is lying at the point of death.

MRS. ELVSTED (*shrieks*). Oh God! Oh God——!

TESMAN. To the hospital! And at the point of death.

HEDDA (*involuntarily*). So soon then——

MRS. ELVSTED (*wailing*). And we parted in anger, Hedda!

HEDDA (*whispers*). Thea—Thea—be careful!

MRS. ELVSTED (*not heeding her*). I must go to him! I must see him alive!

BRACK. It is useless, Madam. No one will be admitted.

MRS. ELVSTED. Oh, at least tell me what has happened to him? What is it?

TESMAN. You don't mean to say that he has himself—— Eh?

HEDDA. Yes, I am sure he has.

TESMAN. Hedda, how can you——?

BRACK (*keeping his eyes fixed upon her*). Unfortunately you have guessed quite correctly, Mrs. Tesman.

MRS. ELVSTED. Oh, how horrible!

TESMAN. Himself, then! Fancy that!

HEDDA. Shot himself!

BRACK. Rightly guessed again, Mrs. Tesman.

MRS. ELVSTED (*with an effort at self-control*). When did it happen, Mr. Brack?

BRACK. This afternoon—between three and four.

TESMAN. But, good Lord, where did he do it? Eh?

BRACK (*with some hesitation*). Where? Well—I suppose at his lodgings.

MRS. ELVSTED. No, that cannot be; for I was there between six and seven.

BRACK. Well, then, somewhere else. I don't know exactly. I only know that he was found——. He had shot himself—in the breast.

MRS. ELVSTED. Oh, how terrible! That he should die like that!

HEDDA (*to Brack*). Was it in the breast?

BRACK. Yes—as I told you.

HEDDA. Not in the temple?

BRACK. In the breast, Mrs. Tesman.

HEDDA. Well, well—the breast is a good place, too.

BRACK. How do you mean, Mrs. Tesman?

HEDDA (*evasively*). Oh, nothing—nothing.

TESMAN. And the wound is dangerous, you say—eh?

BRACK. Absolutely mortal. The end has probably come by this time.

MRS. ELVSTED. Yes, yes, I feel it. The end! The end! Oh, Hedda——!

TESMAN. But tell me, how have you learned all this?

BRACK (*curtly*). Through one of the police. A man I had some business with.

HEDDA (*in a clear voice*). At last a deed worth doing!

TESMAN (*terrified*). Good heavens, Hedda! what are you saying?

HEDDA. I say there is beauty in this.

BRACK. H'm, Mrs. Tesman——

TESMAN. Beauty! Fancy that!

MRS. ELVSTED. Oh, Hedda, how can you talk of beauty in such an act!

HEDDA. Eilert Lövborg has himself made up his account with life. He has had the courage to do—the one right thing.

MRS. ELVSTED. No, you must never think that was how it happened! It must have been in delirium that he did it.

TESMAN. In despair!

HEDDA. That he did not. I am certain of that.

MRS. ELVSTED. Yes, yes! In delirium! Just as when he tore up our manuscript.

BRACK (*starting*). The manuscript? Has he torn that up?

MRS. ELVSTED. Yes, last night.

TESMAN (*whispers softly*). Oh, Hedda, we shall never get over this.

BRACK. H'm, very extraordinary.

TESMAN (*moving about the room*). To think of Eilert going out of the world in this way! And not leaving behind him the book that would have immortalized his name——

MRS. ELVSTED. Oh, if only it could be put together again!

TESMAN. Yes, if it only could! I don't know what I would not give——

MRS. ELVSTED. Perhaps it can, Mr. Tesman.

TESMAN. What do you mean?

MRS. ELVSTED (*searches in the pocket of her dress*). Look here. I have kept all the loose notes he used to dictate from.

HEDDA (*a step forward*). Ah——!

TESMAN. You have kept them, Mrs. Elvsted! Eh?

MRS. ELVSTED. Yes, I have them here. I put them in my pocket when I left home. Here they still are——

TESMAN. Oh, do let me see them!

MRS. ELVSTED (*hands him a bundle of papers*). But they are in such disorder—all mixed up.

TESMAN. Fancy, if we could make something out of them, after all! Perhaps if we two put our heads together——

MRS. ELVSTED. Oh, yes, at least let us try——

TESMAN. We will manage it! We must! I will dedicate my life to this task.

HEDDA. You, George? Your life?

TESMAN. Yes, or rather all the time I can spare. My own collections must wait in the meantime. Hedda—you understand, eh? I owe this to Eilert's memory.

HEDDA. Perhaps.

TESMAN. And so, my dear Mrs. Elvsted, we will give our whole minds to it: There is no use in brooding over what can't be undone—eh? We must try to control our grief as much as possible, and——

MRS. ELVSTED. Yes, yes, Mr. Tesman, I will do the best I can.

TESMAN. Well then, come here. I can't rest until we have looked through the notes. Where shall we sit? Here? No, in there, in the back room. Excuse me, my dear Judge. Come with me, Mrs. Elvsted.

MRS. ELVSTED. Oh, if only it were possible! (TESMAN *and* MRS. ELVSTED *go into the back room. She takes off her hat and cloak. They both sit at the table under the hanging lamp, and are soon deep in an eager examination of the papers.* HEDDA *crosses to the stove and sits in the arm-chair. Presently* BRACK *goes up to her.*)

HEDDA (*in a low voice*). Oh, what a sense of freedom it gives one, this act of Eilert Lövborg's.

BRACK. Freedom, Mrs. Hedda? Well, of course, it is a release for him——

HEDDA. I mean for me. It gives me a sense of freedom to know that a deed of deliberate courage is still possible in this world,—a deed of spontaneous beauty.

BRACK (*smiling*). H'm—my dear Mrs. Hedda——

HEDDA. Oh, I know what you are going to say. For you are a kind of specialist too, like—you know!

BRACK (*looking hard at her*). Eilert Lövborg was more to you than perhaps you are willing to admit to yourself. Am I wrong?

HEDDA. I don't answer such questions. I only know that Eilert Lövborg has had the courage to live his life after his own fashion. And then—the last great act, with its beauty! Ah! that he should have the will and the strength to turn away from the banquet of life—so early.

BRACK. I am sorry, Mrs. Hedda,—but I fear I must dispel an amiable illusion.

HEDDA. Illusion?

BRACK. Which could not have lasted long in any case.

HEDDA. What do you mean?

BRACK. Eilert Lövborg did not shoot himself—voluntarily.

HEDDA. Not voluntarily?

BRACK. No. The thing did not happen exactly as I told it.

HEDDA (*in suspense*). Have you concealed something? What is it?

BRACK. For poor Mrs. Elvsted's sake I idealized the facts a little.

HEDDA. What are the facts?

BRACK. First, that he is already dead.

HEDDA. At the hospital?

BRACK. Yes—without regaining consciousness.

HEDDA. What more have you concealed?

BRACK. This—the event did not happen at his lodgings.

HEDDA. Oh, that can make no difference.

BRACK. Perhaps it may. For I must tell you—Eilert Lövborg was found shot in—in Mademoiselle Diana's boudoir.

HEDDA (*makes a motion as if to rise, but sinks back again*). That is impossible, Judge Brack! He cannot have been there again to-day.

BRACK. He was there this afternoon. He went there, he said, to demand the return of something which they had taken from him. Talked wildly about a lost child——

HEDDA. Ah—so that was why——

BRACK. I thought probably he meant his manuscript; but now I hear he destroyed that himself. So I suppose it must have been his pocket-book.

HEDDA. Yes, no doubt. And there—there he was found?

BRACK. Yes, there. With a pistol in his breast-pocket, discharged. The ball had lodged in a vital part.

HEDDA. In the breast—yes.

BRACK. No—in the bowels.

HEDDA (*looks up at him with an expression of loathing*). That too! Oh, what curse is it that makes everything I touch turn ludicrous and mean?

BRACK. There is one point more, Mrs. Hedda—another disagreeable feature in the affair.

HEDDA. And what is that?

BRACK. The pistol he carried——

HEDDA (*breathless*). Well? What of it?

BRACK. He must have stolen it.

HEDDA (*leaps up*). Stolen it! That is not true! He did not steal it!

BRACK. No other explanation is possible. He must have stolen it—— Hush!

(TESMAN *and* MRS. ELVSTED *have risen from the table in the back room, and come into the drawing room.*)

TESMAN (*with the papers in both his hands*). Hedda dear, it is almost impossible to see under that lamp. Think of that!

HEDDA. Yes, I am thinking.

TESMAN. Would you mind our sitting at your writing-table—eh?

HEDDA. If you like. (*Quickly.*) No, wait! Let me clear it first!

TESMAN. Oh, you needn't trouble, Hedda. There is plenty of room.

HEDDA. No, no, let me clear it, I say! I will take these things in and put them on the piano. There! (*She has drawn out an object, covered with sheet music, from under the bookcase, places several other pieces of music upon it, and carries the whole into the inner room, to the left.* TESMAN *lays the scraps of paper on the writing-table, and moves the lamp there from the corner table.* He and MRS. ELVSTED *sit down and proceed with their work.* HEDDA *returns.*)

HEDDA (*behind* MRS. ELVSTED's *chair, gently ruffling her hair*). Well, my sweet Thea,—how goes it with Eilert Lövborg's monument?

MRS. ELVSTED (*looks dispiritedly up at her*). Oh, it will be terribly hard to put in order.

TESMAN. We must manage it. I am determined. And arranging other people's papers is just the work for me. (HEDDA *goes over to the stove, and seats herself on one of the footstools.* BRACK *stands over her, leaning on the arm-chair.*)

HEDDA (*whispers*). What did you say about the pistol?

BRACK (*softly*). That he must have stolen it.

HEDDA. Why stolen it?

BRACK. Because every other explanation ought to be impossible, Mrs. Hedda.

HEDDA. Indeed?

BRACK (*glances at her*). Of course Eilert Lövborg was here this morning. Was he not?

HEDDA. Yes.

BRACK. Were you alone with him?

HEDDA. Part of the time.

BRACK. Did you not leave the room whilst he was here?

HEDDA. No.

BRACK. Try to recollect. Were you not out of the room a moment?

HEDDA. Yes, perhaps just a moment—out in the hall.

BRACK. And where was your pistol-case during that time?

HEDDA. I had it locked up in——

BRACK. Well, Mrs. Hedda?

HEDDA. The case stood there on the writing-table.

BRACK. Have you looked since, to see whether both the pistols are there?

HEDDA. No.

BRACK. Well, you need not. I saw the pistol found in Lövborg's pocket, and I knew it at once as the one I had seen yesterday—and before, too.

HEDDA. Have you it with you?

BRACK. No; the police have it.

HEDDA. What will the police do with it?

BRACK. Search till they find the owner.

HEDDA. Do you think they will succeed?

BRACK (*bends over her and whispers*). No, Hedda Gabler —not so long as I say nothing.

HEDDA (*looks frightened at him*). And if you do not say nothing,—what then?

BRACK (*shrugs his shoulders*). There is always the possibility that the pistol was stolen.

HEDDA (*firmly*). Death rather than that.

BRACK (*smiling*). People say such things—but they don't do them.

HEDDA (*without replying*). And supposing the pistol was not stolen, and the owner is discovered? What then?

BRACK. Well, Hedda—then comes the scandal.

HEDDA. The scandal!

BRACK. Yes, the scandal—of which you are mortally afraid. You will, of course, be brought before the court— both you and Mademoiselle Diana. She will have to explain how the thing happened—whether it was an accidental shot or murder. Did the pistol go off as he was trying to take it out of his pocket, to threaten her with? Or did she tear the pistol out of his hand, shoot him, and push it back into his pocket? That would be quite like her; for she is an able-bodied young person, this same Mademoiselle Diana.

HEDDA. But *I* have nothing to do with all this repulsive business.

BRACK. No. But you will have to answer the question: Why did you give Eilert Lövborg the pistol? And what conclusions will people draw from the fact that you did give it to him?

HEDDA (*lets her head sink*). That is true. I did not think of that.

BRACK. Well, fortunately, there is no danger, so long as I say nothing.

HEDDA (*looks up at him*). So I am in your power, Judge Brack. You have me at your beck and call, from this time forward.

BRACK (*whispers softly*). Dearest Hedda—believe me—I shall not abuse my advantage.

HEDDA. I am in your power none the less. Subject to your will and your demands. A slave, a slave then! (*Rises impetuously.*) No, I cannot endure the thought of that! Never!

BRACK (*looks half-mockingly at her*). People generally get used to the inevitable.

HEDDA (*returns his look*). Yes, perhaps. (*She crosses to the writing-table. Suppressing an involuntary smile, she imitates* TESMAN's *intonations.*) Well? Are you getting on, George? Eh?

TESMAN. Heaven knows, dear. In any case it will be the work of months.

HEDDA (*as before*). Fancy that! (*Passes her hands softly through* MRS. ELVSTED's *hair.*) Doesn't it seem strange to you, Thea? Here are you sitting with Tesman—just as you used to sit with Eilert Lövborg?

MRS. ELVSTED. Ah, if I could only inspire your husband in the same way.

HEDDA. Oh, that will come too—in time.

TESMAN. Yes, do you know, Hedda—I really think I be-

gin to feel something of the sort. But won't you go and
sit with Brack again?

HEDDA. Is there nothing I can do to help you two?

TESMAN. No, nothing in the world. (*Turning his head.*)
I trust to you to keep Hedda company, my dear Brack.

BRACK (*with a glance at* HEDDA). With the very greatest of pleasure.

HEDDA. Thanks. But I am tired this evening. I will go
in and lie down a little on the sofa.

TESMAN. Yes, do, dear—eh? (HEDDA *goes into the back
room and draws the curtains. A short pause. Suddenly she
is heard playing a wild dance on the piano.*)

MRS. ELVSTED (*starts from her chair*). Oh—what is that?

TESMAN (*runs to the doorway*). Why, my dearest Hedda
—don't play dance music to-night! Just think of Aunt
Rina! And of Eilert, too!

HEDDA (*puts her head out between the curtains*). And of
Aunt Julia. And of all the rest of them. After this, I will
be quiet. (*Closes the curtains again.*)

TESMAN (*at the writing-table*). It's not good for her to
see us at this distressing work. I'll tell you what, Mrs.
Elvsted,—you shall take the empty room at Aunt Julia's.
and then I will come over in the evenings, and we can sit
and work there—eh?

HEDDA (*in the inner room*). I hear what you are saying,
Tesman. But how am *I* to get through the evenings out
here?

TESMAN (*turning over the papers*). Oh, I daresay Judge
Brack will be so kind as to look in now and then, even
though I am out.

BRACK (*in the arm-chair, calls out gaily*). Every blessed
evening, with all the pleasure in life, Mrs. Tesman! We
shall get on capitally together, we two!

HEDDA (*speaking loud and clear*). Yes, don't you flatter
yourself we will, Judge Brack? Now that you are the one

cock in the basket—— (*A shot is heard within.* TESMAN, MRS. ELVSTED, *and* BRACK *leap to their feet.*)

TESMAN. Oh, now she is playing with those pistols again. (*He throws back the curtains and runs in, followed by* MRS. ELVSTED. HEDDA *lies stretched on the sofa, lifeless. Confusion and cries.* BERTA *enters in alarm from the right.*)

TESMAN (*shrieks to* BRACK). Shot herself! Shot herself in the temple! Fancy that!

BRACK (*half-fainting in the arm-chair*). Good God!—people don't do such things.

THE LADY FROM THE SEA

CAST OF CHARACTERS

DOCTOR WANGEL.

ELLIDA WANGEL, *his second wife.*

BOLETTE,
HILDE *(not yet grown up),* } *his daughters by his first wife.*

ARNHOLM *(second master at a college).*

LYNGSTRAND.

BALLESTED.

A STRANGER.

YOUNG PEOPLE OF THE TOWN.

TOURISTS.

VISITORS.

(The action takes place in a small fjord town, Northern Norway.)

ACT I

(SCENE.—DOCTOR WANGEL'S *house, with a large veranda garden in front of and around the house. Under the veranda a flagstaff. In the garden an arbor, with table and chairs. Hedge, with small gate at the back. Beyond, a road along the seashore. An avenue of trees along the road. Between the trees are seen the fjord, high mountain ranges and peaks. A warm and brilliantly clear summer morning.*)

(BALLESTED, *middle-aged, wearing an old velvet jacket, and a broad-brimmed artist's hat, stands under the flagstaff, arranging the ropes. The flag is lying on the ground. A little way from him an easel, with an outspread canvas. By the easel on a camp-stool, brushes, a palette, and box of colors.*)

(BOLETTE WANGEL *comes from the room opening on the veranda. She carries a large vase with flowers, which she puts down on the table.*)

BOLETTE. Well, Ballested, does it work smoothly?

BALLESTED. Certainly, Miss Bolette, that's easy enough. May I ask—do you expect any visitors to-day?

BOLETTE. Yes, we're expecting Mr. Arnholm this morning. He got to town in the night.

BALLESTED. Arnholm? Wait a minute—wasn't Arnholm the man who was tutor here several years ago?

BOLETTE. Yes, it is he.

BALLESTED. Oh, really! Is he coming into these parts again?

BOLETTE. That's why we want to have the flag up.

BALLESTED. Well, that's reasonable enough.

(BOLETTE *goes into the room again. A little after* LYNGSTRAND *enters from the road and stands still, interested by the easel and painting gear. He is a slender youth, poorly but carefully dressed, and looks delicate.*)

LYNGSTRAND (*on the other side of the hedge*). Good morning.

BALLESTED (*turning round*). Hello! Good morning. (*Hoists up flag*). That's it! Up goes the balloon. (*Fastens the ropes, and then busies himself about the easel.*) Good morning, my dear sir. I really don't think I've the pleasure of——

LYNGSTRAND. I'm sure you're a painter.

BALLESTED. Of course I am. Why shouldn't I be?

LYNGSTRAND. Yes, I can see you are? May I take the liberty of coming in a moment?

BALLESTED. Would you like to come in and see?

LYNGSTRAND. I should like to immensely.

BALLESTED. Oh! there's nothing much to see yet. But come in. Come a little closer.

LYNGSTRAND. Many thanks. (*Comes in through the garden gate.*)

BALLESTED (*painting*). It's the fjord there between the islands I'm working at.

LYNGSTRAND. So I see.

BALLESTED. But the figure is still wanting. There's not a model to be got in this town.

LYNGSTRAND. Is there to be a figure, too?

BALLESTED. Yes. Here by the rocks in the foreground a mermaid is to lie, half-dead.

LYNGSTRAND. Why is she to be half-dead?

BALLESTED. She has wandered hither from the sea, and can't find her way out again. And so, you see, she lies there dying in the brackish water.

LYNGSTRAND. Ah, I see.

BALLESTED. The mistress of this house put it into my head to do something of the kind.

LYNGSTRAND. What shall you call the picture when it's finished?

BALLESTED. I think of calling it "The Mermaid's End."

LYNGSTRAND. That's capital! You're sure to make something fine of it.

BALLESTED (*looking at him*). In the profession, too, perhaps?

LYNGSTRAND. Do you mean a painter?

BALLESTED. Yes.

LYNGSTRAND. No, I'm not that; but I'm going to be a sculptor. My name is Hans Lyngstrand.

BALLESTED. So you're to be a sculptor? Yes, yes; the art of sculpture is a nice, pretty art in its way. I fancy I've seen you in the street once or twice. Have you been staying here long?

LYNGSTRAND. No; I've only been here a fortnight. But I shall try to stop till the end of the summer.

BALLESTED. For the bathing?

LYNGSTRAND. Yes; I wanted to see if I could get a little stronger.

BALLESTED. Not delicate, surely?

LYNGSTRAND. Yes, perhaps I am a little delicate; but it's nothing dangerous. Just a little tightness on the chest.

BALLESTED. Tush!—a bagatelle! You should consult a good doctor.

LYNGSTRAND. Yes, I thought of speaking to Doctor Wangel one of these times.

BALLESTED. You should. (*Looks out to the left.*) There's another steamer, crowded with passengers. It's really marvelous how traveling has increased here of late years.

LYNGSTRAND. Yes, there's a good deal of traffic here, I think.

BALLESTED. And lots of summer visitors come here, too.

I often hear our good town will lose its individuality with all these foreign goings on.

LYNGSTRAND. Were you born in the town?

BALLESTED. No; but I have accla—acclimatized myself. I feel united to the place by the bonds of time and habit.

LYNGSTRAND. Then you've lived here a long time?

BALLESTED. Well—about seventeen or eighteen years. I came here with Skive's Dramatic Company. But then we got into difficulties, and so the company broke up and dispersed in all directions.

LYNGSTRAND. But you yourself remained here?

BALLESTED. I remained, and I've done very well. I was then working chiefly as decorative artist, don't you know.

(BOLETTE *comes out with a rocking-chair, which she places on the veranda.*)

BOLETTE (*speaking into the room*). Hilde, see if you can find the embroidered footstool for father.

LYNGSTRAND (*going up to the veranda, bows*). Good morning, Miss Wangel.

BOLETTE (*by the balustrade*). What! Is it you, Mr. Lyngstrand? Good morning. Excuse me one moment, I'm only —— (*Goes into room.*)

BALLESTED. Do you know the family?

LYNGSTRAND. Not well. I've only met the young ladies now and again in company; and I had a chat with Mrs. Wangel the last time we had music up at the "View." She said I might come and see them.

BALLESTED. Now, do you know, you ought to cultivate their acquaintance.

LYNGSTRAND. Yes; I'd been thinking of paying a visit. Just a sort of call. If only I could find some excuse——

BALLESTED. Excuse! Nonsense! (*Looking out to the left.*) Damn it! (*Gathering his things.*) The steamer's by the pier already. I must get off to the hotel. Perhaps some of the new arrivals may want me. For I'm a hairdresser, too, don't you know.

LYNGSTRAND. You are certainly very many-sided, sir.

BALLESTED. In small towns one has to try to acclam—acc*li*matize oneself in various branches. If you should require anything in the hair line—a little pomatum or such like—you've only to ask for Dancing-master Ballested.

LYNGSTRAND. Dancing master!

BALLESTED. President of the "Wind Band Society," by your leave. We've a concert on this evening up at the "View." Good-bye, good-bye!

(*He goes out with his painting gear through the garden gate.* HILDE *comes out with the footstool.* BOLETTE *brings more flowers.* LYNGSTRAND *bows to* HILDE *from the garden below.*)

HILDE (*by the balustrade, not returning his bow*). Bolette said you had ventured in to-day.

LYNGSTRAND. Yes; I took the liberty of coming in for a moment.

HILDE. Have you been out for a morning walk?

LYNGSTRAND. Oh, no! nothing came of the walk this morning.

HILDE. Have you been bathing, then?

LYNGSTRAND. Yes; I've been in the water a little while. I saw your mother down there. She was going into her bathing machine.

HILDE. Who was?

LYNGSTRAND. Your mother.

HILDE. Oh! I see. (*She puts the stool in front of the rocking-chair.*)

BOLETTE (*interrupting*). Didn't you see anything of father's boat out on the fjord?

LYNGSTRAND. Yes; I thought I saw a sailing boat that was steering inland.

BOLETTE. I'm sure that was father. He's been to visit patients on the islands. (*She is arranging things on the table.*)

LYNGSTRAND (*taking a step up the stairs to the veranda*). Why, how everything's decorated here with flowers!

BOLETTE. Yes; doesn't it look nice?

LYNGSTRAND. It looks lovely! It looks as if it were some festival day in the house.

HILDE. That's exactly what it is.

LYNGSTRAND. I might have guessed it! I'm sure it's your father's birthday.

BOLETTE (*warningly to* HILDE). Hm—hm!

HILDE (*taking no notice of her*). No, mother's.

LYNGSTRAND. Oh! your mother's!

BOLETTE (*in low voice, angrily*). Really, Hilde!

HILDE (*the same*). Let me be! (*To* LYNGSTRAND.) I suppose you're going home to breakfast now?

LYNGSTRAND (*going down steps*). Yes, I suppose I must go and get something to eat.

HILDE. I'm sure you find the living very good at the hotel!

LYNGSTRAND. I'm not staying at the hotel now. It was too expensive for me.

HILDE. Where are you staying, then?

LYNGSTRAND. I'm staying up at Mrs. Jensen's.

HILDE. What Mrs. Jensen's?

LYNGSTRAND. The midwife.

HILDE. Excuse me, Mr. Lyngstrand, but I really have other matters to attend to——

LYNGSTRAND. Oh! I'm sure I ought not to have said that.

HILDE. Said what?

LYNGSTRAND. What I said.

HILDE (*looking contemptuously at him*). I don't understand you in the least.

LYNGSTRAND. No, no. But I must say good-bye for the present.

BOLETTE (*comes forward to the steps*). Good-bye, good-bye, Mr. Lyngstrand. You must excuse us now. But another day—when you've plenty of time—and inclination—you really must come in and see father and the rest of us.

LYNGSTRAND. Yes; thanks, very much. I shall be delighted.

(*Bows, and goes out through the garden gate. As he goes along the road he bows again towards the veranda.*)

HILDE (*in low voice*). Adieu, Monsieur! Please remember me to Mother Jensen.

BOLETTE (*in a low voice, shaking her arm*). Hilde! You naughty child! Are you quite crazy? He might have heard you.

HILDE. Pshaw! Do you think I care about *that?*

BOLETTE (*looking out to the right*). Here's father.

(WANGEL, *in traveling dress and carrying a small bag, comes from the footpath.*)

WANGEL. See! I'm back again, little girls! (*He enters through the garden gate.*)

BOLETTE (*going towards him at the bottom of the garden*). Oh! It is delightful that you've come!

HILDE (*also going up to him*). Now have you got off for the whole day, father?

WANGEL. Oh! no. I must go down to the office for a little while presently. I say—do you know if Arnholm has come?

BOLETTE. Yes; he arrived in the night. We sent to the hotel to inquire.

WANGEL. Then you've not seen him yet?

BOLETTE. No; but he's sure to come here this morning.

WANGEL. Yes; he's sure to do that.

HILDE (*pulling him*). Father, now you must look round.

WANGEL (*looking towards the veranda*). Yes, I see well enough, child. It's quite festive.

BOLETTE. Now, don't you think we've arranged it nicely?

WANGEL. I must say you have. Are—are we alone at home now?

HILDE. Yes; she's gone to——

BOLETTE (*interrupting quickly*). Mother has gone to bathe.

WANGEL (*looks lovingly at* BOLETTE, *and pats her head. Then he says, hesitating*). Look here, little ones. Do you want to keep this up all day? And the flag hoisted, too?

HILDE. Surely you understand that, father!

WANGEL. Hm! Yes; but you see——

BOLETTE (*looks at him and nods*). Surely you can understand we've been doing all this in honor of Mr. Arnholm. When such a good friend comes to see you for the first time——

HILDE (*smiling, and shaking him*). Think! he who used to be Bolette's tutor, father!

WANGEL (*with a half-smile*). You're a pair of sly minxes. Well—good heavens—after all, it's but natural we should remember her who is no more with us. Here, Hilde (*Gives her his bag*), take that down to the office. No, children. I don't like this—the way, I mean. This habit of every year—well—what can one say? I suppose it can't be managed any other way.

HILDE (*about to go out of garden, and, with the bag, stops short, turns, and points out*). Look at that gentleman coming up here. I'm sure it's your tutor.

BOLETTE (*looks in that direction*). He? (*Laughs.*) That is good! Do you think that middle-aged fellow is Arnholm?

WANGEL. Wait a moment, child. Why, by Jove, I do believe it is he. Yes, it certainly is.

BOLETTE (*staring at him in quiet amazement*). Yes; I almost think——

(ARNHOLM, *in elegant morning dress, with gold spectacles, and a thin cane, comes along the road. He looks over-worked. He looks in at the garden, bows in friendly fashion, and enters by the garden gate.*)

WANGEL (*going to meet him*). Welcome, dear Arnholm! Heartily welcome back to your old quarters again!

ARNHOLM. Thanks, thanks, Doctor Wangel. A thousand thanks. (*They shake hands and walk up the garden together.*) And there are the children! (*Holds out his hands and looks at them.*) I should hardly have known these two again.

WANGEL. No, I believe you.

ARNHOLM. And yet—perhaps Bolette—yes, I should have known Bolette again.

WANGEL. Hardly, I think. Why, it is eight—nine years since you saw her. Ah, yes! Many a thing has changed here meanwhile.

ARNHOLM (*looking round*). I really don't see it; except that the trees have grown remarkably, and that you've set up that arbor.

WANGEL. Oh! no—outwardly.

ARNHOLM (*smiling*). And then, of course, you've two grown-up daughters here now.

WANGEL. Grown up! Well, there's only one grown up.

HILDE (*aside*). Just listen to father!

WANGEL. But now let's sit down up there on the veranda. It's cooler than here. Won't you?

ARNHOLM. Thanks, thanks, dear doctor.

(*They go up.* WANGEL *motions him to the rocking-chair.*)

WANGEL. That's right! Now make yourself comfortable, and rest, for you seem rather tired after your journey.

ARNHOLM. Oh, that's nothing. Here, amid these surroundings——

BOLETTE (*to* WANGEL). Hadn't we better have some soda and syrup in the sitting room? It's sure to be too hot out here soon.

WANGEL. Yes, girls. Let's have some soda and syrup, and perhaps a drop of Cognac, too.

BOLETTE. Cognac, too!

WANGEL. Just a little, in case anyone should like some.

BOLETTE. All right. Hilde, go down to the office with the bag.

(BOLETTE *goes into the room, and closes the door after her.* HILDE *takes the bag, and goes through the garden to the back of the house.*)

ARNHOLM (*who has followed* BOLETTE *with his eyes*). What a splendid—. They are both splendid girls, who've grown up here for you.

WANGEL (*sitting down*). Yes; you think so, too?

ARNHOLM. Why, it's simply amazing, how Bolette!—and Hilde, too! But now, you yourself, dear doctor. Do you think of staying here all your life?

WANGEL. Yes; I suppose so. Why, I've been born and bred here, so to say. I lived here so very happily with—her who left us so early—she whom you knew when you were here before, Arnholm.

ARNHOLM. Yes, yes!

WANGEL. And now I live here so happily with her who has taken her place. Ah! On the whole, fate has been very good to me.

ARNHOLM. You have no children by your second marriage?

WANGEL. We had a little boy, two—two and a half years ago. But he didn't stay long. He died when he was four—five months old.

ARNHOLM. Isn't your wife at home to-day?

WANGEL. Oh, yes. She's sure to be here soon. She's down there bathing. She does so every blessed day no matter what the weather.

ARNHOLM. Is she ill, then?

WANGEL. Not exactly ill, although she has been extremely nervous for the last few years—that is to say, she is now and then. I can't make out what really ails her. But to plunge into the sea is her joy and delight.

ARNHOLM. Yes; I remember that of old.

WANGEL (*with an almost imperceptible smile*). To be

sure! You knew Ellida when you were teacher out there at Skjoldviken.

ARNHOLM. Certainly. She used often to visit at the Parsonage. But I mostly met her when I went to the light-house to see her father.

WANGEL. Those times out there, you may believe me, have set deep marks upon her. The people in the town here can't understand her at all. They call her the "Lady from the Sea."

ARNHOLM. Do they?

WANGEL. Yes. And so—now, you see, speak to her of the old days, dear Arnholm, it will do her good.

ARNHOLM (*looks at him in doubt*). Have you any reason for thinking so?

WANGEL. Assuredly I have.

ELLIDA (*her voice is heard outside the garden*). Are you there, Wangel?

WANGEL (*rising*). Yes, dear.

(MRS. ELLIDA WANGEL, *in a large, light wrap, and with wet hair hanging loose over her shoulders, comes from between the trees of the arbour.* ARNHOLM *rises.*)

WANGEL (*smiling, and holding out his hands to her*). Ah! So now we have our Mermaid!

ELLIDA (*goes quickly up the veranda, and seizes his hands*). Thank God that I see you again! When did you come?

WANGEL. Just now; a little while since. (*Pointing to* ARNHOLM.) But won't you greet an old acquaintance?

ELLIDA (*holding out her hand to* ARNHOLM). So here you are! Welcome! And forgive me for not being at home——

ARNHOLM. Don't mention it—don't stand on any ceremony.

WANGEL. Was the water nice and fresh to-day?

ELLIDA. Fresh! Oh! The water here never is fresh. It is so tepid and lifeless. Ugh! The water in the fjord here is sick.

ARNHOLM. Sick?

ELLIDA. Yes, sick. And I believe it makes one sick, too.

WANGEL (*smiling*). You're giving our bathing resort a good name!

ARNHOLM. I should rather believe, Mrs. Wangel, that you have a peculiar relation to the sea, and to all that belongs to it.

ELLIDA. Perhaps; I almost think so myself. But do you see how festively the girls have arranged everything in your honor?

WANGEL (*embarrassed*). Hm! (*Looks at his watch.*) Well, I suppose I must be quick and——

ARNHOLM. Is it really for me?

ELLIDA. Yes. You may be sure we don't decorate like this every day. Ugh! How suffocatingly hot it is under this roof. (*Goes down into the garden.*) Come over here. Here at least there is a little air. (*Sits down in arbor.*)

ARNHOLM (*going thither*). I think the air quite fresh here.

ELLIDA. Yes, you—who are used to the stifling air of the town! It's terrible there in the summer, I hear.

WANGEL (*who has also gone into the garden*). Hm, dear Ellida, you must just entertain our friend alone for a little while.

ELLIDA. Are you busy?

WANGEL. Yes, I must go down to the office. And then I must change. But I won't be long.

ARNHOLM (*sitting down in arbor*). Now, don't hurry, dear doctor. Your wife and I will manage to kill the time.

WANGEL (*nodding*). Oh, yes! I'm sure you will. Well, good-bye for the present. (*He goes out through the garden.*)

ELLIDA (*after a short pause*). Don't you think it's pleasant sitting out here?

ARNHOLM. I think I've a pleasant seat now.

ELLIDA. They call this my arbor, because I had it fitted up, or rather Wangel did for me.

ARNHOLM. And you usually sit here?

ELLIDA. Yes, I pass most of the day here.

ARNHOLM. With the girls, I suppose?

ELLIDA. No, the girls—usually sit on the veranda.

ARNHOLM. And Wangel himself?

ELLIDA. Oh! Wangel goes to and fro—now he comes to me, and then he goes to his children.

ARNHOLM. And is it you who wish this?

ELLIDA. I think all parties feel most comfortable in this way. You know we can talk across to one another—if we happen to find there is anything to say.

ARNHOLM (*after thinking awhile*). When I last crossed your path—out at Skjoldviken, I mean—Hm! That is long ago now.

ELLIDA. It's quite ten years since you were there with us.

ARNHOLM. Yes, about that. But when I think of you out there in the lighthouse! The heathen, as the old clergyman called you, because your father had named you, as he said, after an old ship, and hadn't given you a name fit for a Christian.

ELLIDA. Well, what then?

ARNHOLM. The last thing I should then have believed was that I should see you again down here as the wife of Wangel.

ELLIDA. No; at that time Wangel wasn't—at that time the girls' first mother was still living. Their real mother, so——

ARNHOLM. Of course, of course! But even if that had not been—even if he had been free—still, I could never have believed this would come about.

ELLIDA. Nor I. Never on earth—then.

ARNHOLM. Wangel is such a good fellow. So honorable. So thoroughly good and kind to all men.

ELLIDA (*warmly and heartily*). Yes, he is indeed.

ARNHOLM. But he must be so absolutely different from you, I fancy.

ELLIDA. You are right there. So he is.

ARNHOLM. Well, but how did it happen? How did it come about?

ELLIDA. Ah! dear Arnholm, you mustn't ask me about

that. I couldn't explain it to you, and even if I could, you would never be able to understand, in the least.

ARNHOLM. Hm! (*In lower tone.*) Have you ever confided anything about me to your husband? Of course, I meant about the useless step—I allowed myself to be moved to.

ELLIDA. No. You may be sure of that. I've not said a word to him about—about what you speak of.

ARNHOLM. I am glad. I felt rather awkward at the thought that——

ELLIDA. There was no need. I have only told him what is true—that I liked you very much, and that you were the truest and best friend I had out there.

ARNHOLM. Thanks for that. But tell me—why did you never write to me after I had gone away?

ELLIDA. I thought that perhaps it would pain you to hear from one who—who could not respond as you desired. It seemed like re-opening a painful subject.

ARNHOLM. Hm. Yes, yes, perhaps you were right.

ELLIDA. But why didn't you write?

ARNHOLM (*looks at her and smiles, half reproachfully*). I make the first advance? Perhaps expose myself to the suspicion of wanting to begin all over again? After such a repulse as I had had?

ELLIDA. Oh no! I understand very well. Have you never since thought of forming any other tie?

ARNHOLM. Never! I have been faithful to my first memories.

ELLIDA (*half jestingly*). Nonsense! Let the sad old memories alone. You'd better think of becoming a happy husband, I should say.

ARNHOLM. I should have to be quick about it, then, Mrs. Wangel. Remember, I'm already—I'm ashamed to say—I'm past thirty-seven.

ELLIDA. Well, all the more reason for being quick. (*She*

is silent for a moment, and then says, earnestly, in a low voice.) But listen, dear Arnholm; now I am going to tell you something that I could not have told you then, to save my life.

ARNHOLM. What is it?

ELLIDA. When you took the—the useless step you were just speaking of—I could not answer you otherwise than I did.

ARNHOLM. I know that you had nothing but friendship to give me; I know that well enough.

ELLIDA. But you did not know that all my mind and soul were then given elsewhere.

ARNHOLM. At that time!

ELLIDA. Yes.

ARNHOLM. But it is impossible. You are mistaken about the time. I hardly think you knew Wangel then.

ELLIDA. It is not Wangel of whom I speak.

ARNHOLM. Not Wangel? But at that time, out there at Skjoldviken—I can't remember a single person whom I can imagine the possibility of your caring for.

ELLIDA. No, no, I quite believe that; for it was all such bewildering madness—all of it.

ARNHOLM. But tell me more of this.

ELLIDA. Oh! it's enough if you know I was bound then; and you know it now.

ARNHOLM. And if you had not been bound?

ELLIDA. Well?

ARNHOLM. Would your answer to my letter have been different?

ELLIDA. How can I tell? When Wangel came the answer was different.

ARNHOLM. What is your object, then, in telling me that you were bound?

ELLIDA (*getting up, as if in fear and unrest*). Because I must have someone in whom to confide. No, no; sit still.

ARNHOLM. Then your husband knows nothing about this?

ELLIDA. I confessed to him from the first that my thoughts had once been elsewhere. He never asked to know more, and we have never touched upon it since. Besides, at bottom it was simply madness. And then it was over directly—that is to a certain extent.

ARNHOLM (*rising*). Only to a certain extent? Not quite?

ELLIDA. Yes, yes, it is! Oh, good heavens! Dear Arnholm, it is not what you think. It is something so absolutely incomprehensible, I don't know how I could tell it you. You would only think I was ill, or quite mad.

ARNHOLM. My dearest lady! Now you really must tell me all about it.

ELLIDA. Well, then, I'll try to. How will you, as a sensible man, explain to yourself that—(*Looks round, and breaks off.*) Wait a moment. Here's a visitor.

(LYNGSTRAND *comes along the road, and enters the garden. He has a flower in his button-hole, and carries a large, handsome bouquet done up in paper and silk ribbons. He stands somewhat hesitatingly and undecidedly by the veranda.*)

ELLIDA (*from the arbor*). Have you come to see the girls, Mr. Lyngstrand?

LYNGSTRAND (*turning round*). Ah, madam, are you there? (*Bows, and comes nearer.*) No, it's not that. It's not the young ladies. It's you yourself, Mrs. Wangel. You know you gave me permission to come and see you——

ELLIDA. Of course I did. You are always welcome here.

LYNGSTRAND. Thanks; and as it falls out so luckily that it's a festival here to-day——

ELLIDA. Oh! Do you know about that?

LYNGSTRAND. Rather! And so I should like to take the liberty of presenting this to Mrs. Wangel. (*Bows, and offers her the bouquet*).

ELLIDA (*smiling*). But, my dear Mr. Lyngstrand, oughtn't you to give these lovely flowers to Mr. Arnholm himself? For you know it's really he——

LYNGSTRAND (*looking uncertainly at both of them*). Excuse me, but I don't know this gentleman. It's only—I've only come about the birthday, Mrs. Wangel.

ELLIDA. Birthday? You've made a mistake, Mr. Lyngstrand. There's no birthday here to-day.

LYNGSTRAND (*smiling slyly*). Oh! I know all about that! But I didn't think it was to be kept so dark.

ELLIDA. What do you know?

LYNGSTRAND. That it is Madam's birthday.

ELLIDA. Mine?

ARNHOLM (*looks questioningly at her*). To-day? Surely not.

ELLIDA (*to* LYNGSTRAND). Whatever made you think that?

LYNGSTRAND. It was Miss Hilde who let it out. I just looked in here a little while ago, and I asked the young ladies why they were decorating the place like this, with flowers and flags.

ELLIDA. Well?

LYNGSTRAND. And so Miss Hilde said, "Why, to-day is mother's birthday."

ELLIDA. Mother's!—I see.

ARNHOLM. Aha! (*He and* ELLIDA *exchange a meaning look.*) Well, now that the young man knows about it——

ELLIDA (*to* LYNGSTRAND). Well, now that you know——

LYNGSTRAND (*offering her the bouquet again*). May I take the liberty of congratulating you?

ELLIDA (*taking the flowers*). My best thanks. Won't you sit down a moment, Mr. Lyngstrand? (ELLIDA, ARNHOLM, *and* LYNGSTRAND *sit down in the arbor.*) This—birthday business—was to have been kept secret, Mr. Arnholm.

ARNHOLM. So I see. It wasn't for us uninitiated folk!

ELLIDA (*putting down the bouquet*). Just so. Not for the uninitiated.

LYNGSTRAND. 'Pon my word, I won't tell a living soul about it.

ELLIDA. Oh, it wasn't meant like that. But how are you getting on? I think you look better than you did.

LYNGSTRAND. Oh! I think I'm getting on famously. And by next year, if I can go south——

ELLIDA. And you are going south, the girls tell me.

LYNGSTRAND. Yes, for I've a benefactor and friend at Bergen, who looks after me, and has promised to help me next year.

ELLIDA. How did you get such a friend?

LYNGSTRAND. Well, it all happened so very luckily. I once went to sea in one of his ships.

ELLIDA. Did you? So you wanted to go to sea?

LYNGSTRAND. No, not at all. But when mother died, father wouldn't have me knocking about at home any longer, and so he sent me to sea. Then we were wrecked in the English Channel on our way home; and that was very fortunate for me.

ARNHOLM. What do you mean?

LYNGSTRAND. Yes, for it was in the shipwreck that I got this little weakness—of my chest. I was so long in the ice-cold water before they picked me up; and so I had to give up the sea. Yes, that was very fortunate.

ARNHOLM. Indeed! Do you think so?

LYNGSTRAND. Yes, for the weakness isn't dangerous; and now I can be a sculptor, as I so dearly want to be. Just think; to model in that delicious clay, that yields so caressingly to your fingers!

ELLIDA. And what are you going to model? Is it to be mermen and mermaids? Or is it to be old Vikings?

LYNGSTRAND. No, not that. As soon as I can set about it,

I am going to try if I can produce a great work—a group, as they call it.

ELLIDA. Yes; but what's the group to be?

LYNGSTRAND. Oh! something I've experienced myself.

ARNHOLM. Yes, yes; always stick to that.

ELLIDA. But what's it to be?

LYNGSTRAND. Well, I thought it should be the young wife of a sailor, who lies sleeping in strange unrest, and she is dreaming. I fancy I shall do it so that you will see she is dreaming.

ARNHOLM. Is there anything else?

LYNGSTRAND. Yes, there's to be another figure—a sort of apparition, as they say. It's her husband, to whom she has been faithless while he was away, and he is drowned at sea.

ARNHOLM. What?

ELLIDA. Drowned?

LYNGSTRAND. Yes, he was drowned on a sea voyage. But that's the wonderful part of it—he comes home all the same. It is night-time. And he is standing by her bed looking at her. He is to stand there dripping wet, like one drawn from the sea.

ELLIDA (*leaning back in her chair*). What an extraordinary idea! (*Shutting her eyes.*) Oh! I can see it so clearly, living before me!

ARNHOLM. But how on earth, Mr.—Mr.— I thought you said it was to be something you had experienced.

LYNGSTRAND. Yes. I did experience that—that is to say, to a certain extent.

ARNHOLM. You saw a dead man?

LYNGSTRAND. Well, I don't mean I've actually seen this— experienced it in the flesh. But still——

ELLIDA (*quickly, intently.*) Oh! tell me all you can about it! I must understand about all this.

ARNHOLM (*smiling*). Yes, that'll be quite in your line. Something that has to do with sea fancies.

ELLIDA. What was it, Mr. Lyngstrand?

LYNGSTRAND. Well, it was like this. At the time when we were to sail home in the brig from a town they called Halifax, we had to leave the boatswain behind in the hospital. So we had to engage an American instead. This new boatswain——

ELLIDA. The American?

LYNGSTRAND. Yes, one day he got the captain to lend him a lot of old newspapers and he was always reading them. For he wanted to teach himself Norwegian, he said.

ELLIDA. Well, and then?

LYNGSTRAND. It was one evening in rough weather. All hands were on deck—except the boatswain and myself. For he had sprained his foot and couldn't walk, and I was feeling rather low, and was lying in my berth. Well, he was sitting there in the forecastle, reading one of those old papers again.

ELLIDA. Well, well!

LYNGSTRAND. But just as he was sitting there quietly reading, I heard him utter a sort of yell. And when I looked at him, I saw his face was as white as chalk. And then he began to crush and crumple the paper, and to tear it into a thousand shreds. But he did it so quietly, quietly.

ELLIDA. Didn't he say anything? Didn't he speak?

LYNGSTRAND. Not directly; but a little after he said to himself, as it were: "Married—to another man. While I was away."

ELLIDA (closes her eyes, and says, half to herself). He said that?

LYNGSTRAND. Yes. And think—he said it in perfect Norwegian. That man must have learnt foreign languages very easily——

ELLIDA. And what then? What else happened?

LYNGSTRAND. Well, now the remarkable part is coming—that I shall never forget as long as I live. For he added, and that quite quietly, too: "But she is mine, and mine she shall remain. And she shall follow me, if I should come home and fetch her, as a drowned man from the dark sea."

ELLIDA (*pouring herself out a glass of water. Her hand trembles*). Ah! How close it is here to-day.

LYNGSTRAND. And he said this with such strength of will that I thought he must be the man to do it.

ELLIDA. Don't you know anything about—what became of the man?

LYNGSTRAND. Oh! madam, he's certainly not living now.

ELLIDA (*quickly*). Why do you think that?

LYNGSTRAND. Why? Because we were shipwrecked afterwards in the Channel. I had got into the longboat with the captain and five others. The mate got into the stern-boat; and the American was in that too, and another man.

ELLIDA. And nothing has been heard of them since?

LYNGSTRAND. Not a word. The friend who looks after me said so quite recently in a letter. But it's just because of this I was so anxious to make it into a work of art. I see the faithless sailor-wife so life-like before me, and the avenger who is drowned, and who nevertheless comes home from the sea. I can see them both so distinctly.

ELLIDA. I, too. (*Rises.*) Come; let us go in—or, rather, go down to Wangel. I think it is so suffocatingly hot. (*She goes out of the arbor.*)

LYNGSTRAND (*who has also risen*). I, for my part, must ask you to excuse me. This was only to be a short visit because of the birthday.

ELLIDA. As you wish. (*Holds out her hand to him.*) Good-bye, and thank you for the flowers.

(LYNGSTRAND *bows, and goes off through the garden gate.*)

ARNHOLM (*rises, and goes up to* ELLIDA). I see well enough that this has gone to your heart, Mrs. Wangel.

ELLIDA. Yes; you may well say so. Although——

ARNHOLM. But still—after all, it's no more than you were bound to expect.

ELLIDA (*looks at him surprised*). Expect!

ARNHOLM. Well, so it seems to me.

ELLIDA. Expect that anyone should come back again!—come to life again like that!

ARNHOLM. But what on earth!—is it that mad sculptor's sea story, then?

ELLIDA. Oh, dear Arnholm, perhaps it isn't so mad after all!

ARNHOLM. Is it that nonsense about the dead man that has moved you so? And I who thought that——

ELLIDA. What did you think?

ARNHOLM. I naturally thought that was only a make-believe of yours. And that you were sitting here grieving because you had found out a family feast was being kept secret; because your husband and his children live a life of remembrances in which you have no part.

ELLIDA. Oh! no, no! That may be as it may. I have no right to claim my husband wholly and solely for myself.

ARNHOLM. I should say you had.

ELLIDA. Yes. Yet, all the same, I have not. That is it. Why, I, too, live in something from which they are shut out.

ARNHOLM. You! (*In lower tone.*) Do you mean?—you, you do not really love your husband!

ELLIDA. Oh! yes, yes! I have learnt to love him with all my heart! And that's why it is so terrible—so inexplicable—so absolutely inconceivable!

ARNHOLM. Now you must and shall confide all your troubles to me. Will you, Mrs. Wangel?

ELLIDA. I cannot, dear friend. Not now, in any case. Later, perhaps.

(BOLETTE *comes out into the veranda, and goes down into the garden.*)

BOLETTE. Father's coming up from the office. Hadn't we better all of us go into the sitting-room?

ELLIDA. Yes, let us.

(WANGEL, *in other clothes, comes with* HILDE *from behind the house.*)

WANGEL. Now, then, here I am at your service. And now we shall enjoy a good glass of something cool.

ELLIDA. Wait a moment. (*She goes into the arbor and fetches the bouquet.*)

HILDE. I say! All those lovely flowers! Where did you get them?

ELLIDA. From the sculptor, Lyngstrand, my dear Hilde.

HILDE (*starts*). From Lyngstrand?

BOLETTE (*uneasily*). Has Lyngstrand been here again?

ELLIDA (*with a half-smile*). Yes. He came here with these. Because of the birthday, you understand.

BOLETTE (*looks at* HILDE). Oh!

HILDE (*mutters*). The idiot!

WANGEL (*in painful confusion to* ELLIDA). Hm!—yes, well you see—I must tell you, my dear, good, beloved Ellida——

ELLIDA (*interrupting*). Come, girls! Let us go and put my flowers in the water together with the others. (*Goes up to the veranda.*)

BOLETTE (*to* HILDE). Oh! after all she is good at heart.

HILDE (*in a low tone with angry look*). Fiddlesticks! She only does it to take in father.

WANGEL (*on the veranda, presses* ELLIDA's *hand*). Thanks —thanks! My heartfelt thanks for that, dear Ellida.

ELLIDA (*arranging the flowers*). Nonsense! Should not I, too, be in it, and take part in—in mother's birthday?

ARNHOLM. Hm!

(*He goes up to* WANGEL, *and* ELLIDA, BOLETTE, *and* HILDE *remain in the garden below.*)

ACT II

(SCENE.—*At the "View," a shrub-covered hill behind the town. A little in the background a beacon and a vane. Great stones arranged as seats around the beacon, and in the foreground. Farther back is seen the outer fjord, with islands and outstanding headlands. The open sea is not visible. It is a summer's evening, and twilight. A golden-red shimmer in the air and over the mountain-tops in the far distance. A quartette is faintly heard singing below in the background. Young townsfolk, ladies and gentlemen, come up in pairs, from the right, and, talking familiarly, pass out beyond the beacon. A little after,* BALLESTED *enters, as guide to a party of foreign tourists with their ladies. He is laden with shawls and traveling bags.*)

BALLESTED (*pointing upwards with a stick*). Sehen, Sie, meine Herrschaften, dort, out there, liegt eine andere mountain. That wollen wir also besteigen, and so herunter. (*He goes on with the conversation in French, and leads the party off to the left.* HILDE *comes quickly along the up-hill path, stands still, and looks back. Soon after* BOLETTE *comes up the same way.*)

BOLETTE. But, dear, why should we run away from Lyngstrand?

HILDE. Because I can't bear going up-hill so slowly. Look —look at him crawling up!

BOLETTE. Ah! But you know how delicate he is.

HILDE. Do you think it's very—dangerous?

BOLETTE. I certainly do.

HILDE. He went to consult father this afternoon. I should like to know what father thinks about him.

BOLETTE. Father told me it was a thickening of the lungs, or something of the sort. He won't live to be old, father says.

HILDE. No! Did he say it? Fancy—that's exactly what I thought.

BOLETTE. For heaven's sake don't show it!

HILDE. How can you imagine such a thing? (*In an undertone.*) Look, here comes Hans crawling up. Don't you think you can see by the look of him that he's called Hans?

BOLETTE (*whispering*). Now do behave! You'd better!

    (LYNGSTRAND *comes in from the right, a parasol in his hand.*)

LYNGSTRAND. I must beg the young ladies to excuse me for not getting along as quickly as they did.

HILDE. Have you got a parasol too, now?

LYNGSTRAND. It's your mother's. She said I was to use it as a stick. I hadn't mine with me.

BOLETTE. Are they down there still—father and the others?

LYNGSTRAND. Yes; your father looked in at the restaurant for a moment, and the others are sitting out there listening to the music. But they were coming up here presently, your mother said.

HILDE (*stands looking at him*). I suppose you're thoroughly tired out now?

LYNGSTRAND. Yes; I almost think I'm a little tired now. I really believe I shall have to sit down a moment. (*He sits on one of the stones in the foreground.*)

HILDE (*standing in front of him*). Do you know there's to be dancing down there on the parade?

LYNGSTRAND. Yes; I heard there was some talk about it.

HILDE. I suppose you think dancing's great fun?

BOLETTE (*who begins gathering small flowers among the heather*). Oh, Hilde! Now do let Mr. Lyngstrand get his breath.

LYNGSTRAND (*to* HILDE). Yes, Miss Hilde; I should very much like to dance—if only I could.

HILDE. Oh, I see! Haven't you ever learnt?

LYNGSTRAND. No, I've not. But it wasn't *that* I meant. I meant I couldn't because of my chest.

HILDE. Because of that weakness you said you suffered from?

LYNGSTRAND. Yes; because of that.

HILDE. Aren't you very sorry you've that—weakness?

LYNGSTRAND. Oh, no! I can't say I am (*smiling*), for I think it's because of it that everyone is so good, and friendly, and kind to me.

HILDE. Yes. And then, besides, it's not dangerous.

LYNGSTRAND. No; it's not at all dangerous. So I gathered from what your father said to me.

HILDE. And then it will pass away as soon as ever you begin traveling.

LYNGSTRAND. Of course it will pass away.

BOLETTE (*with flowers*). Look here, Mr. Lyngstrand, you are to put this in your button-hole.

LYNGSTRAND. Oh! A thousand thanks, Miss Wangel. It's really too good of you.

HILDE (*looking down the path*). There they are, coming along the road.

BOLETTE (*also looking down*). If only they know where to turn off. No; now they're going wrong.

LYNGSTRAND (*rising*). I'll run down to the turning and call out to them.

HILDE. You'll have to call out pretty loud.

BOLETTE. No; it's not worth while. You'll only tire yourself again.

LYNGSTRAND. Oh, it's so easy going down-hill. (*Goes off to the right.*)

HILDE. Down-hill—yes. (*Looking after him.*) Why, he's actually jumping! And he never remembers he'll have to come up again.

BOLETTE. Poor fellow!

HILDE. If Lyngstrand were to propose, would you accept him?

BOLETTE. Are you quite mad?

HILDE. Of course, I mean if he weren't troubled with that "weakness." And if he weren't to die so soon, would you have him *then*?

BOLETTE. I think you'd better have him yourself!

HILDE. No, that I wouldn't! Why, he hasn't a farthing. He hasn't enough even to keep himself.

BOLETTE. Then why are you always going about with him?

HILDE. Oh, I only do that because of the weakness.

BOLETTE. I've never noticed that you in the least pity him for it!

HILDE. No, I don't. But I think it so interesting.

BOLETTE. What is?

HILDE. To look at him and make him tell you it isn't dangerous; and that he's going abroad, and is to be an artist. He really believes it all, and is so thoroughly happy about it. And yet nothing will ever come of it; nothing whatever. For he won't live long enough. I feel that's so fascinating to think of.

BOLETTE. Fascinating!

HILDE. Yes, I think it's most fascinating. I take that liberty.

BOLETTE. Hilde, you really are a dreadful child!

HILDE. That's just what I want to be—out of spite. (*Looking down.*) At last! I shouldn't think Arnholm liked coming up-hill. (*Turns round.*) By the way, do you know what I noticed about Arnholm at dinner?

BOLETTE. Well?

HILDE. Just think—his hair's beginning to come off— right on the top of his head.

BOLETTE. Nonsense! I'm sure that's not true.

HILDE. It is! And then he has wrinkles round both his

eyes. Good gracious, Bolette, how could you be so much in love with him when he used to read with you?

BOLETTE (*smiling*). Yes. Can you believe it? I remember I once shed bitter tears because he thought Bolette was an ugly name.

HILDE. Only to think! (*Looking down.*) No! I say, do just look down here! There's the "Mermaid" walking along and chatting with him. Not with father. I wonder if those two aren't making eyes at one another.

BOLETTE. You ought to be ashamed of yourself! How can you stand there and say such a thing of her? Now, when everything was beginning to be so pleasant between us.

HILDE. Of course—just try and persuade yourself of that, my child! Oh, no! It will never be pleasant between us and her. For she doesn't belong to us at all. And we don't belong to her either. Goodness knows what father dragged her into the house for! I shouldn't wonder if some fine day she went mad under our very eyes.

BOLETTE. Mad! How can you think such a thing?

HILDE. Oh! it wouldn't be so extraordinary. Her mother went mad, too. She died mad—I know that.

BOLETTE. Yes, heaven only knows what you don't poke your nose into. But now don't go chattering about this. Do be good—for father's sake. Do you hear, Hilde?

(WANGEL, ELLIDA, ARNHOLM and LYNGSTRAND *come up from the right.*)

ELLIDA (*pointing to the background*). Out there it lies.

ARNHOLM. Quite right. It must be in that direction.

ELLIDA. Out there is the sea.

BOLETTE (*to* ARNHOLM). Don't you think it is delightful up here?

ARNHOLM. It's magnificent, I think. Glorious view!

WANGEL. I suppose you never used to come up here?

ARNHOLM. No, never. In my time I think it was hardly accessible; there wasn't any path even.

WANGEL. And no grounds. All this has been done during the last few years.

BOLETTE. And there, at the "Pilot's Mount," it's even grander than here.

WANGEL. Shall we go there, Ellida?

ELLIDA (*sitting down on one of the stones*). Thanks, not I; but you others can. I'll sit here meanwhile.

WANGEL. Then I'll stay with you. The girls can show Arnholm about.

BOLETTE. Would you like to go with us, Mr. Arnholm?

ARNHOLM. I should like to, very much. Does a path lead up there too?

BOLETTE. Oh yes. There's a nice broad path.

HILDE. The path is so broad that two people can walk along it comfortably, arm in arm.

ARNHOLM (*jestingly*). Is that really so, little Missie? (*To* BOLETTE.) Shall we two see if she is right?

BOLETTE (*suppressing a smile*). Very well, let's go. (*They go out to the left, arm in arm.*)

HILDE (*to* LYNGSTRAND). Shall we go too?

LYNGSTRAND. Arm in arm?

HILDE. Oh, why not? For aught I care!

LYNGSTRAND (*taking her arm, laughing contentedly*). This is a jolly lark.

HILDE. Lark?

LYNGSTRAND. Yes; because it looks exactly as if we were engaged.

HILDE. I'm sure you've never walked out arm in arm with a lady before, Mr. Lyngstrand. (*They go off.*)

WANGEL (*who is standing beside the beacon*). Dear Ellida, now we have a moment to ourselves.

ELLIDA. Yes; come and sit down here, by me.

WANGEL (*sitting down*). It is so free and quiet. Now we can have a little talk together.

ELLIDA. What about?

Wangel. About yourself, and then about us both. Ellida, I see very well that it can't go on like this.

Ellida. What do you propose instead?

Wangel. Perfect confidence, dear. A true life together—as before.

Ellida. Oh, if that could be! But it is so absolutely impossible!

Wangel. I think I understand you, from certain things you have let fall now and again.

Ellida (*passionately*). Oh, you do not! Don't say you understand!

Wangel. Yes. Yours is an honest nature, Ellida—yours is a faithful mind.

Ellida. It is.

Wangel. Any position in which you could feel safe and happy must be a completely true and real one.

Ellida (*looking eagerly at him*). Well, and then?

Wangel. You are not suited to be a man's second wife.

Ellida. What makes you think that?

Wangel. It has often flashed across me like a foreboding. To-day it was clear to me. The children's memorial feast—you saw in me a kind of accomplice. Well, yes; a man's memories, after all, cannot be wiped out—not so mine, anyhow. It isn't in me.

Ellida. I know that. Oh! I know that so well.

Wangel. But you are mistaken all the same. To you it is almost as if the children's mother were still living—as if she were still here invisible amongst us. You think my heart is equally divided between you and her. It is this thought that shocks you. You see something immoral in our relation, and that is why you no longer can or will live with me as my wife.

Ellida (*rising*). Have you seen all that, Wangel—seen into all this?

WANGEL. Yes; to-day I have at last seen to the very heart of it—to its utmost depths.

ELLIDA. To its very heart, you say? Oh, do not think that!

WANGEL (*rising*). I see very well that there is more than this, dear Ellida.

ELLIDA (*anxiously*). You know there is more?

WANGEL. Yes. You cannot bear your surroundings here. The mountains crush you, and weigh upon your heart. Nothing is open enough for you here. The heavens above you are not spacious enough. The air is not strong and bracing enough.

ELLIDA. You are right. Night and day, winter and summer, it weighs upon me—this irresistible home-sickness for the sea.

WANGEL. I know it well, dear Ellida (*laying his hands upon her head*). And that is why the poor sick child shall go home to her own again.

ELLIDA. What do you mean?

WANGEL. Something quite simple. We are going away.

ELLIDA. Going away?

WANGEL. Yes. Somewhere by the open sea—a place where you can find a true home, after your own heart.

ELLIDA. Oh, dear, do not think of that! That is quite impossible. You can live happily nowhere on earth but here!

WANGEL. That must be as it may. And, besides, do you think I can live happily here—without you?

ELLIDA. But I am here. And I will stay here. You have me.

WANGEL. Have I, Ellida?

ELLIDA. Oh! don't speak of all this. Why, here you have all that you love and strive for. All your life's work lies here.

WANGEL. That must be as it may, I tell you. We are going away from here—are going somewhere—out there. That is quite settled now, dear Ellida.

ELLIDA. What do you think we should gain by that?

WANGEL. You would regain your health and peace of mind.

ELLIDA. Hardly. And then you, yourself! Think of yourself, too! What of you?

WANGEL. I would win you back again, my dearest.

ELLIDA. But you cannot do that! No, no, you can't do that, Wangel! That is the terrible part of it—heart-breaking to think of.

WANGEL. That remains to be proved. If you are harboring such thoughts, truly there is no other salvation for you than to go hence. And the sooner the better. Now this is irrevocably settled, do you hear?

ELLIDA. No! Then in heaven's name I had better tell you everything straight out. Everything just as it is.

WANGEL. Yes, yes! do.

ELLIDA. For you shall not ruin your happiness for my sake, especially as it can't help us in any way.

WANGEL. I have your word now that you will tell me everything just as it is.

ELLIDA. I'll tell you everything as well as I can, and as far as I understand it. Come here and sit by me. (*They sit down on the stones.*)

WANGEL. Well, Ellida, so——

ELLIDA. That day when you came out there and asked me if I would be yours, you spoke so frankly and honestly to me about your first marriage. It had been so happy, you said.

WANGEL. And so it was.

ELLIDA. Yes, yes! I am sure of that, dear! It is not for that I am referring to it now. I only want to remind you that I, on my side, was frank with you. I told you quite openly that once in my life I had cared for another. That there had been a—a kind of engagement between us.

WANGEL. A kind of——

ELLIDA. Yes, something of the sort. Well, it only lasted

such a very short time. He went away; and after that I put an end to it. I told you all that.

WANGEL. Why rake up all this now? It really didn't concern me; nor have I once asked you who he was!

ELLIDA. No, you have not. You are always so thoughtful for me.

WANGEL (*smiling*). Oh, in this case I could guess the name well enough for myself.

ELLIDA. The name?

WANGEL. Out in Skjoldviken and thereabouts there weren't many to choose from; or, rather, there was only a single one.

ELLIDA. You believe it was Arnholm!

WANGEL. Well, wasn't it?

ELLIDA. No!

WANGEL. Not he? Then I don't in the least understand.

ELLIDA. Can you remember that late in the autumn a large American ship once put into Skjoldviken for repairs?

WANGEL. Yes, I remember it very well. It was on board that ship that the captain was found one morning in his cabin—murdered. I myself went out to make the *post-mortem*.

ELLIDA. Yes, it was you.

WANGEL. It was the second mate who had murdered him.

ELLIDA. No one can say that. For it was never proved.

WANGEL. There was enough against him anyhow, or why should he have drowned himself as he did?

ELLIDA. He did not drown himself. He sailed in a ship to the north.

WANGEL (*startled*). How do you know?

ELLIDA (*with an effort*). Well, Wangel—it was this second mate to whom I was—betrothed.

WANGEL (*springing up*). What! Is it possible!

ELLIDA. Yes, it is so. It was to him!

WANGEL. But how on earth, Ellida! How did you come

to betroth yourself to such a man? To an absolute stranger! What is his name?

ELLIDA. At that time he called himself Friman. Later, in his letters he signed himself Alfred Johnston.

WANGEL. And where did he come from?

ELLIDA. From Finmark, he said. For the rest, he was born in Finland, had come to Norway there as a child with his father, I think.

WANGEL. A Finlander, then?

ELLIDA. Yes, so he called himself.

WANGEL. What else do you know about him?

ELLIDA. Only that he went to sea very young. And that he had been on long voyages.

WANGEL. Nothing more?

ELLIDA. No. We never spoke of such things.

WANGEL. Of what did you speak, then?

ELLIDA. We spoke mostly about the sea.

WANGEL. Ah! About the sea——

ELLIDA. About storms and calm. Of dark nights at sea. And of the sea in the glittering sunshiny days we spoke also. But we spoke most of the whales, and the dolphins, and the seals who lie out there on the rocks in the midday sun. And then we spoke of the gulls, and the eagles, and all the other sea birds. I think—isn't it wonderful?—when we talked of such things it seemed to me as if both the sea beasts and sea birds were one with him.

WANGEL. And with you?

ELLIDA. Yes; I almost thought I belonged to them all, too.

WANGEL. Well, well! And so it was that you betrothed yourself to him?

ELLIDA. Yes. He said I must.

WANGEL. You must? Had you no will of your own, then?

ELLIDA. Not when he was near. Ah! afterwards I thought it all so inexplicable.

WANGEL. Were you often together?

ELLIDA. No; not very often. One day he came out to our place, and looked over the lighthouse. After that I got to know him, and we met now and again. But then that happened about the captain, and so he had to go away.

WANGEL. Yes, yes. Tell me more about that.

ELLIDA. It was just daybreak when I had a note from him. He said in it I was to go out to him at the Bratthammer. You know the headland there between the lighthouse and Skjoldviken?

WANGEL. I know, I know!

ELLIDA. I was to go out there at once, he wrote, because he wanted to speak to me.

WANGEL. And you went?

ELLIDA. Yes. I could not do otherwise. Well, then he told me he had stabbed the captain in the night.

WANGEL. He said that himself! Actually said so!

ELLIDA. Yes. But he had only acted rightly and justly, he said.

WANGEL. Rightly and justly! Why did he stab him then?

ELLIDA. He wouldn't speak out about that. He said it was not fit for me to hear.

WANGEL. And you believed his naked, bare word?

ELLIDA. Yes. It never occurred to me to do otherwise. Well, anyhow, he had to go away. But now, when he was to bid me farewell——. No; you never could imagine what he thought of——

WANGEL. Well? Tell me.

ELLIDA. He took from his pocket a key-ring—and drew a ring that he always wore from his finger, and he took a small ring I had. These two he put on the key-ring. And then he said we should wed ourselves to the sea.

WANGEL. Wed?

ELLIDA. Yes, so he said. And with that he threw the key-ring, and our rings, with all his might, as far as he could into the deep.

WANGEL. And you, Ellida, you did all this?

ELLIDA. Yes—only think—it then seemed to me as if it must be so. But, thank God!—he went away.

WANGEL. And when he was gone?

ELLIDA. Oh! You can surely understand that I soon came to my senses again—that I saw how absolutely mad and meaningless it had all been.

WANGEL. But you spoke just now of letters. So you have heard from him since?

ELLIDA. Yes, I have heard from him. First I had a few short lines from Archangel. He only wrote he was going to America. And then he told me where to send an answer.

WANGEL. And did you?

ELLIDA. At once. I wrote him, of course, that all must be at an end between us; and that he must no longer think of me, just as I should no longer think of him.

WANGEL. But did he write again?

ELLIDA. Yes, he wrote again.

WANGEL. And what was his answer to your communication?

ELLIDA. He took no notice of it. It was exactly as if I had never broken with him. He wrote quite composedly and calmly that I must wait for him. When he could have me he would let me know, and then I was to go to him at once.

WANGEL. So he would not release you?

ELLIDA. No. Then I wrote again, almost word for word as I had before; or perhaps more firmly.

WANGEL. And he gave in?

ELLIDA. Oh, no! Don't think that! He wrote quietly, as before—not a word of my having broken with him. Then I knew it was useless, and so I never wrote to him again.

WANGEL. And you never heard from him?

ELLIDA. Oh, yes! I have had three letters since then. Once he wrote to me from California, and a second time from China. The last letter I had from him was from Australia.

He wrote he was going to the gold-mines; but since then he has made no sign.

WANGEL. This man has had a strange power over you, Ellida.

ELLIDA. Yes, yes! The terrible man!

WANGEL. But you mustn't think of that any more. Never again—never! Promise me that, my dear, beloved Ellida. Now we must try another treatment for you. Fresher air than here within the fjords. The salt, fresh air of the sea! Dear, what say you to that?

ELLIDA. Oh! don't speak of it! Don't think of it! There is no help in this for me. I feel that so well. I can't shake it off—not even there.

WANGEL. What, dear?—What do you really mean?

ELLIDA. I mean the horror of it, this incomprehensible power over the mind.

WANGEL. But you have shaken it off—long since—when you broke with him. Why, all this is long past now.

ELLIDA (springing up). No; that it is not—it is not!

WANGEL. Not past?

ELLIDA. No, Wangel, it is not past; and I fear it never will be—never, in all our life.

WANGEL (in a pained voice). Do you mean to say that in your innermost heart you have never been able to forget this strange man?

ELLIDA. I had forgotten him; but then it was as if he had suddenly come back again.

WANGEL. How long ago is that?

ELLIDA. It's about three years ago, now, or a little longer. It was just when I expected the child.

WANGEL. Ah! at that time? Yes, Ellida—now I begin to understand many things.

ELLIDA. You are mistaken, dear. What has come to me? Oh! I believe nothing on earth will ever make it clear.

WANGEL (looking sadly at her). Only to think that all

these three years you have cared for another man. Cared for another. Not for me—but for another!

ELLIDA. Oh! you are so utterly mistaken! I care for no one but you.

WANGEL (*in a subdued voice*). Why, then, in all this time have you not lived with me as my wife?

ELLIDA. Because of the horror that comes from the strange man.

WANGEL. The horror?

ELLIDA. Yes, the horror. A horror so terrible—such as only the sea could hold. For now you shall hear, Wangel.

(*The young townsfolk come back, bow, and pass out to the right. Together with them come* ARNHOLM, BO-LETTE, HILDE, *and* LYNGSTRAND.)

BOLETTE (*as she passes by*). Well, are you still walking about up here?

ELLIDA. Yes, it is so cool and pleasant up here on the heights.

ARNHOLM. We, for our part, are going down for a dance.

WANGEL. All right. We'll soon come down—we also.

HILDE. Good-bye, for the present!

ELLIDA. Mr. Lyngstrand, will you wait one moment? (LYNGSTRAND *stops.* ARNHOLM, BOLETTE *and* HILDE *go out. To* LYNGSTRAND.) Are you going to dance too?

LYNGSTRAND. No, Mrs. Wangel. I don't think I dare.

ELLIDA. No, you should be careful, you know—your chest. You're not quite well yet, you see.

LYNGSTRAND. Not quite.

ELLIDA (*with some hesitation*). How long may it be now since you went on that voyage?

LYNGSTRAND. That time when I contracted this weakness?

ELLIDA. Yes, that voyage you told me about this morning?

LYNGSTRAND. Oh! it's about—wait a moment—yes, it's a good three years now.

ELLIDA. Three years, then.

LYNGSTRAND. Perhaps a little more. We left America in February, and we were wrecked in March. It was the equinoctial gales we came in for.

ELLIDA (*looking at* WANGEL). So it was at that time——

WANGEL. But, dear Ellida——

ELLIDA. Well, don't let me detain you, Mr. Lyngstrand. Now go down, but don't dance.

LYNGSTRAND. No, I'll only look on. (*He goes out.*)

ELLIDA. Johnston was on board too, I am quite certain of it.

WANGEL. What makes you think so?

ELLIDA (*without answering*). He learnt on board that I had married another while he was away. And so that very hour this came over me.

WANGEL. The horror?

ELLIDA. Yes, all of a sudden I see him alive right in front of me; or, rather a little in profile. He never looks at me, only he is there.

WANGEL. How do you think he looks?

ELLIDA. Exactly as when I saw him last.

WANGEL. Ten years ago?

ELLIDA. Yes; out there at Bratthammeren. Most distinctly of all I see his breastpin, with a large bluish-white pearl in it. The pearl is like a dead fish's eye, and it seems to glare at me.

WANGEL. Good God! You are more ill than I thought. More ill than you yourself know, Ellida.

ELLIDA. Yes, yes! Help me if you can, for I feel how it is drawing closer and more close.

WANGEL. And you have gone about in this state three whole years, bearing for yourself this secret suffering, without confiding in me.

ELLIDA. But I could not; not till it became necessary for your own sake. If I had confided in you I should also have had to confide to you the unutterable.

WANGEL. Unutterable?

ELLIDA. No, no, no! Do not ask. Only one thing, nothing more. Wangel, when shall we understand that mystery of the boy's eyes?

WANGEL. My dear love, Ellida, I assure you it was only your own fancy. The child had exactly the same eyes as other normal children have.

ELLIDA. No, he had not. And you could not see it! The child's eyes changed color with the sea. When the fjord lay bathed in sunshine, so were his eyes. And so in storm. Oh, I saw it, if you did not!

WANGEL (*humoring her*). Maybe. But even if it were true, what then?

ELLIDA (*in lower voice, and coming nearer*). I have seen such eyes before.

WANGEL. Well? Where?

ELLIDA. Out at Bratthammeren, ten years ago.

WANGEL (*stepping back*). What does it mean?

ELLIDA (*whispers, trembling*). The child had the strange man's eyes.

WANGEL (*cries out reluctantly*). Ellida!

ELLIDA (*clasps her hands despairingly about her head*). Now you understand why I would not, why I *dared* not, live with you as your wife. (*She turns suddenly and rushes off over the heights.*)

WANGEL (*hurrying after her and calling*). Ellida, Ellida! My poor unhappy Ellida!

ACT III

(SCENE.—*A more remote part of* DOCTOR WANGEL'S *garden. It is boggy and overshadowed by large old trees. To the right is seen the margin of a dank pond. A low, open fence separates the garden from the footpath, and the fjord in the background. Beyond is the range of mountains, with its peaks. It is afternoon, almost evening.* BOLETTE *sits on a stone seat, and on the seat lie some books and a work-basket.* HILDE *and* LYNGSTRAND, *both with fishing-tackle, walk along the bank of the pond.*)

HILDE (*making a sign to* LYNGSTRAND). I can see a large one.

LYNGSTRAND (*looking*). Where?

HILDE (*pointing*). Can't you see? He's down there. Good gracious! There's another! (*Looks through the trees.*) Out there. Now he's coming to frighten him away!

BOLETTE (*looking up*). Who's coming?

HILDE. Your tutor, Miss!

BOLETTE. Mine?

HILDE. Yes. Goodness knows he never was mine.

(ARNHOLM *enters from between the trees.*)

ARNHOLM. Are there fish in the pond now?

HILDE. There are some very ancient carp.

ARNHOLM. No! Are the old carp still alive?

HILDE. Yes; they're pretty tough. But now we're going to try and get rid of some of them.

ARNHOLM. You'd better try out there at the fjord.

LYNGSTRAND. No; the pond is—well, so to say—more mysterious.

HILDE. Yes; it's fascinating here. Have you been in the sea?

ARNHOLM. Yes; I've come straight from the baths.

HILDE. I suppose you kept in the enclosure?

ARNHOLM. Yes; I'm not much of a swimmer.

HILDE. Can you swim on your back?

ARNHOLM. No.

HILDE. I can. (*To* LYNGSTRAND.) Let's try out there on the other side. (*They go off along the pond.*)

ARNHOLM (*coming closer to* BOLETTE). Are you sitting all alone here, Bolette?

BOLETTE. Yes; I generally do.

ARNHOLM. Isn't your mother down here in the garden?

BOLETTE. No—she's sure to be out with father.

ARNHOLM. How is she this afternoon?

BOLETTE. I don't quite know. I forgot to ask.

ARNHOLM. What books have you there?

BOLETTE. The one's something about botany. And the other's a geography.

ARNHOLM. Do you care about such things?

BOLETTE. Yes, if only I had time for it. But, first of all, I've to look after the housekeeping.

ARNHOLM. Doesn't your mother help you—your step-mother—doesn't she help with that?

BOLETTE. No, that's my business. Why, I saw to that during the two years father was alone. And so it has been since.

ARNHOLM. But you're as fond as ever of reading.

BOLETTE. Yes, I read all the useful books I can get hold of. One wants to know something about the world. For here we live so completely outside of all that's going on—or almost.

ARNHOLM. Now don't say that, dear Bolette.

BOLETTE. Yes! I think we live very much as the carp down there in the pond. They have the fjord so near them, where the shoals of wild fishes pass in and out. But the poor, tame house-fishes know nothing, and they can take no part in that.

ARNHOLM. I don't think it would fare very well with them if they could get out there.

BOLETTE. Oh, it would be much the same, I expect.

ARNHOLM. Moreover, you can't say that one is so completely out of the world here—not in the summer anyhow. Why, nowadays this is quite a rendezvous for the busy world —almost a terminus for the time being.

BOLETTE. Ah, yes! you who yourself are only here for the time being—it is easy for you to make fun of us.

ARNHOLM. I make fun? How can you think that?

BOLETTE. Well, all that about this being a rendezvous, and a terminus for the busy world—that's something you've heard the townsfolk here saying. Yes—they're in the habit of saying that sort of thing.

ARNHOLM. Well, frankly, I've noticed that, too.

BOLETTE. But really there's not an atom of truth in it. Not for us who always live here. What good is it to us that the great strange world comes hither for a time on its way North to see the midnight sun? We ourselves have no part in that; we see nothing of the midnight sun. No! We've got to be good, and live our lives here in our carp pond.

ARNHOLM (*sitting down by her*). Now tell me, dear Bolette, isn't there something or other—something definite you are longing for?

BOLETTE. Perhaps.

ARNHOLM. What is it, really? What is it you are longing for?

BOLETTE. Chiefly to get away.

ARNHOLM. That above all, then?

BOLETTE. Yes; and then to learn more. To really know something about everything.

ARNHOLM. When I used to teach you, your father often said he would let you go to college.

BOLETTE. Yes, poor father! He says so many things. But

when it comes to the point he—there's no real stamina in father.

ARNHOLM. No, unfortunately you're right there. He has not exactly stamina. But have you ever spoken to him about it—spoken really earnestly and seriously?

BOLETTE. No, I've not quite done that.

ARNHOLM. But really you ought to. Before it is too late, Bolette, why don't you?

BOLETTE. Oh! I suppose it's because there's no real stamina in me either. I certainly take after father in that.

ARNHOLM. Hm—don't you think you're unjust to yourself there?

BOLETTE. No, unfortunately. Besides, father has so little time for thinking of me and my future, and not much desire to either. He prefers to put such things away from him whenever he can. He is so completely taken up with Ellida.

ARNHOLM. With whom? What?

BOLETTE. I mean that he and my stepmother—(*breaks off*). Father and mother suffice one another, as you see.

ARNHOLM. Well, so much the better if you were to get away from here.

BOLETTE. Yes; but I don't think I've a right to; not to forsake father.

ARNHOLM. But, dear Bolette, you'll have to do that sometime, anyhow. So it seems to me the sooner the better.

BOLETTE. I suppose there is nothing else for it. After all, I must think of myself, too. I must try and get occupation of some sort. When once father's gone, I have no one to hold to. But, poor father! I dread leaving him.

ARNHOLM. Dread?

BOLETTE. Yes, for father's sake.

ARNHOLM. But, good heavens! Your stepmother? She is left to him.

BOLETTE. That's true. But she's not in the least fit to do all that mother did so well! There is so much she doesn't see, or that she won't see, or that she doesn't care about. I don't know which it is.

ARNHOLM. Hm, I think I understand what you mean.

BOLETTE. Poor father! He is weak in some things. Perhaps you've noticed that yourself? He hasn't enough occupation, either, to fill up his time. And then she is so thoroughly incapable of helping him; however, that's to some extent his own fault.

ARNHOLM. In what way?

BOLETTE. Oh! father always likes to see happy faces about him. There must be sunshine and joy in the house, he says. And so I'm afraid he often gives her medicine which will do her little good in the long run.

ARNHOLM. Do you really think that?

BOLETTE. Yes; I can't get rid of the thought. She is so odd at times. (*Passionately.*) But isn't it unjust that I should have to stay at home here? Really it's not of any earthly use to father. Besides, I have a duty towards myself, too, I think.

ARNHOLM. Do you know what, Bolette? We two must talk these matters over more carefully.

BOLETTE. Oh! That won't be much use. I suppose I was created to stay here in the carp pond.

ARNHOLM. Not a bit of it. It depends entirely upon yourself.

BOLETTE (*quickly*). Do you think so?

ARNHOLM. Yes, believe me, it lies wholly and solely in your own hands.

BOLETTE. If only that were true! Will you perhaps put in a good word for me with father?

ARNHOLM. Certainly. But first of all I must speak frankly and freely with you yourself, dear.

BOLETTE (*looks out to the left*). Hush! don't let them notice anything. We'll speak of this later.

(ELLIDA *enters from the left. She has no hat on, but a large shawl is thrown over her head and shoulders.*)

ELLIDA (*with restless animation*). How pleasant it is here! How delightful it is here!

ARNHOLM (*rising*). Have you been for a walk?

ELLIDA. Yes, a long, long lovely walk up there with Wangel. And now we're going for a sail.

BOLETTE. Won't you sit down?

ELLIDA. No, thanks; I won't sit down.

BOLETTE (*making room on seat*). Here's a pleasant seat.

ELLIDA (*walking about*). No, no, no! I'll not sit down— not sit down!

ARNHOLM. I'm sure your walk has done you good. You look quite refreshed.

ELLIDA. Oh, I feel so thoroughly well—I feel so unspeakably happy. So safe, so safe! (*Looking out to the left.*) What great steamer is that coming along there?

BOLETTE (*rising, and also looking out*). It must be the large English ship.

ARNHOLM. It's passing the buoy. Does it usually stop here?

BOLETTE. Only for half an hour. It goes farther up the fjord.

ELLIDA. And then sails away again to-morrow—away over the great open sea—right over the sea. Only think! to be with them. If one could. If only one could!

ARNHOLM. Have you never been any long sea voyage, Mrs. Wangel?

ELLIDA. Never; only those little trips in the fjord here.

BOLETTE (*with a sigh*). Ah, no! I suppose we must put up with the dry land.

ARNHOLM. Well, after all, that really is our home.

ELLIDA. No; I don't think it is.

ARNHOLM. Not the land?

ELLIDA. No; I don't believe so. I think that if only men had from the beginning accustomed themselves to live on the sea, or *in* the sea perhaps, we should be more perfect than we are—both better and happier.

ARNHOLM. You really think that?

ELLIDA. Yes. I should like to know if we should not. I've often spoken to Wangel about it.

ARNHOLM. Well, and he?

ELLIDA. He thinks it might be so.

ARNHOLM (*jestingly*). Well, perhaps! But it can't be helped. We've once for all entered upon the wrong path, and have become land beasts instead of sea beasts. Anyhow, I suppose it's too late to make good the mistake now.

ELLIDA. Yes, you've spoken a sad truth. And I think men instinctively feel something of this themselves. And they bear it about with them as a secret regret and sorrow. Believe me—herein lies the deepest cause for the sadness of men. Yes, believe me, in this.

ARNHOLM. But, my dearest Mrs. Wangel, I have not observed that men are so extremely sad. It seems to me, on the contrary, that most of them take life easily and pleasantly— and with a great, quiet, unconscious joy.

ELLIDA. Oh! no, it is not so. The joy is, I suppose, something like our joy at the long pleasant summer days—it has the presentiment of the dark days coming. And it is this presentiment that casts its shadows over the joy of men, just as the driving clouds cast their shadow over the fjords. It lies there so bright and blue—and of a sudden——

ARNHOLM. You shouldn't give way to such sad thoughts. Just now you were so glad and so bright.

ELLIDA. Yes, yes, so I was. Oh, this—this is so stupid of me. (*Looking about her uneasily.*) If only Wangel would come! He promised me so faithfully he would. And yet he does not come. Dear Mr. Arnholm, won't you try and find him for me?

ARNHOLM. Gladly——

ELLIDA. Tell him he must come here directly now. For now I can't see him——

ARNHOLM. Not see him?

ELLIDA. Oh! you don't understand. When he is not by me I often can't remember how he looks. And then it is as if I had quite lost him. That is so terribly painful. But do go, please. (*She paces round the pond.*)

BOLETTE (*to* ARNHOLM). I will go with you—you don't know the way.

ARNHOLM. Nonsense, I shall be all right.

BOLETTE (*aside*). No, no, no. I am anxious. I'm afraid he is on board the steamer.

ARNHOLM. Afraid?

BOLETTE. Yes. He usually goes to see if there are any acquaintances of his. And there's a restaurant on board——

ARNHOLM. Ah! Come then.

(*He and* BOLETTE *go off.* ELLIDA *stands still awhile, staring down at the pond. Now and again she speaks to herself in a low voice, and breaks off. Along the footpath beyond the garden fence a* STRANGER *in traveling dress comes from the left. His hair and beard are bushy and red. He has a Scotch cap on, and a traveling bag with strap across his shoulders.*)

THE STRANGER (*goes slowly along by the fence and peeps into the garden. When he catches sight of* ELLIDA *he stands still, looks at her fixedly and searchingly, and speaks in a low voice*). Good evening, Ellida!

ELLIDA (*turns round with a cry*). Oh dear! have you come at last!

THE STRANGER. Yes, at last.

ELLIDA (*looking at him astonished and frightened*). Who are you? Do you seek anyone here?

THE STRANGER. You surely know that well enough, Ellida.

ELLIDA (*starting*). What is *this!* How do you address me? Whom are you looking for?

THE STRANGER. Well, I suppose I'm looking for you.

ELLIDA (*shuddering*). Oh! (*She stares at him, totters back, uttering a half-suffocating cry.*) The eyes—the eyes!

THE STRANGER. Are you beginning to recognize me at last? I knew you at once, Ellida.

ELLIDA. The eyes! Don't look at me like that! I shall cry for help!

THE STRANGER. Hush, hush! Do not fear. I shan't hurt you.

ELLIDA (*covering her eyes with her hands*). Do not look at me like that, I say!

THE STRANGER (*leaning with his arms on the garden fence*). I came with the English steamer.

ELLIDA (*stealing a frightened look at him*). What do you want with me?

THE STRANGER. I promised you to come as soon as I could——

ELLIDA. Go—go away! Never, never come here again! I wrote to you that everything must be over between us—everything! Oh! you know that!

THE STRANGER (*imperturbably, and not answering her*). I would gladly have come to you sooner; but I could not. Now, at last I am able to, and I am here, Ellida.

ELLIDA. What is it you want with me? What do you mean? Why have you come here?

THE STRANGER. Surely you know I've come to fetch you.

ELLIDA (*recoils in terror*). To fetch me! is that what you mean?

THE STRANGER. Of course.

ELLIDA. But surely you know that I am married?

THE STRANGER. Yes, I know.

ELLIDA. And yet—and yet you have come to—to fetch me!

THE STRANGER. Certainly I have.

ELLIDA (*seizing her head with both her hands*). Oh! this misery—this horror! This horror!

THE STRANGER. Perhaps you don't want to come?

ELLIDA (*bewildered*). Don't look at me like that.

THE STRANGER. I was asking you if you didn't want to come.

ELLIDA. No, no, no! Never in all eternity! I will not, I tell you. I neither can nor will. (*In lower tone.*) I dare not.

THE STRANGER (*climbs over the fence, and comes into the garden*). Well, Ellida, let me tell you one thing before I go.

ELLIDA (*wishes to fly, but cannot. She stands as one paralyzed with terror, and leans for support against the trunk of a tree by the pond*). Don't touch me! Don't come near me! No nearer! Don't touch me, I say!

THE STRANGER (*cautiously coming a few steps nearer*). You need not be so afraid of me, Ellida.

ELLIDA (*covering her eyes with her hands*). Don't look at me like that.

THE STRANGER. Do not be afraid—not afraid.

(WANGEL *comes through the garden, from the left.*)

WANGEL (*still half-way between the trees*). Well, you've had to wait for me a long while.

ELLIDA (*rushes towards him, clings fast to his arm, and cries out*). Oh! Wangel! Save me! *You* save me—if you can!

WANGEL. Ellida! What in heaven's name——

ELLIDA. Save me, Wangel! Don't you see him there? Why, he is standing there!

WANGEL (*looking thither*). *That* man? (*Coming nearer.*) May I ask you who you are, and what you have come into this garden for?

THE STRANGER (*motions with a nod towards* ELLIDA). I want to talk to her.

WANGEL. Oh! indeed. So I suppose it was you. (*To* ELLIDA.) I hear a stranger has been to the house and asked for you?

THE STRANGER. Yes, it was I.

WANGEL. And what do you want with my wife? (*Turning round.*) Do you know him, Ellida?

ELLIDA (*in a low voice and wringing her hands*). Do I know him! Yes, yes, yes!

WANGEL (*quickly*). Well!

ELLIDA. Why, it is he, Wangel!—he himself! He who you know——

WANGEL. What! What is it you say? (*Turning.*) Are you the Johnston who once——

THE STRANGER. You may call me Johnston for aught I care! However, that's not my name.

WANGEL. It is not?

THE STRANGER. It is—no longer. No!

WANGEL. And what may you want with my wife? For I suppose you know the lighthouse-keeper's daughter has been married this long time, and whom she married, you of course also know.

THE STRANGER. I've known it over three years.

ELLIDA (*eagerly*). How did you come to know it?

THE STRANGER. I was on my way home to you, Ellida. I came across an old newspaper. It was a paper from these parts, and in it there was that about the marriage.

ELLIDA (*looking straight in front of her*). The marriage! So it was that!

THE STRANGER. It seemed so wonderful to me. For the rings—why that, too, was a marriage, Ellida.

ELLIDA (*covering her face with her hands*). Oh!——

WANGEL. How dare you?

THE STRANGER. Have you forgotten that?

ELLIDA (*feeling his look, suddenly cries out*). Don't stand there and look at me like that!

WANGEL (*goes up to him*). You must deal with me, and not with her. In short—now that you know the circumstances—what is it you really want here? Why do you seek my wife?

THE STRANGER. I promised Ellida to come to her as soon as I could.

WANGEL. Ellida—again!——

THE STRANGER. And Ellida promised faithfully she would wait for me until I came.

WANGEL. I notice you call my wife by her first name. This kind of familiarity is not customary with us here.

THE STRANGER. I know that perfectly. But as she first, and above all, belongs to me——

WANGEL. To you, still——

ELLIDA (*draws back behind* WANGEL). Oh! he will never release me!

WANGEL. To you? You say she belongs to you?

THE STRANGER. Has she told you anything about the two rings—my ring and Ellida's?

WANGEL. Certainly. And what then? She put an end to that long ago. You have had her letters, so you know this yourself.

THE STRANGER. Both Ellida and I agreed that what we did should have all the strength and authority of a real and full marriage.

ELLIDA. But you hear, I will not! Never on earth do I wish to know anything more of you. Do not look at me like that. I will not, I tell you!

WANGEL. You must be mad to think you can come here, and base any claim upon such childish nonsense.

THE STRANGER. That's true. A claim, in your sense, I certainly have not.

WANGEL. What do you mean to do, then? You surely do not imagine you can take her from me by force, against her own will?

THE STRANGER. No. What would be the good of that? If Ellida wishes to be with me she must come freely.

ELLIDA (*starts, crying out*). Freely!

WANGEL. And you actually believe that——

ELLIDA (*to herself*). Freely!

WANGEL. You must have taken leave of your senses! Go your ways. We have nothing more to do with you.

THE STRANGER (*looking at his watch*). It is almost time for me to go on board again. (*Coming nearer.*) Yes, yes, Ellida, now I have done my duty. (*Coming still nearer.*) I have kept the word I gave you.

ELLIDA (*beseechingly drawing away*). Oh! don't touch me!

THE STRANGER. And so now you must think it over till to-morrow night——

WANGEL. There is nothing to think over here. See that you get away.

THE STRANGER (*still to* ELLIDA). Now I'm going with the steamer up the fjord. To-morrow night I will come again, and then I shall look for you here. You must wait for me here in the garden, for I prefer settling the matter with you alone; you understand?

ELLIDA (*in low, trembling tone*). Do you hear that, Wangel?

WANGEL. Only keep calm. We shall know how to prevent this visit.

THE STRANGER. Good-bye for the present, Ellida. So to-morrow night——

ELLIDA (*imploringly*). Oh! no, no! Do not come to-morrow night! Never come here again!

THE STRANGER. And should you then have a mind to follow me over the seas——

ELLIDA. Oh, don't look at me like that!

THE STRANGER. I only mean that you must then be ready to set out.

WANGEL. Go up to the house, Ellida.

ELLIDA. I cannot! Oh, help me! Save me, Wangel!

THE STRANGER. For you must remember that if you do not go with me to-morrow all is at an end.

ELLIDA (*looks tremblingly at him*). Then all is at an end? For ever?

THE STRANGER (*nodding*). Nothing can change it then, Ellida. I shall never again come to this land. You will never see me again, nor hear from me either. Then I shall be as one dead and gone from you for ever.

ELLIDA (*breathing with difficulty*). Oh!

THE STRANGER. So think carefully what you do. Good-bye! (*He goes to the fence and climbs over it, stands still, and says.*) Yes, Ellida; be ready for the journey to-morrow night. For then I shall come and fetch you. (*He goes slowly and calmly down the footpath to the right*).

ELLIDA (*looking after him for a time*). Freely, he said; think—he said that I must go with him freely!

WANGEL. Only keep calm. Why, he's gone now, and you'll never see him again.

ELLIDA. Oh! how can you say that? He's coming again to-morrow night!

WANGEL. Let him come. He shall not meet you again in any case.

ELLIDA (*shaking her head*). Ah, Wangel! do not believe you can prevent him.

WANGEL. I can, dearest; only trust me.

ELLIDA (*pondering, and not listening to him*). Now when he's been here to-morrow night—and then when he has gone over seas in the steamer——

WANGEL. Yes; what then?

ELLIDA. I should like to know if he will never, never come back again.

WANGEL. No, dear Ellida. You may be quite sure of that. What should he do here after this? Now that he has learnt from your own lips that you will have nothing more to do with him. With that the whole thing is over.

ELLIDA (*to herself*). To-morrow, then, or never!

WANGEL. And should it ever occur to him to come here again——

ELLIDA. Well?

WANGEL. Why, then, it is in our power to make him harmless.

ELLIDA. Oh! do not think that!

WANGEL. It is in our power, I tell you. If you can get rid of him in no other way, he must expiate the murder of the captain.

ELLIDA (*passionately*). No, no, no! Never that! We know nothing about the murder of the captain! Nothing whatever!

WANGEL. Know nothing? Why, he himself confessed it to you!

ELLIDA. No, nothing of that. If you say anything of it I shall deny it. He shall not be imprisoned. He belongs out there—to the open sea. He belongs out there!

WANGEL (*looks at her and says slowly*). Ah! Ellida— Ellida!

ELLIDA (*clinging passionately to him*). Oh, dear, faithful one—save me from this man!

WANGEL (*disengaging himself gently*). Come, come with me!

(LYNGSTRAND *and* HILDE, *both with fishing tackle, come in from the right, along the pond.*)

LYNGSTRAND (*going quickly up to* ELLIDA). Now, Mrs. Wangel, you must hear something wonderful.

WANGEL. What is it?

LYNGSTRAND. Fancy! We've seen the American!

WANGEL. The American?

HILDE. Yes, I saw him, too.

LYNGSTRAND. He was going round the back of the garden, and thence on board the great English steamer.

WANGEL. How do you know the man?

LYNGSTRAND. Why, I went to sea with him once. I felt

so certain he'd been drowned—and now he's very much alive!

WANGEL. Do you know anything more about him?

LYNGSTRAND. No. But I'm sure he's come to revenge himself upon his faithless sailor-wife.

WANGEL. What do you mean?

HILDE. Lyngstrand's going to use him for a work of art.

WANGEL. I don't understand one word.

ELLIDA. You shall hear afterwards.

(ARNHOLM *and* BOLETTE *come from the left along the footpath outside the garden.*)

BOLETTE (*to those in the garden*). Do come and see! The great English steamer's just going up the fjord.

(*A large steamer glides slowly past in the distance.*)

LYNGSTRAND (*to* HILDE *behind the garden fence*). To-night he's sure to come to her.

HILDE (*nods*). To the faithless sailor-wife—yes.

LYNGSTRAND. Fancy, at midnight!

HILDE. That must be so fascinating!

ELLIDA (*looking after the ship*). To-morrow, then!

WANGEL. And then never again.

ELLIDA (*in a low, imploring tone*). Oh! Wangel, save me from myself!

WANGEL (*looks anxiously at her*). Ellida—I feel there is something behind this——

ELLIDA. There is—the temptation!

WANGEL. Temptation?

ELLIDA. The man is like the sea!

(*She goes slowly and thoughtfully through the garden, and out to the left.* WANGEL *walks uneasily by her side, watching her closely.*)

ACT IV

(SCENE.—DOCTOR WANGEL's *garden-room. Doors right and left. In the background, between the windows, an open glass door, leading out on to the veranda. Below this a portion of the garden is visible. A sofa and table down left. To the right a piano, and farther back a large flower-stand. In the middle of the room a round table, with chairs. On the table is a rose-tree in bloom, and other plants round it. Morning.*)

In the room, by the table, BOLETTE *is sitting on the sofa, busy with some embroidery.* LYNGSTRAND *is seated on a chair at the upper end of the table. In the garden below* BALLESTED *sits painting.* HILDE *stands by watching him.*)

LYNGSTRAND (*with his arms on the table, sits silent awhile, looking at* BOLETTE's *work*). It must be awfully difficult to do a border like that, Miss Wangel?

BOLETTE. Oh, no! It's not very difficult, if only you take care to count right.

LYNGSTRAND. To count? Must you count, too?

BOLETTE. Yes, the stitches. See!

LYNGSTRAND. So you do! Just fancy! Why, it's almost a kind of art. Can you design, too?

BOLETTE. Oh, yes! When I've a copy.

LYNGSTRAND. Not unless?

BOLETTE. No.

LYNGSTRAND. Well, then, after all, it's not a real art?

BOLETTE. No; it is rather only a sort of—handicraft.

LYNGSTRAND. But still, I think that perhaps you could learn art.

BOLETTE. If I haven't any talent?

393

LYNGSTRAND. Yes; if you could always be with a real true artist——

BOLETTE. Do you think, then, I could learn it from him?

LYNGSTRAND. Not exactly learn in the ordinary sense; but I think it would grow upon you little by little—by a kind of miracle as it were, Miss Wangel.

BOLETTE. That would be wonderful.

LYNGSTRAND (*after a pause*). Have you ever thought about—I mean, have you ever thought deeply and earnestly about marriage, Miss Wangel?

BOLETTE (*looking quickly at him*). About—no!

LYNGSTRAND. I have.

BOLETTE. Really? Have you?

LYNGSTRAND. Oh yes! I often think about things of that sort, especially about marriage; and, besides, I've read several books about it. I think marriage must be counted a sort of miracle;—that a woman should gradually change till she is like her husband.

BOLETTE. You mean has like interests?

LYNGSTRAND. Yes, that's it.

BOLETTE. Well, but his abilities,—his talents,—and his skill?

LYNGSTRAND. Hm—well—I should like to know if all that too——

BOLETTE. Then, perhaps, you also believe that everything a man has read for himself, and thought out for himself, that this, too, can grow upon his wife?

LYNGSTRAND. Yes, I think it can. Little by little; as by a sort of miracle. But, of course, I know such things can only happen in a marriage that is faithful, and loving, and really happy.

BOLETTE. Has it never occurred to you that a man, too, might, perhaps, be thus drawn over to his wife? Grow like her, I mean.

LYNGSTRAND. A man? No, I never thought of that.

BOLETTE. But why not one as well as the other?

LYNGSTRAND. No; for a man has a calling that he lives for; and *that's* what makes a man so strong and firm, Miss Wangel. He has a calling in life.

BOLETTE. Has every man?

LYNGSTRAND. Oh no! I am thinking more especially of artists.

BOLETTE. Do you think it right of an artist to get married?

LYNGSTRAND. Yes, I think so. If he can find one he can heartily love, I——

BOLETTE. Still, I think he should rather live for his art alone.

LYNGSTRAND. Of course he must; but he can do that just as well, even if he marries.

BOLETTE. But how about her?

LYNGSTRAND. Her? Who?

BOLETTE. She whom he marries. What is she to live for?

LYNGSTRAND. She, too, is to live for his art. It seems to me a woman must feel so thoroughly happy in *that*.

BOLETTE. Hm, I don't exactly know——

LYNGSTRAND. Yes, Miss Wangel, you may be sure of that. It is not merely all the honor and respect she enjoys through him; for that seems almost the least important to me. But it is this—that she can help him to create, that she can lighten his work for him, be about him and see to his comfort, and tend him well, and make his life thoroughly pleasant. I should think that must be perfectly delightful to a woman.

BOLETTE. Ah! you don't yourself know how selfish you are!

LYNGSTRAND. I, selfish! Good heavens! Oh, if only you knew me a little better than you do! (*Bending closer to her.*) Miss Wangel, when once I am gone—and that will be very soon now——

BOLETTE (*looks pityingly at him*). Oh, don't think of anything so sad!

LYNGSTRAND. But, really, I don't think it is so very sad.

BOLETTE. What do you mean?

LYNGSTRAND. Well, you know that I set out in a month. First from here, and then, of course, I'm going south.

BOLETTE. Oh, I see! Of course.

LYNGSTRAND. Will you think of me sometimes, then, Miss Wangel?

BOLETTE. Yes, gladly.

LYNGSTRAND (*pleased*). No, promise!

BOLETTE. I promise.

LYNGSTRAND. By all that is sacred, Miss Bolette?

BOLETTE. By all that is sacred. (*In a changed manner.*) Oh, but what can come of it all? Nothing on earth can come of it!

LYNGSTRAND. How can you say that! It would be so delightful for me to know you were at home here thinking of me!

BOLETTE. Well, and what else?

LYNGSTRAND. I don't exactly know of anything else.

BOLETTE. Nor I either. There are so many things in the way. Everything stands in the way, I think.

LYNGSTRAND. Oh, another miracle might come about. Some happy dispensation of fortune, or something of the sort; for I really believe I shall be lucky now.

BOLETTE (*eagerly*). Really? You do believe that?

LYNGSTRAND. Yes, I believe it thoroughly. And so—after a few years—when I come home again as a celebrated sculptor, and well off, and in perfect health——

BOLETTE. Yes, yes! Of course, we will hope so.

LYNGSTRAND. You may be perfectly certain about it. Only think faithfully and kindly of me when I am down there in the south; and now I have your word that you will.

BOLETTE. You have (*shaking her head*). But, all the same, nothing will surely come of it.

LYNGSTRAND. Oh! yes, Miss Bolette. At least this will come of it. I shall get on so much more easily and quickly with my art work.

BOLETTE. Do you believe that, too?

LYNGSTRAND. I have an inner conviction of it. And I fancy it will be so cheering for you, too—here in this out-of-the-way place—to know within yourself that you are, so to say, helping me to create.

BOLETTE (*looking at him*). Well; but you on your side?

LYNGSTRAND. I?

BOLETTE (*looking out into the garden*). Hush! Let us speak of something else. Here's Mr. Arnholm.

(ARNHOLM *is seen in the garden below. He stops and talks to* HILDE *and* BALLESTED.)

LYNGSTRAND. Are you fond of your old teacher, Miss Bolette?

BOLETTE. Fond of him?

LYNGSTRAND. Yes; I mean do you care for him?

BOLETTE. Yes, indeed I do, for he is a true friend—and adviser, too—and then he is always so ready to help when he can.

LYNGSTRAND. Isn't it extraordinary that he hasn't married!

BOLETTE. Do you think it is extraordinary?

LYNGSTRAND. Yes, for you say he's well-to-do.

BOLETTE. He is certainly said to be so. But probably it wasn't so easy to find anyone who'd have him.

LYNGSTRAND. Why?

BOLETTE. Oh! He's been the teacher of nearly all the young girls that he knows. He says that himself.

LYNGSTRAND. But what does that matter?

BOLETTE. Why, good heavens! One doesn't marry a man who's been your teacher!

LYNGSTRAND. Don't you think a young girl might love her teacher?

BOLETTE. Not after she's really grown up.

LYNGSTRAND. No—fancy that!

BOLETTE (*cautioning him*). Sh! sh!

(*Meanwhile* BALLESTED *has been gathering together his things, and carries them out from the garden to the right.* HILDE *helps him.* ARNHOLM *goes up the veranda, and comes into the room.*)

ARNHOLM. Good morning, my dear Bolette. Good morning, Mr.—Mr.—hm——

(*He looks displeased, and nods coldly to* LYNGSTRAND, *who rises.*)

BOLETTE (*rising up and going up to* ARNHOLM). Good morning, Mr. Arnholm.

ARNHOLM. Everything all right here today?

BOLETTE. Yes, thanks, quite.

ARNHOLM. Has your stepmother gone to bathe again today?

BOLETTE. No. She is upstairs in her room.

ARNHOLM. Not very bright?

BOLETTE. I don't know, for she has locked herself in.

ARNHOLM. Hm—has she?

LYNGSTRAND. I suppose Mrs. Wangel was very much frightened about that American yesterday?

ARNHOLM. What do *you* know about that?

LYNGSTRAND. I told Mrs. Wangel that I had seen him in the flesh behind the garden.

ARNHOLM. Oh! I see.

BOLETTE (*to* ARNHOLM). No doubt you and father sat up very late last night, talking?

ARNHOLM. Yes, rather late. We were talking over serious matters.

BOLETTE. Did you put in a word for me, and my affairs, too?

ARNHOLM. No, dear Bolette, I couldn't manage it. He was so completely taken up with something else.

BOLETTE (*sighs*). Ah! yes; he always is.

ARNHOLM (*looks at her meaningly*). But later on to-day we'll talk more fully about—the matter. Where's your father now? Not at home?

BOLETTE. Yes, he is. He must be down in the office. I'll fetch him.

ARNHOLM. No, thanks. Don't do that. I'd rather go down to him.

BOLETTE (*listening*). Wait one moment, Mr. Arnholm; I believe that's father on the stairs. Yes, I suppose he's been up to look after her.

(WANGEL *comes in from the door on the left.*)

WANGEL (*shaking* ARNHOLM'S *hand*). What, dear friend, are you here already? It was good of you to come so early, for I should like to talk a little further with you.

BOLETTE (*to* LYNGSTRAND). Hadn't we better go down to Hilde in the garden?

LYNGSTRAND. I shall be delighted, Miss Wangel.

(*He and* BOLETTE *go down into the garden, and pass out between the trees in the background.*)

ARNHOLM (*following them with his eyes, turns to* WAN-GEL). Do you know anything about that young man?

WANGEL. No, nothing at all.

ARNHOLM. But do you think it right he should knock about so much with the girls?

WANGEL. Does he? I really hadn't noticed it.

ARNHOLM. You ought to see to it, I think.

WANGEL. Yes, I suppose you're right. But, good Lord! what's a man to do? The girls are so accustomed to look after themselves now. They won't listen to me, nor to Ellida.

ARNHOLM. Not to her either?

WANGEL. No; and besides I really cannot expect Ellida to trouble about such things. She's not fit for that (*breaking off*). But it wasn't *that* which we were to talk of. Now tell me, have you thought the matter over—thought over all I told you of?

ARNHOLM. I have thought of nothing else ever since we parted last night.

WANGEL. And what do you think should be done?

ARNHOLM. Dear Wangel, I think you, as a doctor, must know that better than I.

WANGEL. Oh! if you only knew how difficult it is for a doctor to judge rightly about a patient who is so dear to him! Besides, this is no ordinary illness. No ordinary doctor and no ordinary medicines can help her.

ARNHOLM. How is she to-day?

WANGEL. I was upstairs with her just now, and then she seemed to me quite calm; but behind all her moods something lies hidden which it is impossible for me to fathom; and then she so changeable, so capricious—she varies so suddenly.

ARNHOLM. No doubt that is the result of her morbid state of mind.

WANGEL. Not altogether. When you go down to the bed-rock, it was born in her. Ellida belongs to the sea-folk. That is the matter.

ARNHOLM. What do you really mean, my dear doctor?

WANGEL. Haven't you noticed that the people from out there by the open sea are, in a way, a people apart? It is almost as if they themselves lived the life of the sea. There is the rush of waves, and ebb and flow too, both in their thoughts and in their feelings, and so they can never bear transplanting. Oh! I ought to have remembered that. It was a sin against Ellida to take her away from there, and bring her here.

ARNHOLM. You have come to that opinion?

WANGEL. Yes, more and more. But I ought to have told myself this beforehand. Oh! I knew it well enough at bottom! But I put it from me. For, you see, I loved her so! Therefore I thought of myself first of all. I was inexcusably selfish at that time!

ARNHOLM. Hm. I suppose every man is a little selfish under such circumstances. Moreover, I've never noticed that vice in you, Doctor Wangel.

WANGEL (*walks uneasily about the room*). Oh, yes! And I have been since then, too. Why, I am so much, much older than she is. I ought to have been at once as a father to her and a guide. I ought to have done my best to develop and enlighten her mind. Unfortunately nothing ever came of that. You see, I hadn't stamina enough, for I preferred her just as she was. So things went worse and worse with her, and then I didn't know what to do. (*In a lower voice.*) That was why I wrote to you in my trouble, and asked you to come here.

ARNHOLM (*looks at him in astonishment*). What, was it for this you wrote?

WANGEL. Yes; but don't let anyone notice anything.

ARNHOLM. How on earth, dear doctor—what good did you expect me to be? I don't understand it.

WANGEL. No, naturally. For I was on an altogether false track. I thought Ellida's heart had at one time gone out to you, and that she still secretly cared for you a little—that perhaps it would do her good to see you again, and talk of her home and the old days.

ARNHOLM. So it was your wife you meant when you wrote that she expected me, and—and perhaps longed for me.

WANGEL. Yes, who else?

ARNHOLM (*hurriedly*). No, no. You're right. But I didn't understand.

WANGEL. Naturally, as I said, for I was on an absolutely wrong track.

ARNHOLM. And you call yourself selfish!

WANGEL. Ah! but I had such a great sin to atone for. I felt I dared not neglect any means that might give the slightest relief to her mind.

ARNHOLM. How do you really explain the power this stranger exercises over her?

WANGEL. Hm—dear friend—there may be sides to the matter that *cannot* be explained.

ARNHOLM. Do you mean anything inexplicable in itself—absolutely inexplicable?

WANGEL. In any case not explicable as far as we know.

ARNHOLM. Do you believe there is something in it, then?

WANGEL. I neither believe nor deny; I simply don't know. That's why I leave it alone.

ARNHOLM. Yes. But just one thing: her extraordinary, weird assertion about the child's eyes——

WANGEL (*eagerly*). I don't believe a word about the eyes. I *will* not believe such a thing. It must be purely fancy on her part, nothing else.

ARNHOLM. Did you notice the man's eyes when you saw him yesterday?

WANGEL. Of course I did.

ARNHOLM. And you saw no sort of resemblance?

WANGEL (*evasively*). Hm—good heavens! What shall I say? It wasn't quite light when I saw him; and, besides, Ellida had been saying so much about this resemblance, I really don't know if I was capable of observing quite impartially.

ARNHOLM. Well, well, may be. But that other matter? All this terror and unrest coming upon her at the very time, as it seems, this strange man was on his way home.

WANGEL. That—oh! that's something she must have persuaded and dreamed herself into since it happened. She was not seized with this so suddenly—all at once—as she now maintains. But since she heard from young Lyngstrand that Johnston—or Friman, or whatever his name is—was on his way hither, three years ago, in the month of March, she now evidently believes her unrest of mind came upon her at that very time.

ARNHOLM. It was not so, then?

WANGEL. By no means. There were signs and symptoms of it before this time, though it did happen, by chance, that in that month of March, three years ago, she had a rather severe attack.

ARNHOLM. After all, then——?

WANGEL. Yes, but that is easily accounted for by the circumstances—the condition she happened to be in at the time.

ARNHOLM. So, symptom for symptom, then.

WANGEL (*wringing his hands*). And not to be able to help her! Not to know how to counsel her! To see no way!

ARNHOLM. Now if you could make up your mind to leave this place, to go somewhere else, so that she could live amid surroundings that would seem more homelike to her?

WANGEL. Ah, dear friend! Do you think I haven't offered her that, too? I suggested moving out to Skjoldviken, but she will not.

ARNHOLM. Not that either?

WANGEL. No, for she doesn't think it would be any good; and perhaps she's right.

ARNHOLM. Hm. Do you say that?

WANGEL. Moreover, when I think it all over carefully, I really don't know how I could manage it. I don't think I should be justified, for the sake of the girls, in going away to such a desolate place. After all, they must live where there is at least a prospect of their being provided for some day.

ARNHOLM. Provided for! Are you thinking about that already?

WANGEL. Heaven knows, I must think of that too! But then, on the other hand, again, my poor sick Ellida! Oh, dear Arnholm! in many respects I seem to be standing between fire and water!

ARNHOLM. Perhaps you've no need to worry on Bolette's account. (*Breaking off.*) I should like to know where she— where they have gone. (*Goes up to the open door and looks out.*)

WANGEL. Oh, I would so gladly make any sacrifice for all three of them, if only I knew what!

(ELLIDA *enters from the door on the left.*)

ELLIDA (*quickly to* WANGEL). Be sure you don't go out this morning.

WANGEL. No, no! of course not. I will stay at home with you. (*Pointing to* ARNHOLM, *who is coming towards them.*) But won't you speak to our friend?

ELLIDA (*turning*). Oh, are you here, Mr. Arnholm? (*Holding out her hand to him.*) Good morning.

ARNHOLM. Good morning, Mrs. Wangel. So you've not been bathing as usual to-day?

ELLIDA. No, no, no! That is out of the question to-day. But won't you sit down a moment?

ARNHOLM. No, thanks, not now. (*Looks at* WANGEL.) I promised the girls to go down to them in the garden.

ELLIDA. Goodness knows if you'll find them there. I never know where they may be rambling.

WANGEL. They're sure to be down by the pond.

ARNHOLM. Oh! I shall find them right enough. (*Nods, and goes out across the veranda into the garden.*)

ELLIDA. What time is it, Wangel?

WANGEL (*looking at his watch*). A little past eleven.

ELLIDA. A little past. And at eleven o'clock, or half-past eleven to-night, the steamer is coming. If only that were over!

WANGEL (*going nearer to her*). Dear Ellida, there is one thing I should like to ask you.

ELLIDA. What is it?

WANGEL. The evening before last—up at the "View"— you said that during the last three years you had so often seen him bodily before you.

ELLIDA. And so I have. You may believe that.

WANGEL. But, how did you see him?

ELLIDA. How did I see him?

WANGEL. I mean, how did he look when you thought you saw him?

ELLIDA. But, dear Wangel, why, you now know yourself how he looks.

WANGEL. Did he look exactly like that in your imagination?

ELLIDA. He did.

WANGEL. Exactly the same as you saw him in reality yesterday evening?

ELLIDA. Yes, exactly.

WANGEL. Then how was it you did not at once recognize him?

ELLIDA. Did I not?

WANGEL. No; you said yourself afterwards that at first you did not at all know who the strange man was.

ELLIDA (*perplexed*). I really believe you are right. Don't you think that strange, Wangel? Fancy my not knowing him at once!

WANGEL. It was only the eyes, you said.

ELLIDA. Oh, yes! The eyes—the eyes.

WANGEL. Well, but at the "View" you said that he always appeared to you exactly as he was when you parted out there —ten years ago.

ELLIDA. Did I?

WANGEL. Yes.

ELLIDA. Then, I suppose he did look much as he does now.

WANGEL. No. On our way home, the day before yesterday, you gave quite another description of him. Ten years ago he had no beard, you said. His dress, too, was quite different. And that breast-pin with the pearl? That man yesterday wore nothing of the sort.

ELLIDA. No, he did not.

WANGEL (*looks searchingly at her*). Now just think a little, dear Ellida. Or perhaps you can't quite remember how he looked when he stood by you at Bratthammeren?

ELLIDA (*thoughtfully closing her eyes for a moment*). Not quite distinctly. No, to-day I can't. Is it not strange?

WANGEL. Not so very strange after all. You have now

been confronted by a new and real image, and that over-shadows the old one, so that you can no longer see it.

ELLIDA. Do you believe that, Wangel?

WANGEL. Yes. And it overshadows your sick imaginings, too. That is why it is good a reality has come.

ELLIDA. Good? Do you think it good?

WANGEL. Yes. That it has come. It may restore you to health.

ELLIDA (*sitting down on sofa*). Wangel, come and sit down by me. I must tell you all my thoughts.

WANGEL. Yes, do, dear Ellida.

(*He sits down on a chair on the other side of the table.*)

ELLIDA. It was really a great misfortune—for us both—that we two of all people should have come together.

WANGEL (*amazed*). What are you saying?

ELLIDA. Oh, yes, it was. And it's so natural. It could bring nothing but unhappiness, after the way in which we came together.

WANGEL. What was there in that way?

ELLIDA. Listen, Wangel; it's no use going on, lying to our-selves and to one another.

WANGEL. Are we doing so? Lying, you say?

ELLIDA. Yes, we are; or, at least, we suppress the truth. For the truth—the pure and simple truth is—that you came out there and bought me.

WANGEL. Bought—you say bought!

ELLIDA. Oh! I wasn't a bit better than you. I accepted the bargain. Sold myself to you!

WANGEL (*looks at her full of pain*). Ellida, have you really the heart to call it that?

ELLIDA. But is there any other name for it? You could no longer bear the emptiness of your house. You were on the look-out for a new wife.

WANGEL. And a new mother for the children, Ellida.

ELLIDA. That too, perhaps, by the way; although you

didn't in the least know if I were fit for the position. Why, you had only seen me and spoken to me a few times. Then you wanted me, and so——

WANGEL. Yes, you may call it as you will.

ELLIDA. And I, on my side—why, I was so helpless and bewildered, and so absolutely alone. Oh! it was so natural I should accept the bargain, when you came and proposed to provide for me all my life.

WANGEL. Assuredly it did not seem to me a providing for you, dear Ellida. I asked you honestly if you would share with me and the children the little I could call my own.

ELLIDA. Yes, you did; but all the same, I should never have accepted! Never have accepted that at any price! Not sold myself! Better the meanest work—better the poorest life— after one's own choice.

WANGEL (*rising*). Then have the five—six years that we have lived together been so utterly worthless to you?

ELLIDA. Oh! Don't think that, Wangel. I have been as well cared for here as human being could desire. But I did not enter your house freely. That is the thing.

WANGEL (*looking at her*). Not freely!

ELLIDA. No. It was not freely that I went with you.

WANGEL (*in subdued tone*). Ah! I remember your words of yesterday.

ELLIDA. It all lies in those words. They have enlightened me; and so I see it all now.

WANGEL. What do you see?

ELLIDA. I see that the life we two live together—is really no marriage.

WANGEL (*bitterly*). You have spoken truly there. The life we *now* live is not a marriage.

ELLIDA. Nor was it formerly. Never—not from the very first (*looks straight in front of her*). The first—that might have been a complete and real marriage.

WANGEL. The first—what do you mean?

ELLIDA. Mine—with him.

WANGEL (*looks at her in astonishment*). I do not in the least understand you.

ELLIDA. Ah! dear Wangel, let us not lie to one another, nor to ourselves.

WANGEL. Well—what more?

ELLIDA. You see—we can never get away from that one thing—that a freely given promise is fully as binding as a marriage.

WANGEL. But what on earth——

ELLIDA (*rising impetuously*). Set me free, Wangel!

WANGEL. Ellida! Ellida!

ELLIDA. Yes, yes! Oh! grant me that! Believe me, it will come to that all the same—after the way we two came together.

WANGEL (*conquering his pain*). It has come to this, then?

ELLIDA. It has come to this. It could not be otherwise.

WANGEL (*looking gloomily at her*). So I have not won you by our living together. Never, never possessed you quite.

ELLIDA. Ah! Wangel—if only I could love you, how gladly I would—as dearly as you deserve. But I feel it so well —that will never be.

WANGEL. Divorce, then? It is a divorce, a complete, legal divorce that you want?

ELLIDA. Dear, you understand me so little! I care nothing for such formalities. Such outer things matter nothing, I think. What I want is that we should, of our own free will, release each other.

WANGEL (*bitterly, nods slowly*). To cry off the bargain again—yes.

ELLIDA (*quickly*). Exactly. To cry off the bargain.

WANGEL. And then, Ellida? Afterwards? Have you reflected what life would be to both of us? What life would be to both you and me?

ELLIDA. No matter. Things must turn out afterwards as they may. What I beg and implore of you, Wangel, is the most important. Only set me free! Give me back my complete freedom!

WANGEL. Ellida, it is a fearful thing you ask of me. At least give me time to collect myself before I come to a decision. Let us talk it over more carefully. And you yourself—take time to consider what you are doing.

ELLIDA. But we have no time to lose with such matters. I must have my freedom again to-day.

WANGEL. Why to-day?

ELLIDA. Because he is coming to-night.

WANGEL (*starts*). Coming! He! What has this stranger to do with it?

ELLIDA. I want to face him in perfect freedom.

WANGEL. And what—what else do you intend to do?

ELLIDA. I will not hide behind the fact that I am the wife of another man; nor make the excuse that I have no choice, for then it would be no decision.

WANGEL. You speak of a choice. Choice, Ellida! A choice in such a matter!

ELLIDA. Yes, I must be free to choose—to choose for either side. I must be able to let him go away—alone, or to go with him.

WANGEL. Do you know what you are saying? Go with him—give your whole life into his hands!

ELLIDA. Didn't I give my life into *your* hands, and without any ado?

WANGEL. Maybe. But he! He! an absolute stranger! A man of whom you know so little!

ELLIDA. Ah! but after all I knew you even less; and yet I went with you.

WANGEL. Then you knew to some extent what life lay before you. But now? Think! What do you know? You know absolutely nothing. Not even who or what he is.

ELLIDA (*looking in front of her*). That is true; but that is the terror.

WANGEL. Yes, indeed, it is terrible!

ELLIDA. That is why I feel I must plunge into it.

WANGEL (*looking at her*). Because it seems terrible?

ELLIDA. Yes; because of that.

WANGEL (*coming closer*). Listen, Ellida. What do you really mean by terrible?

ELLIDA (*reflectively*). The terrible is that which repels and attracts.

WANGEL. Attracts, you say?

ELLIDA. Attracts most of all, I think.

WANGEL (*slowly*). You are one with the sea.

ELLIDA. That, too, is a terror.

WANGEL. And that terror is in you. You both repel and attract.

ELLIDA. Do you think so, Wangel?

WANGEL. After all, I have never really known you—never really. Now I am beginning to understand.

ELLIDA. And that is why you must set me free! Free me from every bond to you—and yours. I am not what you took me for. Now you see it yourself. Now we can part as friends —and freely.

WANGEL (*sadly*). Perhaps it would be better for us both if we parted—— And yet, I cannot! You are the terror to me, Ellida; the attraction is what is strongest in you.

ELLIDA. Do you say that?

WANGEL. Let us try and live through this day wisely—in perfect quiet of mind. I dare not set you free, and release you to-day. I have no right to. No right for your own sake, Ellida. I exercise my right and my duty to protect you.

ELLIDA. Protect? What is there to protect me from? I am not threatened by any outward power. The terror lies deeper, Wangel. The terror is—the attraction in my own mind. And what can you do against that?

WANGEL. I can strengthen and urge you to fight against it.

ELLIDA. Yes; if I *wished* to fight against it.

WANGEL. Then you do not wish to?

ELLIDA. Oh! I don't know myself.

WANGEL. To-night all will be decided, dear Ellida——

ELLIDA (*bursting out*). Yes, think! The decision so near— the decision for one's whole life!

WANGEL. And then to-morrow——

ELLIDA. To-morrow! Perhaps my real future will have been ruined.

WANGEL. Your real——

ELLIDA. The whole, full life of freedom lost—lost for me, and perhaps for him also.

WANGEL (*in a lower tone, seizing her wrist*). Ellida, do you love this stranger?

ELLIDA. Do I? Oh, how can I tell! I only know that to me he is a terror, and that——

WANGEL. And that——

ELLIDA (*tearing herself away*). And that it is to him I think I belong.

WANGEL (*bowing his head*). I begin to understand better.

ELLIDA. And what remedy have you for that? What advice to give me?

WANGEL (*looking sadly at her*). To-morrow he will be gone, then the misfortune will be averted from your head; and then I will consent to set you free. We will cry off the bargain to-morrow, Ellida.

ELLIDA. Ah, Wangel, to-morrow! that is too late.

WANGEL (*looking towards garden*). The children—the children! Let us spare them, at least for the present.

(ARNHOLM, BOLETTE, HILDE, *and* LYNGSTRAND *come into the garden.* LYNGSTRAND *says good-bye in the garden, and goes out. The rest come into the room.*)

ARNHOLM. You must know we have been making plans.

HILDE. We're going out to the fjord to-night and——

BOLETTE. No; you mustn't tell.

WANGEL. We two, also, have been making plans.

ARNHOLM. Ah!—really?

WANGEL. To-morrow Ellida is going away to Skjoldviken for a time.

BOLETTE. Going away?

ARNHOLM. Now, look here, that's very sensible, Mrs. Wangel.

WANGEL. Ellida wants to go home again—home to the sea.

HILDE (*springing towards* ELLIDA). You are going away—away from us?

ELLIDA (*frightened*). Hilde! What is the matter?

HILDE (*controlling herself*). Oh, it's nothing. (*In a low voice, turning from her.*) Are only you going?

BOLETTE (*anxiously*). Father,—I see it;—*you*, too, are going—to Skjoldviken!

WANGEL. No, no! Perhaps I shall run out there every now and again.

BOLETTE. And come here to us?

WANGEL. I will——

BOLETTE. Every now and again!

WANGEL. Dear child, it must be. (*He crosses the room.*)

ARNHOLM (*whispers*). We will talk it over later, Bolette. (*He crosses to* WANGEL. *They speak in low tones up stage by the door.*)

ELLIDA (*aside to* BOLETTE). What was the matter with Hilde? She looked quite scared.

BOLETTE. Have you never noticed what Hilde goes about here, day in, day out, hungering for?

ELLIDA. Hungering for?

BOLETTE. Ever since you came into the house?

ELLIDA. No, no. What is it?

BOLETTE. One loving word from you.

ELLIDA. Oh! If there should be something for me to do *here!*

(*She clasps her hands together over her head, and looks fixedly in front of her, as if torn by contending thoughts and emotions.* WANGEL *and* ARNHOLM *come across the room whispering.* BOLETTE *goes to the side room, and looks in. Then she throws open the door.*)

BOLETTE. Father, dear—the table is laid—if you——

WANGEL (*with forced composure*). Is it, child? That's well. Come, Arnholm! We'll go in and drink a farewell cup —with the "Lady from the Sea." (*They go out through the right.*)

ACT V

(SCENE.—*The distant part of* DOCTOR WANGEL'S *garden, and the carp pond. The summer night gradually darkens.* ARNHOLM, BOLETTE, LYNGSTRAND *and* HILDE *are in a boat, punting along the shore to the left.*)

HILDE. See! We can jump ashore easily here.

ARNHOLM. No, no; don't!

LYNGSTRAND. I can't jump, Miss Hilde.

HILDE. Can't you jump either, Arnholm?

ARNHOLM. I'd rather not try.

BOLETTE. Then let's land down there, by the bathing steps.

(*They push off. At the same moment* BALLESTED *comes along the footpath, carrying music-books and a French horn. He bows to those in the boat, turns and speaks to them. The answers are heard farther and farther away.*)

BALLESTED. What do you say? Yes, of course it's on account of the English steamer; for this is her last visit here this year. But if you want to enjoy the pleasures of melody, you mustn't wait too long. (*Calling out.*) What? (*Shaking his head.*) Can't hear what you say!

(ELLIDA, *with a shawl over her head, enters, followed by* DOCTOR WANGEL.)

WANGEL. But, dear Ellida, I assure you there's plenty of time.

ELLIDA. No, no, there is not! He may come any moment.

BALLESTED (*outside the fence*). Hallo! Good evening, doctor. Good evening, Mrs. Wangel.

WANGEL (*noticing him*). Oh! is it you? Is there to be music to-night?

414

BALLESTED. Yes; the Wind Band Society thought of making themselves heard. We've no dearth of festive occasions nowadays. To-night it's in honor of the English ship.

ELLIDA. The English ship! Is she in sight already?

BALLESTED. Not yet. But you know she comes from between the islands. You can't see anything of her, and then she's alongside of you.

ELLIDA. Yes, that is so.

WANGEL (*half to* ELLIDA). To-night is the last voyage, then she will not come again.

BALLESTED. A sad thought, doctor, and that's why we're going to give them an ovation, as the saying is. Ah! yes— ah! yes. The glad summer-time will soon be over now. Soon all ways will be barred, as they say in the tragedy.

ELLIDA. All ways barred—yes!

BALLESTED. It's sad to think of. We have been the joyous children of summer for weeks and months now. It's hard to reconcile yourself to the dark days—just at first, I mean. For men *can* accli—a—acclimatize themselves, Mrs. Wangel. Ay, indeed they can. (*Bows, and goes off to the left.*)

ELLIDA (*looking out at the fjord*). Oh, this terrible suspense! This torturing last half-hour before the decision!

WANGEL. You are determined, then, to speak to him yourself?

ELLIDA. I must speak to him myself; for it is freely that I must make my choice.

WANGEL. You have no choice, Ellida. You have no right to choose—no right without my permission.

ELLIDA. You can never prevent the choice, neither you nor anyone. You can forbid me to go away with him—to follow him—in case I should choose to do that. You can keep me here by force—against my will. That you can do. But that I should choose, choose from my very soul—choose him, and not you—in case I would and did choose thus—this you cannot prevent.

WANGEL. No; you are right. I cannot prevent that.

ELLIDA. And so I have nothing to help me to resist. Here, at home, there is no single thing that attracts me and binds me. I am so absolutely rootless in your house, Wangel. The children are not mine—their hearts, I mean—never have been. When I go, if I do go, either with him to-night, or to Skjold-viken to-morrow, I haven't a key to give up, an order to give about anything whatsoever. I am absolutely rootless in your house—I have been absolutely outside everything from the very first.

WANGEL. You yourself wished it.

ELLIDA. No, no, I did not. I neither wished nor did not wish it. I simply left things just as I found them the day I came here. It is you, and no one else, who wished it.

WANGEL. I thought to do all for the best for you.

ELLIDA. Yes, Wangel, I know it so well! But there is retribution in that, a something that avenges itself. For now I find no binding power here—nothing to strengthen me—nothing to help me—nothing to draw me towards what should have been the strongest possession of us both.

WANGEL. I see it, Ellida. And that is why from to-morrow you shall have back your freedom. Henceforth you shall live your own life.

ELLIDA. And you call that my own life! No! My own true life lost its bearings when I agreed to live with you. (*Clenches her hand in fear and unrest.*) And now—to-night—in half an hour, he whom I forsook is coming—he to whom I should have cleaved for ever, even as he has cleaved to me! Now he is coming to offer me—for the last and only time—the chance of living my life over again, of living my own true life—the life that terrifies and attracts—and I *can* not forego that—not freely.

WANGEL. That is why it is necessary your husband—and your doctor—should take the power of acting from you, and act on your behalf.

ELLIDA. Yes, Wangel, I quite understand. Believe me, there are times when I think it would be peace and deliverance if with all my soul I could be bound to you—and try to brave all that terrifies—and attracts. But I cannot! No, no, I cannot do that!

WANGEL. Come, Ellida, let us walk up and down together for a while.

ELLIDA. I would gladly—but I dare not. For he said I was to wait for him here.

WANGEL. Come! There is time enough.

ELLIDA. Do you think so?

WANGEL. Plenty of time, I tell you.

ELLIDA. Then let us go, for a little while.

(*They pass out in the foreground. At the same time* ARNHOLM *and* BOLETTE *appear by the upper bank of the pond.*)

BOLETTE (*noticing the two as they go out*). See there——

ARNHOLM (*in low voice*). Hush! Let them go.

BOLETTE. Can you understand what has been going on between them these last few days?

ARNHOLM. Have you noticed anything?

BOLETTE. Have I not!

ARNHOLM. Anything peculiar?

BOLETTE. Yes, one thing and another. Haven't you?

ARNHOLM. Well—I don't exactly know.

BOLETTE. Yes, you have; only you won't speak out about it.

ARNHOLM. I think it will do your stepmother good to go on this little journey.

BOLETTE. Do you think so?

ARNHOLM. I should say it would be well for all parties that she should get away every now and then.

BOLETTE. If she does go home to Skjoldviken to-morrow, she will never come back again to here!

ARNHOLM. My dear Bolette, whatever makes you think that?

BOLETTE. I am quite convinced of it. Just you wait; you'll see that she'll not come back again; not anyhow as long as I and Hilde are in the house here.

ARNHOLM. Hilde, too?

BOLETTE. Well, it might perhaps be all right with Hilde. For she is scarcely more than a child. And I believe that at bottom she worships Ellida. But, you see, it's different with me—a stepmother who isn't so very much older than oneself!

ARNHOLM. Dear Bolette, perhaps it might, after all, not be so very long before you left.

BOLETTE (*eagerly*). Really! Have you spoken to father about it?

ARNHOLM. Yes, I have.

BOLETTE. Well, what does he say?

ARNHOLM. Hm! Well, your father's so thoroughly taken up with other matters just now——

BOLETTE. Yes, yes! that's how I knew it would be.

ARNHOLM. But I got this much out of him. You mustn't reckon upon any help from him.

BOLETTE. No?

ARNHOLM. He explained his circumstances to me clearly; he thought that such a thing was absolutely out of the question, impossible for him.

BOLETTE (*reproachfully*). And you had the heart to come and mock me?

ARNHOLM. I've certainly not done that, dear Bolette. It depends wholly and solely upon yourself whether you go away or not.

BOLETTE. What depends upon me?

ARNHOLM. Whether you are to go out into the world— learn all you most care for—take part in all you are hungering after here at home—live your life under brighter conditions, Bolette.

BOLETTE (*clasping her hands together*). Good God! But it's impossible! If father neither can nor will—and I have no one else on earth to whom I could turn——

ARNHOLM. Couldn't you make up your mind to accept a little help from your old—from your former teacher?

BOLETTE. From you, Mr. Arnholm! Would you be willing to——

ARNHOLM. Stand by you! Yes—with all my heart. Both with word and in deed. You may count upon it. Then you accept? Well? Do you agree?

BOLETTE. Do I agree! To get away—to see the world—to learn something thoroughly! All that seemed to be a great, beautiful impossibility!

ARNHOLM. All that may now become a reality to you, if only you yourself wish it.

BOLETTE. And to all this unspeakable happiness you will help me! Oh, no! Tell me, *can* I accept such an offer from a stranger?

ARNHOLM. You can from me, Bolette. From me you can accept anything.

BOLETTE (*seizing his hands*). Yes, I almost think I can! I don't know how it is, but—(*bursting out*) Oh! I could both laugh and cry for joy, for happiness! Then I should know life really after all. I began to be so afraid life would pass me by.

ARNHOLM. You need not fear that, Bolette. But now you must tell me quite frankly—if there is anything—anything you are bound to here.

BOLETTE. Bound to? Nothing.

ARNHOLM. Nothing whatever?

BOLETTE. No, nothing at all. That is—I am bound to father to some extent. And to Hilde, too. But——

ARNHOLM. Well, you'll have to leave your father sooner or later. And some time Hilde also will go her own way in life. That is only a question of time. Nothing more. And so there is nothing else that binds you, Bolette? Not any kind of connection.

BOLETTE. Nothing whatever. As far as that goes, I could leave at any moment.

ARNHOLM. Well, if that is so, dear Bolette, you shall go away with me!

BOLETTE (*clapping her hands*). O God! what joy to think of it!

ARNHOLM. For I hope you trust me fully?

BOLETTE. Indeed, I do!

ARNHOLM. And you dare to trust yourself and your future fully and confidently into my hands, Bolette? Is that true? You will dare to do this?

BOLETTE. Of course; how could I not do so? Could you believe anything else? You, who have been my old teacher —my teacher in the old days, I mean.

ARNHOLM. Not because of that. I will not consider that side of the matter; but—well, so you are free, Bolette! There is nothing that binds you, and so I ask you, if you could—if you could—bind yourself to me for life?

BOLETTE (*steps back frightened*). What are you saying?

ARNHOLM. For all your life, Bolette. Will you be my wife?

BOLETTE (*half to herself*). No, no, no! That is impossible, utterly impossible!

ARNHOLM. It is really so absolutely impossible for you to——

BOLETTE. But, surely, you cannot mean what you are saying, Mr. Arnholm! (*Looking at him.*) Or—yet—was that what you meant when you offered to do so much for me?

ARNHOLM. You must listen to me one moment, Bolette. I suppose I have greatly surprised you!

BOLETTE. Oh! how could such a thing from you—how could it but—but surprise me!

ARNHOLM. Perhaps you are right. Of course, you didn't —you could not know it was for your sake I made this journey.

BOLETTE. Did you come here for—for my sake?

ARNHOLM. I did, Bolette. In the spring I received a letter

from your father, and in it there was a passage that made me think—hm—that you held your former teacher in—in a little more than friendly remembrance.

BOLETTE. How could father write such a thing?

ARNHOLM. He did not mean it so. But I worked myself into the belief that here was a young girl longing for me to come again.—No, you mustn't interrupt me, dear Bolette! And—you see, when a man like myself, who is no longer quite young, has such a belief—or fancy, it makes an overwhelming impression. There grew within me a living, a grateful affection for you; I thought I must come to you, see you again, and tell you I shared the feelings that I fancied you had for me.

BOLETTE. And now you know it is not so!—that it was a mistake!

ARNHOLM. It can't be helped, Bolette. Your image, as I bear it within myself, will always be colored and stamped with the impression that this mistake gave me. Perhaps you cannot understand this; but still it is so.

BOLETTE. I never thought such a thing possible.

ARNHOLM. But now you have seen that it is possible, what do you say now, Bolette? Couldn't you make up your mind to be—yes—to be my wife?

BOLETTE. Oh! it seems so utterly impossible, Mr. Arnholm. You, who have been my teacher! I can't imagine ever standing in any other relation towards you.

ARNHOLM. Well, well, if you think you really cannot.— Then our old relations remain unchanged, dear Bolette.

BOLETTE. What do you mean?

ARNHOLM. Of course, to keep my promise all the same. I will take care you get out into the world and see something of it. Learn some things you really want to know; live safe and independent. Your future I shall provide for also, Bolette. For in me you will always have a good, faithful, trustworthy friend. Be sure of that.

BOLETTE. Good heavens! Mr. Arnholm, all that is so utterly impossible now.

ARNHOLM. Is that impossible too?

BOLETTE. Surely you can see that! After what you have just said to me, and after my answer—Oh! you yourself must see that it is impossible for me now to accept so very much from you. I can accept nothing from you—nothing after this.

ARNHOLM. So you would rather stay at home here, and let life pass you by?

BOLETTE. Oh! it is such dreadful misery to think of that.

ARNHOLM. Will you renounce knowing something of the outer world? Renounce bearing your part in all that you yourself say you are hungering for? To know there is so infinitely much, and yet never really to understand anything of it? Think carefully, Bolette.

BOLETTE. Yes, yes! You are right, Mr. Arnholm.

ARNHOLM. And then, when one day your father is no longer here, then perhaps to be left helpless and alone in the world; or live to give yourself to another man—whom you, perhaps, will also feel no affection for——

BOLETTE. Oh, yes! I see how true all you say is. But still —and yet perhaps——

ARNHOLM (quickly). Well?

BOLETTE (looking at him hesitatingly). Perhaps it might not be so impossible after all.

ARNHOLM. What, Bolette?

BOLETTE. Perhaps it might be possible—to accept—what you proposed to me.

ARNHOLM. Do you mean that, after all, you might be willing to—that at all events you could give me the happiness of helping you as a steadfast friend?

BOLETTE. No, no, no! Never that, for that would be utterly impossible now. No—Mr. Arnholm—rather take me.

ARNHOLM. Bolette! You will?

BOLETTE. Yes, I believe I will.

ARNHOLM. And after all you will be my wife?

BOLETTE. Yes; if you still think that—that you will have me.

ARNHOLM. Think! (*Seizing her hand.*) Oh, thanks, thanks, Bolette. All else that you said—your former doubts —these do not frighten me. If I do not yet possess your whole heart, I shall know how to conquer it. Oh, Bolette, I will wait upon you hand and foot!

BOLETTE. And then I shall see something of the world? Shall live! You have promised me that?

ARNHOLM. And will keep my promise.

BOLETTE. And I may learn everything I want to?

ARNHOLM. I, myself, will be your teacher as formerly, Bolette. Do you remember the last school year?

BOLETTE (*quietly and absently*). To think—to know— one's self free, and to get out into the strange world, and then, not to need to be anxious for the future—not to be harassed about one's stupid livelihood!

ARNHOLM. No, you will never need to waste a thought upon such matters. And that's a good thing, too, in its way, dear Bolette, isn't it? Eh?

BOLETTE. Indeed it is. That is certain.

ARNHOLM (*putting his arms about her*). Oh, you will see how comfortably and easily we shall settle down together! And how well and safely and trustfully we two shall get on with one another, Bolette.

BOLETTE. Yes. I also begin to—I believe really—it will answer. (*Looks out to the right, and hurriedly frees herself.*) Oh, don't say anything about this.

ARNHOLM. What is it, dear?

BOLETTE. Oh, it's that poor (*pointing*)—see out there.

ARNHOLM. Is it your father?

BOLETTE. No. It's the young sculptor. He's down there with Hilde.

ARNHOLM. Oh, Lyngstrand! What's really the matter with him?

BOLETTE. Why, you know how weak and delicate he is.

ARNHOLM. Yes. Unless it's simply imaginary.

BOLETTE. No, it's real enough! He'll not last long. But perhaps that's best for him.

ARNHOLM. Dear, why should *that* be best?

BOLETTE. Because—because—nothing would come of his art anyhow. Let's go before they come.

ARNHOLM. Gladly, my dear Bolette.

(HILDE *and* LYNGSTRAND *appear by the pond.*)

HILDE. Hi, hi! Won't your honors wait for us?

ARNHOLM. Bolette and I would rather go on a little in advance. (*He and* BOLETTE *go out to the left.*)

LYNGSTRAND (*laughs quietly*). It's very delightful here now. Everybody goes about in pairs—always two and two together.

HILDE (*looking after them*). I could almost swear he's proposing to her.

LYNGSTRAND. Really? Have you noticed anything?

HILDE. Yes. It's not very difficult—if you keep your eyes open.

LYNGSTRAND. But Miss Bolette won't have him. I'm certain of that.

HILDE. No. For she thinks he's got so dreadfully old-looking, and she thinks he'll soon get bald.

LYNGSTRAND. It's not only because of *that*. She'd not have him anyhow.

HILDE. How can you know?

LYNGSTRAND. Well, because there's someone else she's promised to think of.

HILDE. Only to think of?

LYNGSTRAND. While he is away, yes.

HILDE. Oh! then I suppose it's you she's to think of.

LYNGSTRAND. Perhaps it might be.

HILDE. She promised you that?

LYNGSTRAND. Yes—think—she promised me that! But mind you don't tell her you know.

HILDE. Oh! I'll be mum! I'm as secret as the grave.

LYNGSTRAND. I think it's awfully kind of her.

HILDE. And when you come home again—are you going to be engaged to her, and then marry her?

LYNGSTRAND. No, that wouldn't very well do. For I daren't think of such a thing during the first years. And when I shall be able to, she'll be rather too old for me, I fancy.

HILDE. And yet you wish her to think of you?

LYNGSTRAND. Yes; that's so useful to me. You see, I'm an artist. And she can very well do it, because she herself has no real calling. But all the same, it's kind of her.

HILDE. Do you think you'll be able to get on more quickly with your work if you know that Bolette is here thinking of you?

LYNGSTRAND. Yes, I fancy so. To know there is a spot on earth where a young, gentle, reserved woman is quietly dreaming about you—I fancy it must be so—so—well, I really don't exactly know what to call it.

HILDE. Perhaps you mean—fascinating?

LYNGSTRAND. Fascinating! Oh, yes! Fascinating was what I meant, or something like it. (*Looks at her for a moment.*) You are so clever, Miss Hilde. Really you are very clever. When I come home again you'll be about the same age as your sister is now. Perhaps, too, you'll look like your sister looks now. And perhaps, too, you'll be of the same mind she is now. Then, perhaps, you'll be both yourself and your sister —in one form, so to say.

HILDE. Would you like that?

LYNGSTRAND. I hardly know. Yes; I almost think I should. But now, for this summer, I would rather you were like yourself alone, and exactly as you are.

HILDE. Do you like me best as I am?

LYNGSTRAND. Yes, I like you immensely as you are.

HILDE. Hm. Tell me, you who are an artist, do you think I'm right always to wear bright-colored summer dresses?

LYNGSTRAND. Yes! I think you're quite right.

HILDE. You think bright colors suit me, then?

LYNGSTRAND. They suit you charmingly—to my taste.

HILDE. But tell me, as an artist, how do you think I should look in black?

LYNGSTRAND. In black, Miss Hilde?

HILDE. Yes, all in black. Do you think I should look well?

LYNGSTRAND. Black's hardly suitable for the summer. However, you'd probably look remarkably well in black, especially with your appearance.

HILDE (*looking straight in front of her*). All in black, up to the throat; black frilling round that, black gloves, and a long black veil hanging down behind.

LYNGSTRAND. If you were dressed so, Miss Hilde, I should wish I were a painter, and I'd paint you as a young, beautiful, sorrowing widow!

HILDE. Or as a young, sorrowing, betrothed girl!

LYNGSTRAND. Yes, that would be better still. But you can't wish to be dressed like that?

HILDE. I hardly know; but I think it's fascinating.

LYNGSTRAND. Fascinating?

HILDE. Fascinating to think of, yes. (*Suddenly pointing to the left.*) Oh, just look *there!*

LYNGSTRAND (*looking*). The great English steamer; and right by the pier!

(WANGEL *and* ELLIDA *come in past the pond.*)

WANGEL. No; I assure you, dear Ellida, you are mistaken. (*Seeing the others.*) What, are you two here? It's not in sight yet, is it, Mr. Lyngstrand?

LYNGSTRAND. The great English ship?

WANGEL. Yes.

LYNGSTRAND (*pointing*). There she is already, doctor.

ELLIDA. I knew it.

WANGEL. Come!

LYNGSTRAND. Come like a thief in the night, as one might say, so quietly and noiselessly.

WANGEL. You must go to the pier with Hilde. Be quick! I'm sure she wants to hear the music.

LYNGSTRAND. Yes; we were just going there, doctor.

WANGEL. Perhaps we'll follow you. We'll come directly.

HILDE (*whispering to* LYNGSTRAND). They're hunting in couples, too!

> (HILDE *and* LYNGSTRAND *go out through the garden. Music is heard in the distance out at the fjord during the following.*)

ELLIDA. Come! He is here! Yes, yes—I feel it.

WANGEL. You'd better go in, Ellida! Let me talk with him alone.

ELLIDA. Oh! that's impossible—impossible, I say. (*With a cry.*) Ah! do you see him, Wangel?

> (THE STRANGER *enters from the left, and remains on the pathway outside the fence.*)

THE STRANGER (*bowing*). Good evening. You see I am here again, Ellida.

ELLIDA. Yes, yes. The time has come now.

THE STRANGER. And are you ready to start, or not?

WANGEL. You can see for yourself that she is not.

THE STRANGER. I'm not asking about a traveling dress, or anything of that kind, nor about packed trunks. All that is needed for a journey I have with me on board. I've also secured a cabin for her. (*To* ELLIDA.) So I ask you if you are ready to go with me, to go with me—freely?

ELLIDA. Oh! do not ask me! Do not tempt me!

> (*A ship's bell is heard in the distance.*)

THE STRANGER. That is the first bell for going on board. Now you must say "Yes" or "No."

ELLIDA (*wringing her hands*). To decide—decide for one's whole life! Never to be able to undo it again!

THE STRANGER. Never. In half an hour it will be too late.

ELLIDA (*looking shyly and searchingly at him*). Why is it you hold to me so resolutely?

THE STRANGER. Don't you feel, as I do, that we two belong together?

ELLIDA. Do you mean because of the vow?

THE STRANGER. Vows bind no one, neither man nor woman. If I hold so steadfastly to you, it is because I *cannot* do otherwise.

ELLIDA (*in a low, trembling voice*). Why didn't you come before?

WANGEL. Ellida!

ELLIDA (*bursting out*). Ah! All that attracts, and tempts, and lures into the unknown! All the strength of the sea concentrated in this one thing!

(THE STRANGER *climbs over the fence.*)

ELLIDA (*stepping back to* WANGEL). What is it? What do you want?

THE STRANGER. I see it and I hear it in you, Ellida. After all, you will choose me in the end.

WANGEL (*going towards him*). My wife has no choice here. I am here both to choose for her and to defend her. Yes, defend! If you do not go away from here—away from this land—and never come back again—Do you know to what you are exposing yourself?

ELLIDA. No, no, Wangel, not that!

THE STRANGER. What will you do to me?

WANGEL. I will have you arrested as a criminal, at once, before you go on board; for I know all about the murder at Skjoldviken.

ELLIDA. Ah! Wangel, how can you?

THE STRANGER. I was prepared for that, and so—(*takes a revolver from his breast pocket*)—I provided myself with this.

ELLIDA (*throwing herself in front of him*). No, no; do not kill him! better kill me!

THE STRANGER. Neither you nor him, don't fear that. This is for myself, for I will live and die a free man.

ELLIDA (*with growing excitement*). Wangel, let me tell you this—tell it you so that he may hear it. You can indeed keep me here! You have the means and the power to do it. And you intend to do it. But my mind—all my thoughts, all the longings and desires of my soul—these you cannot bind! These will rush and press out into the unknown that I was created for, and that you have kept from me!

WANGEL (*in quiet sorrow*). I see it, Ellida. Step by step you are slipping from me. The craving for the boundless, the infinite, the unattainable will drive your soul into the darkness of night at last.

ELLIDA. Yes! I feel it hovering over me like black noiseless wings.

WANGEL. It shall not come to that. No other deliverance is possible for you. I at least can see no other. And so—so I cry off our bargain at once. Now you can choose your own path in perfect—perfect freedom.

ELLIDA (*stares at him a while as if stricken dumb*). Is it true—true what you say? Do you mean that—mean it with all your heart?

WANGEL. Yes—with all my sorrowing heart—I mean it.

ELLIDA. And can you do it? Can you let it be so?

WANGEL. Yes, I can. Because I love you so dearly.

ELLIDA (*in a low, trembling voice*). And have I come so near—so close to you?

WANGEL. The years and the living together have done that.

ELLIDA (*clasping her hands together*). And I—who so little understood this!

WANGEL. Your thoughts went elsewhere. And now—now you are completely free of me and mine—and—and mine. Now your own true life may resume its real bent again, for now you can choose in freedom, and on your own responsibility, Ellida.

ELLIDA (*clasps her head with her hands, and stares at* WANGEL). In freedom, and on my own responsibility! Responsibility, too? That changes everything.

(*The ship bell rings again.*)

THE STRANGER. Do you hear, Ellida? It has rung now for the last time. Come.

ELLIDA (*turns towards him, looks firmly at him, and speaks in a resolute voice*). I shall never go with you after this!

THE STRANGER. You will not!

ELLIDA (*clinging to* WANGEL). I shall never go away from you after this.

WANGEL. Ellida, Ellida!

THE STRANGER. So it is over?

ELLIDA. Yes. Over for all time.

THE STRANGER. I see. There is something here stronger than my will.

ELLIDA. Your will has not a shadow of power over me any longer. To me you are as one dead—who has come home from the sea, and who returns to it again. I no longer dread you. And I am no longer drawn to you.

THE STRANGER. Good-bye, Mrs. Wangel! (*He swings himself over the fence.*) Henceforth you are nothing but a shipwreck in my life that I have tided over. (*He goes out.*)

WANGEL (*looks at her for a while*). Ellida, your mind is like the sea—it has ebb and flow. Whence came the change?

ELLIDA. Ah! don't you understand that the change came—was *bound* to come when I could choose in freedom?

WANGEL. And the unknown?—It no longer lures you?

ELLIDA. Neither lures nor frightens me. I could have seen it—gone out into it, if only I myself had willed it. I could have chosen it. And that is why I could also renounce it.

WANGEL. I begin to understand little by little. You think and conceive in pictures—in visible figures. Your longing and aching for the sea, your attraction towards this strange man, these were the expression of an awakening and growing desire for freedom; nothing else.

ELLIDA. I don't know about that. But you have been a good physician for me. You found, and you *dared* to use the right remedy—the only one that could help me.

WANGEL. Yes, in utmost need and danger we doctors dare much. And now you are coming back to me again, Ellida?

ELLIDA. Yes, dear, faithful Wangel—now I am coming back to you again. Now I can. For now I come to you freely, and on my own responsibility.

WANGEL (*looks lovingly at her*). Ellida! Ellida! To think that now we can live wholly for one another——

ELLIDA. And with common memories. Yours, as well as mine.

WANGEL. Yes, indeed, dear.

ELLIDA. And for our children, Wangel?

WANGEL. You call them *ours!*

ELLIDA. They who are not mine yet, but whom I shall win.

WANGEL. Ours! (*Gladly and quickly kisses her hands.*) I cannot speak my thanks for those words!

    (HILDE, BALLESTED, LYNGSTRAND, ARNHOLM, *and* BOLETTE *come into the garden. At the same time a number of young townspeople and visitors pass along the footpath.*)

HILDE (*aside to* LYNGSTRAND). See! Why, she and father look exactly as if they were a betrothed couple!

BALLESTED (*who has overheard*). It is summer-time, little Missie.

ARNHOLM (*looking at* WANGEL *and* ELLIDA). The English steamer is putting off.

BOLETTE (*going to the fence*). You can see her best from here.

LYNGSTRAND. The last voyage this year.

BALLESTED. Soon all the sea-highways will be closed, as the poet says. It is sad, Mrs. Wangel. And now we're to lose you also for a time. To-morrow you're off to Skjoldviken, I hear.

WANGEL. No; nothing will come of that. We two have changed our minds—to-night.

ARNHOLM (*looking from one to the other*). Oh!—really!

BOLETTE (*coming forward*). Father, is that true?

HILDE (*going towards* ELLIDA). Are you going to stay with us after all?

ELLIDA. Yes, dear Hilde, if you'll have me.

HILDE (*struggling between tears and laughter*). Fancy! Have you!

ARNHOLM (*to* ELLIDA). But this is quite a surprise——

ELLIDA (*smiling earnestly*). Well, you see, Mr. Arnholm—Do you remember we talked about it yesterday? When you have once become a land-creature you can no longer find your way back again to the sea, nor to the sea-life either.

BALLESTED. Why, that's exactly the case with my mermaid.

ELLIDA. Something like—yes.

BALLESTED. Only with this difference—that the mermaid dies of it, while human beings can acclam—acclimatize themselves. Yes, yes. I assure you, Mrs. Wangel, they *can* ac-climatize themselves.

ELLIDA. In freedom they can, Mr. Ballested.

WANGEL. And when they act on their own responsibility, dear Ellida.

ELLIDA (*quickly holding out her hand to him*). Exactly.

(*The great steamer glides noiselessly out beyond the fjord. The music is heard nearer land.*)